THE 79TH FIGHTER GROUP
Over Tunisia, Sicily, and Italy
in World War II

The 79th Fighter Group
Over Tunisia, Sicily, and Italy
in World War II

Don Woerpel

Schiffer Military History
Atglen, PA

Dust jacket and aircraft profile artwork by S.W. Ferguson, Colorado Springs, CO.

SAY'S DAY

The dust jacket artwork depicts Flying Skulls Red Section Leader Lt. Sammie Say at the height of the battle off Cape Bon, Tunisia, on April 30, 1943. Maggiore Caroli is seen exiting his MC 205 riddled by the Red Leader, while far below, an Italian destroyer, attacked by the other 79th Group Warhawks, burns in the distance. Chapter five describes the fight in full detail.

Book design by Robert Biondi.

Library of Congress Catalog Number: 2001088288.

Printed in China.
ISBN: 0-7643-1322-3

We are always looking for people to write books on new and related subjects. If you have an idea for a book, please contact us at the address below.

Published by Schiffer Publishing Ltd.
4880 Lower Valley Road
Atglen, PA 19310
Phone: (610) 593-1777
FAX: (610) 593-2002
E-mail: Schifferbk@aol.com.
Visit our web site at: www.schifferbooks.com
Please write for a free catalog.
This book may be purchased from the publisher.
Please include $3.95 postage.
Try your bookstore first.

In Europe, Schiffer books are distributed by:
Bushwood Books
6 Marksbury Ave.
Kew Gardens
Surrey TW9 4JF
England
Phone: 44 (0)208 392-8585
FAX: 44 (0)208 392-9876
E-mail: Bushwd@aol.com.
Free postage in the UK. Europe: air mail at cost.
Try your bookstore first.

Contents

Preface and Acknowledgments 6

Chapter 1 El Hamma 10
Chapter 2 The Balloon Goes Up 16
Chapter 3 To Find a War 25
Chapter 4 All Out For Monty 43
Chapter 5 Cape Bon 57
Chapter 6 Turkey Shoot 68
Chapter 7 The Straits of Messina 79
Chapter 8 Not So Sunny Italy 91
Chapter 9 Stalemate 102
Chapter 10 The Stranded Whale 112
Chapter 11 Cassino, Strangle and Rome 129
Chapter 12 Corsican Summer 147
Chapter 13 Rhone Valley Massacre 159
Chapter 14 Back in the Gumbo Again 171
Chapter 15 Italian Finalé 182
Chapter 16 Taking the Scenic Route Home 203
Chapter 17 The Last Tally-ho 216

Appendices
Appendix I: Summary of 79th Fighter Group Combat Operations 224
Appendix II: Assignments 232
Appendix III: Commanding Officers 233
Appendix IV: Station List 234
Appendix V: Insignia 235
Appendix VI: Citations 237
Appendix VII: Equivalent ranks and units 239

79th Fighter Group Aircraft in Profile 240
End Notes 253
Glossary 257
Bibliography 258
Index 260

Preface and Acknowledgments

If American fighter pilots with the Eighth Air Force in England were the undisputed glamour boys of the Army Air Forces during World War II, those who flew in the Mediterranean Theater of Operations were probably best known for being unknown. There were two reasons for their relative obscurity, and neither had anything to do with how they fought; they obviously fought well or you wouldn't be reading this now.

First, the Mediterranean was, for the most part, a British theater of operations. American military strategists had never conceived of the Mediterranean as an area where the war could be won – although it most surely could have been lost there – and were convinced from the beginning that only an assault on the continent of Europe from staging bases in the United Kingdom would provide a quick, decisive victory over Nazi Germany. Thus, operations in the south, no matter how difficult or bloody, would always be viewed in the United States as subsidiary sideshows to the main event in Northwest Europe.

Moreover, the air war in the Mediterranean, especially after the RAF's Western Desert Air Force won aerial supremacy in late 1942, was of a much different nature than the one waged from the British Isles. American fighter pilots flying from English bases had as their battleground the cold, thin skies over the very heart of the enemy's defensive fighter force where, as they escorted Fortress and Liberator crews to targets deep in Germany, they met the full fury of an aroused and desperate Luftwaffe almost daily. With many opportunities for individual air-to-air combat – and the opportunity to increase their personal scores – their exploits soon became well known to the general American public.

By contrast, with but few exceptions – most notably during the waning days of the Tunisian campaign, and again over Italy's Anzio beachhead in early 1944 – large-scale clashes between opposing fighter formations in the south were rare. Many pilots in the theater completed their entire overseas tour without ever seeing an enemy aircraft in the air, and their war became primarily a low-level war of close support and interdiction – unenviable tasks that were hazardous, exacting, and totally without glamour.

Because issues and accomplishments elsewhere were often more dramatic and conspired to isolate them, and because the very nature of the war they waged was not always conducive to the making of frontpage headlines, the exploits of the fighter pilots in the Mediterranean went largely unheralded. And have remained so to this day.

This book is the story of one such group of unheralded Americans who took part in that forgotten campaign. It is the story of the war in the Mediterranean as seen through the eyes of those who flew – and those who kept 'em flying – with the 79th Fighter Group. Although by no means an official report, certainly not complete, perhaps not entirely accurate, I have attempted to tell who they were and what they did, and chronicle their life and times as they fought, toiled and died on the long road to victory that began on the sands west of Alamein in the fall of 1942 and ended some thirty months later in the fog-shrouded mountains of northern Italy. To show how the overall strategy of the war on the ground in that theater influenced the war in the air as it was fought by the men of the 79th, the narrative is set in the broader context of the entire Mediterranean campaign. Hopefully, this provides the book with greater appeal not only for the serious student of military and aviation history, but the casual reader as well.

As with most accounts of the war in the air, the majority of the text, for obvious reasons, deals with the exploits of the minority – the pilots. I therefore tender my apologies to the faithful and tireless ground crews for this disparity. Without their skill and dedication no victory would have been possible. Their war was one of repetition and boredom; dull, monotonous work that required a special brand of courage. Unfortunately, a day-by-day account of their vitally important tasks would also tend to make dull and monotonous reading.

I obviously didn't realize it at the time, but the idea for this book was conceived on the last day of August 1944. On that sultry Thursday morning my father, clutching in his hand a crumpled telegram he had received from the War Department just twenty minutes earlier, had the heart-wrenching task of telling my grandmother that her youngest son had been reported Missing in Action over southern France. Several weeks later the family's worst fears were realized when another telegram confirmed that "Uncle Herb" had been killed. As a young boy of nine-going-on-ten who thought fighter pilots in general – and my uncle in particular – were all ten-feet tall, this family tragedy affected me profoundly. World War II, and the quest to learn about my uncle's military service and how he died has dominated my life ever since. Eventually, that quest evolved into a history of the 79th Fighter Group entitled *A Hostile Sky* published in 1977, and the "new and improved" version that you are reading now.

I didn't plan a revised edition when I began the original project some twenty-nine years ago, it just worked out that way. After *A Hostile Sky* was published I assumed that would be the end of the story. But over the years, as more information became available, I began to consider a revised and expanded edition, and this book is the result.

Hopefully, my attempt to tell the story of the 79th Fighter Group the second time around is better than the first. Unfortunately, it's obvious now more than ever that the story is still very far from complete. Of some 2,200 men who at one time or another during the war called the 79th their home away from home, I have only reached about two hundred, or less than ten percent of the total number of men who served with the Group during the war. That leaves ninety percent who have not been heard from. And while much of what I got from those I did reach has made its way into this book, much was also left out for one reason or another, usually because I wasn't smart enough to figure out how to use what they gave me.

It is also quite possible that the description of an event that happened at a particular time or place isn't exactly the way some of those who were there may remember it. One reason, of course, is that no two people ever view the same event in quite the same way, which presented a problem when my source of information about a particular event was two or more people. Another reason is that in many instances the "official" record of the event is at odds with a participant's memory of it. Often it was obvious that the "official" version was correct, but many times it was just as obvious that it was wrong. All of which made sorting fact from fiction interesting, to say the least. Be that as it may, responsibility for any and all errors of fact or omission is mine, and mine alone.

In late 1971, when I first began to seriously consider writing a history of the 79th Fighter Group, two total strangers ultimately provided the guidance and impetus needed to get the project off the ground. On a whim, I wrote to Ernest R. McDowell, whose day job was traffic manager for a scientific instrument firm in Chicago, but whose avocation was the history of military aviation. He had written several books on the subject, including one on the 325th Fighter Group – *Checkertail Clan* – and he took time from his busy schedule to answer a myriad of questions that I pestered him with almost daily. He also pointed me in the right direction for further research, and by a stroke of very good fortune put me in touch with Richards H. Hoffman, MD. An original member of the 79th Fighter Group, and its flight surgeon for much of the war, Hoffman was articulate and witty, and possessed an almost uncanny ability to recall with clarity details of events that were then more than three decades old. He provided me with an unending wealth of information, anecdotes and photographs to draw upon, and all contributed immeasurably to the development of this history. Of at least equal importance was his unwavering faith in the project. Countless times during the six years it took to put the original book together, an encouraging letter from him lifted my sagging spirits and gave me the inspiration needed to continue. I never met the man personally, but the book was as much his as it was mine. Sadly, he died of cancer shortly after it was published.

To both "Doc" Hoffman and Ernie McDowell I will be eternally grateful. Without their help and support I would still be taxiing with my flaps down.

Official research material for the book consisted of several thousand pages of combat journals, war diaries, daily operations reports, biographical data and other documents from the National Archives and Records Center in Washington, DC; the Albert F. Simpson Historical Research Center at the Air University at Maxwell Air Force Base in Alabama; the Book and Magazine Branch of the USAF's Office of Information, and the Research Division of the United States Air Force Museum at Dayton, Ohio. In all instances my requests were courteously and efficiently processed. To those who assisted me in my quest for information at the above facilities I offer my most sincere thanks.

Of special interest were the Daily Operations Reports and Squadron War Diaries. The Ops Reports summarized each mission flown by the Group – number of aircraft, type of mission, time up and time down, target, weather, ammunition and explosives carried and expended, type and intensity of anti-aircraft fire encountered, enemy aircraft encountered and results, aircraft losses, casualties, etc. The report generally included a brief narrative detailing type of formation flown, bombing procedure, and a summary of results. That narrative was much more thorough and descriptive during the early months of the war than it was after January 1944 when the reporting procedure was streamlined, but such is progress.

Squadron war diaries and outline histories were more informal, and many times more informative, than Daily Operations Reports. Submitted to higher headquarters on a monthly basis with a brief synopsis of day to day operations, the reports not only summarized the squadron's activities for the month – noting squadron strength, changes in command, stations and movement, awards, flight leaders on significant mission, and losses in action – but might also describe what the men had for supper.

One of the largest sources of unofficial research material was gleaned (stolen, would perhaps be a better word) from the pages of *The Falcon*, an illustrated history of the 79th Fighter Group compiled and printed by members of the Group in Germany shortly after the war. Edited by Captain Ragnar G. Lind, and published as a limited edition for the Group's "alumni," it is without question the finest of its kind, and surviving copies of *The Falcon* have become much sought after collectors' items.

A War Diary was also compiled at the Group level – which provided much of the material for *The Falcon* – and Captain Elliott K. Shapira, the 87th Squadron Intelligence Officer was an especially prolific contributor to that diary. In most instances in this book, where War Diary is listed as a source, he is the author.

Much of the material on the following pages reflects the generous willingness of 79th veterans (and their kin) to share experiences through letters, newspaper clippings, artifacts and photographs, and I have never ceased to marvel that so many would entrust prized mementos of their wartime experiences to a complete stranger and the incertitude of the United States Postal Service. I am most appreciative that they did, however, for without their help this project would have crashed and burned on takeoff many years ago.

Those whom I would especially like to thank include both those who contributed to the original research done on the project back in the Seventies, and those who have since added material for the revised edition.

In the original edition published in 1977, I made extensive use of photographs and other material submitted by Calvin Arnold, Paul Church, Ralph Colmer, Henry Craig, William Feimer, Bill Horn, Jack Kauffman, Ed Kelly, Vincent Lappin, James McGuire, Dick Morrissey, George Murto, Frank Sanders, Fred Wright and, of course, "Doc" Hoffman. Other former members of the Group who "contributed to the cause" included J. C. Beeks, Chet Campbell, Brig. Gen. Benjamin B. Cassiday, Jr. (USAF, Ret.), Clyde Churchill, William Claycomb, Jack Cox, Milton Dozeman, Bob Drum, Harry Einstanding, Allen Erick, Al Fetters, Herman Finkelstein, Milo Foreman, Anthony Gagliardo, Joseph Geers, William Gower, Frank Jones, Lou Kinkle, Glenn Lyans, Ed Newbould, William Nichols, Richard Phillips, Sherrill Roark, Fred Spanhut, Earl Trafton, Frank Ward, Dan Weaver, Clair Weinheimer, and Dr. Henry Winsauer.

Among those 79th veterans who contributed new material for the revised book were Bill Abbott, Tom Anderson, Wyman Anderson, Phil Bagian, Robert Bell, William Bishop, Basil Blair, James Blassingham, William "Doug" Brittian, Al Bratt, Dr. L. A. Charpentier, Donald Claycomb, John Cochran, Bill Colgan, Bob Duffield, Merlin Eltzroth, Ed Evans, Jack Faires, Roger Files, Jackson Gilmore, Maj. Gen. Lee Gossick (USAF, Ret.), Martin Granberg, Donald Guilfoyle, Harold Hall, Herb Hanson, Malcolm Hayles, Herb Hazzard, Dick Hilgard, Dr. Charles Jaslow, Bob Kelley, Jack Kelly, Russ Kelly, John Kittrell, Harold Land, Donald Lawless, Paul McArthur, Tom McIntosh, Ed McLaughlin, Malcolm "Joe" McNall, Frank Milstead, Robert Minett, Robert Moody, Warren Morgan, Robert Norman, Conrad "Harry" Odle, Ed Payne, John Pinkham, James Pittard, Edwin Plank, Harry Powell, William Probst, Colonel Wayne Rhynard (USAF, Ret.), Romie R. Royse, Richard Sanderson, Powell Scheumack, Kenneth Schuchman, Wayne Sherer, E. Randolph Silsbee, Bob Spurgin, Robert Sweeney, James Sweeting, Robert Taylor, Jack Tessier, John Tobin, David Vandivort, Eugene T. Van Houten and Max Wysong. In addition, David Rouleau provided photos and material about his brother Louis, an 86th Squadron pilot killed over Italy in 1944, and John F. Martin, Jr. filled me in on the details about the death of his father, Lt. Colonel Johnny Martin, in a flying accident in 1947.

I also owe thanks to historians John Lambert, Gregory Moreira, Paul Vercammen, Chris Shores, Roger Freeman, William N. Hess, Harold Oyster, Wilfred Corey and Len Godbold, as well as to Lorenz Stallmeister of the German Fighter Pilot's Association and Larry L. Bogeman of the USAF's Fighter Test Branch at Wright-Patterson Air Force Base. They all assisted me greatly during the early days of my research. For the revised edition, Jerry Rep, who is the editor and publisher of the

Friends Journal of the Air Force Museum Foundation, provided much information about the incomparable Fred Borsodi, the former fighter commander who met an untimely death near the end of the war demonstrating a Lockheed P-80 Shooting Star. Through Rep I was also able to learn the fate of the captured Ju 88 that Borsodi and Pete Bedford flew back to the States in the fall of 1943.

Providing new material from across the sea were Taddei Dominique, Andre´ Besson, Henri Vignau, Claude Faure, Claude DeLuy, Vincent Remble, Norman L. R. Franks and Andy Stewart.

Dominique is one of a group of Corsican men dedicated to preserving the memory of Allied airmen based on that island during the war. His group has already dedicated a Memorial at Ghisonaccia Airfield (home of the 57th Bomb Wing) and another is being planned for Alto, where the 57th Fighter Group was stationed. They are also working on a French language book about American fighter and bomber units stationed on Corsica. For this book, he provided information about Serragia Airdrome.

Messieurs Besson, Vignau, Faure, DeLuy and Remble live in the south of France, and are actively involved in researching, locating and documenting crash sites of Allied aircraft lost over southern France during the war. They unselfishly shared a wealth of that information with me, some of which shed new light on the fate of several aircraft flown by 79th pilots. All of their information was very useful, and very much appreciated.

Franks lives in England, and has published books covering RAF Air/Sea Rescue operations. Although the information was second-hand via a letter Franks wrote to Ed Newbould of the 79th Fighter Group Association, thanks to him I was able to learn more about the rescue of several 79th pilots downed at sea.

Stewart also lives in England, and is one of a team that restored a German Me 109 captured in North Africa in 1942. He provided much information about *Irmgard,* the 109 that the 79th put back into flying condition in 1943.

The excellent maps in the first book were designed by my cousin, Timothy Herbert Hein. Because of the miracle of modern computers his cartographic talents weren't required for the revised edition, but he came to my rescue in my hour of need back in 1977 and I owe him a very special debt of gratitude.

Finally, to my wife Ann, who couldn't be faulted for thinking that I have spent most of my life letting down empty buckets into empty wells, and am frittering away what's left of it trying to draw them up again. For more than four decades she has shared her home not only with someone who lives as much in the past as the present, but also with hundreds of "war" books and magazines bought with money that she is convinced, I am sure, could have been put to much better use. She has also sat uncomplainingly through more episodes of *Airpower, Twentieth Century* and *Victory at Sea* than she probably cares to remember, and has seen enough reruns of *Twelve O'Clock High* and *Thunderbolt* to be able to recite the screenplay in her sleep. But without her support and incredible patience and understanding my dream of doing this book would have forever remained just that – a dream. I owe her much more than mere words can express.

Don Woerpel
Plover, Wisconsin
August 2000

one

El Hamma

As a result [of the blitz] the armor broke through the Valley of Death without having to suffer the fate of the gallant six hundred

- Desert Air Force historian

As fighter pilots go, Captain Frederic A. Borsodi was a senior citizen at age twenty-seven. The son of a Texas oil man, he graduated from Yale with honors in 1939; dabbled for a time in auto racing (it bored him); won his wings with the Navy at Pensacola (was cashiered out for breaking regulations forbidding newly commissioned pilots to marry), and had been a test pilot with the Pratt & Whitney people before joining the 79th Fighter Group's 86th Squadron (the Comanches) at Hillsgrove, Rhode Island a few months after Pearl Harbor. An outstanding pilot, warrior, and leader of men, Borsodi had been in North Africa since the early fall of 1942.

Now he squirmed uncomfortably in the hot, cramped cockpit of his scarred and weather-beaten Warhawk as it sat on the wide, dirt runway at Causeway landing ground in southern Tunisia, and listened to the monotonous ticking of the P-40's big Packard-built Merlin engine while perspiration darkened the sides of his already oil-stained flight suit. Minutes earlier, twenty-four aircraft – twelve each from the 85th and 87th squadrons – had taken off, the dust kicked up by their prop wash just now beginning to settle slowly back to earth, covering man and machine with a fine, sooty layer of grit and obscuring an already hazy sky. Behind him on the dusty runway, twenty-three Comanche and Hell's Belles* pilots – shoulder harnesses fastened, seat belts snugged tightly, radio connections plugged in – awaited the signal to go to war sitting down. They would make aviation history today with their backsides planted firmly on the seamed edges of parachute packs.

It was the afternoon of March 26, 1943 – a Friday – and the 79th Fighter Group and other Desert Air Force squadrons had been called upon to help General Bernard Law Montgomery's British Eighth Army outflank the formidable Mareth Line in southern Tunisia. Eighth Army had been stalled in front of the Mareth Line for nearly a week after a frontal attack near the sea bogged down, and Monty now decided to bypass it completely. He planned to concentrate his forces in the New Zealand sector west of the Line, bully his way through a narrow defile near El Hamma called the Tebaga Gap, and break into the tank country beyond. Blocking the way were numerous enemy guns – many of them deadly "eighty-eights" – on the heights surrounding the Gap. Unless those guns were silenced the attacking New Zealand infantry would almost certainly suffer heavy casualties. It was up to the Desert Air Force to make sure the "eighty-eights" were put out of action.

Simply put, the air operation plan was this: while several squadrons of fighters and light bombers kept the enemy busy over his own fields in northern Tunisia, Desert Air Force Spitfires would weave a protective cover over the immediate battle area. Then, as the infantry moved up to its start line, three squadrons of light and medium bombers would saturate the area in front of the NZeds while cannon-firing Hurricanes interdicted the roads leading to the battlefield. Starting at Zero Hour minus thirty minutes, two and a half squadrons of Kittyhawks and Warhawks would enter the area every quarter hour to bomb and strafe in front of the advancing New Zealanders. The "eighty-eights" on the high ground were to be given special attention.

In addition to the 79th, other fighter units taking part in the low strafe would be the American 57th and 324th Fighter Groups (although the 324th would not participate as a unit; its three squadrons were attached to the other two American groups), the RAF's 239, 244 and 322 Wings, and 7 South Afri-

* The Hell's Belles (316th) Squadron of the 324th Fighter Group was attached to the 79th for combat experience.

can Wing. The 79th drew the deadly middle period. Its pilots would make their strafing runs without the demoralization of the enemy enjoyed by the last squadrons to enter the area, or the benefit of surprise to be had in the beginning. When the 79th swooped down over the El Hamma road the enemy would be waiting and still full of fight.

A few hours before, as a steady stream of twin-engine bombers droned overhead and the distant rumble of artillery echoed down from the hills to the north, RAF Wing Commander H. F. "Billy" Burton had gathered the 79th's pilots around him on a sand dune at Causeway to personally spell out the mission. Outlining the tactical situation facing Eighth Army, Burton stressed the importance of silencing the guns on the hills south of El Hamma long enough to allow the NZeds to break through the Gap. He told them they could expect as high as fifty percent losses, but if the operation was a success it could shorten the war in North Africa by as much as ten weeks. Because the 79th was new to the North African fighting it would be led into the battle area by a flight of New Zealand Kittyhawks of 239 Wing. Particular emphasis was placed during the briefing on air/ground recognition signals marking the boundary lines between friendly and hostile troops. Positive identification of ground forces was always a ticklish proposition when working in close support over a fluid bomb line; it was all the more so today as most of the Group's pilots had yet to fly their first low-level strafing mission – almost all of their previous sorties had been escorting bombers.

Flanked by Lt. Bernard "Moon" Mullin (left center) and Captain Barney Turner, Captain Fred Borsodi (with helmet and goggles) was, as fighter pilots go, a senior citizen at age twenty-seven. (Hoffman)

At five minutes past four a green flare arced through the haze at Causeway. Fred Borsodi scanned his instrument panel with an experienced eye and was already moving as another

As their landing gear awkwardly retract one at a time, four Falcon Warhawks lift free of Causeway's dust for the March 26 bombing and strafing show near El Hamma. Six anti-personnel bombs can be seen under the wing of the nearest P-40. (Hoffman)

flare split the sky, his charges following closely behind. Breaking ground at close to a hundred miles an hour, gear and flaps were quickly cranked up and the twenty-four P-40s formed up west of the landing ground, climbing steadily until reaching 6,000 feet. They then picked up their New Zealand escort and turned northwest into the sun seeking the red and blue smoke that marked the boundary lines of the 5th New Zealand Brigade.

As they neared the target area, pillars of billowing black smoke rose high into the air from burning vehicles that littered both sides of the road – victims of the first squadrons in the area – and a few moments later the twenty-four Warhawks in Borsodi's "show" nosed over and headed for the deck. At an altitude of less than a hundred feet each pilot toggled six anti-personnel bombs over the enemy's forward positions, then dropped down even lower – to body height – to begin their strafing runs down the road to El Hamma.

Racing over the sand and scrub, Borsodi spotted dirty puffs of smoke from an artillery barrage out of the corner of his eye, and glimpsed a smoldering Kittyhawk in a ditch at the side of the road. Another lay crumpled and spent a few yards away. As the pilots swept over a small rise they found the road in front of them jam-packed with vehicles, and suddenly they were eyeball-to-eyeball with a German soldier furiously manning a gun from the back of a truck. The German had only a few seconds left to live, but he had nerve, and he took Borsodi and Major Jack Watkins out of the fight. Standing up in full view of the on-rushing P-40s he traded the Americans round for round. Watkins was hit at once, and turned for home where he later bellied in safely. Borsodi's craft was rocked by a violent explosion, and smoke poured into the cockpit. He was on fire, and nearly out of control. Unless he acted quickly his bones, too, like the skeletal framework of his dying P-40, would be scattered across the Tunisian countryside. He clawed desperately for bail-out altitude, his ruffled Warhawk spewing flames, smoke and glycol. At 600 feet he rolled the stricken ship on its back and dropped free. His chute snapped open with a bone-jarring jolt, took one downward swing, and dumped him in a heap in the middle of no-man's land as mortar and artillery shells slammed into the earth around him and shrapnel and machine-gun bullets whizzed overhead. He had landed in the midst of a terrific fight between German and New Zealand infantry.

The remaining pilots continued to run the gauntlet, guns hammering, as they flailed everything in front of them with 50-caliber machine-gun fire. Some, like Lieutenants Dick

An 85th Squadron Warhawk stands ready to fly against the deadly "eighty-eights" blocking the New Zealand advance through Tebaga Gap. (Sanders)

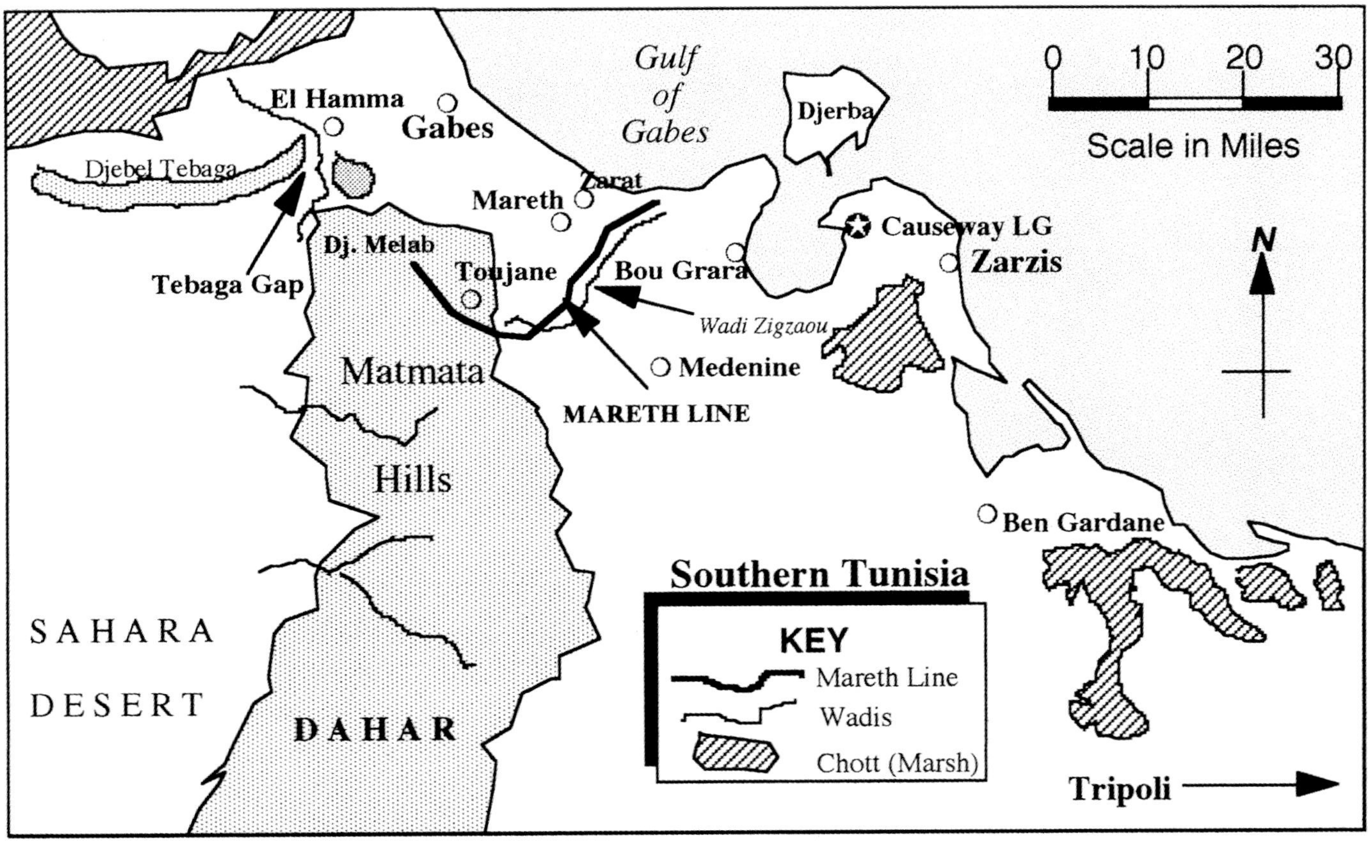

Morrissey and "Tiger" Taylor, made second and even third passes down the road, flying through a maelstrom of enemy fire as the deadly duels between fighter pilots and ground gunners continued.

Then it was over. Less than thirty minutes after they had swooped down over the Afrika Korp's 21st Panzer Division the 79th's contribution to the El Hamma breakthrough was history. Shot up and widely scattered, they limped home to count noses.

Borsodi was missing, but would walk in the next day without a scratch. A British half-track had raced out to pick him up as soon as he hit the ground, and dodging bullets all the way he and his rescuers zigged and zagged back to the friendly side of the line where they spent the night in a slit trench infested with fleas.

Major Fred Delaney of the 316th was also down. He bellied in at the South African's drome, bloodied from a wound in the leg, but safe. So was Jack Watkins, who limped back to Causeway and a wheels-up landing. Captain Dave Brown and Lieutenants Art Weldon and Bob Spurgin, all from Borsodi's show, were missing. On Spurgin's initial pass, flak had torn an eight-inch hole in the wing of his P-40 (named *Beth Hanna*) and he was hit again as he circled back over the mountains for another run. With oil boiling up through the floor of the cockpit, Spurgin headed for home. He never got there. *Beth Hanna* quit on him while still on the wrong side of the line, forcing him to make a wheels-up landing in enemy territory.

Johnny Hoagland of the 85th Squadron and Bob Ligett of the 87th were also missing. Hoagland, nicknamed "General" by his buddies, had his engine shot out and landed unharmed in the middle of no-man's land. Rescued by the crew of a New Zealand bren-gun carrier he eventually made his way back through the lines (after first having a spot of tea with a New Zealand colonel) becoming, like Fred Borsodi, a member of the "Late Arrivals Club." Formed in the Western Desert by the RAF in 1941, membership was gained by making it safely through enemy lines, and entitled the aircrew member to wear the emblem of the winged boot on the left breast of his flying suit.

Ligett, Spurgin, Brown and Weldon were not so lucky. They were reached first by the Germans and would sit out the rest of the war behind barbed wire.

Bit by bit as the pilots straggled back, Intelligence officers began piecing together what had happened over the El Hamma road. Leading the 85th (Flying Skulls) Squadron, Major Jake Schoellkopf IV had put an 88-mm gun out of action, burned a truck and damaged another. Then, with Lieutenant Dick Bunker he shot up some enemy infantry shooting at them from a shallow ditch and damaged two more trucks. Malcolm "Joe" McNall hit three trucks – leaving one in flames – while Joe Connelly strafed a German staff car and six other vehicles before he was hit by ground fire and forced to break off his attack. Captain Johnny Cimaglia, the Skulls Ops Officer, damaged two trucks and left another burning brightly, and strafed a squad of infantry. Fred Hale shot up a tent full of soldiers, while Bob Taylor destroyed two trucks. Ralph Lind blasted a stone building being used as an observation post into crushed rock, shot up two large trucks and three smaller vehicles, and knocked out an anti-tank gun. George Blare knocked a tread off a Mark IV tank, and Sammy Say and Milt Clark shot up a command post, staff cars, motorcycles and numerous soldiers. Say, although not by design, also tore up a respectable length of enemy communications wire with the wingtip of his P-40.

The Skeeters (87th Squadron) were led by Captain Benjamin "Duke" Uhrich, the Squadron Commander. After dropping their wing bombs in a good pattern at the start of the attack, they broke off in pairs to strafe along the road and gun area at the head of the New Zealand corridor. The Duke, flying ol' 97 and with Lieutenant Edward Fitzgerald on his wing, burned two trucks and strafed a row of tents half hidden in a wadi; Fitzgerald added another truck destroyed and two damaged. Frank Huff blew up three trucks, and damaged three others, before a burst of 20-mm flak tore an 11-inch hole in his port wing near the wheelwell. Lee "Goose" Gossick in a P-40 called *The Gruesome Goose* strafed back and forth across the road almost all the way to El Hamma village, silencing an 88-mm gun and setting two trucks and a communications trailer on fire. Clinton "Butch" Owen added two more trucks to the Squadron's tally, and also gunned a number of donkey carts heading north up the road. Meanwhile, Asa A. "Ace" Adair took out an 88-mm gun crew and two trucks. For his efforts, he picked up several holes in his starboard wing.

Wyman D. "Porky" Anderson in *Hokus Porkus* blew up two trucks and a staff car before a cannon shell knocked him

Lt. Dick Morrissey of the Comanches (center) with two RAF pilots atop a downed Me-109 of JG 27. (Kauffman)

Captain Benjamin "Duke" Uhrich, shown here as a 1st lieutenant, led Skeeter Squadron through the deadly fire over the El Hamma road. Uhrich was a father figure to his pilots, who trusted him implicitly. (Wright)

In his Hokus Porkus, Lt. Wyman "Porky" Anderson blew up two trucks and a staff car before ground gunners knocked him out of the fight. (Morrissey)

out of the fight. The shell made a two-inch hole at the point of entry, bulging the wing's upper surface and piercing it with numerous small holes. William "Scotty" Rogers burned seven trucks and a gas bowser, and Morris Watkins took out an 88-mm gun that had shot up Bruce Morrison's Warhawk, but not before Morrison set four trucks on fire.

Paul McArthur and Bob Ligett were strafing a wadi south of El Hamma when both were hit. McArthur saw Ligett belly-in, then he too was hit in the fuel tank. Streaming high octane gasoline from the punctured tank, he swung around a small hill to rake two trucks and a tank with machine-gun fire, then joined up with "Ace" Adair and headed for Neffatia, Libya, home of 7 South African Wing.

The Comanches and Hell's Belles had been hit the hardest. Five of the fifteen aircraft taking part in the show didn't make it back, and the others all suffered battle damage of varying degree. In exchange for their losses, they took out an "eighty-eight," destroyed or damaged sixteen vehicles, and shot up scores of German infantry.

One Comanche pilot, Dick Morrissey, almost "bought it" on his first pass. Leading "B" Flight he swooped low over a wadi to find it filled with enemy soldiers firing at him with automatic weapons. He thought he was a dead duck. Fortunately, his wingman, Bill "Tiger" Taylor, was in a perfect position to rake the ditch with machine-gun fire which forced the enemy to dive for cover as Morrissey and Taylor zoomed over their heads unscathed. A few moments later the two pilots found themselves in a similar situation. This time neither were able to depress their guns. Again it was a close call. "I saw four or five '40s in front of me streaming white smoke from coolant hits, and figured my whole flight was goners, so I dove my ship right at the Jerries," Morrissey said. "I couldn't shoot but I must have scared hell out them because they all hit the dirt."[1] With that, Morrissey's flight looked for its New Zealand escort. They figured they had had enough excitement for one day and were ready to head for home. Instead, the New Zealanders led them back into the thick of the firestorm. After another low-level pass over a wadi filled with angry soldiers firing automatic weapons they finally set course for Causeway, eventually being the last flight to land.

Although costly, the aerial blitz by Desert Air Force fighters and fighter-bombers was an unqualified success. The New Zealanders quickly took advantage of the confusion it caused and poured through Tebaga Gap to mark the first time in the war that Allied airpower had paved the way for a major breakthrough on the ground.

Dick Morrissey's "B" Flight with (left to right), standing: Morrissey, Horace Cumberland and Jack Kauffman. Front: Bob Fuller, Jake Chamberlain and Bill "Tiger" Taylor. (Morrissey)

The shadows are lengthening as 79th ground personnel sweat out the return of their pilots from the El Hamma show. (Hoffman)

For the 79th, it would put on other and perhaps more spectacular shows, but El Hamma would always remain its outstanding contribution to the Tunisian campaign. It wasn't the Group's combat debut – that had taken place twelve days before – but it was still a relative newcomer to the fighting in North Africa. It wouldn't be long, however, before the 79th would become Eighth Army's favorite American fighter group and bask in the title of "Monty's Pets." That it was in North Africa at all, and not in China or the South Pacific, or hunting for German U-boats off the New England coast, was because of the British debacle at Tobruk just nine months earlier.

two

The Balloon Goes Up

"It looks as if it's the whole damned Afrika Korps!"

– British tank commander

Not large, its peacetime population numbered less than 5,000, the importance of Tobruk lay in its strategic location. At one time the main Italian fortress in Libya, and owning the only respectable harbor between Alexandria and Tripoli, it sat directly astride the main supply route on the North African coast just seventy-five miles west of the Egyptian frontier. The British captured Tobruk from the Italians in January 1941, and used the port as a base to supply their desert army. A month later, when the first German troops arrived in North Africa to bolster the faltering Italians, Tobruk became a prime objective for the German general who needed the port to support his advance to Egypt. The British were determined to hold Tobruk at all costs, however, and settled in for a long siege. Both sides knew that whoever held Tobruk held the key to Egypt, the Suez Canal and, ultimately, the Middle East.

For eight months the defenders of Tobruk continued to stand fast against repeated assaults. But time was running out. Six months into 1942 the enemy was once again knocking at the gates. This time with renewed vigor and determination.

The faint hint of another June dawn was just beginning to brighten the eastern horizon as a double column of German armor, covered with the coarse, gritty dust of the Libyan desert, rattled and clanked toward the anti-tank ditch that marked Tobruk's outer line of defense. A hundred yards short of this man-made barrier the column halted, engines idling impatiently, while a young panzer lieutenant in the lead tank scanned the hostile terrain in front of him, and studied with more than cursory interest a group of sappers (engineers) struggling to lay a bridge over the deep tank-traps. Then, right on schedule with the early morning sun came the Stukas, their gull wings and extended undercarriages giving them the appearance of evil, prehistoric birds of prey, as they wheeled and darted overhead to plant their cargo of whistling death on the British positions on the other side of the ditch. At the height of this cacophony of shrieking Stukas and exploding bombs the tanks lurched forward with a gnashing of gears and rumbled at flank speed into the billowing clouds of smoke and debris.

This was the armor of the 5th Panzer Regiment, the vanguard of Generaloberst (Colonel-General) Erwin Rommel's combat group, as the legendary Desert Fox mounted a three-division assault against Tobruk this twentieth day of June 1942.

The sappers and Stukas had done their jobs well. By mid-morning the entire 15th Panzer Division had crossed the hastily constructed bridges and was well inside the British perimeter. Later that afternoon sun-bronzed German infantrymen of the 90th Light Division roamed the streets of the city flushing out stragglers, while Krupp-built tanks sat atop Pilastrino Ridge menacing the bombed and battered harbor below with their long-barreled 75-mm guns. Tobruk was clearly in the bag and both Rommel and the garrison commander – Major-General H. B. Klopper, commanding general of the 2nd South African Division – knew it.

At a quarter to eight the next morning a large white flag, starkly visible against the dark pall of black smoke hovering over the city, fluttered weakly in the warm, still air above Klopper's headquarters. An hour later Rommel stood triumphantly in the center of Tobruk's main thoroughfare, his familiar desert goggles perched high above the brim of his cap, accepting the surrender of the beleaguered fortress from the disheartened South African. "For you the war is over," Rommel told a group of captured officers. "You have fought like lions and been led by donkeys."[1]

Tobruk had fallen at last! Tobruk, the city that had withstood a siege of eight long months, had now been taken in less than twenty-four hours, and echoed to the sound of jackboots on rubble-filled streets as the rank and file of the Afrika Korps washed desert sand from parched throats with captured British beer, and gorged themselves on Irish potatoes, Australian bully beef, and tinned South African pineapples, all part of the massive store of booty collected by Rommel's desert warriors. For with the capture of Tobruk, in addition to removing a major obstacle that blocked his advance to the Nile, tons of precious petrol and provisions, hundreds of serviceable vehicles, a large water-filtration plant, and a valuable if badly shattered port fell into Rommel's hands as well.

As the 33,000 battle-weary troopers of Tobruk's former garrison shuffled behind the wire of prisoner of war cages Rommel, summarily promoted to Generalfeldmarschall (Field Marshal) by a grateful Hitler on June 22, allowed himself the luxury of only a small tin of pineapples and a glass of Scotch whiskey before shifting his gaze eastward toward Egypt and the Suez Canal.

The door to Egypt was now wide open. With the Tobruk bastion eliminated and the rest of British Eighth Army in full retreat, Rommel could roll unhampered to the very banks of the Nile. The entire world realized that the pendulum of the North African battle – a battle that had see-sawed back and forth across the Western Desert for almost two years – had this time clearly swung in favor of Rome and Berlin. The fate of the Allies in Africa – perhaps the world – was sure to be influenced by the fall of this Libyan port city. In addition, the fate of the American 79th Fighter Group, at least as to when and where it would fight, had also been decided with the British disaster at Tobruk.

Generaloberst Erwin Rommel (shown here as a Generalleutnant), the famed Desert Fox of the Afrika Korps, studies a map of the North African battlefield with a member of his staff. With his capture of Tobruk, Rommel would be promoted to Generalfeldmarschall. (Bundesarchiv, Koblenz)

In June 1940 France was about to topple under the weight of the German war machine. The British Expeditionary Force to France had just been taken off the beaches of Dunkirk and, within a fortnight, the German swastika would be fluttering over the Eiffel Tower in Paris. Britain, now standing alone, was sure to fall. It seemed an ideal time for Italy's ambitious Benito Mussolini to share with Adolf Hitler in the fruits of victory. With his eye on French and British possessions in Africa, and particularly coveting the rich oil fields of the Middle East and Italian control of the Suez Canal, the bombastic *Il Duce* (the leader) tardily declared war on France and Great Britain in the second week of June and prepared to strike at Britain's "lifeline" in the Mediterranean. This "lifeline," the route through which passed almost all of Britain's commerce, was the narrow Suez Canal.

A small, densely populated island, England imported most of its food and the raw material needed to wage war from a vast empire in India and Asia. The shortest, fastest route from these rich, distant colonies was through the Red Sea, up the Suez Canal into the Mediterranean, and then past Gibraltar into the Atlantic. If denied this passage, shipping would have to make the long treacherous haul around the southern tip of Africa – a route that ran through the very heart of U-boat country and took almost twice as long. The delay in supplies reaching a hard-pressed England could well prove fatal. Accordingly, although she could ill afford to weaken the defenses of the home island in the face of a German invasion that was expected at any hour, the shorter route had to be protected at all costs, and the British War Ministry began to slowly trickle supplies and reinforcements to General Sir Archibald Wavell's Middle East Command headquartered in Cairo.

By July 1940 Wavell had gathered a force of 100,000 men with which to defend the entire eastern Mediterranean. His area of responsibility stretched from Algeria in the west to beyond the Persian Gulf in the east, and north and south from the

Balkans to Rhodesia. In what would prove to be the main battle arena – the so-called Western Desert between Tripoli and Alexandria – he had only the 37,000 men of Major-General Richard N. "Dick" O'Connor's Western Desert Force holding the line at Mersa Matruh. At sea, the Mediterranean Fleet sailing under the flag of Admiral Sir Andrew Cunningham was woefully out-gunned by the Italian Navy, while in the air the Royal Air Force could muster but a handful of antiquated aircraft – Blenheims, Lysanders, Sunderlands, and fabric-covered Gladiator biplanes – most of them already obsolete before they would ever fire a shot or drop a bomb in anger. This was the embryo Western Desert Air Force (WDAF) of Air Commodore Raymond Collishaw, a Canadian who had fought von Richthofen's "Flying Circus" from the open cockpit of a Sopwith triplane in the 1914-1918 war, scoring 60 victories in the air to place him third on Britain's all-time ace list. His guiding hand over the WDAF in the months ahead would many times more than make up for the numerical advantage enjoyed by the Italian *Regia Aeronautica* (Air Force).

Once in the war, the Italians struck quickly. In August 1940 they invaded British Somaliland and also seized frontier posts in the Sudan and northern Kenya. On September 13 the Italian Tenth Army – nearly 250,000 men strong – followed *Maresciallo d'Italia* (Field Marshal) Rudolfo Graziani out from Bardia and rolled almost unopposed eastward across the desert into Egypt, occupying Sidi Barrani three days later. There Graziani halted, sixty miles from O'Connor's main force at Mersa Matruh, to dig in behind a loose network of fortified outposts that stretched inland from the sea some fifty miles. The fast advance had extended his lines of communications almost to the limit and Graziani felt compelled to accumulate large stores of supplies before resuming the offensive. Despite urgings from Rome to keep pressing the British, pleas that fell on deaf ears and prompted Mussolini to remark that "one should give jobs to people who are looking for at least one promotion; Graziani's only anxiety is to remain a Marshal,"[2] the cautious Italian continued to sit complacently behind his poor-man's Maginot Line when all that stood between him and complete victory were the few understrengthed battalions of O'Connor's Western Desert Force sixty miles to the east.

O'Connor welcomed the unexpected respite. During the next ten weeks, as the two opposing armies faced each other separated only by a few miles of sand, he began to build up strength for an offensive of his own. In October, troops from Australia and New Zealand began arriving in Egypt to bolster his veteran 7th Armored and 4th Indian divisions; Collishaw received two squadrons of new Wellington bombers and a squadron of tank-busting Hurricanes, and the 2nd and 7th Royal Tank Regiments discarded their slow, thin-skinned vehicles for more modern equipment. By the second week of December O'Connor was ready.

Greatly outnumbered, his one advantage over the Italians was his sound grasp of the principles of desert warfare. The battlefield in North Africa was much like the sea, with coastal towns and villages nothing more than harbors serving not only the Mediterranean, but the desert "sea" as well. Bases were best defended by offensive action away from the harbors, while mobility and self-sufficiency was not only desirable but absolutely essential. As a long-time naval power Great Britain understood this perfectly and was quick to adopt naval tactics to the land battles of the Western Desert. Italy did not. Italian soldiers feared and hated the desert and never learned to cope with its hardships and dangers. Their tactics were based on traditional static defensive positions, which were quickly exploited by O'Connor's highly mechanized British and Commonwealth troops in a classic battle of penetration and encirclement.

When he unleashed his armor against Graziani's fortified camps near Sidi Barrani on December 9, O'Connor's fast tanks punched through a gap in the Italian line and drove for the sea. His infantry and slower tanks followed the first force through the gap, then turned and hit Graziani from the rear. The maneuver caught the Italians by complete surprise and after a brief fight that cost the British 624 killed, wounded or missing in exchange for over 38,000 prisoners – "five acres of officers and two hundred acres of other ranks"[3] – O'Connor was off and running. The British general then sent his armored columns boldly across the uncharted sands to block Graziani's escape and soon had most of Tenth Army pinned against the sea south of Benghazi. Surrounded, beaten, and thoroughly demoralized, the remnants of Mussolini's once-proud Expeditionary Force to Africa surrendered on February 7, 1941.

The Western Desert Force, outnumbered by almost seven to one, had destroyed the fighting effectiveness of an entire army in less than two months, and given the British their first major land victory of the war. Had he been allowed to continue his westward advance it is quite probable O'Connor could have swept unchecked across the desert to Tripoli, clearing all of North Africa of the enemy in 1941, thereby shortening the war by many months. But this was not to be. He was ordered to halt the drive and secure his lines near Benghazi. A new crisis was developing in the Balkans and Wavell need O'Connor's veteran divisions (plus most of Collishaw's experienced squadrons) to send as a fire brigade to that troubled spot.

The previous October, as O'Connor and Graziani faced each other across sixty miles of no-man's land, Mussolini had

decided to improve his territorial and maritime position in the eastern Mediterranean by sending his Albanian-based troops crashing across the border into Greece. As usual, the Italian Army wasn't equal to the task and was seriously rebuffed. Displaying superior skill in mountain fighting, the small Greek Army continuously outmaneuvered and outflanked its antagonist. By the end of the year the Italians had been forced back across the frontier and Mussolini's prestige sank to a new low. The Greek government, however, assessed (correctly so) that Hitler would not stand idle while his long-time friend and partner was beaten and humiliated; the German Army was expected to intervene on Italy's behalf at any moment. Late in February 1941, knowing they would be no match for Hitler's well-drilled legions, the Greeks appealed to the British for help.

The request was granted. More of a political gesture than a sound military move, and largely through the insistence of Winston Churchill who feared a German-Italian victory in Greece would induce neutral Turkey to side with the Axis, Wavell was ordered to rush ground, sea and air reinforcements to the Balkans as soon as possible, even at the risk of unguarding Egypt's western frontier.

What was sent was too little, too late. Wavell collected a conglomerate force of 60,000 men from his British, Australian and New Zealand divisions and sent them to Greece where they arrived April 5, one day before Hitler attacked both that country and Yugoslavia. Another 14,000 desert veterans were lifted to the off-shore island of Crete. What happened in the next few weeks, although not an irrevocable British disaster, was nevertheless a serious setback. Against the combined weight of the German Wehrmacht (armed forces) utilizing its infamous blitzkrieg tactics to near perfection, Wavell's fire brigade suffered one reverse after another. When Yugoslavia folded on April 17 the heart of the Greek resistance collapsed with it. The Germans were soon in Athens and the British were forced to stage another Dunkirk-style evacuation, leaving behind all of their precious heavy equipment. The Greek government surrendered the mainland on April 24, and the battle now shifted to Crete where a mixed force of Greek, British and New Zealand troops held out until the last day of May before a German glider and parachute attack – the first major airborne assault in history – made their position there untenable, and they too were evacuated.

The Grecian campaign had lasted only fifty-six days but the cost to British arms had run high. Casualties suffered by Wavell's command totaled more than 38,000 experienced fighting men, plus more than two dozen ships and scores of aircraft. Also lost in the hopeless struggle was the last chance for the Allies to gain an easy victory in North Africa. When Wavell next met the enemy on the sands of the Western Desert he would face not only the Italians, but the resourceful Germans as well.

In the spring of 1941 Hitler was preparing to violate a peace pact signed two years earlier with Russian dictator Joseph Stalin and go to war against the Soviet Union. Needing to secure his southern flank in the Middle East, he had watched with interest the fumbling of the Italians in Libya and Egypt. After Graziani's debacle in February, Hitler offered to send Mussolini ground and air units provided the Italians held their main base at Tripoli, undertook naval and air operations against the British ports of Tobruk and Benghazi, and neutralized the tiny island of Malta – a particularly bothersome thorn located in the middle of the Axis' Mediterranean shipping lanes.

The movement of two German divisions to Tripoli began in late February 1941 and a new German-Italian command, the *Deutsches Afrika Korps* (DAK), was created. The DAK, soon to become better known simply as the Afrika Korps, was led by a daring panzer commander who had caught Hitler's eye during the battle for France the year before – forty-nine-year-old General Erwin Johannes Eugen Rommel.

Thick, black smoke boils up from a British tank after it takes a direct hit from German artillery fire in the desert south of Tobruk. (National Archives)

In addition to the two fresh German divisions just getting off the boat at Tripoli, Rommel's command would also include one of five Italian divisions still in North Africa, but because the bulk of Axis manpower in the theater was still Italian, Rommel was chagrined to discover he would be subordinate to the *Comando Supremo* (Italian Army High Command) and its lackluster Commander-in-Chief, General Gariboldi. To further muddy his operational waters Luftwaffe units of *X Fliegerkorps* (roughly equivalent to an American numbered air force) sent as his air support would answer neither to him nor the *Comando Supremo*, but received orders directly from Berlin.

Rommel would soon prove himself a brilliant tactician and master of desert warfare, his name becoming a household word throughout much of Western Europe. But instead of eventually returning to his native Germany in triumph, Hitler's failure to grasp the full strategic importance of the Middle East, mutual suspicion and distrust among German and Italian commanders, and an unwieldy arrangement of tactical cooperation (or the lack of it) between German ground forces and supporting Luftwaffe units, would all contribute heavily to his subsequent defeat. First, however, he would severely test the will of Britain and her allies.

With the bulk of Wavell's army mired in the hopeless Grecian misadventure Rommel began the opening round in the battle for Egypt on March 24, 1941. It was the beginning of many see-saw battles fought in the Western Desert between the British and the Afrika Korps during the next eighteen months; battles that saw first one side, then the other, momentarily holding the advantage. A British officer, perhaps wistfully thinking of less perilous times, labeled these wild tank charges the "Benghazi Handicap."

At first Rommel rolled eastward with comparative ease. El Aghelia fell almost without a fight; Benghazi was his by April 3, and he was knocking at the gates of Tobruk one week later. There he was checked. Wavell realized that Tobruk was all that remained between Rommel and the Suez and threw in as many reinforcements as he could scrape together for its defense. For five days a bitter battle swirled around that city, but when the dust settled Tobruk was still British. Rommel's first bid for the Suez had failed. He could cross the Egyptian frontier, taking Bardia and Sollum (which he did), but could advance no farther as long as the British garrison at Tobruk threatened his supply lines.

Wavell, meanwhile, was under pressure from Churchill to launch a counterattack and relieve the isolated Tobruk defenders. With only two inexperienced divisions at his disposal the Middle East Commander was mildly apprehensive about his meager force being equal to the task. Nevertheless, he reassured himself that two divisions had been enough to rout the Italians in the same area six months earlier, and on May 15 Wavell struck back at the Afrika Korps in the Bardia-Sollum sector.

But the situation in the desert had changed since he last fought Tenth Army there. O'Connor, his brilliant tank commander, was gone, having been captured by a German patrol in April, and the enemy had converted the 88-mm anti-aircraft gun for use against tanks and infantry with terrifying and devastating results. Finally, Erwin Rommel, the unorthodox and innovative German, was not Rudolfo Graziani the overly-cautious and unimaginative Italian.

Wavell's attempt to relieve Tobruk was doomed from the start and he was badly mauled. Another abortive advance by the British a month later resulted in a resounding defeat for Wavell, and after three days of savage fighting the British withdrew back into Egypt. Churchill, who had goaded his Middle East Commander into a premature confrontation with Rommel, was shattered by the defeat and sacked Wavell in July (the British called it being "bowler-hatted"), replacing him with General Sir Claude Auchinleck, just recently summoned from India. Tall, athletic, notoriously monosyllabic, but with a highly original military mind, "the Auk" was viewed as the Indian army's most outstanding officer. His first task was to reorganize the Western Desert Force. He formed a new army around his handful of veterans – Eighth Army, the name first appearing in print on November 18, 1941 – and picked General Alan Cunningham who had just completed the reconquest of East Africa to lead it. At the same time reinforcements and material

German officers watch from afar as Stuka dive-bombers pound British positions near Tobruk. (National Archives)

from Britain and the United States continued to trickle into the Middle East. Slowly, Auchinleck began to win the race for supplies.

Meanwhile, Rommel's supply problems were just beginning. Hitler's Russian offensive had begun in June* and was siphoning off much of the material badly needed in the desert. That which *was* earmarked for the Afrika Korps was being heavily interdicted by the Royal Navy and RAF; less than half the tonnage coming down from Germany and Italy ever reached its North African destination, the rest lay spoiling on the floor of the Mediterranean. As a result, Rommel was still building up his supply base when Eighth Army, now made up of XIII and XXX Corps and numbering almost 700 tanks, went over on the offensive in the third week of November.

Auchinleck planned to have Cunningham send XXX Corps in a wide southern sweep around enemy lines and then turn north towards Tobruk. Hopefully, Rommel would assess this as Eighth Army's primary effort and turn loose his panzers in that area. Then, with the main battle tanks of the Afrika Korps irrecoverably committed, Cunningham would launch XIII Corps northward to isolate Bardia and Sollum while Tobruk's garrison punched its way out of its small perimeter on prearranged signal to form the anvil upon which Eighth Army would hammer the enemy. That was the theory. In actual practice it didn't go the way Auchinleck envisioned.

When "the Auk" made his move on November 18 Rommel, who was now in charge of all Axis ground forces in the desert, had two panzer divisions on the coast, two divisions of German infantry holding the eastern frontier near Bardia-Sollum, and five Italian divisions investing Tobruk. The Desert Fox was outnumbered in armor by more than 160 tanks, but his Mark IIIs and IVs were vastly superior to the Stuarts, Crusaders, Matildas and Valentines of the British and, more importantly, his "eighty-eights" outgunned the best that Eighth Army had by a good 1,800 yards. The Afrika Korps' edge in qualitative firepower, plus Rommel's erroneous belief that Eighth Army's offensive was nothing more than a reconnaissance in force, threw a monkey-wrench into Auchinleck's carefully laid plans and indirectly resulted in Cunningham being "bowler-hatted."

Rommel first realized he was facing more than just a local attack when forty-eight hours after the attack started he heard a BBC broadcast telling of a major British offensive in the desert. Thus he didn't react to the threat until the second day of the offensive, upsetting Auchinleck's delicate timetable. The British drive was quickly reduced to a series of unsynchronized assaults that were easily dealt with one at a time by the Afrika Korps. By November 23 Cunningham had been badly bloodied and prepared to withdraw. The stubborn "Auk" refused to sanction such a move, however, and losing faith in his Eighth Army commander fired him on the spot. Cunningham was replaced by Major-General Neil Ritchie three days later.

Eighth Army renewed its attack on November 27. After one more abortive attempt to relieve Tobruk a link-up with its garrison was finally effected two days later. This time it held. As British battle tanks churned up great clouds of dust south of the city Rommel realized he had been outmaneuvered and ordered a general withdrawal to the west. Ritchie relentlessly pursued him, sending his under-gunned and thin-hulled armor in a wide sweep designed to get behind the retreating enemy. Rommel was forced to retire even farther or risk losing his entire army. On December 15 he went past Benghazi, and by the end of the year had dug in near El Agheila, his original starting point some nine months earlier.

Here his position was strong. An impassable swamp guarded his southern flank while the Gulf of Sirte anchored his line in the north. With the front temporarily stalemated both sides began to gather supplies for another clash, a task made easier for Rommel who was near his main depot at Tripoli, than it was for Auchinleck whose supply line stretched all the way back to the Nile Delta. Both generals quickly discovered that indeed the desert was, as a captured German officer remarked after the campaign, "the tactician's paradise, but the quartermaster's hell."

On January 21, 1942 Rommel attacked again. Eighth Army was caught off balance and fell back to the Gazala-Bir Hacheim line some forty miles west of Tobruk, giving up Benghazi and abandoning large stocks of supplies that helped Rommel sustain his advance. But then once again the front was stalemated. Auchinleck's position was weak, but Rommel had advanced so far in so short a time that a pause to replenish was required. Again both sides struggled to win the quartermaster's war. This time the distance of each army from its respective supply depot was about equal.

As Malta-based aircraft and the Royal Naval continued to harass Axis supply convoys in the Mediterranean, Rommel was acutely aware that British strength was building up faster than his own. Knowing that the longer he waited the weaker he would become, he decided to strike before he lost the logistical war. On the night of May 27/28 he attacked the Gazala Line, a series of fortified positions south and west of Tobruk that stretched from Gazala on the coast some 40 miles south to Bir Hacheim,

* Hitler had originally planned to attack Russia (Operation BARBAROSSA) on May 15, 1941, but the defeat of the Italian armies in North Africa and Greece forced him to intervene on Italy's behalf, postponing BARBAROSSA until June 22. The five-week delay ultimately proved fatal.

a fortified "box" defended by the Free French. For the next three weeks, from Bir Hacheim to a desert crossroads a few miles to the north called Knightsbridge, there raged one of the fiercest tank battles of the entire war. When it was over the burned out hulks of hundreds of British and American-built tanks littered the bleak, arid landscape. With little left to oppose them, and the Western Desert Air Force driven back out of range, Rommel's panzers rolled up to the outskirts of Tobruk on the night of June 20, spanned the anti-tank ditches on makeshift bridges, and moved boldly into the city. Twenty-six hours later Tobruk was German, Rommel was a shiny new Generalfeldmarschall, and Eighth Army was in headlong retreat to the east.

At the apex of his career and with Egypt's distant pyramids beckoning, Rommel dashed quickly eastward along the coastal track in pursuit of a shattered Eighth Army. If he made it to the banks of the Nile the Middle East would be lost to the Allies. "To lose the Middle East meant to lose the southern supply route to the USSR and the main ferry route to India. India itself would be rendered difficult if not impossible to defend, and the lifeline to China would be correspondingly endangered. Loss of the oil wells in Iran and Iraq would be a severe blow, tantamount to cessation of Allied air and naval activity in the Indian Ocean. The economic gain to the Axis, although admittedly substantial, would not be so great as the economic and strategic loss to the Allies."[4] And always, there loomed the foreboding specter of a German link-up with the Japanese somewhere east of the Nile.

The fall of Tobruk was also a crushing blow to British prestige. The defense of the fortress against months of heavy siege had become a matter of fierce national pride – a symbol of tenacity and determination reflecting the very spirit of Eighth Army. Even the name . . . Tobruk . . . had become invested with a special sort of glamour. Thus, "of all the reverses ever suffered by British arms, few have caused a greater shock than the fall of Tobruk. It was quite unexpected and appeared inexplicable to all who were not there."[5] That its loss was clearly something much more serious in the eyes of the average British soldier than just another running of the "Benghazi Handicap" is evidenced by these words of an Eighth Army officer returning from the desert to England aboard ship when news of the defeat came over the radio:

> "There is a cold hand upon my heart. I feel sick and utterly miserable. Tobruk has fallen. Gone! It is hard to believe. I've had the wireless sets frantically searching the air for more and more details; but they are not to be had. All we know is Rommel penetrated the defenses there yesterday and that the show is now over. A tenseness is creeping into the atmosphere abroad [sic]. There are questions, questions, questions – all day long. It is a frightful blow."[6]

Winston Churchill was in Washington attending a conference with President Roosevelt when word of the capitulation reached him. Visibly shaken by the staggering news, and admitting to be the "most miserable Englishman in America since Burgoyne surrendered at Saratoga,"[7] he made an eloquent appeal to FDR for help, especially for bombers and fighters to bolster the RAF in the desert. As a result, an arrangement known as the Arnold-Portal-Towers Agreement was hastily signed. It provided that one American heavy bomb group, two medium bomb groups, and two fighter groups (the 33rd and 57th) would be sent to the Middle East as soon as possible, with another four groups to arrive early in 1943. These groups would be operationally controlled by the RAF Middle East and, in the case of the mediums and fighters, by the Western Desert Air Force, but were to be handled administratively by General Lewis H. Brereton's United States Army Middle East Air Force (USAMEAF), the immediate predecessor of what would eventually become the US Ninth Air Force.

Shortly after the Americans were plunged into the war at Pearl Harbor Allied planners had met in Washington to shape and plot their global strategy. It was decided Germany constituted the most perilous threat to the Allied cause and that all available resources would be utilized to counter the advances of the senior Axis partner while a holding action would be conducted against the Japanese in the Pacific. It was also at this conference that Churchill first proposed an Anglo-American invasion of Northwest Africa in conjunction with an Eighth Army advance westward across the desert as a means of tightening the ring around Germany. The American delegation, not wanting to fritter away resources on a Mediterranean adventure, were in complete disagreement with the British proposal, opting instead for a cross-Channel attack on the German-occupied northern French coast mounted from the British Isles.

The issue was still deadlocked when the fall of Tobruk and Rommel's subsequent rapid advance eastward settled the matter. To remove the menace of Rommel from Egypt (and to partially pacify Stalin, who was clamoring for a "second front") President Roosevelt directed his Chiefs of Staff on July 25, 1942 to implement the invasion of Northwest Africa at the earliest possible date.

To help meet the requirements for this invasion, now codenamed TORCH and scheduled for November 8, 1942, the US Twelfth Air Force was formed. Under the command of Brigadier-General James H. Doolittle who had just returned from his daring Tokyo raid, the fledgling Twelfth began drawing men and material from other commands to form the nucleus of the new air force. One of the units requested by Doolittle for use over the TORCH invasion beaches was the 33rd Fighter Group, a unit that had been undergoing extensive training since January 1941. The 33rd, however, was slated as the second fighter group (behind the 57th) to go to Egypt under the provisions of the Arnold-Portal-Towers Agreement. Desperately short of fighter aircraft, the War Department nevertheless recognized the validity of Doolittle's request for at least a trained, if not tried and proven, group over the TORCH assault beaches, and released the 33rd to the Twelfth Air Force. However, it was also recognized that fighter aircraft and combat crews were just as desperately needed in Egypt. In addition, it was felt that air superiority over the Eighth Army front in the Western Desert would be beneficial to the TORCH landings in Northwest Africa.

Therefore, the War Department set in motion the paperwork necessary to send another fighter group to Egypt in place of the 33rd. The group chosen was one just then being formed – the 79th Fighter Group.

three

To Find a War

"We found right off the bat that the Germans knew an awful lot more about things than we did, and that all we had was our eagerness."

– General Philip G. Cochran

The war in the desert was still Rommel's to win when someone from the Long Range Desert Group (a British commando-type unit operating in enemy territory) first proposed installing a squadron of the American 57th Fighter Group behind and south of the German lines near the Libyan-Egyptian frontier. From there, so the theory went, they could sneak their Curtiss P-40s in under radar cover and hit the unsuspecting enemy from the rear. Lt.-Colonel Frank Mears, the 57th's skipper, bought the idea and in early November 1942 a truck convoy carrying squadron support personnel rolled south behind a column of Matilda tanks to prepare a temporary landing ground behind enemy lines. Riding with the ground crew was 1st Lieutenant Fred A. Wright, Jr., a pilot from the 79th Fighter Group on detached service with the 57th.

The convoy had followed a faint desert track in a southwesterly direction for several dusty hours when shortly before dusk two Messerschmitt Me 109Gs whistled down the length of the column low enough to kick up small plumes of dust with their prop wash. Their sandy-brown camouflage made them barely visible in the fading Egyptian sunlight as they chandelled sharply to port, dumped gear and flaps, and prepared to set down on the hard, sun-baked floor of the desert. The German pilots had incorrectly identified the convoy as one of their own, an excusable but oft-times fatal error in the hit-and-run fighting west of Alamein. It wasn't until a nervous tank gunner garbaged up the air around them with a half dozen cannon shells that they realized their mistake, hurriedly cleaned up their kites, and headed for a quieter piece of sky. An hour later a flight of twin-engined Ju 88s, informed of the convoy's location by the pair of errant fighters, were overhead with bombs tumbling earthward. No damage was done, but with the element of surprise now lost the column returned to its base near Alexandria later that night.

For Fred Wright, who had been in North Africa less than two weeks, it was his initial brush with combat and his first close-hand look at Willi Messerschmitt's highly-touted fighter. Although the ground was a frustrating place for a fighter pilot to be when enemy planes were overhead, he would soon be assigned an aircraft in the 57th's "Six Five" Squadron. The next time he met the Luftwaffe he would be airborne.

A native of Gulfport, Mississippi and graduate of pilot class 42-D, he joined the 57th in the early summer of 1942 at Groton, Connecticut. When the 57th sailed for Egypt aboard the carrier *Ranger* in July a small cadre, including Fred Wright, stayed behind to form the nucleus of the 79th Fighter Group. Now, sixteen weeks later, although officially assigned to the 79th, he was back with his original outfit on a temporary basis.

Activated on February 9, 1942 at Florida's Dale Mabry Field near Tallahassee, the 79th and its three squadrons – the 85th, 86th and 87th – exchanged personnel eleven weeks later with the 81st Pursuit Group (the Army Air Forces changed its "pursuit" designation to "fighter" in May 1942) at Morris Field, Charlotte, North Carolina. On paper the 81st went to Florida and the 79th to North Carolina without personnel or equipment, each unit absorbing the other. In reality it was simply a redesignation; a changing of numbers rather than a changing of men.

In late June the 79th left Morris Field (which later in the war would have the dubious distinction of having the highest VD rate of any stateside base in the AAF), and traveled to New England. There, on a rainy evening in early July the new commanding officer of the Group, Lt.-Colonel Peter McGoldrick, moved his headquarters section and 85th Squadron into an air base near Bedford, Massachusetts. McGoldrick, who had graduated at Kelly Field with Pilot Class 40-A in March 1940, set up shop in a grassy orchard, installing his staff in a nondescript cow barn cleared of cattle and swallows, but not of cobwebs. With the thirty-year-old West Pointer were Major Earl E. Bates, the Group's Operations Officer, and Captain J. Frederick Schoellkopf IV, skipper of the 85th Squadron. The 86th, with Captain Jack West* settled into Theodore Greene Field at Hillsgrove, Rhode Island, while Captain Charles E. Grogan's 87th set up camp at Rentschler Field near Hartford, Connecticut. The lines of communication between headquarters and the squadrons were kept open by a battered and temperamental Waco biplane that flew between the three fields.

As personnel culled from bases and training depots all along the east coast began fleshing out the original cadre formed by the 57th, the 79th started a summer of intensive training. The new "sports" checked out in the P-40 and flew training missions daily, with one or two coastal intercept missions becoming actual operations, while mechanics peered into the innards of the big Allison engine to learn its secrets, and other ground crew began to develop and fine-tune their skills as well.

One of the new "sports" was Charles Jaslow. As part of the small cadre from the 57th left behind when that group headed overseas, Jaslow had been with the 57th at Bradley Field since graduating from flying school in April. His squadron commander had been the colorful Philip G. Cochran, who would later gain fame in North Africa as "Mr. P-40," and in Burma where he headed the 1st Air Commando Group. He was also the inspiration for Colonel Flip Corkin, a character in Milton Caniff's popular comic strip, *Terry and the Pirates.* Jaslow remembers him as the man who saved his flying career after he demolished a P-40 in May 1942, fresh out of flying school.

It was only Jaslow's third hop in a P-40, and he cracked up attempting a short-field takeoff. Unhurt, he climbed out of the wrecked airplane. Within seconds a jeep pulled up with Cochran in it and the ambulance right behind him. Jaslow was taken to the base hospital, and when the flight surgeon found nothing wrong with him, Cochran immediately took him back to the flight line and shoved him into the cockpit of the nearest P-40. "Get it in the air, sport!" he said. With Cochran watching him like a hawk, Jaslow took off, did a circuit around the field, and landed. "I'm firmly convinced that if he hadn't gotten me back in the air right after my accident I would never have flown again," Jaslow said. "He didn't give me time to think about it."[1]

Lt. Fred Wright of the Skeeters, attached to the 57th Fighter Group for combat experience in the fall of 1942, with Miss Squirm, a P-40 obviously inherited from 112 Squadron RAF. (Wright)

As the training intensified, the 79th slowly began shaping up, a task made more difficult when the War Department pirated a substantial number of officers and noncoms in late July to form yet another group – the 325th. The Allies were in trouble all over the globe and the AAF was frantically racing against time to put combat crews in the field. By late September the 79th was ready.

Sunday, September 27 started out much like any other Sunday afternoon, with the usual rumors floating around – "they were going to England . . . they were going to China . . . they were going to stay in the United States as part of a static defense group" – and many suffered from the usual daze following Saturday night. Some of the younger officers were entertaining friends in a nearby farm house when word came that Colonel McGoldrick wanted his staff to gather in the "barn," where he told them the 79th had been placed on overseas alert. The Group's social life ended abruptly. Leaves were canceled, equipment packed and crated, the weary P-40s inherited from the 57th Group just three months earlier were turned over to the new 325th, and last minute phone calls were placed to hometowns all over the United States. Several years after the war Katherine Woerpel Radke, writing in the Waterloo (Wis.) *Courier*, recalled the inadequacy of words during those last minute farewells:

> "The call [from her brother, later killed over France] was like thousands of others made in those days. We talked of family, generalities, even the weather, while the wires oozed with the words held in check that became more evi-

* West would leave within a few weeks to help organize another group, and Tarleton "Jack" Watkins would take over the 86th.

dent as the light banter of conversation continued. When the operator advised 'time is up,' the brother, very much in character, quickly said, 'Well, this is it, we're heading out. Keep your chin up.' In one of the most dramatic moments of our lives, which called for some sage remark, I could come through with nothing but such stupid words as, 'Keep your neck clean.'"

That night, under the watchful eye of more than a hundred of Bedford's citizens, the ground echelon left "secretly" by rail, arriving at its staging area at Indiantown Gap, Pennsylvania late the next afternoon. Six hectic days were spent at the Gap, home of the Pennsylvania National Guard, before they moved once again, this time to Hampton Roads near Norfolk, Virginia. There they were assembled at dockside beneath the glass roof of a rectangular shed. Loaded down with rifles, helmets, musette bags and a myriad of other gear; in need of shaves and eyes red from a sleepless night, they filed out of the shed as their names were called and struggled up the ladders of a large, gray troopship known to them then only as HR-18.

They surveyed their new floating home. The vessel, belching thick black smoke from two oversized stacks, was soon discovered to be the former Cunard luxury liner *Mauretania,* a ship with a famous name and proud heritage. The original *Mauretania* was built in 1907 and held the North Atlantic speed record for twenty-two years. It was broken up for scrap in 1935 and a second *Mauretania* – the one that would take the 79th to war – was launched four years later. It was operated by Cunard White Star Ltd. prior to being taken over by the British Ministry of War Transport, and after the war it resumed regular passenger service for the Cunard line until scraped in 1965. An anonymous enlisted man described the first few days aboard ship:

"The morning sun was the only official witness when we staggered (and when you have a full pack with barracks bag you stagger) onto the great liner that was once polished bright and shiny but was now merely polished. We climbed three stories in this floating Empire State Building and plunked ourselves and our luggage down on what was called the Main Deck Aft. Landlubbers like myself, from the prairies of Kansas, soon learned that 'aft' was rear and 'deck' meant two things: the place nearest the water and the place where you got hot in warm weather and cold in cool weather.

". . . when we chugged away from the dock it was a toss-up to see which way the ship would turn so that you could be on the side to get a last glimpse of the United States, and space next to the rail was selling like hotcakes for six-bits and up.

". . . rolling on the high seas, we had our first boat-drill. 'Action Stations!' the loudspeaker roared, and on went the water canteens and out to the boat stations we went. Finding Boat Station 8 when you have four floors of troops trying to do the same was confusing, but eventually we got it down to perfection.

Fred Wright's wingman, his P-40 still sporting early-war national insignia, moves in close. (Wright)

"The sea immediately did not agree with many individuals, and it was at this point that most of us Army men were glad we hadn't joined the Navy. Eating was a problem. Two meals a day of mutton, and the meals were so light we almost had to nail the tables to the deck so they wouldn't fly away.

"Several days from shore we ran into Old Man Sun. Shirts were ripped off and on came the shorts. The ship's canteen did a rush business selling shorts, and when they were all sold out, down came the order telling us wearing of shorts was forbidden. It's things like that that get soldiers in a fighting mood."[2]

When the *Mauretania* left Hampton Roads on October 7 she sailed alone.

"For ten days she steamed in solitary majesty, changing course every fifteen minutes as a precaution against enemy submarines lurking along the eastern seaboard of the United States. Southward from the Virginia Capes she sailed, through a graveyard of Allied merchantmen, but here, for forty-eight hours at least, was aerial escort by Lockheed Hudsons, Catalina flying boats, and white-camouflaged Fortresses.

"From the North American coastal waters the *Mauretania* entered the treacherous Caribbean. Rumor had marked every latitude as the spot of a recent torpedoing and the nights buzzed with tales of enemy submarines. The *Mauretania,* with her cargo of over 7,000 air force, ordnance, engineering and medical personnel, was a definite Iron Cross for any German U-boat commander.

"After ten days a strip of land was sighted; a bit of green – Brazil! German-built aircraft with Brazilian markings flew overhead, the irregular 'whomp-whomp' of their unsynchronized engines easily discernible. The ship dropped anchor at Rio de Janeiro to take on water and fuel while an outmoded destroyer of the Brazilian Navy circled constantly, screening the *Mauretania* with smoke. There was no blackout in Rio, and the lights in the evening reflected the broad avenues, the modern apartments, the inviting bars. All was clear to the naked eye – clearer and more tantalizing through binoculars. Yet, for reasons of security, no one was permitted to leave the ship.

"On the morning of October 20 she sailed again. By this time everyone knew it was Africa; but what part, and then where? Life steadied. During the warm days and beautiful balmy nights it was impossible to believe there was a

Lt.-Colonel Peter McGoldrick, first wartime commander of the 79th, and first member of the Group to die in combat. Flying with the 57th to gain combat experience, McGoldrick was killed on November 6 strafing a motor convoy near Charing Cross, Egypt. (Hoffman)

Major Earl Bates with Lil Joe II, the only aircraft in the Group to carry the Falcon insignia. He took over the 79th after McGoldrick was killed. (Lappin)

war raging on the other side of the ocean; it seemed more like a vacation cruise.

"Suddenly, the weather changed drastically. The wind howled and roared, reaching near hurricane force as the ship rolled in the mountainous seas. There were flurries of snow in the air and graceful Arctic terns swept lazily overhead. The *Mauretania* had dipped far south, well into the 'Roaring Forties,' to avoid a wolfpack that had struck a convoy off the African Cape. Everyone changed quickly from suntans to woolens, and speculation was rife as to how long a lifeboat could withstand the battering of the sea.

"On October 30 two South African gunboats escorted the ship into the harbor at Durban and everyone was granted a welcome forty-eight hour shore leave. Durban was famous among seafaring people for its hospitality, and did not disappoint the *Mauretania's* passengers when they went ashore to feast on steak and eggs, and warm British beer. Since leaving the States they had subsisted on cold fish, boiled potatoes, and mutton – Durban was a welcome change.

"Two days later, after a false start prompted by a submarine scare, they sailed again, passing through Mozambique Channel close enough to the island of Madagascar to see flashes of gunfire from an artillery duel. Hugging the east coast of Africa the *Mauretania* slipped into the Red Sea, glided effortlessly past Aden, and finally docked at Port Tewfik, Egypt on November 12 – 10,000 miles and thirty-eight days from home."[3]

Debarking, they arrived at the RAF transit camp at Kasfareet near Great Bitter Lake the same day, and for the first time felt the disturbance of sand under their collars and gazed upon British Wimpys,* Spitfires and Hurricanes. A squadron historian noted:

American pilots were tutored by combat-wise RAF officers. Shown here is Wing Commander Billy Drake of 112 Squadron. In six months of fighting over the desert he accounted for fifteen enemy aircraft. (Kauffman)

"We were quartered in brick barracks that were far from luxurious. Everyone slept on hard concrete floors. We froze at night, sweat during the day, and fought hordes of pernicious flies night and day. We almost perished on the British rations, some of the offerings in the mess being beyond reasonable description. At night we watched two-year-old movies under the stars, and during the day there was swimming in the Suez – if you liked ice water. We had our first contact with the British, beginning a relationship first characterized by prejudice, but later on one of mutual confidence and trust.

* Nickname for the Wellington bomber, which was named for the hamburger-loving character Wellington J. Wimpy in the *Popeye* comic strip.

The 79th's first overseas base was Landing Ground 174, some forty miles west of Alexandria. (Kauffman)

A bleak and barren wasteland, LG-174 was soon transformed into a livable base. As were most landing grounds in the Western Desert, LG-174 was nothing more than a wide, flat tract of land with runway boundaries marked by empty fifty-five gallon gasoline drums. (Hoffman)

"The desert landscape, bleak and uncompromising, filled us with awe. The day we were scheduled to leave we had our first taste of desert sandstorm, or *khamsin* as they were called by the natives. The fine brown particles of sand blew in from the hills to the west, obliterating everything from view, seeping through every crack in the building. We huddled on the concrete floor with blankets over our heads.

"On the night of November 17 we boarded a creaky, antiquated train for Amaryia, Egypt, twenty miles southwest of Alexandria. After an all-night train ride that took us through Cairo we arrived at a bleak, desolate stretch of sand and scrub where British lorries took us to our final destination – in the midst of yet another sandstorm. The black tarmac road was swept with twisting rivers of sand driven by the high winds as we turned off the road into nowhere. Our hearts sank. There was nothing to be seen through the haze of the storm except the dull, yellow floor of the desert, and an occasional clump of thorny brush. The storm lifted slightly as we reached our camp area, indistinguishable from the rest of the landscape, with only a few forlorn and lonesome tents flapping in the wind, and desolation as far as the eye could see. We had arrived at our first overseas base, a flat, open stretch of desert some forty miles west of Alexandria – Landing Ground 174. There we were met by members of the advance party and most of the pilots who told us that Colonel McGoldrick had been killed."[4]

McGoldrick and some of his pilots had gone on ahead of the rest of the Group to fly with the 57th, gaining experience they could then pass along to the others. On November 6 his flight attacked a convoy of German motor transport near Charing Cross, Egypt. As he was swinging around for a second strafing pass his Warhawk was hit by ground fire. Attempting a wheels-up landing nearby, he was killed instantly when the P-40 skidded into a minefield and blew up. Major Earl E. Bates, the Group Ops Officer and an old fighter hand since 1935, took over command of the 79th.

Shortly after the ground echelon left Bedford, the pilots checked in briefly at Grenier Field at Manchester, New Hampshire, where they remained until October 22, then moved on down to Miami. The next day they began pulling out of Miami's 36th Street Airport in Air Transport Command (ATC) C-54s on the first leg of their long journey to Cairo.

Using the Antilles Island chain as a stepping stone across the Caribbean (airfields had been constructed along the route on sites obtained from the British in the 1940 exchange for fifty outmoded destroyers) they flew to Natal, Brazil where they boarded Pan American Clippers for the west coast of Africa. The 2,800-mile trip across the South Atlantic usually required a refueling stop at tiny Ascension Island 1,400 miles out of Natal. Ascension featured thirty-four square miles of lava and rock-strewn bleakness – "a crow would break his leg trying to land here," surveyors said[5] – and countless thousands of noisy "wide-awakes" or native sooty terns. The large birds were a hazard to flight operations as they flew excitedly over their nests to a height of 200 feet or more, getting in the way of the large transports with an impact great enough to smash a

Boresighting the six guns of a P-40 kicked up just enough dust to sour an armorer's disposition. (Kauffman)

An annoying feature of all desert bases were the numerous dust storms (khamsins) that boiled up out of the west on a moment's notice. (Hoffman)

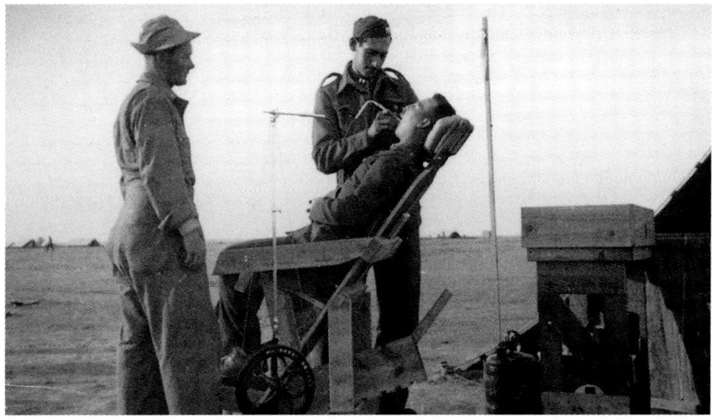

Captain Irving Fernebok attends to the dental needs of a patient at his desert "clinic." Cpl. Walter Rowe supplies the footpower to operate the drill. (Hoffman)

window in the pilot's compartment. As the overloaded Clippers strained to reach this former British cable station and its 6,000-foot runway, most of the passengers were aware of a popular ATC ditty then making the rounds on the African run: "If we don't hit Ascension, my wife gets a pension . . ."

After a brief stop the Clippers, with fuel tanks topped off, clawed through huge flocks of "wide-awakes" and set course for either Fisherman's Lake, Liberia or the Gold Coast village of Accra.

At Accra, described as "a happily disturbed colony of khaki ants where everyone is enroute to a war, and vehicles of every description clutter the streets like boom time in Nevada City,"[6] Pan American Airways operated a P-40 assembly plant. As crated aircraft arrived by ship at nearby Takoradi they were trucked to Accra and erected by maintenance crews. When the P-40s later rolled out of the assembly plant in flying condition small flights, usually with a Boston (Douglas A-20, a light bomber) guiding the way, headed out across the wide waist of Africa for Cairo. Primitive airstrips had been hacked out of the veldt along the ferry route that passed over Nigeria, French Equatorial Africa and the Sudan, and the pilots slipped in and out of such exotic sounding places as Kano, Fort Lamy, El Fasher and Khartoum, before reaching the old, established airport of Heliopolis outside of Cairo.

Charles Jaslow's flight was typical:

> ". . . we would set out each morning at dawn, gathered around the A-20. The first day we landed at Kano for refueling and then on to Maiduguri [in the bush country at the edge of the Sahara Desert] for overnight. Pan Am had set up all the stations across Africa so the accommodations and food were good. At Maiduguri they had pet leopards and I played with one and almost got bitten.
>
> "The next morning we left at dawn again . . . we were in our planes and ready to go as soon as the sun rose. We landed at Fort Lamy for refueling and left as soon as we could for Khartoum where we landed just as night was closing in – it was close. We spent the night at Khartoum University sleeping on cots on the veranda. The next day (our third day out) we took off for Wadi Halfa for refueling. They had to refuel our planes from five-gallon cans and it took forever. It was also very hot. Our planes were 'red-lined' at 120 degrees – we weren't supposed to start or run the engines if the temperature gauge was over 120 – but at Wadi Halfa the gauges read more than 120 before we started the engines, so we lined up in a row, cranked up the engines and took off straight ahead. And prayed! That night we landed at Cairo."[7]

The 57th Fighter Group, the first of the Arnold-Portal-Towers fighter groups sent to Africa, had reached Khartoum by the end of July. But instead of going directly into combat, the Group was sent to Palestine to train with the Western Desert Air Force. As badly needed as they were, the arrival of American aircraft and airmen caused training, maintenance, and policy problems for the British.

To begin with, desert flying required specialized training – even combat-savvy Battle of Britain fliers underwent a period of indoctrination before being posted to front-line desert squadrons – and it would have been senseless slaughter to put American pilots, with no combat experience and little knowledge of the desert, up against seasoned Luftwaffe and Italian veterans as soon as they arrived overseas.

Also, with ground facilities at a premium in the Western Desert and American service crews usually arriving in the theater later than their pilots, a strain was put on the RAF maintenance program. For every American plane serviced, a British Kittyhawk, Hurricane or Spitfire remained unattended. Thus, although American combat crews and aircraft were beginning to reach the North African war zone in ever-increasing numbers, it did not necessarily mean there were more aircraft available to put in the air against the enemy.

Lastly, there was some fear among high-ranking RAF officers that the flow of lend-lease Kittyhawks – the British import version of the P-40 – to British units would decrease as the Americans strived to build up their own fighting force.

These difficulties were soon resolved by integrating the American units with British squadrons until the former were able to stand on their own. In this way the three squadrons of the 57th Fighter Group were smoothly filtered into the Western Desert Air Force. Pilots began training with RAF 233 Wing,* and later flew operational missions with 239 Wing before entering combat as a group for the first time in early October. Likewise, when members of the 79th's air echelon arrived in Egypt they were fed into the squadrons of the 57th Group to begin *their* period of desert apprenticeship. Knowledge gained here would then be passed on to the new arrivals. Thus it was that Colonel McGoldrick had been flying combat and had been killed, and Fred Wright, who was a flight leader with the 79th Group's 87th Squadron, found himself on temporary duty with the 57th Fighter Group in the first week of November 1942.

By November 1942, however, the tactical situation in North Africa that had seemed so grim in early summer, and had prompted the 79th's move to Egypt, had turned in favor of the Allies.

After Rommel seized Tobruk in June he had pushed east along the coast at a fast pace, hoping to keep Eighth Army off balance as he drove for the Nile. But Auchinleck, stubborn and determined as ever, rallied his routed army for a tenacious stand at Mersa Matruh that slowed Rommel's advance long enough to allow Eighth Army to fall back and dig in on a line near the small railroad junction of El Alamein.

Here the front narrowed. To the north lay the blue waters of the Mediterranean; thirty-five miles south the quicksand of the Qattara Depression created a natural barrier. Only forty miles from Alexandria, this line was clearly the "last ditch" for the British. If Rommel wasn't stopped here there was nothing to prevent him from reaching Cairo. Most bets were on Rommel. The Italians felt so confident they shipped a brass band to Africa, along with a large, white stallion for Mussolini to ride when he led victory parades in Alexandria and Cairo. Conversely, with the Afrika Korps alarmingly close, the Royal Navy steamed out of Alexandria on July 1 and British officials in

Alexandria was a favorite furlough city for Allied troops of all nations on leave from "The Blue." (Kauffman)

Cpl. Joseph Pumphrey adorns tail section of 79th Warhawk with fine example of his artwork. Note photo taped to rudder. (Hoffman)

* A RAF wing was equivalent to an American group, usually consisting of three squadrons operating either independently or as a homogenous unit. Unlike its American counterpart, the RAF squadron was not permanently attached to the parent organization but was interchangeable from wing to wing as the occasion dictated. The RAF group was a rung above the wing on the organizational ladder, handling operational and administrative duties of two or more wings.

Cairo became so skittish they began burning secret documents, spreading so much black paper ash into the sky that the date became known as "Ash Wednesday."

British fears were premature. Rommel was in no position to attack just yet, and on July 7 he dug in opposite Eighth Army. His rapid advance had created a logistical nightmare for his quartermaster corps, with supply lines now reaching all the way back to Tobruk, Benghazi, and even Tripoli. In addition, Hitler's campaign in Russia was bleeding other German war theaters white; only a meager shipment of supplies was allotted for Rommel's desert campaign. He would have to fight with what he had or could capture.

Many crack Luftwaffe units had also been pulled out of North Africa to support German ground forces in Russia, giving the Western Desert Air Force a much-needed respite of sorts, and allowing Malta-based air and naval forces a clean shot at Axis convoys running the Italy-to-Africa gauntlet. Enemy shipping at the time stood about one chance in four of reaching a North African port while the British, bolstered by an American war production that was finally beginning to operate at full capacity, continued to pour men and material into the Middle East at an ever-increasing rate.

Major Tarleton "Jack" Watkins, commanding officer of the 86th Squadron, in front of his desert home at Landing Ground 174. With an A-20 group in Hawaii the day the Japanese showed up there unannounced, he retired after the war as a brigadier general. (Kauffman)

During July and throughout much of August, as both sides feverishly prepared for the inevitable showdown by stocking arms, munitions and other accouterments of battle, the front was relatively quiet; only limited attacks were mounted as patrols probed for weak spots in the line. Churchill used this lull to once again change commanders, and during the second week of August the arrival of General Harold R. L. G. Alexander and Lt.-General Bernard Law Montgomery to lead Middle East Command and Eighth Army, respectively, pumped new life into the sagging British and Commonwealth forces.

Alexander was the very epitome of a professional British Army soldier. A strict disciplinarian – his insistence on deportment and military courtesy was legend – he was also known for his imperturbability and charm, a personality trait that endeared him to his own troops and the Americans as well.

Montgomery, meanwhile, was destined to become one of the most publicized and controversial figures of the war. Relentlessly professional in his attitude toward soldiering, and austere to a fault in his personal life, he also had that rare gift

Shot down behind the lines while flying with the 57th, Lt. Jack Kelly of the Comanches was back on flight status within twenty-four hours. (Kelly)

For the price of a pack of "V" cigarettes (five cigarettes to a pack), Lt. Lee "Goose" Gossick of the Skeeters has fresh eggs delivered to the front door of his canvas home by an Arab carrying a live hen in a sack. (Gossick)

A few empty ammo boxes and a hand-operated clippers provides all the tools needed to equip the Flying Skulls' tonsorial parlor at a desert base. (Craig)

for capturing the imagination and confidence of the men he led. But modesty was not one of his virtues, and he was usually at odds with most American commanders because of his inability or unwillingness to improvise, and his condescending and supercilious demeanor.

By the end of August Rommel felt strong enough to attack. German intelligence had reported the British spread dangerously thin at the southern end of the Alamein line near the Qattara Depression. He planned to feint an attack in the north near the sea, then conduct a holding action in the center of the line while delivering his main blow against the weak southern positions. As soon as he penetrated the line he would turn north and strike for the coast, thereby encircling Eighth Army and cutting British lines of communications.

Unfortunately for Rommel, this was exactly what Montgomery expected him to do and he prepared his defense accordingly. When Rommel launched his offensive on the night of August 30/31, he immediately ran into trouble – any real hope he had entertained of cutting off Eighth Army was soon dashed – and within forty-eight hours he was forced to withdraw back to his original start line. The discreet thing to do would have been to withdraw back into Libya, nearer his supply point while drawing the British away from theirs, but a cable from Berlin forbade such a move. He was ordered to hold where he was. Rommel had no choice but to strengthen his position at El Alamein and hope he could ward off the counterattack that was sure to come.

For almost two months Rommel fortified his line while his British opponent shuffled troops, assembled equipment and supplies, and worked out a detailed plan of attack. The RAF and Royal Navy once again helped Montgomery win the quartermaster's war, and by late October Monty outnumbered his German adversary by more than two to one. He was ready to go on the offensive.

In the early evening hours of October 23 a tumultuous artillery barrage lit up the entire thirty-five mile front for fifteen deafening minutes as some 800 Eighth Army guns pounded pre-selected targets. Then the fire lifted to become a creeping barrage and Montgomery attacked all along the line, his tankers and riflemen moving out across no-man's land and into the "marsh," the deep German and Italian minefields. From the Mediterranean to the Depression they advanced: Tommy, South African, Indian and Greek. Men from Australia, France and New Zealand; two battalions of French Foreign Legionnaires, and a flying column of Spahis. Some, like the Highlanders, marched to the same strains of music heard at Ticonderoga, Lucknow and Waterloo, moving forward, bayonets at the ready, behind their regimental bagpipers. This was the opening round of one of the decisive battles of World War II – El Alamein, the end of the beginning in North Africa.

The bitter fighting raged under the hot sun for nearly ten days until, on November 2, Eighth Army broke through the German positions and into the open country beyond. Rommel had clearly lost the battle; to prevent losing his army as well, he ordered an immediate withdrawal despite contrary instructions from Berlin.

The run of German-Italian conquests in Africa had been decisively checked. Never again would the *Panzerarmee Afrika* (as the Afrika Korps was now officially known) mount an offensive of any consequence; gone forever was the dream, savored by German and Italian alike, of sipping whiskey and soda in the bar of Cairo's Shepheard's Hotel. Although still seven months and many lives from the finish, the North African campaign and been conclusively decided on the cruel, hot sands between the Qattara Depression and the Sea.

With the enemy now on the defensive and falling back to the west, there was no immediate need to commit the 79th to combat. For the next two months it would stay at Landing Ground 174 training under desert conditions.

In the first few days after their arrival tents were pitched and banked (the men lived in British "EPIP" tents designed for use in India that featured a canvas covering over the tent with a one-foot space to allow air to flow through and keep it "cool"); lights and communications established; slit trenches dug (but never used), and other refinements added until gradually the barren wasteland was transformed into a livable, permanent base. As were most airstrips in the desert, LG-174 was nothing more than a flat piece of land with runway boundaries marked with 55-gallon fuel drums. Called landing grounds when built by the British, airdromes when built by the Americans, few, if any structures were of a permanent nature, and barracks, hangars, repair shops and other buildings usually related to an active airdrome were virtually non-existent.

The popular conception (the British called it "the cinema impression") of a desert did not apply to the area surrounding 174. "There was much less sand than one might expect, and the sandstorms so often mentioned were more frequently choking clouds of dust rather than sand. Vast stretches were hard, firm going (except after rain), and resembled flat rock more than anything else. There were practically no features in the landscape other than occasion shallow depressions. Where the Western Desert was true to convention however, was in its lack of water. A pipeline had been constructed all the way from Alexandria, and this supply eked out with the rather brackish water obtained from local wells. Even so, the normal water ration was one gallon per head, per day, for all purposes . . . Among the more disagreeable features [of the desert] were the flies, a filthy, pertinacious, excruciating pestilence. As for the climate, it was not so trying after a time, and most people found it healthy enough except when the hot winds, or *khamsins,* were blowing. These winds were completely horrible. Physically,

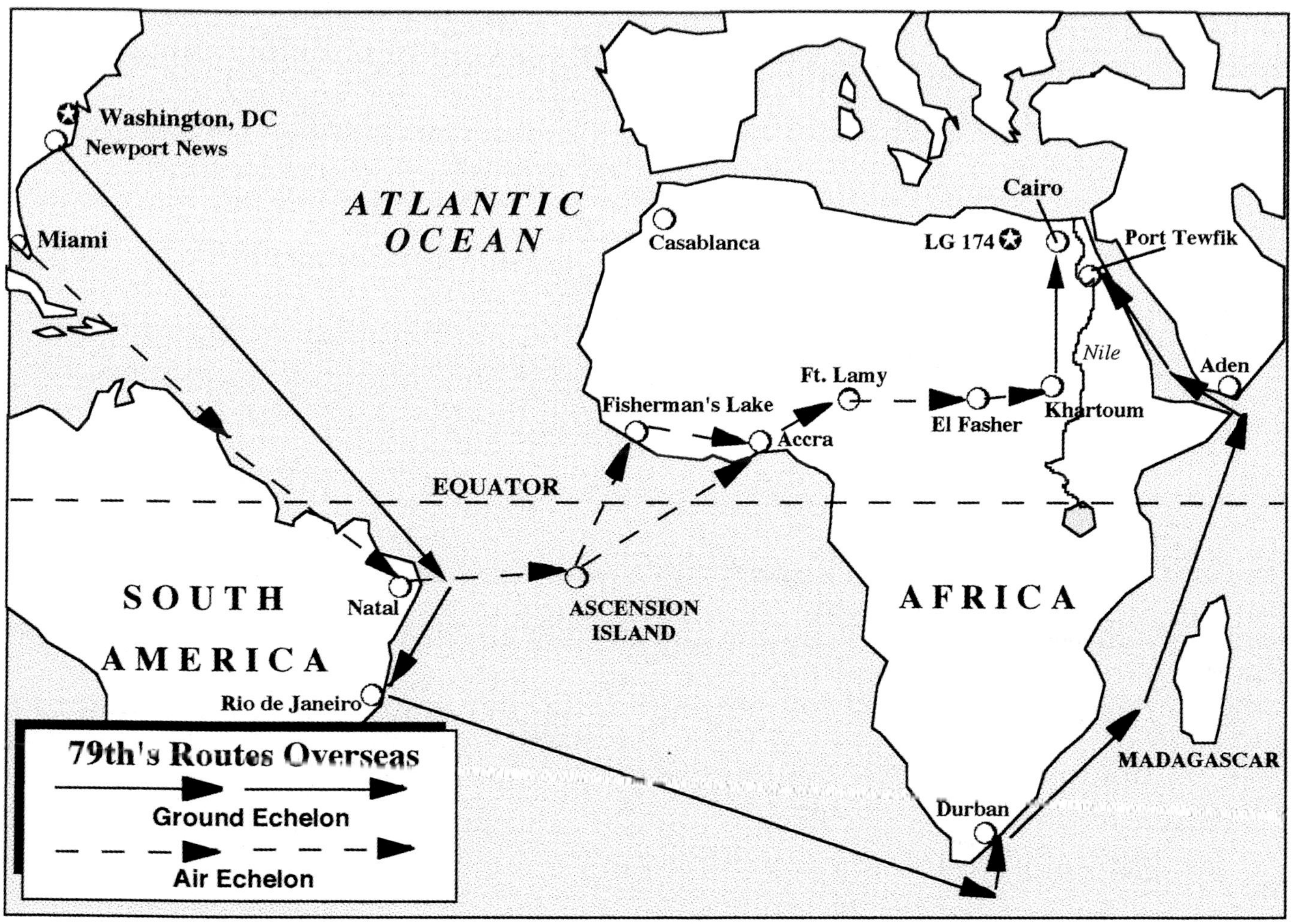

they seemed devoid of oxygen. Morally, they made the most placid temperature morose."[8] The hot winds could raise temperatures by as much as 35 degrees in an hour or two, sapping the strength of friend and foe alike. "Bedouin law permitted a man to kill his wife after five days of it."[9] Wind, rain and sandstorm (the 79th would experience over a dozen of the latter during its two-month stay at LG-174) were the major problems encountered, with sand and wind the bane of the maintenance men. Dry particles of sand and dust would percolate into seemingly sealed aircraft compartments, fouling instruments and causing faulty readings; special care had to be taken to ensure that dust didn't get into the shell extractor chutes under the wings, as these openings if not covered would permit sand to enter and jam the guns, while wrenches and pliers had to be handled as carefully as surgical instruments so that sand would not enter vital aircraft parts and contaminate the machine, which like the human body, is readily susceptible to infection.

In the heat that sometimes reached 120 degrees in the shade, the metal skin of a Warhawk was burning hot to the ungloved hand, while 100 octane fuel became extremely difficult to work with – air locks occurred and fuel evaporation was tremendous. Crew chiefs often worked with only a screwdriver and a pair of pliers; planes were patched with rolls of adhesive tape supplied by the medics; engines were serviced in the open with maintenance crews using fuel drums for ladders. Ground crews were also plagued by a lack of transportation, having only one vintage Dodge truck in the beginning. The sheet metal shop consisted of a small wooden bench set up in the open, and the communications people, much to their dismay, soon discovered there was only *one* radio frequency in the entire Western Desert.

Even the Group Dental Officer had his problems. Captain Irving J. Fernebok had been an oral surgeon in civilian life with two lavish Manhattan offices and the latest word in modern equipment. Now he fashioned many of his own instruments from bits and pieces of scrap metal, and set up his "clinic" (featuring a homemade Rube Goldberg-type chair) in the sand. Corporal Walter Rowe, his assistant, supplied the necessary foot power to operate the primitive drill. An inestimable amount of pain was avoided, however, when the captain had the foresight to persuade each officer to smuggle a box of Novocain aboard the *Mauretania* when she sailed in October. Novocain and other pain-killing drugs were not among the more plentiful items to be found in Egypt.

And finally, the sandstorms seemed to boil up at the most inopportune times: as the armorers were pulling the guns of a P-40 for cleaning, or at chow time, with the wind scrambling pots and pans in every direction. As one man put it, "we were in the land where Christ was born, and wished to Christ we were back in the land where *we* were born."

Halfaya ("Hellfire") Pass between Egypt and Libya. Debris from recent fighting can be seen in the right foreground. (Hoffman)

By far the most popular feature of 174 was its easy accessibility to the varied delights of Alexandria, or "Alex," as it was called, only forty-eight miles away. Overnight passes gave everyone the opportunity to explore its mysteries. Despite the blackout, meatless days, and shortages of many items, Alex was the center of relaxation for battle-weary troops of almost every Allied nation returning from "The Blue," as the British called the desert. Memorable spots were Ramley Station, the Union Bar, the Fleet Club and Sisters Street. A French restaurant near the bay called Monaco's was also popular, offering steaks and featuring a potent cocktail known as the "Nile Dream."

The bar and club of the 13th Hellenic Greek Squadron, flying Blenheims from a field two miles from 174, offered the more venturesome an opportunity to practice Greek. Unfortunately, distance and direction in the desert, especially at night, could be deceiving, and many were those who curled up in the sand under the stars to wait for dawn and some idea as to just "where 'n the hell camp was." It was along about this time that a good many compasses disappeared from the salvage planes.

It was also at 174 that the Group insignia was designed. Enlisting the aid of Mr. Alan Rowe, conservator of the Graeco-Roman Museum in Alexandria, and Mr. Badie Effendi, the museum artist, Egyptian mythology was incorporated into the design as a tribute to Colonel McGoldrick. According to Egyptian legend Horus, the son of the sun god Osirus, was the avenger of his father's death and was represented as a falcon on the obelisks of ancient historians. Consequently, a falcon was adopted as the chief symbol in the Group's insignia, conveying the idea that the 79th would be the avenger of its fallen commander. Subsequently, the Group became known as the falcon group – or the Falcons. Squadron insignia was also designed, and the 85th, 86th, and 87th squadrons were called the "Flying Skulls," the "Comanches," and "Skeeters," respectively.

The 85th (Flying Skull) Squadron constructed an officers club complete with a bar made from the wing of a Me 109, and walls decorated with examples of Corporal Joseph Pumphrey's artwork. Pumphrey, an armorer from Copperton, Utah, had designed the Squadron's insignia, and was soon to gain fame throughout the entire theater for his P-40 rudder art. An enlisted men's PX was set up; a baseball league formed, and squadron newsletters published. At Thanksgiving the cooks somehow managed to provide a turkey dinner complete with all the trimmings, and their first Christmas in the desert was brightened when the DC-3 mail plane from Cairo arrived with one hundred cases of American beer.

While the bulk of the Group was still in the backwash of the war many of the pilots were already playing for keeps as they flew combat with the 57th Fighter Group.

All that was left of Mussolini's once-proud Castel Benito Airdrome near Tripoli was a mass of wrecked aircraft and gutted, twisted hangars. (Hoffman)

Lieutenant Sammy Say, a Flying Skull pilot attached to the 57th's Six-Four (Black Scorpions) Squadron drew first blood for the entire Group when he damaged a Me 109 December 8 while escorting bombers over the Egyptian-Libyan border, and quickly, other Falcon pilots also broke into the scoring column, although victory claims were definitely on the conservative side. The P-40s at the time were not equipped with gun cameras, and to follow a shot-up victim to the deck to learn his fate was inviting trouble, while RAF experience had proved the folly of exaggeration in aerial combat.

Major Tarleton (Jack) Watkins, the Comanche's skipper, damaged a Me 109 on December 10 while attacking a German airfield near Marble Arch, Tripolitania, and Captain Fred Borsodi of the same squadron damaged another on December 13. Two days later Borsodi chalked up the first air-to-air kill by a 79th pilot in a fight with Messerschmitts near El Aghelia.

Watkins, although getting credit for a "damaged" in his fight with the 109s on December 10, undoubtedly ended up being a "probable" in the Luftwaffe victory column that day. He survived the encounter but his P-40 was wrecked beyond repair. It was his third mission, and Fred Borsodi was on his wing:

> "We got bounced by Messerschmitts as we were coming off the target, and a dogfight developed," Watkins explained years later. "Two 109s came by me in a gentle climb, and stupid me I decided to pull up behind the leader and shoot him down while Fred took care of his wingman. I closed to within fifty feet and was just getting ready to fire when my plane was shot out from under me by the German wingman. Apparently, when we pulled up from our bombing run, Fred was blinded by the sun and skidded well out to the right to keep from running into me; unknowingly, I had no protection. It was my fault, but the first burst took a large chunk out of my rudder, and while rolling onto my back I got hit again by both machine-gun

and cannon fire. One burst went over my shoulder and through the control stick, several rounds took the top off my main fuel tank right under my feet, and several more hit the armor plate protecting my back. Fortunately, the only cannon shell that could have penetrated the armor plate was stopped by the battery."[10]

Watkins went into a spiraling dive, pulling out at about 600 feet some ten miles on the wrong side of the lines. He limped home waiting for his P-40 to become unglued at any moment, and bellied in near the landing ground. His plane, which he had borrowed from "Fuzzy" Fairland of the 66th, was named *The Purple Shaft.* It was a total wreck. Watkins said "Fuzzy" wasn't happy with what he had done to his airplane.

Lt. Sammy Say (standing left) and other Flying Skull pilots sample some homemade "Stuka Juice." Made by distilling a large barrel of wine and mixed with canned fruit juice, it smelled like a skunk but fortunately no one went blind. (Hoffman)

On January 11 the Skeeters started off the new year on the right foot when Lieutenants Lee "Goose" Gossick and Jesse Jory claimed a damaged and a probable, respectively, in a fight with 109s southwest of Buerat, Libya, and Lieutenant Dick Morrissey of the 86th damaged yet another 109 on January 13.

All this was not without loss, however. In addition to Colonel McGoldrick's death on November 6, two other 79th pilots were killed while gaining experience with the 57th Fighter Group. Lieutenant Robert Guillebeau of the Comanches was killed December 10 in a scrap with 109s northwest of El Agheila, and the Flying Skulls lost Captain Raymond Palermo in a mid-air collision over the 57th's landing ground at Hamuriet on January 16. In addition, several pilots were wounded, including Lieutenant Jimmy Reutershan of the 86th who was hit in the hand by shell fragments when his flight was bounced by fifteen 109s on January 11. He ended up in a Cairo hospital with American nurses who got to see one of their first not-too-badly damaged fighter pilots. Lieutenant Bill Abbott of the 85th, was also hit in the hand on January 14 while flying close-cover escort for fighter-bombers and crash-landed safely near Gheddabia. He eventually ending up in the same hospital with Reutershan. Lieutenant Bob Minett of the 86th wasn't wounded, but lost an engine while on a dive-bombing mission near Tripoli with the 57th's Exterminator's Squadron (the 66th) and bellied-in behind enemy lines, making his way back to base safely with the help of friendly Arabs. Lieutenant John (Jack) Kelly of the 86th Squadron also had a "behind-the-lines" experience starting when he got shot down on January 13:

"It was my first time out, and I was flying wing on Captain Albert Zipser, the flight leader, when we got into a fight with a highly experienced German squadron," Kelly said. "My position in this flight was essentially as a flying armor plate for the flight leader, but I was flying a really dumb tight wing and in no position to see anything but Zipser's plane. That's how we did it in those days; later, we trailed far enough back to allow the trailing pilot to protect himself while still covering the leader. After a few hairy maneuvers I was still tight on Zipser's wing when all of a sudden I got hammered. I figured I was in real trouble, as I was in a steep dive and on fire. My canopy was already open so I climbed over the side and bailed out. Luckily, I didn't hit the tail, and I pulled the ripcord as soon as I was clear. When I hit the ground, I gathered up by chute and ran as fast and as far away from where I had landed as I could, eventually falling to the ground exhausted. I lay there for a long time, and when I thought it was safe raised my head slightly to see if anyone was looking for me. Off in the distance I could see the burning wreck of my plane, and a German staff car. I ducked down again and didn't move for several hours. At one point an Arab passed within fifty feet of me, but because of the scrub brush he didn't see me. I learned later that the Germans paid a reward to the locals for information leading to the capture of Allied airmen. Later that afternoon, after seeing no sign of life, I decided to walk toward the sea and our lines. Just as it started to get dark I could make out half a dozen soldiers some forty yards away with their rifles pointed straight at me. Since I only had a .45-cal. automatic I wasn't interested in a shoot-out, so I sat on my chute pack, pulled a corner of silk out and weakly waved it as a gesture of surrender. As they cautiously approached, one of them yelled, 'It's a Yank!' Apparently, they had seen me bail out that morning and wondered what had happened to the pilot."[11]

Causeway Landing Ground near Zarzis, Tunisia. Located on a flat, semi-tidal sandspit overlooking the Bay of Bou Grara, Causeway was where the 79th first went to war as a unit. An abandoned Macchi MC-200 can be seen at right center. (Kauffman)

The soldiers were part of a Scottish outfit out in front of the rest of Eighth Army, who treated Kelly as an honored guest. The next day he walked and hitchhiked his way back to base where he discovered his squadron mates had given him up for dead and had divided up his possessions. Aside from a bruised chest muscle caused when his parachute jerked open, he was unharmed and back on flight status within twenty-four hours.

Eighth Army had rolled swiftly westward across the desert since the breakthrough at Alamein, retaking Tobruk and Benghazi in November and entering El Agheila two weeks before Christmas. By the first of January Montgomery was only two hundred miles from Tripoli. Still at Landing Ground 174, the 79th was now hundreds of miles behind the front, and rumors began circulating that they would be moving soon. In late January, the rumors proved true.

On the morning of January 20, 1943, the day a British bomber crashed there – the bombardier was rescued by sergeants Leslie Rogers, Wilbert Holland and Leonard Bachetti of the 85th Squadron, who braved the flames to break into the nose of the plane to pull him out just minutes before it exploded – A-Party, consisting of half the personnel from each department, left LG-174. B-Party followed eight days later. This practice of splitting the Group into two separate but self-contained parties was standard operating procedure with the Desert Air Force (the offspring of the Western Desert Air Force) and would mark every move the 79th would make in the future. The forward party (A-Party) would move to the new landing ground and set up camp – utilizing fuel, food, and ammunition laid down by a British service unit until locating its own supply sources – while the rest of the Group remained behind still operating from the old site. When A-Party had the new landing ground ready to receive aircraft, B-Party would then move up to join them. Many times after the Group entered combat the pilots would take off on a mission from the old field and land at the new. In this way they were always able to maintain operations without interruption. The RAF had learned from experience that it was better to have its squadrons self-sufficient rather than relying on a service unit for transportation. Without its own transport it would have been impossible for the Group to be as highly mobile as it was. Later, in Tunisia, the 79th's A-Party was on the road less than ninety minutes after receiving orders to move and, before Alamein, a South African squadron pulled out of its landing ground just as a column of German tanks clanked into view on the other side of the field.

As the 79th, now boasting over a hundred vehicles – British trucks and Dodges and Fords painted desert yellow; American Jeeps and GMCs in olive drab; two-wheeled trailers; operations trailers; a dental trailer, gas bowsers, and water trucks – rolled out of 174 their thoughts went back over the past two months:

> "174 . . . three little numerals . . . an inconspicuous spot on the Desert Air Force map; a desolate, barren hell sprinkled with British tents, camouflaged Warhawks, grimy GIs and desert shrubs . . . three little numerals for the three little squadrons fresh off the boat, huddled together to escape the penetrating dust . . . 174 . . . a small oasis of Yanks amid all the troops of Her Majesty's Empire . . . 174 . . . grinding teeth with the desert morsels of chow served up by 'Pop' Davis and the other cooks . . . 174 . . . happy memories of the Greeks, their drinks and genial hospitality . . . chug-a-lug parties . . . repairing aircraft without tools . . . guard duty from 0200 to 0600, and the Wogs (natives) firing into the tent area . . . 174 . . . the

'gilly-gilly man' . . . camel caravans in the night . . . gin and powdered lemon juice . . . canned beer and peanuts.

"The motor convoy turned off the main Alexandria highway at a sign indelible now in the mind of every man who was there, a large black sign, and in white letters a foot high the words 'Western Desert.' Soon, vivid reminders of the war: charred wrecks of vehicles, barbed wire fences, great litters of empty shell casings, and a cluster of huts labeled El Alamein. Beyond were salvage yards that held hundreds upon hundreds of vehicles – both enemy and Allied – then a mile-long dump of empty petrol tins and, irreverently in the same area, interminable rows of white crosses, both Latin and Maltese.

"On they rolled, westward over the road that thousands of sweating South African blacks, POWs, and the ever-present Royal Engineers labored painfully to keep in semi-repair. Soon they passed a small crossroads, a hallowed spot for the 79th – Charing Cross. Then Halfaya Pass and the slow precipitous ascent in Libya, and the breathtaking view from the top of the pass. Below to the east, Egypt and the blue Mediterranean, the long black thread of the highway snaking upward; and to the west, the verdure of the Libyan coastal strip.

"A few miles beyond battered Tobruk camp was made at Landing Ground 150 near El Gazala, a rough and stony field surrounded by rugged terrain and numerous caves dug out by the Italians. Still in reserve, the 79th remained at LG-150 for ten days, flying still more training missions. The waiting was becoming difficult.

"Then westward again, the trucks rolling along the coastal road. From sea level clean, green expanses of farmland swept up to the rugged mountain masses from whose crest southward stretched the Libyan desert plateau. Up the convoy went, winding through great chasms of green forest, up over peaks and ridges; the immensity and natural beauty overwhelming. Descending through Derna Pass, down the sheer cliff side for two thousand feet, the road inched downward in curves at times so sharp truck and trailer were unable to negotiate them without unhitching. From the little harbor town of Derna the road followed the seashore until the convoy turned south on a dusty track that eventually led to a new landing ground sixty miles from Misurata, Tripolitania – Darraugh North."[12]

Darraugh North was a dusty, miserable hell-hole, the aircraft grounded much of the time because of violent sandstorms. It was here, however, that most of the obstacles to desert flying were overcome, the bugs worked out. Crew chiefs perfected the technique of setting valves and performing other engine maintenance through the obscurity of blowing sand; armorers

Air Vice-Marshal Harry Broadhurst (left), Air Officer Commanding, Desert Air Force. (Morrissey)

designed an improvement in the bomb shackle installation of wing racks, and Communications improvised a brace attachment for the antenna mast that prevented the antenna from snapping off in a high-speed pull-out. Different approaches to desert takeoffs were also experimented with. The fighter fields of North Africa, with their dusty runways, produced a visibility problem when the lead aircraft kicked up great clouds of dust at takeoff, obscuring the vision of those behind it. At 174 a twenty-four abreast takeoff was tried briefly, but the congestion at the end of the runway negated whatever benefit was derived by the improved visibility, and that method was discarded. Another time two runways were bulldozed out in the shape of an "X." To save join-up time, and petrol, two aircraft would sit at all four corners of the runway facing each other. Coordinating the takeoff with flares and r/t (radio/telephone) chatter, "it was interesting to say the least," said one pilot[13], "watching a pair of P-40s barreling down on you, hoping they would get airborne before ending up in your lap." When Fred Wright was at Beni Uhlid with the 57th they had a Spitfire squadron on the other side of the landing ground. In case of an alert it had been decided to get the Warhawks off first, with the Spits following – each flight taking off over the other fellows'

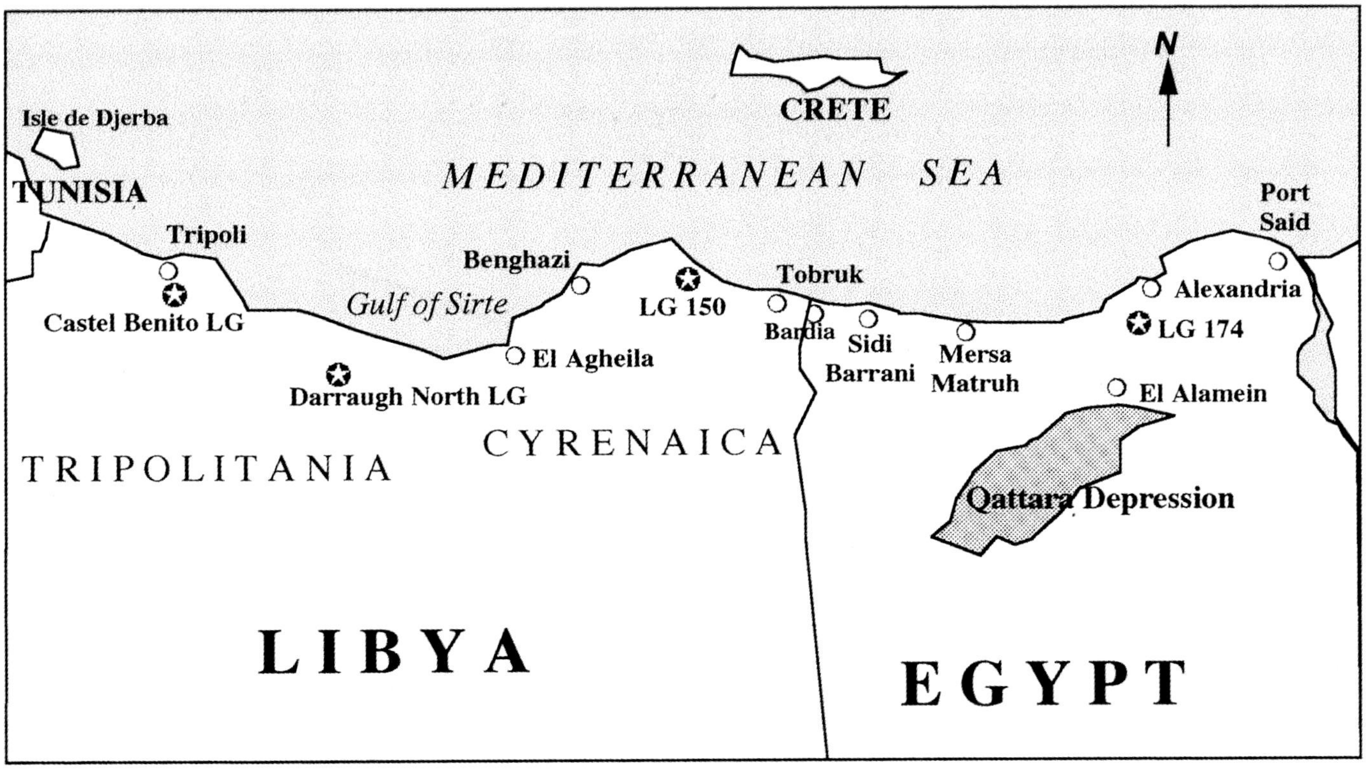

area. In a practice run the Warhawks had just started rolling toward the Spits when they, too, began moving down the runway. With sixteen aircraft all fighting for the same limited airspace, both flights somehow made the takeoff without incident. Once airborne, however, the Spitty leader broke in on the r/t, "I say, Yank, that was a bit of a go, don't you think?"[14] Experimenting at Darraugh North the 79th found the best method, when possible, was a takeoff of about six aircraft line abreast.

By the end of February Eighth Army was up against the Mareth Line in Tunisia and the 79th, still out of effective fighter range, still following as a reserve unit, moved into what was left of Mussolini's highly-publicized Castel Benito airdrome fifteen miles south of Tripoli. It was there, six years earlier, that Mussolini had proclaimed in a powerful voice the coming greatness of fascist Italy.

Castel Benito was an oasis of green turf and evergreens – a welcome change – and gutted hangars, and scores of wrecked German and Italian aircraft. Tripoli itself was a bitter disappointment. In spite of appearances, the normal amenities of city life were sadly lacking. Shops were scantily filled and cleanliness was only facade deep. The Luftwaffe made a nightly appearance over the harbor, providing the Falcons with a front row seat to the pyrotechnic display and prompting an epidemic of slit-trench digging. The discovery of a wine factory nearby helped make their stay at Castel Benito, and the waiting for combat, a little more bearable. Not exactly the nectar of the Gods, rather this "Stuka Juice" was probably aged with acetone; but it was alcoholic, and fortunately no one went blind.

On March 11 the Group left Castel Benito and trucked along the coastal road to Tunisia's Causeway Landing Ground. Located ten miles north of the village of Zarzis, Causeway was a flat, semi-tidal sand spit jutting out towards the picturesque Isle de Djerba overlooking the glassy Bay of Bou Grara. The squadrons set up camps in the sand dunes around the landing ground perimeter, while Group Headquarters personnel moved in among the olive groves and poppy fields a mile away. Tents were pitched near the water, and a nearby sulfur spring in a palm-studded oasis soon became a popular spot for after hours relaxation.

The 79th was now up to its full allotment of three squadrons of twenty-five aircraft each. In addition, one squadron of the 324th Fighter Group – the 316th Hell's Belles Squadron – was attached, as it began its period of on-the-job desert training. The other two squadrons of the 324th were flying with the veteran 57th.

Although administratively controlled by General Strickland's IX Fighter Command, a part of General Brereton's Ninth Air Force which had been formed on November 12, the 79th was under the tactical reins of the Desert Air Force now commanded by Air Vice-Marshal Harry Broadhurst (a Battle of Britain veteran with twelve victories) and was controlled operationally by the RAF's 211 Group which had at its disposal radar stations and fighter control squadrons for interception; a detachment of Royal Engineers for airdrome construction and repair, and an armored car squadron and anti-aircraft brigade to protect its landing grounds. Besides the Tomahawks, Kittyhawks and Warhawks its aircraft inventory consisted of British Hurricanes and Spitfires, and American A-20s (Bostons) and A-30s (Baltimores), the latter two types being twin-engined light bombers flown by British and Commonwealth crews.

As the British anti-aircraft batteries were sited and communications to 211 Group established, word was received that the 79th's first combat mission – a bomber-escort – had been laid on for March 14. After many, many months of tedious training, 10,000 miles by sea and 1,500 dusty miles across the desert, the 79th Fighter Group had finally caught up with the war.

four

All Out for Monty

"This defense-stunning adaptation of the German blitz method worked very effectively, although frowned on by Broadhurst's distant RAF superiors as a breach of Air Staff doctrine."

– B. H. Liddell Hart, British historian

Twenty-three Warhawks lifted free of Causeway's dust on the afternoon of March 14, marking the Group's combat debut as they shepherded a flight of 12th Bomb Group Mitchells (B-25s) over the Mareth Line. The mission was uneventful, almost anti-climactic, and results of the bombing went unobserved because of heavy cloud cover. Anti-aircraft fire however, especially near Zarat, was intense and accurate, and Sammy Say of the Flying Skulls, the first in the Group to break into the scoring column while with the 57th, chalked up another first when his aircraft became the first in the squadron to be damaged by ack-ack. A fighter-bomber sweep over a road northwest of Medinine was run on the 15th, and the next day the 79th had its first brush with the enemy in the air when Lieutenant Carl Simpson damaged one of four Me 109s attempting to break up a bomber formation the Skulls were escorting over the Gulf of Gabes.

Starting March 20 a string of twenty-seven consecutive bomber-escort shows were flown by the Group as DAF mediums began softening up enemy positions on the Mareth Line. They didn't go unchallenged. With the presence of more and more Allied bombers over the Mareth Line, encounters with the Luftwaffe and *Regia Aeronautica* became more frequent. By early 1943 the Allies owned most of the sky over southern Tunisia, but the enemy in the air was still a force to be reckoned with. Although suffering from a steady rate of attrition and numerically outnumbered, the German Luftwaffe, and to a lesser extent the Italian *Regia Aeronautica,* still possessed fine machines and very capable, experienced pilots.

The Me 109G (or Gustav, for "G" in the German phonetic alphabet), especially in the hands of a German *experte* (an experienced pilot with a high number of aerial victories) was more than a match for the Hurricanes, Kittyhawks and Warhawks of the DAF. The Spitfire V could pretty much hold its own against the 109G, but it wasn't until Spit IXs began arriving in the theater that the Allies in North Africa had a fighter that could meet the nimble Gustav on even terms.

The 79th's ground crew salvaged a 109G (*Irmgard* was written on the side, obviously the name of the pilot's wife or girlfriend) that had belly landed in a salt marsh near Causeway, and other than a bent propeller the plane showed no evidence of battle damage; it was easily put back into flying condition. Realizing that flying a late-model German fighter would provide invaluable experience, Captain Fred Jory, a flight leader with the Skeeters, was told to prepare a list of squadron pilots ranked in descending order who, in his opinion, would not prang the bird before others had a chance to fly it. It was a measure of Jory's evaluation skills that the training program was completed without incident until the very last pilot on the schedule washed it out when he hit the button to lower the gear (which worked just the opposite of Allied fighters) and retracted it instead. Nevertheless, all who flew it were impressed with its performance. "They [the Germans] had ideas about flaps, trim alignment, gear and coolant systems that made ours look amateurish by comparison," said Fred Wright. "It was really some kind of airplane for its time, and only the heavier armament of the Warhawk evened out the odds somewhat." Cramped, unforgiving, tricky to land and having a tendency to roll onto its back if lifted off the ground too soon, training fields all over Germany were strewn with the bodies of those who had "bought the farm" trying to master its idiosyncrasies. But those who survived became tough, hard-nosed warriors and were among the best pilots in the world at the time. One unit, Jagd-

This Me-109G, quite possibly Irmgard, under new management. Salvaged from the battlefield, Irmgard was put into flying condition by Lts. Jesse Jory and John Dzamba of the Skeeters and gave the squadron's pilots an opportunity to fly a late-model German fighter. (Hoffman)

geschwader 77,* was filled with well-trained, experienced *experten* who had seen extensive action over England, Russia and Malta before arriving in North Africa. Very capably led, and flying the redoubtable Me 109G, it was JG 77 that the 79th and other Desert Air Force pilots encountered most often over Tunisia.

The Kommodore of JG 77 at the time the 79th entered combat was twenty-four-year old Major Joachim Müncheberg, a deeply-tanned, wavy-haired veteran who had fought the gallant "Few" during the Battle of Britain in 1940; the Russians in front of Moscow in 1941 (where he was shot down three times in less than eight weeks); and again against the Royal Air Force during the siege of Malta, before he arrived in North Africa. At the time of his death on March 23, 1943, he had tallied over 500 operational sorties and was credited with 135 aerial victories – 102 of them against the Western Allies.

After the popular Müncheberg was killed in a crash near kilometer stone number 82 on the Gabes-Gafsa road, he was replaced by Major Johannes "Macki" Steinhoff. At twenty-nine Steinhoff was somewhat older than Müncheberg, but like his predecessor he too had fought on the Channel front and over Russia before being posted to North Africa. He stayed in command of JG 77 throughout the Tunisian campaign, and participated in the battles over Sicily and Italy before being transferred to Northern Europe in early 1944. Two weeks before the end of the war Steinhoff was seriously burned in the crash of a Me-262 jet. By that time he had scored 176 victories, the bulk of them against the Soviets, and ended his combat career as the 22nd-ranking *experten* in the Luftwaffe. After the war he became Inspector General of the new West German Air Force, becoming highly popular with his former foes in the United States and England.

An idea of the caliber of pilots facing the 79th and other DAF units during the fight for Tunisia can perhaps be fathomed by a brief description of the three *gruppen kommandeurs* of JG 77 and some of their top people.

Hauptmann (Captain) Heinz "Pritzl" Bär had his I/JG 77 at Fatnassa, Tunisia until March 26, then his unit moved to Bou Thadi. This *gruppe* had arrived in North Africa in October 1942, having previously fought in Russia and over Malta. Bär (pronounced "Bear") flew over 1,000 operational missions during the war – one of many German pilots who fought from the beginning in 1939 until VE-Day – and was credited with the destruction of 220 Allied aircraft, 124 of which were British or American, and at least thirty-nine between January and May 1943. In addition, he emerged as the top-scoring jet ace of World War II with sixteen victories while flying the Me-262. With an outstanding personality, keen sense of humor and sparkling wit, he was a pilot's pilot and very popular with his

* A Jagdgeschwader was roughly equivalent to a RAF group. It usually consisted of three *gruppen* of thirty-six aircraft each, plus a *stab* (staff) section, with each *gruppe* made up of three *staffeln* (squadrons) of twelve planes each. Number One *Gruppe* of Jagdgeschwader 77, for instance, was designated I/JG 77, Number Two *Gruppe*, II/JG 77, etc.

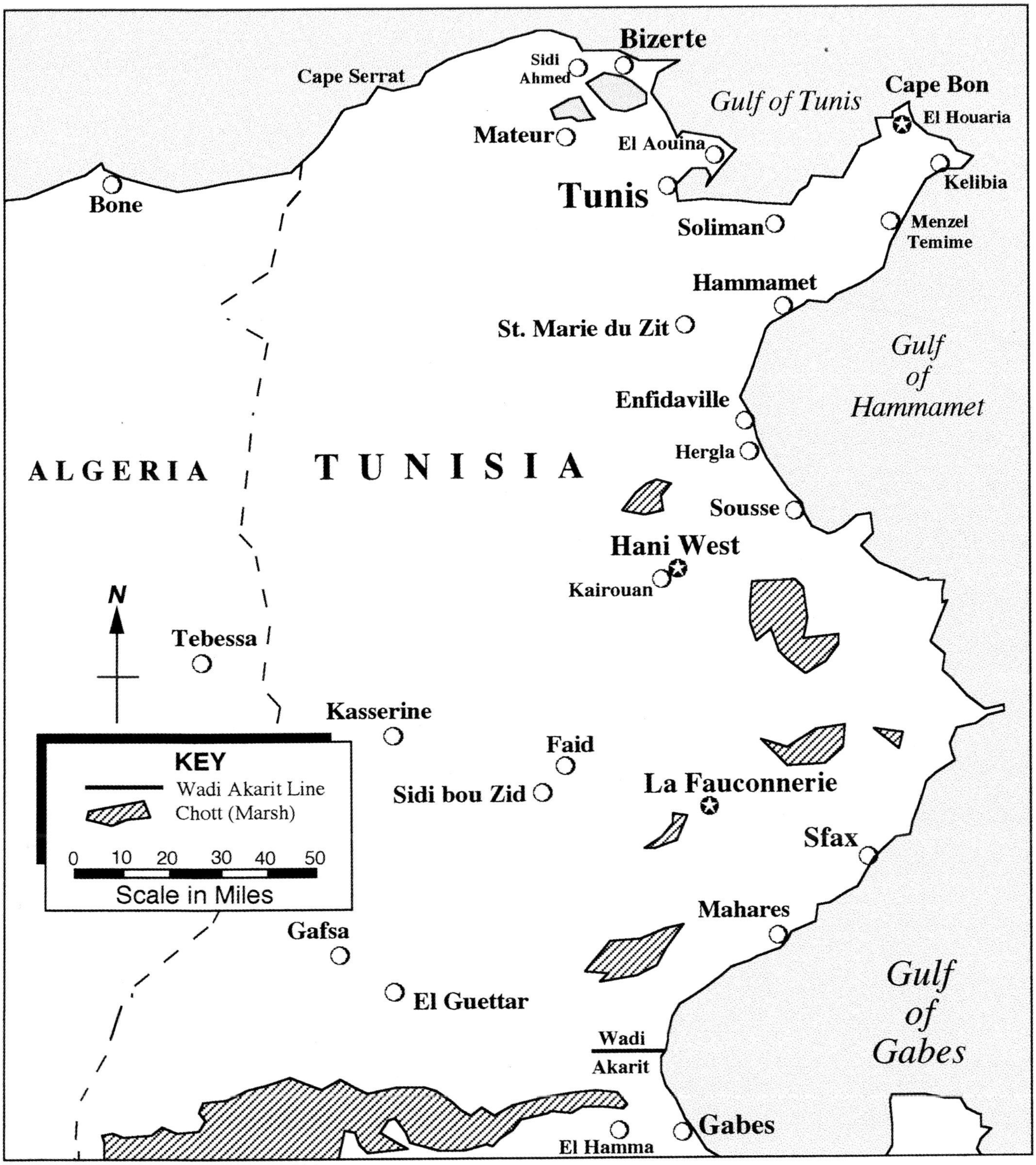
Bizerte
Sidi Ahmed
Cape Serrat
Gulf of Tunis
Cape Bon
El Houaria
Mateur
El Aouina
Kelibia
Bone
Tunis
Soliman
Menzel Temime
Hammamet
St. Marie du Zit
Gulf of Hammamet
Enfidaville
Hergla
ALGERIA
TUNISIA
Sousse
Hani West
Kairouan
N
Tebessa
Kasserine
Faid
KEY
Wadi Akarit Line
Chott (Marsh)
0 10 20 30 40 50
Scale in Miles
Sidi bou Zid
La Fauconnerie
Sfax
Mahares
Gafsa
El Guettar
Gulf of Gabes
Wadi Akarit
Gabes
El Hamma

men. Bär survived the war but ironically was killed in a light sports plane that spun in and crashed over Brunswick in 1957.

II/JG 77 was commanded by Hauptmann Anton Hackl, another first-to-last pilot who survived the war with 192 claims, thirty-two of them hard-to-kill four-engined B-17s and 24s. The Gustavs of his unit were at La Fauconnerie until April 8, then moved to St. Marie du Zit south of Tunis, and later, to Soliman South at the base of the Cape Bon peninsula.

The third *Gruppe* of Jagdgeschwader 77 was that of Hauptmann Kurt "Kuddell" Ubben, also flying Gustavs, and based at Matmata until April 8. Then it too moved to St. Marie du Zit and Soliman South. Ubben's personnel score at the time of his death over northern France in April 1944 stood at 110.

By far the most successful German pilot in the Tunisian fighting was Leutnant (2nd Lieutenant) Ernst Wilhelm Reinert of II/JG 77. Reinert claimed fifty-one victories over the desert in less than four months, and finished the war with a total of 174. Flying with Reinert was Oberleutnant (1st Lieutenant) Siegfried Freytag, known as "The Star of Malta," a tribute to his earlier success over that hotly-contested island. On the day before the 79th went operational Reinert claimed his 136th victim and Freytag his eighty-seventh.

Other *experten* of JG 77 included Leutnants Heinz-Edgar Berres and Arnim Kohler of I/JG 77, and Oberfeldwebel (a junior pilot rank of which there is no equivalent in other air forces) Herbert Kaiser and Leutnant Emil Omert with "Kuddell" Ubben's *gruppe* – III/JG 77. Berres, the *gruppen* adjutant, was victorious fifty-three times before a 239 Wing Spitfire caught up with him over Sicily in July 1943. Kohler survived the war with sixty-nine planes to his credit, while Omert and Kaiser had seventy and sixty-eight victories respectively. Both also survived the hostilities.

In Tunisia in the spring of 1943, Jagdgeschwader 77, even with an acute shortage of supplies and spare parts, and neglected and all but forgotten by Berlin was, with its fine stable of young pilots and combat-savvy *gruppen kommandeurs*, still a very dangerous and formidable adversary.

Other enemy air units in Tunisia had men of equal talent and experience, but for the most part were based farther north and did not come in contact with Desert Air Force fliers until late in the campaign. They included the pilots of two *gruppen* of JG 53 near Bizerte and La Marsa, who wrestled their spindly-legged 109s into the air time and again to grapple with American bombers and fighters of Northwest African Strate-

Major Joachim Müncheberg, kommodore of JG 77 until killed in a scrap with 52nd Group Spitfires in March 1943. At the time of his death he had 135 aerial victories and over 500 operational flights to his credit. (Bundesarchiv, Koblenz)

Hauptmann Johannes Steinhoff inherited command of JG 77 after Müncheberg's death. Under his able leadership JG 77 proved a most formidable adversary for 79th Group and other Allied pilots in the dusty Tunisian skies. (Bundesarchiv, Koblenz)

gic Air Force and XII Fighter Command* approaching Tunisia from the west. Hauptmann Wolfgang Tonne was one of JG 53's outstanding pilots with 122 victories before he was killed in a landing accident on April 20, 1943. At La Smala des Souassis one *gruppe* of JG 51 also fought mainly against the Allied threat from the west, but sometimes also ventured south to pounce on DAF mediums hitting the Mareth Line. Hauptmann Hartmann Grasser was a top-scoring pilots with that unit. And near Kairouan, a Focke-Wulf 190 outfit – II/JG 2 – boasted of Leutnant Erich Rudorffer who would become Germany's seventh-ranked *experten* with 222 aerial victories by the end of the war.

The German fliers were always dangerous and formidable – years of experience and superb leadership at the tactical level made up for numerical disparity and short-sighted vision in Berlin – and even the much-maligned Italians accounted for themselves well during their last weeks in North Africa. The Italians had "brave, capable and even dashing leaders at the squadron level and below, but corruption and incompetence at the top."[1]

In March 1943 the *Regia Aeronautica* had four *squadriglia* (squadrons) of Macchi MC-202 *Folgore* (Lightning) fighters based in Tunisia, and moved two more down from Sicily in April. Part of 6° and 16° *Gruppo* (groups) were based near Gabes, and 18° *Gruppo* was at a landing ground near El Hamma until forced out by the advancing Allies. In addition, there was at least one *gruppo* flying a slightly inferior fighter – the MC-200 *Saetta* (Thunderbolt) – stationed along Tunisia's east coast during April and the first few days in May.

The Italians had by this time obviously lost heart in the war and did not usually press home their attacks with the same gritty determination shown by the Germans. In the handling of their aircraft however, they were superb. And the performance of the MC-202 compared favorably with the Me 109, and clearly outclassed the American-built Curtiss fighters in maneuverability. It was the fastest of the Italian fighters, and could turn inside anything flown in combat by either side in North Africa. If the Macchi had a weakness it was that it was undergunned (early models featured only two 12.7-mm machine-guns mounted over the engine) and carried a limited fuel supply. External tanks extended the range on later models, and the addition of 7.7-mm machine-guns and wing-mounted Mauser MG151 cannon improved the Macchi's firepower, but it would never match the P-40 in either category.

Leutnant Ernst Wilhelm Reinert of II/JG 77 was the most successful pilot over Tunisia. In less than four months he scored fifty-one times and finished the war as the Luftwaffe's twenty-fourth ranked experten with 174 victories in the air. (Bundesarchiv, Koblenz)

On March 21 fourteen plus "snappers" (Me 109s and MC-202s) bounced the Flying Skulls flying top-cover for a flight of Mitchells over Gabes. Captain John Cimaglia damaged a Macchi but Lieutenant Melvin Davis of Oshkosh, Wisconsin turned up missing. No one saw him go down, although Jack Watkins of the Comanches, who were flying medium cover, spotted an oil slick on the water in the vicinity where Davis' plane was last seen. At the end of the war he was still unaccounted for.

By mid-afternoon of March 22 twelve Skeeter P-40s were 10,000 feet over the Eighth Army bomb line. Two thousand feet below a dozen Baltimores and six Bostons, their bomb loads having just tumbled from open bays, were banking sharply to the south when a mixed gaggle of Me 109s and MC-202s

* Allied air and ground forces were reorganized in February 1943. Opposing Rommel and von Armin was the 18th Army Group of General Alexander. Under him was British First Army, the French Corps, Patton's US II Corps and Montgomery's Eighth Army. Air Chief Marshal Sir Arthur Tedder headed up the Mediterranean Air Command that included Northwest African Air Forces commanded by General Carl "Tooey" Spaatz. Under Spaatz were Northwest African Coastal Air Force comprising XII Fighter Command and RAF elements; the Northwest African Strategic Air Force composed of XII Bomber Command and RAF night bombers; and Northwest African Tactical Air Force that included RAF 241 Group, IX Fighter Command, XII Air Support Command, and the RAF's Desert Air Force.

struck the escorting Skeeters. In the melee that followed Fred Wright damaged a Macchi that fell off to the left streaming smoke, and Lieutenant Asa A. "Ace" Adair (believed by many to be the model for Milt Caniff's "Hotshot Charlie" in Caniff's popular comic strip *Terry and the Pirates*),* caught a 109 low over the coastal road leading to Mareth, hit it with a burst of machine-gun fire, and the Messerschmitt plowed into the ground before the pilot could bail out. Adair then damaged another 109, while Lieutenants Bob Ligett and Paul McArthur teamed up on the destruction of one more.

Less than an hour later 86th and 87th pilots were over the bomb line again, this time escorting B-25s. One of the bombers was hit by anti-aircraft fire enroute to the target and limped away watched over by four Warhawks. Within minutes the crippled B-25 fell out of control and crashed, killing the entire crew. As the rest of the formation was coming off the target fifteen 109s jumped the top cover and a swirling, whirling dogfight erupted. Lieutenant Kensley Miller probably destroyed one of the Messerschmitts, but Lieutenant Frank Huff had his hydraulic system shot away and headed for the coast. He eventually made a safe belly landing near Castel Benito.

While Miller, Huff and company were mixing it up with the German fighters, Captain Virgil Ingram, Jr., piloting a 12th Bomb Group B-25 stricken with a starboard engine made useless by flak, was struggling to reach his home field near Medinine. Two miles from the 79th's landing ground at Causeway the crippled bomber stalled and crashed. The next day, with representatives of the 12th Bomb Group present, Ingram and his four-man crew were buried with full military honors.

Another Luftwaffe experten to be reckoned with over Tunisia was Leutnant Heinz-Edgar Berres, gruppen adjutant of I/JG 77. He finished the war with fifty-three victories. (Bundesarchiv, Koblenz)

As the slow, solemn notes of "Taps" echoed across Causeway's sand dunes the Hawks were again back upstairs, this time over Zarat. Lieutenant George "Maxie" Maxwell of the Comanche's destroyed a 109 that probed too close to the bomber formation his squadron was protecting, but Major Delaney, the amiable CO of the 316th, was hit in the wing by ground fire, and Lieutenant William "Scotty" Rogers of the 87th washed out his bird in a landing accident – a feat he would duplicate within twenty-four hours. Just one mission was scheduled for March 25, a bomber-escort show to the Sfax landing grounds. The fighters missed their rendezvous with the Baltimores because of a weather front in the area, so Major Jacob (Fred) Schoellkopf, the Skulls skipper, elected to take his people hunting for targets of opportunity on the Sfax-Mahares road. While ten Skeeters orbited high overhead the Skulls went down on the deck shooting up gun emplacements, vehicles, and a pair of tanks the Germans had failed to camouflage. The ground fire was intense. Lieutenant Phillip Miller was hit in the leg by shrapnel, and Lieutenant Franklin T. Johnson of Los Angeles was missing, his P-40 last seen plunging on fire into the Gulf of Gabes. Johnson was later reported a prisoner of war. After the remainder of the flight landed, Schoellkopf told all who would listen that strafing was a job for a multi-engined aircraft, preferably one with armor plating covering all its vital parts. If anyone disagreed, they would have good reason to change their mind the next day when the Falcons went all out for Monty at El Hamma, the aerial "blitz" that paved the way for his left hook around the Mareth Line.

* Fred Wright was convinced that Adair was indeed the model for "Hotshot Charlie" as Caniff had met Adair when the former visited Phil Cochran at Bradley Field early in the war, and Adair displayed the same attitude and characteristics later made famous by the comic strip character. Dr. Charles Jaslow, another original member of the 87th Squadron disputes that, saying that although Adair "did some wild and crazy things" Caniff only met him once and didn't know enough about him to base a comic strip on.

Built by the French before the war, the Mareth Line ran from the sea near Zarat southwest to the Matmata Hills in southern Tunisia. It was protected on the west by a vast stretch of wild desert and salt marshes (chotts), and in front by a natural tank barrier known as the Wadi Zigzaou. The French had constructed steel and concrete fortifications with mutually supporting fields of fire, and more bunkers and gun emplacements were dug, scores of tank traps built, and the area liberally sown with mines when Rommel's Afrika Korps moved in behind the Line at the end of the year following its long retreat from Egypt. Rommel would have preferred to dig in farther north at Wadi Akarit, but was overruled by Berlin; a line in the sand had been drawn at Mareth, and that is where the Afrika Korps would stand and fight.

Skeeter pilots get the "gen" from Squadron Executive Officer Major Ralph Porter (dark glasses) during a desert briefing at Causeway. With helmet and goggles are (left to right) Lts. Ed Fitzgerald, Lee "Goose" Gossick," Porter, John Kirsch and Jesse Jory. (Jaslow)

To prepare for the battle, Rommel's command structure was reorganized. The old Afrika Korps that Eighth Army veterans had fought all the way from El Alamein was redesignated First Italian Army and placed under the Italian General Giovanni Messe. Both Messe and Generaloberst Jurgen von Arnim (who had been sent to command the Fifth Panzer Army on the Algerian front after the Allies under General Eisenhower invaded North Africa – Operation TORCH – at Casablanca, Oran and Algiers on November 8) answered to Rommel, who was named commander-in-chief of Army Group Afrika, the supreme Axis command in Tunisia. Rommel in turn answered to Generalfeldmarschall Albrecht von Kesselring, Commander-in-Chief South, headquartered in Italy. At the same time all German and Italian air units in North Africa were unified under a single command called *Fliegerkorps Tunis*.

By the middle of February Rommel's Army Group Afrika was being squeezed into an ever-tightening pocket. US II Corps from TORCH had advanced as far east as Gafsa in central Tunisia, and was threatening Rommel's Mareth positions from the rear, while Montgomery was edging closer to Mareth from the south, but at an exasperatingly slow pace.

At the risk of uncovering his line in front of Eighth Army, Rommel launched a counterattack against the more immediate threat from the west, and his panzers tore up the inexperienced Americans in the battle of Kasserine Pass, driving II Corps back to the Algerian frontier. Montgomery, meanwhile, moved three of his divisions up to the Medinine area in southern Tunisia on February 24 where he made limited contact with the enemy – and to some extent relieved the pressure being applied against II Corps – but he was not yet ready to launch a full-scale assault against the Mareth Line.

As Monty marked time south of Mareth, Rommel sent Messe and his First Italian Army in a three-pronged attack down the Mareth-Medinine road on March 6. Sick and disheartened, his health and morale shattered by long weeks of retreat, this was to be the last battle directed by the Desert Fox in North

With a 500-lb. bomb tucked under the belly of Lil Joe II, Group Commander Earl Bates taxies out for a fighter-bomber mission near the Mareth Line. (Hoffman)

Africa. It was hardly an auspicious finalé. Six hours after the attack started the rush slowed, then ground to a complete halt. Messe was forced to withdraw. He left behind fifty-two irreplaceable tanks – almost one quarter of his available armor in southern Tunisia. Rommel left for Germany shortly thereafter, turning over command of Army Group Afrika to von Arnim.

For Monty, this last clash with his long-time antagonist was but a bothersome interlude; a preliminary bout. With the enemy counterattack checked he could now get down to the business of preparing for the main event at Mareth.

Monty's plan was simple: force the Mareth Line and advance on Sfax, the next usable port with many suitable landing grounds. He would use the three divisions of General Oliver Leese's XXX Corps for a frontal attack near the sea to punch a hole through the line for General Brian Horrock's X Corps armor to exploit. At the same time the New Zealand Corps (General Bernard Freyberg)* would swing wide in an outflanking march through the Matmata Hills toward El Hamma to menace the enemy's rear and pin down his reserves. The US II Corps, meanwhile, would advance once again on Gafsa, seizing that city for a supply point, and tie up as many German and Italian divisions as possible.

From the start the attack went badly. Launched on a narrow sector near the coast on the night of March 20/21, the first assault made only a small bulge in the enemy line before it skidded to a halt. A renewed attack the next night fared even worse as minefields and the soft bed of the wadi hindered the advance of tanks and other supporting vehicles. Caught in the open without their armor, attacking infantry was subjected to murderous enfilading fire, and a counterattack by the 15th Panzer Division drove XXX Corps back to its original start line.

The setback prompted a change in Montgomery's strategy. He began to give serious consideration to an outflanking maneuver through the Tebaga Gap, a passage roughly four miles long and three miles wide that ran between the djebels Tebaga and Melab some twenty miles behind the Mareth Line's main fortifications. If he could punch through the Gap he would come out on the coastal plain below the village of El Hamma and have a clear shot down the road to the port of Gabes, fifteen miles to the east. Getting through the narrow passage would be difficult, however, because the enemy controlled the surrounding high ground, and had numerous "eighty-eights" zeroed in on the valley below. An alternative would be to mount yet another outflanking move, this time around the Gap and behind Djebel Tebaga, but that was really no alternative at all because it would allow the enemy time to consolidate his forces in that area.

Monty was still pondering the problem when Harry Broadhurst, the Desert Air Force AOC (Air Officer Commanding), proposed having his DAF fighters and fighter-bombers blast a path in front of the advancing infantry as they rushed through the Gap onto the plain below El Hamma. Such an attack had never been tried by the British before, as close support of ground troops had always been by light bombers, but Broadhurst felt that the cannon and machine-gun fire from low-flying fighters might prove more deadly and disrupting to the enemy than bombs dropped by bombers from comparatively high altitude.

Montgomery liked the idea. He sent a message to his corps commanders to prepare for a daylight assault through Tebaga Gap beginning March 25. The 1st Armored Division wouldn't be in place by then, however, so D-Day was pushed back until the afternoon of the 26th. The success of the attack – codenamed SUPERCHARGE – hinged primarily on two factors: First, the infantry would be assaulting in daylight (jumping off at four o'clock in the afternoon) and moving from west to east; both the daylight attack, and the direction from which it would come, would be something new for Eighth Army. In addition to whatever benefit the surprise of a daytime attack would achieve, the setting sun would also be in the eyes of the German and Italian defenders. Secondly, and most importantly, was the schedule of heavy preliminary bombing of selected enemy strongpoints, and the continuous air support from the fighter squadrons during the assault itself. It would be the DAF's own version of the German-invented blitzkrieg.

Broadhurst and Montgomery both realized there was considerable risk involved and that casualties to the air units could be severe, but as Monty's chief of staff (Major-General Sir Francis de Guingand) explained, it was felt the risk was worth taking "because in our own experience with low-flying attacks the defense took some time to recover equilibrium, and . . . some sort of temporary paralysis often set in."[3]

To coordinate the air support with the ground assault, RAF Group Captain Jackie Darwen* would be in an armored car

* The NZeds were recklessly courageous men whose independent spirit and unconcern with the standard forms of military discipline became one of the most enduring legends of the war. On one occasion a high-ranking British general was inspecting a New Zealand unit when he mentioned to General Freyberg: "Your people don't salute much, do they?" Freyberg shrugged and answered: "You should try waving to them. They always wave back."[2]

* Darwen's wife was killed in an air raid during the London Blitz while dancing with her husband at the *Cafe de Paris*. From then on he harbored a passionate hatred for the enemy and flew with complete disregard for his own personal safety, a habit that did not particularly endear him to his wingmen. Darwen was killed over Italy in October 1943 when his P-40 was hit by flak at 8,000 feet.[4]

near the front, located "cheek by jowl" with the commander of the assault brigade. De Guingand told ground commanders it was important that Darwen be in a good position to see the battle so he could then give pilots the "low-down on how they are doing . . . the air force is going flat out on this low strafing. It may be very expensive owing to the flak and enemy opposition, but they have agreed to cooperate wholeheartedly because [Montgomery] has told them it is the big thing in this stage of the campaign. They will not be able to stage such an intensive effort two days running."[5]

Late in the afternoon of March 26, as British infantry and armor moved toward the entrance of the Tebaga Gap, the Desert Air Force began its aerial blitz. The bombing and strafing lasted for nearly three hours. When it was over and dusk settled on the valley, Freyberg's New Zealanders, bayonets at the ready, poked into the Gap flushing out the dazed and bewildered defenders. Horrock's X Corps armor followed, pushing on towards El Hamma in the moonlight almost unchallenged.

The Desert Air Force had done its job. For a short yet vital time the air attacks had kept the enemy's head down, and caused widespread disorganization among the German and Italian troops on the ground. The New Zealanders – or "Newzies" as the American pilots called them – took advantage of the confusion and broke through the Gap with relatively light casualties.

El Hamma was the classic example of perfect fighter and fighter-bomber employment in cooperation with a ground attack, and would serve later as a model when the powerful American Ninth and Twelfth Air Forces paved the way for the Allied victory in Europe.

As predicted, the cost to the airmen had been high. The DAF flew 412 sorties during the "blitz," with eleven pilots listed as missing, six of them from the 79th – Fred Borsodi, Johnny Hoagland, Robert Spurgin, Dave Brown, Bob Ligett and Art Weldon – although Borsodi and Hoagland would later turn up safe. The other pilots in the Group all made it back safely, but many came back with their aircraft full of holes. Most agreed that the mission was, as the saying went, "rough, brother, rough!"

In the early evening hours of March 26, Montgomery radioed the 79th's commander, Colonel Earl E. Bates: "Please convey to all pilots the grateful thanks of myself and the entire army for their truly magnificent efforts. The results have been first class. I sincerely trust you have not suffered many losses."[6]

After Eighth Army poured through the blitzed Tebaga Gap on March 26 the five Italian divisions that had been by-passed in the Mareth Line were in immediate danger of being cut off. Acting quickly before their escape route to the north was pinched shut, von Arnim fought a delaying action near El Hamma for two days to give his Italian troops time to extricate themselves from the Mareth Line. They slipped from Monty's grasp and moved, most of them on foot, behind the Wadi Akarit some eighteen miles above Gabes.

The center of activity at all forward landing grounds was the squadron Operations tent. (Kauffman)

Here was ideal defensive terrain, certainly the best in Tunisia, and probably the best in all of North Africa. Rugged mountains and impassable salt marshes to the west, and the sea to the east, made it virtually impossible to outflank. The flat, open stretch near the coast was extensively mined and anti-tank ditches built by German and Italian engineers covered the area in front of the wadi. A metalled road wound its way along the coast from Gabes to Sfax, and that too was intersected by water-logged ditches and heavily mined.

Rommel had long advocated the Wadi Akarit line as the *only* practical position in Tunisia from which to stave off the advancing Allies. But Berlin, obsessed more with real estate than with tactical expediency, had ordered him to make his stand at Mareth when he withdrew from Libya in January. Had Rommel had his way then, and occupied the Akarit line with the forces since decimated at Medinine, Mareth and Tebaga Gap, the end in Africa would undoubtedly have been delayed much beyond the actual surrender in May. This in turn would have set back the forthcoming invasion of Sicily, and further strained relations between Moscow and the Anglo-Americans. Fortunately, Hitler, an amateur tactician at best, was in the habit of overriding his competent, capable generals.

Monty spent the next few days after breaching the Gap preparing to assault the Wadi Akarit. The Desert Air Force, although hampered by bad weather, used the time to send its medium and light bombers against airfields in the Sfax area. The field at Sfax el Maou was a primary target. It was a veritable nest of Me 109s and MC-202s, and the staging area for inbound Sicilian-based Ju 88s and twin-engined Me-210s.

Monday, March 29 started out as just another "routine" day for the 79th. Six uneventful shows to Sfax and back escorting Bostons and Baltimores were run in the morning, but two late afternoon strafing missions resulted in two more telegrams with the chilling words, *The Secretary of War desires me to express his regrets . . .* being delivered back home. It started when twelve Comanche Warhawks were low and vulnerable over the coastal road south of Mahares. They had just finished beating up a convoy of motor transport, flaming ten trucks and damaging fifty-eight, when jumped by four Me 109s of II/JG 77 led by Leutnant Ernst Reinert.[7] With no room to maneuver, George Harris and Captain Kenneth Boggs were shot up badly. Harris limped home (it would be another eight days before his number would come up), but Boggs, the Group's Assistant Operations Officer, had the tail section of his P-40 shot completely away and he crashed and burned. A few days later his body was discovered by members of the Coldstream Guard and he was buried beside the wreckage of his aircraft.

On the last mission of the day Lieutenant Harland Highfield of Wilmington, Delaware was hit by small arms fire, also while strafing along the Marahes road, and bellied-in. He spent the rest of the war as a POW. Major Richards H. "Doc" Hoffman, the Group flight surgeon and a tentmate of Boggs, made a note in his diary that night: "The boys made a lot of missions today – six or seven. The last two were strafing and tough as usual. Poor ol' Boggs didn't come back. They saw him try to belly-in, but his ship rolled over and over and burned. Highfield of the 87th is also missing. That makes eight we've lost so far."[8]

The next day five more escort missions were run to Sfax. The Luftwaffe chose not to challenge in the air but flak exploded a Baltimore from 55 Squadron with a direct hit in the bomb bay, and shot out the starboard engine of another that struggled back watched over by Lieutenants George Harris and Donald McKay of the Comanches.

On the last day of March they took the mediums to Sfax again, this time Mitchells of the 12th and 340th Bomb Groups, and again it was costly for the bomber crews. Three of the Mitchells were hit by flak over the target. One made it to Causeway where it force-landed; the crew of the second bailed out near the Isle de Djerba, and the third fell out of formation with one engine on fire. With only one mill turning the bomber was easy meat for the hunters of Jagdgeschwader 77 so Fred Wright and his wingman, Lieutenant Jesse Jory, dropped down from their high-cover perch and started cross-weaving over the crippled B-25. Over the Gulf of Gabes four bogies dived on them, line astern, from out of the sun. Wright skidded to port with full left rudder and snapped a short, desperate burst at the "tail-end Charlie"* before stalling out. When he recovered, the sky was empty except for Jory and the still-plodding B-25. Later, back at Causeway, Wright was explaining to "Duke" Uhrich (Major Benjamin F. "Duke" Uhrich had replaced Major Charles E. Grogan as the 87th's CO in January 1943 when Grogan became Group Ops Officer) what had happened, and was mentally cussing himself for his poor shooting, when the ops officer of a Spit V wing rang up. His lads, it seemed, had mistaken Wright and Jory for a pair of Macchis hounding a Mitchell – the bogies had been Spitfires. One of the Spits, the RAF type went on, had several fresh bullet holes stitched across its fuselage.

Skeeter pilots relax between missions. Lts. Emery Dietrick (without shirt) and Captain Benjamin "Duke" Uhrich (seated center) and Lt. Asa "Ace" Adair at far right. Others are unidentified. (Wright)

On April 2 sixteen Warhawks of the 87th Squadron were escorting Bostons and Baltimores over the Akarit line. The Skeeters in turn had a top cover of four Spit IXs of the Polish Fighting Team, a volunteer unit of highly experienced Polish pilots attached to 145 Squadron, 244 Wing. They were wild men in the air. Once a Polish pilot chased two Ju 88s over the rooftops of Sfax with such vigor that one crashed into a house, and the other a church steeple, without having to fire a shot. Unofficially known as "Skalski's Circus" they were led by Squadron Leader Stanislaw Skalski who finished the war as Poland's top-scoring ace with eighteen victories. Today they sat high in the wings waiting to pounce on anything that threatened the Skeeters or the bombers.

After the bomb run the formation was bounced by a gaggle of 109s from two *gruppen* of Jagdgeschwader 77. Skalski nailed a 109 as it dove through the top-cover and the German spun in from 7,000 feet. Lieutenant Eugeniusz Horbaczewski, who was known to take great risks to secure a kill, chased another Gustav for better than thirty miles before he knocked it out of the sky,[9]

* Traditionally the pilot with the keenest eyesight, quite often the first sign of enemy fighters was "Charlie" on the end of a parachute.

Major Tarleton "Jack" Watkins (left) and Lt. George Harris with Comanche Warhawk. Harris was killed a few days after this photo was taken attempting to ditch his flak-stricken P-40. (Morrissey)

while the other two Poles destroyed still another Messerschmitt and damaged two more. But by now the rest of the Germans were down at the Skeeters' level and heading for the bombers.

Lieutenant Charles "Jazz" Jaslow, flying a P-40 with *Sweet Bets* painted on its nose and the Disney cartoon figure "Dopey" with the words *Passionate Dwarf* painted on the tail, turned into a 109, firing as he honked his heavy Warhawk around in a tight turn, and watched the Jerry crash in a spray of frothy water. Lieutenant Morris Watkins damaged another, the 109 last seen streaming glycol, and Lieutenant Frank Huff drove off the third with a determined firing pass. But the Skeeters weren't to have it all their own way. Lieutenant Ed McDonnel of Brooklyn, New York, was hit hard by one of the Messerschmitts (probably Leutnant Heinz-Edgar Berres)[10] and bailed out. He landed in shallow water, unconscious and face up. When his buddies searched the area later they found only his empty parachute floating on the surface. The Falcons had been hurt again, but their perfect record of protecting the bombers against enemy air opposition remained unblemished.

In the line at Wadi Akarit the First Italian Army of General Meese had two panzer grenadier regiments; two German light divisions (the 90th and 164th), and four Italian divisions, with the 15th Panzers in reserve. At four o'clock in the morning of April 6, the veteran 4th Indian Division spearheaded Eighth Army's attack against this formidable force. At the same time the American II Corps, already moving out from Gafsa on the road to Maknassy, struck at the enemy's right flank. An artillery barrage from all 496 guns of XXX Corps opened the assault, and at first light the Desert Air Force threw its weight behind the attack. It was to be another long, busy and expensive day for the 79th.

By late afternoon 86th and 316th squadrons were strafing along the main coastal road near Achichina when they ran into a hornet's nest in the form of a red, enemy-held blockhouse that filled the air with anti-aircraft fire. Within seconds the flight had four planes down. George Harris, flying a P-40 he called *Blivot,* attempted the near impossible trying to ditch at sea (fighters, especially P-40s, were notoriously difficult to ditch successfully) and has never been heard from. Don McKay bellied in near the coast and was seen running from his downed aircraft, but he too was still listed as missing when the war ended. Lieutenant Ober Leatherman was seen to crash, his P-40 exploding on impact, and Lieutenant George W. Gilpin of the 316th also failed to return, although no one saw him go down. The graves of Gilpin and Leatherman were later found by their wrecked planes. All of the surviving pilots had aircraft that were shot up to one degree or another, and Wayne "Moldy" Rhynard, who was leading the Comanches' "D" Flight, came home with 120 feet of telephone wire trailing behind him that he had clipped with his wing.

Lt. Charles "Jazz" Jaslow with Sweet Bets, a P-40F he named after his "best girl" at the time. An original pilot with the 79th's Skeeter Squadron, Jaslow would go through five P-40s for one reason or another during his eighty-mission combat tour. (Jaslow)

The next day a Fw 190 flew brashly over the Causeway landing ground but was out of range before it could be intercepted. Later that afternoon Lee "Goose" Gossick destroyed an all-black 109 with white wingtips and Wyman "Porky" Anderson damaged another in a fight that erupted when twelve 109s bounced the Skeeters and a flight of Baltimores on the way to Messouna. Gossick got his 109 by turning into it after being jumped from behind, firing a short burst, then giving it a couple of extra squirts as he followed it to the deck. Gossick leveled off at 2,000 feet, but the 109 kept going straight down and Flight Officer Raymond Ermis saw it crash. Anderson, meanwhile, was jumped by three 109s from the rear, but discouraged his attackers when he turned into one and sent it scurrying into a nearby cloud with a burst of machine-gun fire. The 109 emerged from the cloud a few seconds later and was last seen diving for home trailing a long plume of white smoke. At the same time that Gossick and Anderson were mixing it up with the enemy fighters, "Jazz" Jaslow, James Pittard, Ed Fitzgerald, "Scotty" Rogers and Vernon Tyson were keeping the other Messerschmitts at bay, and the Baltimores completed their bomb runs unmolested.

On April 8 Brooklynite Ralph Lind was killed when hit by ground fire while the Flying Skulls were strafing tanks and motor transport on a road south of Messouna, his plane exploding in mid-air before he could bail out, and Thomas Anderson went down in no-man's land. Phillip Miller was also hit, but made a safe landing near a British camp. Anderson was hit just as he leveled off for his strafing run – "they had time to zero in on us because they could see us coming from a long way off, and the anti-aircraft fire was intense" [11] – and his plane flipped over on its back with its wing and tail surfaces shredded. He managed to recover at about 200 feet, but his P-40 was vibrating so badly he could barely keep it in the air and decided to belly-in. Knocked unconscious at impact, when he woke up he was on a stretcher and in the care of New Zealand troops who got him to a British dressing station. The next day he was taken to a field hospital in Tripoli where it was discovered his back was fractured in three places. Anderson was then flown to Cairo where he was in a body cast for about five months, before being shipped back to the States.

Because of Hitler's meddling in tactical affairs von Arnim did not have a chance to properly fortify the strong natural positions at Wadi Akarit. He was also short of ammunition and had lost 14,000 men either killed, wounded or missing between the time he pulled his divisions out of the Mareth Line and moved in behind the one at Akarit. As a result, it took Montgomery less than twenty-four hours to leverage him out of what many considered one of the best natural defensive positions in North Africa.

Comanche pilots (left to right), standing: Lts. Perry Bailey, Wayne Rhynard, George Harris and George Maxwell. Kneeling: Lts. Jack Gumbleton, Danny Mayer and Bill Hanson. Only Rhynard, Maxwell and Gumbleton would survive the war. (Morrissey)

But once again Monty's attempt to bottle up the enemy was futile. Methodical, overly cautious, and waiting until all the pieces were in place before pursing a beaten foe (a trait that never ceased to exasperate his critics), Montgomery had again allowed the bulk of the First Italian Army to escape. Leaving only a rearguard, Messe withdrew to the north and the next favorable defensive terrain at Enfidaville, a small village about five miles in from the sea some 150 miles above the Wadi Akarit line.

By the end of the day on April 8 the 79th was out of effective fighter range of the retreating enemy. The Group prepared to move to a new landing ground at La Fauconnerie.

La Fauconnerie, which literally translates into "Falcon's nest," was located about twenty-five miles northwest of Sfax, and sat atop a high plateau overlooking mile after mile of olive orchards. When an advance party headed by Lt.-Colonel Grogan, Major Guy Stewart (the Group communications officer), and "Doc" Hoffman arrived at La Fauconnerie the embers of campfires left by the Germans were still warm, while wrecked and smoldering aircraft and vehicles of Anton Hackl's *gruppe* littered the field. Mines were still being dug out by the Royal Engineers, and small bands of unattached German and Italian soldiers roamed the neighborhood. On their trek across the desert from Causeway in a reconnaissance car called *The Texsylvannia Special*, the advance party had become lost, was almost captured, and at one time startled a British infantry colonel when it actually got in front of advance elements of Eighth Army.[12]

As the fleeing enemy retreated even farther north the 79th found it was still out of fighter range at La Fauconnerie. While an advance party scouted for a new landing ground twenty missions were run during the next four days, escorting mine-sweepers clearing the harbors at Sousse and Sfax.

On April 17 the 79th moved into Hani West landing ground, located in an alfalfa field just outside the Holy Moslem city of Kairouan. Joining the Group was yet another squadron of the 324th Fighter Group – the 315th – in addition to the 316th Hell's Belles Squadron that had fought alongside the Falcons since the beginning. Hot, treeless, bug infested, and inhabited by snakes, Hani West was not as comfortable as Causeway with its olive groves and warm, sulfur water artesian well (which had done much to soothe the aches and pains of the tireless ground crew as they worked sixteen hours a day to keep 'em flying), but the French Quarter in Kairouan, with its wide, tree-lined avenues, suggested an atmosphere of Europe and civilization, and was a welcome change.

five

Cape Bon

"The most dangerous sea passage in the world was not the Sicilian Channel as the British knew it in 1942, but as Italian sailors knew it during the first four months of 1943"

– Commander M. A. Bragadin, Italian Navy

Shortly after the Allied TORCH landings in November the enemy began to supplement its water-borne supply of the Tunisian battlefield with an airlift of phenomenal proportions. Large aerial fleets of Ju 52s and cumbersome six-engined Me-323 *Gigant* transports took off from Italian bases heavy with supplies and reinforcements, staged through Sicily where they picked up fighter escort, and crossed over to Tunisia and their main air terminals near Tunis. By the first of April the volume of enemy air traffic landing on the Cape Bon peninsula had risen to over 150 transports a day – enough to meet the daily requirements of one-third of all German troops in North Africa.

During January, February and March a plan called Operation FLAX was devised by the Allies to disrupt this flow of men and material from Italy. Information gathered by radar and photo reconnaissance plotted the flights; times of departures and arrivals were noted; refueling centers, staging fields, and the number and type of escort recorded. Meanwhile, nothing was done by the Allies to tip their hand. They patiently waited for just the right moment to strike.

That moment came in the first week of April. The volume of air traffic moving across the Sicilian Strait was now heavy enough to permit crippling losses at a stage in the Tunisian campaign when the enemy could least afford it. Weather conditions were also now favorable for what the Allies had in mind. The plan was for P-38 Lightnings to sweep the Sicilian Strait, synchronizing their efforts with escorted shipping sweeps by medium bombers, while other bombers and fighters worked over the terminal airdromes near Tunis and staging fields on Sicily. On April 5 the Allies officially declared open season on the enemy's airlift. The day was less than six hours old when Operation FLAX began to pay dividends.

Twenty twin-boomed P-38s of the 82nd Fighter Group were escorting B-25s on a sea sweep northeast of Cape Bon when they intercepted fifty-three German aircraft approaching Tunis. The American pilots were soon joined by twenty-six Lightnings of the 1st Fighter Group, and between them they quickly shot down fourteen Ju 52 transports and thirteen other types for the loss of six P-38s. American fighters escorting the heavies to Sicilian targets accounted for still more, and when the total for the opening day of FLAX was tallied the enemy was short 201 valuable aircraft, 161 of them having been caught on the ground.

The butchery continued on April 10 and 11 when P-38 and B-25 crews claimed seventy-one shot down over the sea or caught on overcrowded fields. But the *coup de grace* to the shuttle system of Generalleutnant Ulrich Buchholz, the *Lufttransportfuehrer Mittelmeer,* was soon to be administered by Desert Air Force fighters.

The 79th had just begun operating out of Hani West, joining the 57th which had moved into El Djem North on April 15, in running fighter sweeps off the tip of Cape Bon. With Army Group Afrika being squeezed into an ever-narrowing bridgehead there was little room, or need, for the close support operations that had been the hallmark of these two DAF units and they were free to roam the skies north of Cape Bon searching for Buchholz' transports.

Throughout much of the day on Palm Sunday, April 18, the two groups sent up large standing patrols over the northern approaches to the peninsula. All morning and well into the afternoon they cruised monotonously at 8,000 feet in skies frustratingly clear of enemy air traffic. Late in the afternoon four squadrons of the 57th and a top-cover of eleven Spitfires from the RAF's 92 Squadron relieved the 79th and began the last sweep of the day. It would end in what historians would call the Palm Sunday Massacre, but to the pilots of the 57th Fighter Group it would forever be known simply as the "Goose Shoot."

The "Goose Shoot" got off to a slow start. For over an hour the American pilots searched in vain as the sun dipped lower in the western sky and fuel gauges dropped steadily. Suddenly, as they were about to pack it in for the day, the rays of the setting sun glinted off a large formation (later determined as sixty-five Ju 52s, five Me-110s and sixteen 109s and 202s) skimming the waves six miles off Cape Bon. Buchholz was using the fast-fading light to sneak in another convoy.*

With one squadron of Warhawks and the Spits staying high to deal with the escorting enemy fighters, the rest of the Group dove to the deck and pounced on the transports. Too close to the sea to take effective evasive action the unwieldy, slow-moving, tri-motored Junkers Ju 52s that the Germans called *Tanta Ju* ("Auntie Ju") were torn apart one by one, fuel tanks blazing as they plunged into the water or came to an inglorious end on the beaches near Ras el Ahmar. Initial American claims were fantastically high (not unusual in the blur of fast-moving combat), but final figures released after the war reveal that fifty-nine transports, one Me-110, and nine escorting single-engined fighters were lost this Palm Sunday afternoon. Of the fifty-seven Allied fighters involved in the massacre, six Warhawks and a Spitfire failed to return to their Tunisian airdromes.

Early the next morning Kittyhawks of 7 South African Wing jumped on a formation of Italian SM-82 cargo planes and their escorting Macchi fighters near the island of Pantelleria, claiming twelve. Three days later the same South Africans intercepted twenty six-engined Me-323s. As sixteen of these giant birds fell flaming into the Mediterranean their smoking wreckage marked the funeral pyre of the Axis daytime air-supply shuttle system between Italy and Tunisia. A few half-hearted attempts were made to slip through at night, but a lack of transport aircraft and crews qualified to fly them in darkness, plus radar-equipped RAF Beaufighters and Hurricanes soon cut short that threat. For Army Group Afrika to have any chance of survival it would now have to rely on supplies brought in by surface shipping alone. Accordingly, there was a steady increase in enemy water traffic between Italy and Cape Bon during the last half of April. Every conceivable type of surface vessel was pressed into service to run supplies to the North African battlefield, sailing from Naples to Tunis through the treacherous Sicilian Channel that Italian sailors ruefully referred to as "the death route." Destroyers, barges, and the highly dangerous *Siebelfahren* were used, the latter being shallow-draft, pontoon-raft ferries originally designed for use in the aborted invasion of Britain in 1940. Usually traveling in convoys, each *Siebel* ferry could carry 450 men or ten vehicles, and was armed to the teeth with 88-mm anti-aircraft guns and many lesser weapons. It was also suspected that German and Italian hospital shops were being used for other than humanitarian purposes, but Allied pilots were nevertheless under strict orders to give them a wide berth.

Captain Charles Jackson (dark shirt), the Comanche Intelligence Officer, and Major Richards H. Hoffman, the Group Flight Surgeon, with members of the French Foreign Legion. (Hoffman)

From April 19 until the end of the month the 79th flew a total of forty-two missions, the bulk of them against this influx of enemy shipping, and many were fiercely contested by the pilots of *Fliegerkorps Tunis*.

On April 20 a large sweep in Group strength was conducted between Cape Bon and the Italian island of Pantelleria. They had been airborne only twenty minutes when four 109s slashed at the Flying Skulls. Lieutenant Bill Abbott turned into one, firing at it head-on from close range, and the 109 went cartwheeling into the sea. Lieutenant Carl Simpson damaged another that fell off to the right streaming smoke and glycol, and a few minutes later Comanche pilots got their chance when a flight of Ju 88s and belly-tank-toting 109s were sighted low over the water heading northeast. As Fred Borsodi and his wingman, Lieutenant Pete Bedford, turned into two of the enemy fighters with guns blazing, the German pilots quickly punched off their cumbersome auxiliary tanks – but not quickly enough. Borsodi's victim turned into a bright, orange ball of flaming aviation fuel while Bedford's German, deciding that

* Whether the convoy was inbound with reinforcements and supplies or returning to Sicily is still being argued. Most historians believe the convoy was outbound from Tunisia while many of the Allied pilots participating in the "Goose Shoot" are convinced the transports were inbound.

discretion was the better part of valor, bailed out. The two Comanches then went for the 88s, each sending one of the twin-engined bombers into the water. That night the victory scoreboard at Hani West was richer by five German aircraft.

Shortly before noon on the 21st the 79th was up again in Group strength looking for shipping in the Gulf of Tunis. Twelve Warhawks each from the 85th and 86th, all lugging a 500-pound bomb, joined their immediate top-cover of sixteen Skeeter P-40s and rendezvoused with their high-cover of sixteen Spits over Hergla. The Spitfires were from 1 South African Squadron, 417 Squadron, and Skalski's Polish "Circus."

The minutes passed quickly and two 100-foot motor barges were bombed and strafed, but managed to scoot away relatively unscathed. Accustomed to land targets, the pilots achieved little success against shipping at first; they would soon improve with practice.

As the Skulls pulled up scattered and strung out from their bombing and strafing run a lone 109 that had been lurking in the low, scudding clouds hit Lieutenant John Anderson. From Jamestown, New York, the last anyone saw of him he was dangling from the end of his chute.

After this solitary pass by the 109 on Johnny Anderson the air came alive with enemy fighters and a running dogfight developed. Charles "Kim" Bolack, flying in the Skulls' Red Section, turned into one and got in a good, solid burst from about 150 yards. The 109 went down smoking badly and apparently out of control. Bolack, however, claimed only a probable. "Butch" Owen and Francis Hennin, up high with the Skeeters, watched as three 109s dropped through their flight on fire and plunged into the sea – the Spits were busy – and Leo Berinati shot another 109 out of the sky. Ed Fitzgerald was being hounded by three green and brown 109s over Cape Bon until he blew one up with a nice deflection shot, and Jack Kelly of the 86th caught a Gustav down on the deck running for Sicily, got in a long burst, and the plane dug a wingtip into the water and disappeared behind a frothy curtain of spray. Earlier, Kelly had taken a pot shot at a destroyer, and got shot at in return, with no noticeable ill-effects for either side. Minus Johnny Anderson, and with George Blare's aircraft shot full of holes the flight returned to Hani West.

The next day the 79th suffered its first non-combat fatality when Flight Officer Chester Janicki of Ziegler, Illinois plunged into the bottom of a lake during gunnery practice. During shadow gunnery the sun's reflection made it difficult to estimate altitude, and it was probably this phenomenon that contributed to Janicki's death. That same day Fred Borsodi was struck by anti-aircraft fire while on an otherwise uneventful sweep over the Gulf of Tunis and bellied-in. Borsodi escaped unhurt, but his Warhawk was a total write-off.

Lt. Pete Bedford who, with Fred Borsodi, downed two Me-109s and a pair of Ju-88s near the island of Pantelleria on April 20. (Kauffman)

For the next six days the Group was back at a familiar task, escorting DAF mediums hitting targets near the Eighth Army bomb line or working over airfields in the Soliman area. The Group maintained its spotless reputation of protecting the bomber crews (many bomb groups were beginning to specifically request the 79th for escort), and the only "incident" during this period was when Lieutenant William Glasgow turned a $40,000 P-40* into a twisted, tangled heap of worthless junk after a spectacular landing accident – a "whizzo prang" in RAF vernacular – on April 23. Somehow, miraculously, Glasgow proved true an old pilots' adage about any landing being a good one if you walked away from it, and emerged with only a chipped front tooth.

* A P-40F-10 through P-40F-20 series cost $38,296.

Lts. Johnny "General" Hoagland (left) and Charles "Kim" Bolack (right) of the Flying Skulls. The other pilot is unidentified. (Morrissey)

Struck by anti-aircraft fire while on an otherwise uneventful sweep over the Gulf of Tunis, Fred Borsodi attempted a wheels-up landing on the beach. He escaped unhurt, but his Warhawk was a total write-off. (Kauffman)

Early on April 29 four bomber-escort shows were run against gun positions along the Eighth Army front near Enfidaville. No fighters rose to oppose them, but a Boston was badly mauled by flak and had to be nursed to a wheels-up landing at a forward fighter strip – not, however, before three of its crew went over the side clutching parachute rip-cords.

Later in the morning two Focke-Wulfs and a Messerschmitt dove through a formation of Comanche and Hell's Belles (316th) aircraft east of the ancient city of Carthage. No damage was done to either side, but as the day wore on the air action began to heat up. Shortly after noon, twelve aircraft from all four squadrons, two-thirds of them packing 500-pound bombs, picked up a dozen escorting Spitfires from 92 Squadron over Hergla and headed for the Gulf of Tunis. Their target was a large ship flashed to them by 211 Group shortly after takeoff.

On this beautiful, clear spring afternoon visibility was unlimited and they had no trouble locating the target a few miles off shore. Two squadrons were already vertical and well into their bomb runs when they noticed red cross markings on the side of the vessel. Swinging wide at the bottom of their dive, they managed to avoid hitting the "hospital ship"* and directed their attention instead to several smaller craft in the area. As the Comanches were forming up over Cape Bon they ran head-on into fifteen 109s and 202s that sent everyone scrambling in different directions. Bill Hanson quickly latched on to a Macchi, and the Italian pilot took to the silk when bullet holes began creeping up the length of his fuselage. The old Curtiss Warhawk may not have been as nimble as the Macchi or other fighters in the enemy's arsenal, but the sting of its powerful .50-caliber guns still proved an effective persuader. Major Jack Watkins was at 8,000 feet when a very aggressive Messerschmitt pilot bounced him from up-sun. Leaning his '40 to port so hard it began to tremble in a pre-stall shudder, Watkins got inside the 109, squirted a short burst that sent fragments of wing flying off, and the German plane plummeted straight down into the sea like a bomb. At the same time Jack Kauffman, flying a P-40 he called *Ababa,* was going 'round and 'round with another Hun in turns so tight the weight of his body straining against the shoulder harness threatened to tear it loose from its moorings. After what seem an eternity, he managed to turn inside the 109, squeezed the trigger, and followed the tracers as they converged at a point near the Messerschmitt's wing root. The German plane belched short puffs of black smoke, flipped over on its back, and the pilot dropped clear. Instantly, fighter pilot instinct forced Kauffman to swivel his head lest there was another Jerry on his tail. What he saw wasn't a 109, but it gave him a jolt all the same: tucked in nice and tight under his wing sat Bill "Tiger" Taylor, his wingman, who had hung in there protecting his rear throughout the entire mad, wild, tumbling free-for-all.[1]

Meanwhile, Captain Barney Turner and Lieutenant Conly were both mixing it up with a pair of Macchis off Cape Bon. Turner chased his to the deck and finished it off with several short bursts, while Conly's Macchi was last seen going down trailing smoke. Conly didn't see the Macchi crash, but spotted white rings on the water a few moments later where it would

* DAF squadrons were instructed by 211 Group on May 11 to attack all inbound hospital ships, while outbound or "doubtful" ships were to be left alone. It was later learned that large numbers of armed German troops were evacuated from Tunis aboard "hospital" ships.

Miraculously, the pilot of this P-40, Lt. William Glasgow, walked away from the wreck with only a chipped front tooth. Glasgow's luck would hold again in December when he escaped from a prison camp in Italy, but it would run out shortly after the war when he was killed in a flying accident in the States. (Hoffman)

have gone in, so claimed a probable. Scanning the sky to look for the rest of his flight, Conly ran into another Macchi, which he quickly shot into the sea. While all this was going on, Lieutenant Al Brewer was having an altercation with a Messerschmitt driver. Brewer won the argument, but didn't see the 109 actually crash so only claimed a probable. Jack Kelly and John Gumbleton also encountered 109s over the Cape Bon area, firing several bursts at them before the Messerschmitts broke off combat and scooted for home. With five enemy aircraft destroyed and two probably destroyed April 29 had turned into a pretty good day for the Falcons. Adding frosting to the cake, all four squadrons returned home without a scratch.

By mid-morning of the 30th they were up again over the Gulf of Tunis bombing barges, *Siebel* ferries and dock installations. A near tragedy occurred when the Comanches closed in on a flight of twin-engined bombers and shots were exchanged between the two formations, resulting in extensive damage to Pete Bedford's P-40, before the bombers were identified as friendly B-26 Marauders, a type new to the theater.

Four hours later all four squadrons were airborne again. An Italian destroyer was soon sighted hugging the coast between Tunis and Cape Bon and the Skeeters and Comanches thundered down to attack. Two direct hits knocked large chunks off the bow and the ship rocked and bucked from the many near misses that bracketed it and sent up large geysers of water. With his ship smoking badly, the Italian captain turned the destroyer completely around and inched back toward Tunis and comparative safety. Hounded, crippled, and barely making six

The Comanches' Lt. Jack Kauffman. What he saw behind him wasn't a Jerry but it gave him a jolt just the same. (Kauffman)

knots, the destroyer had gone only a few hundred yards when it stopped dead in the water. Sensing a kill, the pilots screamed in across the waves with masthead-high strafing attacks. They were about to give it the deep-six when fifteen Me 109s sporting blue and dark green camouflage slammed into their formation and a wild fight reminiscent of the day before soon ensued. Barney Turner and Thomas McCarty were jumped by four 109s, but turned back into them and Turner shot one into the sea for his second victory in as many days. Meanwhile, Wayne "Moldy" Rhynard was fighting for his life just above the wavetops, jinking and turning wildly with three 109s that took turns making a run at him. By turning into his antagonist each time one got within firing range, Rhynard managed to stay alive, and after five or six attacks finally got on the tail of one which he promptly shot down. He then got behind another one, watched his tracers strike home, and the 109 left the scene trailing smoke. That was apparently enough for the third Messerschmitt driver who took off in the direction of the island of Zembra.[2]

While Rhynard was mixing it up with the Messerschmitts, Lieutenant Bob Allard got into it with another 109, saw his tracers hit home, and the German did a split-s from about 600 feet. It was unlikely that even the most experienced pilot could recover from such a maneuver at that altitude, so Allard claimed a probable. Lieutenant John Hutt rounded out the scoring for the Comanches when he knocked pieces of engine cowling off a 109 that had jumped him while pulling out of his bomb run at 3,000 feet, claiming a damaged.

During this wild aerial free-for-all, Lieutenants Thomas McCarty and Bill Hanson collided. The wreckage of their P-40s fell on a third a few hundred feet below – one driven by Lieutenant Perry Bailey. Two chutes popped free of the tangled pieces of metal. McCarty was picked up by an Italian hospital ship five hours later – cold, wet and half-drowned – and it was rumored that Bailey had been fished out of the water by an American freighter. At the end of the war however, both Bailey and Hanson were still unaccounted for. McCarty was taken to a POW camp in Italy but escaped five months later.

As soon as the rest of the flight re-armed and re-fueled they resumed their anti-shipping patrol over the Gulf. Their vigilance was soon rewarded with the sight of an Italian destroyer steaming over the horizon inbound from Sicily. Hovering over it were ten enemy fighters. Like their falcon namesake, twenty-four Warhawks of the 87th and 316th pushed over from 9,000 feet and dove to attack. Within two minutes the destroyer was mortally damaged. Fires raged out of control on the deck, and she was listing badly to port from three direct hits. Belching thick, black smoke the ship zig-zagged awkwardly away from the scene in the general direction of Cape Bon. It would later capsize and sink near Sidi Daoud. The destroyer's skipper would lament: "It is impossible to sail these waters during daylight hours."[3]

A handy man to have around, and everyone's favorite wingman, was Lt. Bill "Tiger" Taylor. (Kauffman)

Ten Macchis, five of them new MC-205 *Veltros* (Greyhounds), a progressive development of the MC-202, had tried in vain to break up the attack on the destroyer, but were driven off by the Skulls who were flying top-cover. Sammy Say was leading the Skull's Red Section and flamed a 202, while "Kim" Bolack and Malcolm "Joe" McNall went for another Macchi. McNall hit it in the engine, and the Macchi began spewing coolant and smoke, prompting the pilot to bail out. The rest of the enemy planes scattered.

To balance somewhat the loss of McCarty, Hanson and Bailey, the Group had destroyed two Me 109s and two Macchis, and probably destroyed another Messerschmitt. In addition, they were credited with sinking one and a half destroyers – sharing credit for the first one with another group that polished it off after the 79th got into the free-for-all with the Messerschmitts – to mark the first time ever that an enemy man-of-war had been sunk by bomb-carrying P-40s.

The Italian *Supermarina* (Naval High Command) had long realized the futility of trying to run the aerial and submarine blockade between Sicily and Tunisia, but had been asked by the Army to continue to transport troops to Tunisia in its destroyers for morale reasons, if nothing else. As a result, on April 30 the Italian Navy lost three destroyers (the 57th Group also sank one) with 900 soldiers aboard for no useful end,[4] finally forcing the *Comando Supremo* to grudgingly echo the sentiments of the destroyer captain whose deck had been blown out from under him by the 79th's pilots off Sidi Daoud.

While working over an Italian destroyer in the Gulf of Tunis the Comanches got into a fight with more than a dozen 109s, and Lt. Barney Turner (above) got his second victory in as many days. (Kauffman)

With the 79th and other Allied air units harassing enemy shipping in the Sicilian Straits, time was fast running out for von Arnim's army on the ground in Tunisia. Allied forces from the west had joined up briefly with Montgomery's Eighth Army near Gafsa on April 7 and, again, this time more permanently, at Kairouan four days later. By April 12 Monty was in Sousse. With only 60,000 effective fighting men left to oppose a quarter of a million Allied soldiers pressing in on him from three fronts, and outnumbered in armor by more than fourteen to one, von Arnim was in a hopeless situation; time was fast running out.

But Alexander was also having *his* problems. Knowing that the invasion of Sicily (decided upon in January and set for July) could not take place until the enemy was ejected from North Africa, he was understandably anxious to write a quick end to the Tunisian campaign. He immediately set in motion plans for his "final" offensive: while Eighth Army contained Messe at Enfidaville, and US II Corps advanced on Bizerte, First Army would make the main thrust up the Medjerda Valley in front of Tunis. On the night of April 19 Alexander's "final" push began. Four days later, after penetrating the enemy front to a depth of only eight miles, the offensive was stopped cold. With victory so near, yet just out of reach, Alexander would have to try a different tack.

He transferred two of Monty's best divisions – the 4th Indian and 7th Armored – to the First Army front. There the main blow would be delivered by two infantry divisions and four battalions of tank-borne infantry. Following closely would be the 6th and 7th armored divisions. At the same time Eighth Army would advance north toward Hammamet with the purpose of sealing off the Cape Bon peninsula, while II Corps once again struck out for Bizerte. This new offensive, codenamed VULCAN was to be launched May 6.

After his big fight over Cape Bon, Jack Kauffman's Warhawk undergoes engine maintenance. (Vercammen)

After an artillery barrage that planted one round of high-explosives on every two yards of the two-mile front, and with strong air support overhead beginning at first light, the last major land battle of the North African campaign began on schedule. As the offensive gained momentum, and steamrollered toward Bizerte and Tunis on three separate fronts, enemy resistance quickly crumbled; von Arnim's once-proud army fast became dispirited, broken, unorganized rabble. By the afternoon of May 7 British armor rolled through the streets of Tunis. Bizerte fell the next day. German troops, who had never been trained to fight guerrilla fashion in small independent groups, surrendered in droves. Enemy resistance collapsed completely, and the bag of prisoners, which included some 80,000 Italians and 160,000 Germans, was a bigger haul than had surrendered to the Russians at Stalingrad three months earlier.

For Luftwaffe units still trapped on the peninsula these were days to try mens' souls. With Allied air roaming over the battlefield at will the German pilots were hard-pressed. To avoid having their few remaining aircraft chewed up while they sat on the ground, most of the enemy pilots would fly over to Sicily or the nearby island of Pantelleria at dusk each evening, returning to Cape Bon at dawn to the one or two airfields still in their possession. On the day Tunis fell to the Allies, Generalleutnant Karl Koechy, commander of the Tunisian *Luftgau* (air garrison) ordered airdrome and unit commanders to get their planes and crews out at their own discretion. Some commanders were caught unprepared by this order, while others, like Major Johannes Steinhoff of JG 77, whose earlier experience with a similar situation in Russia had taught him the value of a contingency plan, was already one step ahead of Karl Koechy.

Without the knowledge of his superiors, Steinhoff had arranged beforehand for the transfer of his equipment and "black men" (ground crews, so called because of the color of their overalls) to Trapani on the northwest coast of Sicily. Each day,

Lt. Wayne "Moldy" Rhynard of the Comanches with his crew chief, T/Sgt. Bates Shuping (second from right) and other members of his ground crew, S/Sgt. Matthew Killeward (left) and Pvt. Richard Malone. After finishing his tour with the 79th Rhynard did a second tour with the Eighth Air Force in England and took over the 357th Fighter Group in the fall of 1945. By then his nickname had been changed from "Moldy" to "Fox," as in Reynard the Fox of Aesop's Fables. (Rhynard)

The victim of a Falcon bombing and strafing attack, this Italian warship has run aground a few hundred yards off the east coast of Tunisia. (Kauffman)

Lts. Bill Hanson, Jim Reutershan and Jack Kauffman shortly before Hanson (left) was killed in a mid-air collision over the Gulf of Tunis. (Morrissey)

waiting until Allied combat patrols were relieving each other, the *gruppe's* Messerschmitts took off from bases in Tunisia and headed across the Sicilian Strait. Inside the fuselage of each 109 knelt one of the "black men," without a parachute and with no hope of escaping in an emergency, squeezed in behind the pilot. In addition to the obvious hazards, nails in the boots of the first few men flown out caused the compasses in the aircraft to deviate [5]

Many pilots made the hazardous trip time and time again, and it is to their everlasting credit that they tried to get the "black men" out. But their best was not good enough; there were too many men (only a few days before replacements were still being brought in from Italy), too little time, and not enough transportation. Those being left behind were desperate. Many had been away from home for over two years and offered money, volunteered to be lashed to the wings – anything to get away.[6] But it was not to be. Despite the gallant efforts of many individuals, only a handful of serviceable aircraft with their pilots and mechanics succeeded in escaping. More than 600 enemy aircraft, many which, given the time, could have been repaired and returned to service, were left behind – mute testimony to the dominance of Allied airpower in the western Mediterranean in the late spring of 1943.

As the Tunisian campaign wound down the 79th continued its campaign against enemy shipping. On May 5, while the Skeeters and Hell's Belles were dropping 500-pound bombs on a medium-sized one-stacker in the Gulf, claiming one direct hit on the stern and several near misses, three 109s bounced the Flying Skulls over the target. Lieutenant William Ryburn of Erwin, Tennessee shot the rudder off one of the Messerschmitts, while Flight Lieutenant J. F. Westerna, flying top-cover with the Spitfires of 601 (County of London) Squadron, downed another.[7] Two 109s and a Macchi then attacked the Comanches, but broke away without hitting anything when the Comanches returned fire.

The next day three bomber-escorts, a fighter-bomber show against motor transport, and an anti-shipping mission were flown. They lost one of the Mitchells to flak; lost Lieutenant John C. Cahill of the 316th to ground fire, and sent another Italian destroyer to its doom.

On the first escort show of the day, the Skulls were riding herd on fifteen Mitchells when one of the bombers was hit by flak and went down in flames (three chutes were seen to open) and another, also a victim of flak, limped back to base watched over by four P-40s. The other two escort missions were uneventful, although a lone Messerschmitt dived on the Skeeters as they covered eighteen Baltimores bombing the harbor at Tunis, but the 109 was quickly chased off without having to fire a shot. On the fighter-bomber show, a convoy of motor transport was shot up near Tunis by the Skulls, Skeeters and Hell's Belles, but the Belles lost Lieutenant Cahill who was hit by anti-aircraft fire from an armored vehicle that was part of the convoy. With his P-40 on fire, Cahill set it down wheels-up and was last seen running from his plane. He was later reported to be a prisoner of war. The anti-shipping mission was a four-squadron affair – the 85th, 86th, 87th and 316th – with a squadron of Spitfires thrown in for good measure. Twelve aircraft each from the 87th and 316th carried 500-pound bombs, while the other two squadrons and the Spits flew top-cover. Being fired on by both ship and shore batteries, the Skeeters had first crack at the destroyer, and promptly blew it up with direct hits on both bow and stern. The 316th then went after another destroyer, getting a direct hit and several near misses, and the ship stopped dead in its tracks, smoking badly, but refused to go under.

Four missions against shipping in the Gulf of Tunis were run on May 7, and two more on the afternoon of May 8 left three 5,000-ton merchantmen smoking and brought out the Luftwaffe. The 316th had just finished bombing a merchant ship on the east side of the peninsula, showering it with near misses and causing it to list badly, when they and their top cover were jumped by ten 109s from out of the sun. Captain Robert Dempsey of the 316th (later killed over Sicily) drew first blood, knocking one of the 109s out of the sky with some fancy deflection shooting. Meanwhile, the Comanches were jumped by seven 109s that also came out of the sun but not close enough to engage, while the Skeeters and Flying Skulls were busy with some twenty 109s and Fw 190s that dove on them in pairs. With George Blare on his wing, Sammy Say of the Skulls fired at a 109 as it rolled to the left, the pilot bailed out, and the pilotless Messerschmitt went into a shallow spin from 7,000 feet and crashed into the sea. Johnny "General" Hoagland, a charter member of the "Late Arrivals Club," shot up another 109 and watched as it too went into the water, while Lieutenant Fred Hale tagged still another, plus a slow-flying Fiesler Storch he caught hugging the waves while returning to the coast.

In the Storch was Oberfeldwebel Karl Hosmann,[8] a successful fighter pilot with I/JG 77 who had four P-40s, three Spitfires, a Boston and a Mitchell to his credit since the first of the year. He had also been involved in at least one prior scrap with pilots of the 79th when on April 2 he was in a fight with the Skeeters and their Polish top-cover over Wadi Akarit. On this May afternoon, however, Hosmann was part of a group of unmarried German pilots volunteering to make an extra trip back to Cape Bon to retrieve some of the "black men." After one landing at Menzel Temime (one of the few airfields in Tunisia still in German hands), his 109 was destroyed on the ground by marauding Allied fighters. Wounded slightly in the hand during this attack, Hosmann was helped into the Storch and it took off for Pantelleria. Hale, of course, saw to it that the Storch and Karl Hosmann never arrived.*

As the North African campaign winds down, some of the original Skeeter pilots take a break. Lts. Wyman "Porky" Anderson and Kensley Miller are in the weapons carrier, while standing (left to right) are Lts. Jesse Jory, Frank Huff, Charles "Jazz" Jaslow, Morris Watkins, Francis Hennin, Paul McArthur and James Hundley, with Lts. Asa "Ace" Adair, John Kirsch, Ed Fitzgerald, Harold Crossley and Captain Lee "Goose" Gossick in front. (Gossick)

The next day, May 9, Captain John Cimaglia of the Flying Skulls was leading a strike against shipping when he was hit by anti-aircraft fire. He jettisoned his bomb load and nursed the faltering Warhawk to a wheels-up landing in a salt marsh west of Tunis. Cimaglia climbed out of his damaged P-40 unhurt, and with the help of civilians hailed an ambulance that took him to the headquarters of a British infantry brigade. There he was cordially greeted by the brigade commander.

Unknown to Cimaglia his wingman, Lieutenant Johnny Martin, had followed him down and landed safely in a wheat field about 1,000 yards away. "I had just finished dinner with the brigade commander and was sitting back to enjoy a large glass of excellent French wine when in walked Martin," the Skull's Ops Officer said. "I don't know if I was happy to see him or not."[10]

The two pilots were given a lift back to Martin's plane and by removing their parachutes and stowing them in the P-40's baggage compartment both managed to squeeze into the cramped cockpit. With Martin's 160 pounds settled comfortably on top of Cimaglia, they took off and returned to Hani West, startling tower personnel when the two men climbed down from the single-place Warhawk.

On May 10 the Skeeters were up hunting for targets of opportunity. Lieutenants George T. Lee and Paul MacArthur were at 10,000 feet when they spotted a lone Fw 190 probably flown by Leutnant Alfred Psczolla[11] of II/SG-2 (*Schlachtgeschwader* or ground attack unit) on the deck heading northeast. While MacArthur covered his tail Lee dove to the deck

* Fred Hale died in an auto accident on the Pennsylvania Turnpike in 1946. In a bizarre twist, the accident involved another former 79th pilot, Charles Jaslow. Jaslow, a freshman dental student at the University of Michigan at the time, was driving to New York with three other students when they were involved in a minor accident. While waiting for a tow-truck, a motorist stopped to offer assistance. To Jaslow's "utter amazement" the driver was Hale, whom he hadn't seen since 1943 in Italy. Hale offered Jaslow and his friends a lift, which they accepted. A few miles down the road the car hit a patch of ice, skidded off the highway and rolled over several times. Jaslow was the only survivor.[9]

and shot the 190 into the sea – the last Falcon victory of the Tunisian campaign.*

Three days later, just before von Arnim surrendered his battered army to Alexander, the Afrika Korps signed off with a message to Berlin: "The Deutsches Afrika Korps has fought to the condition to where it can fight no more. It will rise again. *Heia Safari!* (Good Hunting!)"[12]

That same day Alexander signaled Churchill: "Sir, it is my duty to report that the Tunisian campaign is over. All enemy resistance has ceased. We are masters of the North African shores."[13]

With North Africa now firmly in Allied hands, the invasion of Sicily could proceed as planned. It had been decided in January that following the end of enemy resistance in Tunisia, the next target on the invasion hit-list would be Sicily. Code-named HUSKY, it was scheduled for early July. But first, something had to be done about Pantelleria, a small, Italian-owned island off the tip of Cape Bon that functioned chiefly as a listening post to keep Rome informed of air and naval traffic in the Sicilian Channel. To invade Sicily without first knocking out Pantelleria and its smaller neighbors in the Pelagie island group – Lampedusa, Lampione and Linosa – would allow the enemy to broadcast a running commentary on what the Allies were up to in that part of the world. Mussolini boasted that the island was impregnable, comparing it to Gibraltar and Heligoland. It wasn't, as he soon found out.

Lt. Johnny Martin of the Flying Skulls admires P-40 rudder art. During the hectic last days of the Tunisian fighting, Martin "rescued" his Ops officer from a British brigade commander. (Hoffman)

* Between the time the Group went into combat as a unit on March 14 until the end in Africa on May 13, its pilots flew 195 missions (3,836 sorties), destroying twenty-nine enemy aircraft in the air, probably destroying five, and damaging seventeen. These include the victory by Lieutenant Robert Dempsey of the 316th, but not the one by Fred Borsodi while he was with the 57th Group. On the other side of the ledger, the 79th lost twenty-five aircraft on operational sorties and six through accidents during that period. Pilot losses included twenty killed, missing or prisoners of war, including two from the 316th. The three 79th pilots killed prior to March 14 are not included in this total.

six

Turkey Shoot

". . . the fact remains, [our] air forces bombed the island into submission. There were no bloody beaches at Pantelleria or Lampedusa."

– Official AAF history of World War II

Lying almost exactly halfway between Sicily and the tip of the Cape Bon peninsula, Pantelleria's forty-two square miles of lava, pumice, and ugly rugged cliffs of volcanic rock juts out of the Sicilian narrows like a sentinel guarding the southern approaches to Sicily and the Italian mainland. And indeed, in 1943, that it was.

The island sprouted observation posts equipped with RDF (radio direction finding) gear and other electronic hardware used to monitor all naval and air traffic passing through the 90-mile-wide strait between Cape Bon and Sicily – a surveillance the Allies could ill-afford if they hoped to achieve tactical surprise on the Sicilian invasion beaches in July. Further, Pantelleria housed a large airfield with underground hangars and repair shops capable of handling over eighty single-engined fighters, and numerous coves and grottos hidden along the island's jagged shoreline provided supply and refueling bases for enemy submarines, E-boats (similar to American PT-boats) and other small vessels. That the island in Axis hands posed a serious threat to the success of HUSKY was undeniable; it's role as a listening post, and as a flanking base for enemy air and naval power, could seriously menace Allied shipping in that part of the world. For those reasons alone, Pantelleria would have to be neutralized. There were also other advantages to be gained by the island's capture.

An essential prerequisite to a successful landing in Sicily was adequate fighter cover. But in May 1943 the only air bases the Allies had in the theater were on the tiny island of Malta or in North Africa. The fields on Malta were already jammed almost literally wingtip to wingtip with aircraft, and the North African-based fighters (with the exception of twin-engined P-38s) were out of effective range from Sicily. With Pantelleria's Marghana airfield in Allied hands part of the problem would be solved, as at least five squadrons of Spitfires or P-40s could be based there and would be within easy reach of the Sicilian invasion beaches. In addition, both Pantelleria and Lampedusa had sites suitable for the installation of weather and homing stations, and could also provide bases for air/sea rescue units, while Marghana's 5,000-foot runway would offer a safe haven for crippled or fuel-starved Allied bombers struggling to reach their North African bases. It was therefore vitally essential that Pantelleria and the rest of the islands in the Pelagie group be taken as soon as possible. But a conventional approach to the reduction of these islands posed several difficult problems.

Never the "Italian Gibraltar" or the "Mediterranean Heligoland"* that Mussolini boasted of, Pantelleria had nevertheless been extensively fortified by the Italians for over seventeen years. The island's entire water supply was underground; so was its electric plant and ammunition and supply dumps. Among the steep, craggy cliffs more than hundred heavy guns, countless pillboxes and machine-gun nests, and scores of other strongpoints were hewn out of the hard rock and reinforced with concrete, while hundreds of thick stone fences and squat, square houses of rock and masonry dotted the landscape, each providing a miniature fortress that would have to be taken apart stone by stone in costly hand-to-hand combat if the island was stormed. If defended by a stubborn, determined garrison the reduction of Pantelleria could prove costly to the point of jeopardizing the invasion of Sicily and, in so doing, lend truth to the Fascist claim that the island was impregnable. But Pantelleria was not defended by such a garrison, and therein lay its weakness.

* Heligoland was a heavily fortified island in the North Sea used by the Germans as a naval base during both world wars.

Vice-Admiral Gino Pavesi, Pantelleria's military governor, had about 12,000 poorly-armed men under his command for defense of the island. Another 4,500 manned the trenches of Lampedusa. A ragged, seedy lot at best, untested under the fire of combat and of questionable morale, Pavesi's troops had witnessed with awe the might of Allied airpower during the last weeks of the Tunisian campaign. Isolated from the mainland of Italy they could expect little in the nature of air support or reinforcements if attacked, and they knew it. At any rate, they had little heart for a war that was now going badly for the Italian people. Nevertheless, the quality and moral fiber of its garrison notwithstanding, Pantelleria still presented an obstacle to be reckoned with.

An invasion force with enough clout to successfully storm the island fortress would tie up men, ships and landing craft badly needed elsewhere, and probably set back the invasion of Sicily by at least a month. Worst of all, perhaps, was the nagging fear that a stiff resistance by Gino Pavesi's bobtailed garrison would not only upset HUSKY's timetable, but perhaps preclude the invasion altogether. Such a show of strength would also give the Italian army a lift in morale at a time when just the opposite effect was desired. Yet, Pantelleria had to be dealt with. But how?

General Eisenhower, who in February had been appointed Supreme Allied Commander in North Africa, thought a heavy and prolonged air and naval bombardment might be sufficient to break the will of the garrison, softening up the island's defenses to the point where a landing could be achieved relatively unopposed and with minimal losses. Such a bombardment might even force a surrender without the need for an assault landing. With Sicily's D-Day drawing near, and anxious to evaluate the effects of a concentrated and determined bombing campaign against heavily defended and strongly fortified gun emplacements, Ike elected to initiate a massive bombing campaign against Pantelleria and Lampedusa. On May 9 he ordered Air Marshal Sir Arthur Tedder to make available the full strength of Allied airpower in the Mediterranean (over 1,000 operational aircraft) for use in the aerial assault, code-named Operation CORKSCREW.

During the waning days of the Tunisian campaign Pantelleria had been hit only sporadically in nuisance-type air raids designed chiefly to let Pavesi's men know they had not been forgotten. Now, beginning May 18, the volume and intensity of attacks over the island increased dramatically. More than a hundred sorties a day, every day, were flown by the fighters and mediums, most of them against Marghana airfield and the harbor facilities at Porto di Pantelleria, the island's largest city and only port. By the end of the month the airfield was thoroughly cratered, most of Pantelleria's aircraft had been destroyed on the ground (eighty-four shot-up and abandoned aircraft were later found on the field[1]) and all above-ground installations were burned out. The port had been equally battered. On June 1 the air assault was shifted to concentrate on the island's coastal batteries and gun emplacements. Of the eighty major gun batteries on Pantelleria, it was calculated that about two-thirds could be taken out as a direct result of the air strikes, and the remainder rendered useless by the secondary effects of the bombing – disruption of communications, demoralization of gun crews, and damage to scientific equipment and instruments. Under the planned program of almost continuous bombing the enemy would have little chance to repair the damage.

Lt. Jack Kauffman's Ababa stands ready to fly against Pantelleria's gun positions. (Kauffman)

American B-17 Flying Fortresses also lent their weight to the attack beginning June 1, when the heavies, along with P-38s and P-40s, unloaded more than 200 tons of bombs over Pantellerian targets. Three days later another 200 tons of high explosives were showered over the island. Tedder's second phase of the bombing program opened June 6 with round-the-clock attacks that grew in intensity each day – 600 tons on June 7, 700 tons on June 8, and 800 tons on June 9 – reaching

SWITZERLAND
AUSTRIA
HUNGARY
Lyon
Udine
Venice
Rhone River
FRANCE
I T A L Y
YUGOSLAVIA
Genoa
Cesenatico
Marseille
Fano
Jesi
St. Raphael
LIGURIAN SEA
ADRIATIC SEA
N
Bastia
ELBA
CORSICA
Rome
Anzio
Foggia
0 50 100
Miles
TYRRHENIAN SEA
Naples
Bari
Salerno
SARDINIA
MEDITERRANEAN SEA
Messina
SICILY
PANTELLERIA
ALGERIA
TUNISIA
MALTA

A captured Opel Kapitän left behind by the retreating Germans on the Cape Bon peninsula, with a Comanche P-40 in the background. (Vercammen)

a crescendo June 11 as a British infantry brigade prepared to go ashore.

For the 79th Fighter Group, as with most Allied air units in Africa, its job did not stop with the surrender of von Arnim's army in Tunisia. The first Allied trans-Mediterranean convoy since 1941 left Gibraltar on May 17 bound for the Suez Canal, and from May 13 through the 23rd the Group ran sixty-three dull, butt-numbing ship escort missions. Hugging the coast of North Africa the convoy was continuously protected by land-based aircraft. RAF Beaufighters from Malta covered the ships by night, while soft-spoken Spitfires hovered over them at dawn and dusk. The 79th's Warhawks provided cover the rest of the time, and also escorted friendly destroyers prowling the waters off the Cape looking for stragglers. Because of the distances involved it was impossible to maintain an hourly watch over the ships from Hani West, so the 79th operated out of two airfields in relays. Pilots would take off from Hani West – usually in flights of two or four aircraft – land at el Maou airdrome near Sfax (home of the 12th Bomb Group) to refuel and be briefed on the convoy's position, then head out on escort duty, returning to Sfax for more fuel before landing back at their home drome near Kairouan. Enemy aircraft were conspicuous by their absence during this time, and the convoy reached Alexandria without loss. The only "incident" as far as the Falcons were concerned was on May 21 when the Skeeters, flying the last mission of the day, came home in the dark – none of the pilots had flown at night since leaving the States seven months earlier – and Captain William "Scotty" Rogers taxied into a belly tank as he turned off the runway, causing an explosion and fire. He escaped with minor burns, but his '40 was a total wreck. For Rogers, pranging his kite on landing was not something new. He demolished one on March 24 when he overshot the landing ground, and washed out another the next day when he couldn't get his gear down and had to land wheel's-up.

On June 2, pilots and planes and the B-Party ground echelon moved into a hot, sprawling dry lake-bed near El Houaria on the very tip of the Cape Bon peninsula. Two days later they began flying against Pantelleria's well-dug-in gun positions.

Until the second phase of Tedder's air campaign began on June 6 only a few feeble, impotent attempts had been made by the Luftwaffe and *Regia Aeronautica* to contest the Allied bombing. But as Tedder stepped up his aerial attacks the enemy countered by sharply increasing patrol activity over the island. It was too little, too late. During the next ninety-six hours the 79th's fighter pilots would enjoy their best air-to-air combat success of the entire war, shooting twenty-eight Axis aircraft out of the sky, probably destroying another, and damaging four – with the loss of only one aircraft and no pilots.

The fireworks started on the afternoon of June 7 when Lieutenants Milt Clark and Dick Bunker of the 85th each knocked a pair of MC-202s into the sea while escorting A-20s off the northwest coast of Pantelleria. The following day the same squadron was jumped by ten 109s in the same general area, and after a short but furious fight brought their total score to eighteen. Clark, William Ryburn and John Cimaglia each got a 109, while Cimaglia, Kim Bolack and Johnny Martin claimed a 202 apiece. "General" Hoagland petitioned for a probable after seeing his tracers go into the canopy of a 109 that conveniently pulled up in front of him (the 109 went into a vertical dive pouring smoke but wasn't seen to crash), and Bill Abbott damaged another that scurried out of the area and was last seen heading for Pantelleria smoking badly. At the same time the Comanches were escorting a squadron of Bostons when twelve enemy fighters sliced through their formation. The bandits were in and out so quickly they offered nothing but a fleeting shot, but Major Watkins hammered the trailing Macchi enough to claim a damaged.

Lt. Charles "Kim" Bolack of the Flying Skulls. The Macchi he bagged over Pantelleria on June 8 brought his squadron's score to sixteen destroyed in the air. (Hoffman)

The Group ran a hundred uneventful sorties on the 9th – bomber escorts and fighter sweeps notable mostly for much useless radio chatter – until late in the afternoon when six Fw 190s, two of them sporting distinctive red noses, passed under a flight of Comanche aircraft. Fred Borsodi, with Pete Bedford on his wing, turned and followed two of them, firing at the 190s from long range. Suddenly, another Focke-Wulf with Dick Morrissey hot on its tail dove down in front of Borsodi and Bedford. Morrissey got in several bursts that knocked pieces off the 190's tail section and the German wobbled his wings and pulled over in front of Bedford as Morrissey overran him. Bedford shredded the 190's rudder still further and knocked its starboard gear out of the well. As Bedford passed by, the German jettisoned his canopy and started climbing to the right. Borsodi then finished him off, hosing a stream of steel-jacketed shells into the 190 until it caught fire and the pilot bailed out five miles south of Sicily. On the way back to base Lieutenant Horace Cumberland fired a burst into the belly of another Fw 190, but his tracers bounced harmlessly off the underside of the thick-skinned aircraft.

Meanwhile, six 109s had passed over the top of Major Watkins flight. Two of them peeled off to press home a frontal attack on the Comanches. Watkins met the German leader with his heavier-gunned Warhawk, fired two long bursts, and the 109 spun into the water. That made twelve destroyed, one probably destroyed, and two damaged in three days with no losses to the Group. Any way you looked at it, the murky skies over Pantelleria were fast becoming a happy-hunting ground. On the morrow the Skeeters, who thus far trailed the other two squadrons in the scoring, would have their finest hour.

On June 10, as the massive aerial bombardment of Pantelleria neared its thundering climax, the 79th's plucky airborne warriors were up well before dawn, shuttling back and forth between El Houaria and the island, scouring assigned

The hunting was good – and would get even better. Lts. Joe Connelly (right) and Johnny Martin shared a Macchi that dove through their section with a Spitfire hot on its tail. (Hoffman)

sectors for worthwhile targets or escorting mediums as the bombers toggled their share of the 6,200 tons of explosives unloaded over Admiral Pavesi's hapless garrison since the assault began. In the early evening hours the Flying Skulls were bringing home a squadron of Bostons when they ran head-on into a fight involving P-40s, Spitfires, and some fifteen bandits. One of the Macchis, desperate to elude a hotly-pursing Spitfire, pulled blindly up in front of the Skulls Red section. With Joe Connelly and Johnny Martin leading the charge, and looking not unlike a hungry pack of baying beagles in pursuit of a lone, scared rabbit, the entire section went for the Italian. Martin and Connelly soon had him boxed in, hit the 202 from both sides, the Macchi caught fire and went into a shallow dive, and the pilot bailed out. Falcon pilots had been in the air for better than fourteen hours, and this was the first real action in an otherwise uneventful (for them at least) early June day. Five minutes later the Skeeters would electrify the entire Northwest African Air Force when they reduced the enemy's fighter strength by fifteen in as many minutes. It was the sort of dogfight that fighter pilots dream of.

Sixteen Skeeter Warhawks, their pilots answering today to the radio call-sign "Clatter," had droned out of dusty El Houaria earlier in the afternoon to begin their last sweep of the day. Sixteen young men with hard-boned faces burned bronze by the hot desert sun; wearing yellow life jackets, faded khaki shirts, and leather helmets; pistols holstered around their shoulders, hunting knives strapped to their legs, and scarves of discarded parachute silk wound smartly around their necks, were now 5,000 feet over the northeast corner of smoke-shrouded Pantelleria when a lone MC-202 (probably a straggler from the fight the Skulls had run into earlier) came stooging through the Skeeter's top-section. Paul McArthur pulled around on it and fired several bursts. Pieces flew off the Macchi and coolant poured out. The Alabama pilot gave it another squirt. The Italian rolled his plane over on its back and bailed out trailing a partially-opened chute. One down!

A few moments later the Argus eyes of Lt.-Colonel Charles Grogan sighted a large hospital plane hugging the waves twenty miles off the coast. Hovering around it were ten Me 109s. Grogan jinked his P-40 once, then again, to clear his tail, and

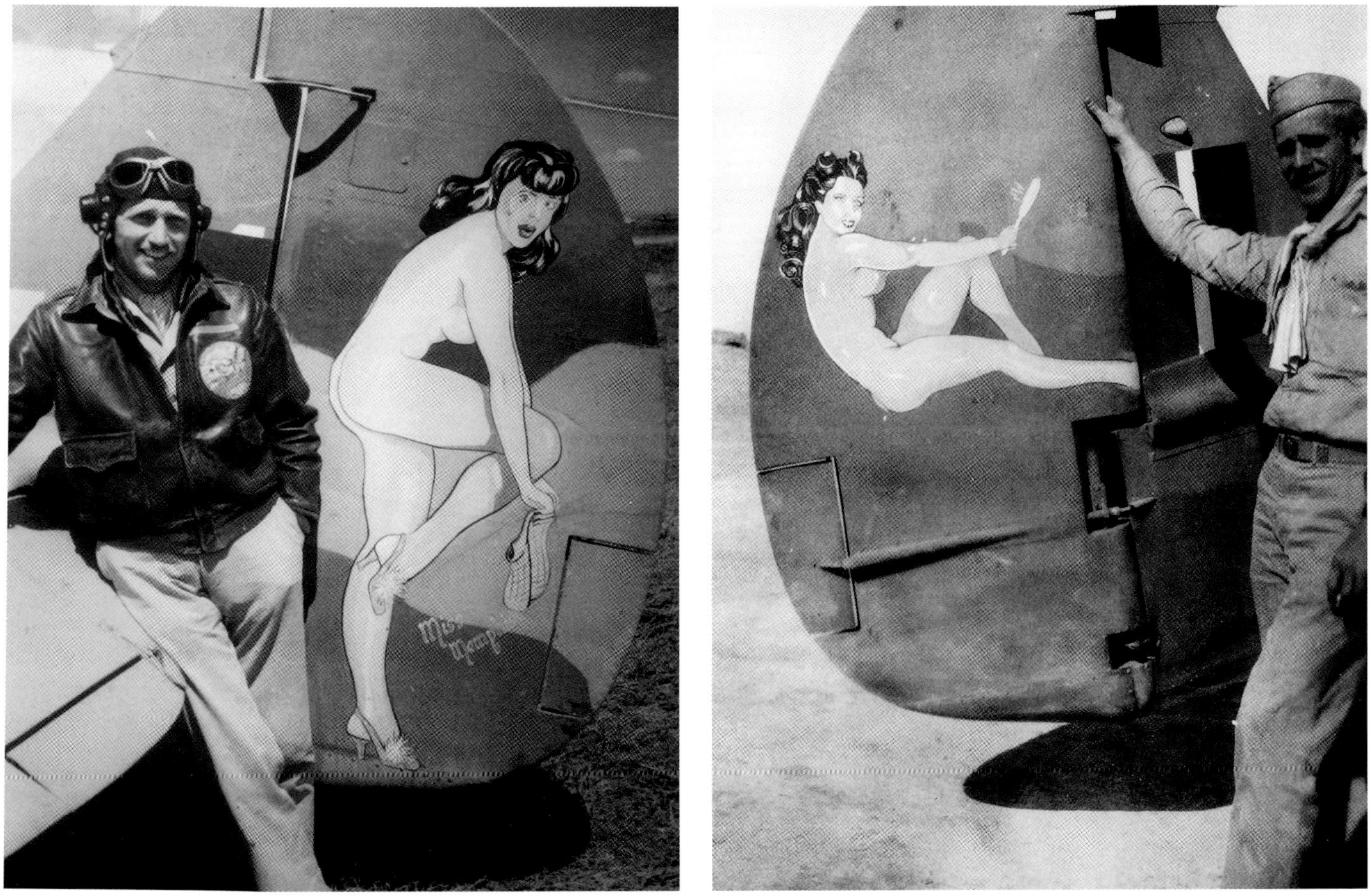

Two more examples of the artwork adorning the rudders of Flying Skull P-40s. Lt. Tom Cox (left) and Lt. John Hutt pose with some of Cpl. Pumphrey's unclad beauties. (Hoffman and Morrissey)

tore down after the Messerschmitts. The old Warhawk, considered by many as obsolete even before Pearl Harbor, had its faults. But diving with a full head of steam wasn't one of them. With Grogan closing fast the German went into aerial convulsions trying to evade him, turned left when he should have turned right, and the P-40's wingtip sliced neatly through the 109's control surfaces. Grogan headed for home minus several feet of his port wing while the Jerry cartwheeled into the sea. Two down . . . and suddenly the entire sky became a jumble of twisting, turning, diving, climbing aircraft.

Morris Watkins, flying on Grogan's wing, rode the tail of a 109, his guns knocking large chunks of metal fabric off the German fighter, and the 109 went in beneath a plume of water and debris. That made three! The six wing guns of Johnny Kirsch tore another 109 to wreckage and the enemy fighter went into a death plunge. Four down! Kensley Miller got the fifth, a 109 that burst into flames, and "Ace" Adair chased another to within twenty miles of Sicily before the Messerschmitt went into the water with an apparent dead man at the controls. Number six! Frank Huff had his Yellow section (Huff, "Jazz" Jaslow, Leo Berinati and John Dzamba) at 7,000 feet when he spotted two 109s orbiting over a downed pilot and lessened their number by one. Seven! Leo Berinati was within gliding distance of Sicily when he caught the other with three long bursts and the 109 half-rolled into the sea. Eight . . . and the fight was just heating up.

"Porky" Anderson got number nine, a Macchi that George Lee and Ed Fitzgerald had been badgering, then kicked hard

Lt. Paul McArthur, who would become the 79th's top-scoring pilot with five confirmed victories, relaxes along the Tripoli waterfront. During the Skeeters' "Turkey Shoot" on June 10 he bagged two Macchis and a pair of 109s, and damaged another Messerschmitt before forced to bail out. He got his fifth kill over Sicily in August 1943. (Wright)

Lt. Jesse "Fred" Jory (left) and Captain Lee "Goose" Gossick of the Skeeters. (Gossick)

right rudder and went head-on for another. This Italian, too, would leave his bones on the floor of the Strait as the Macchi came apart under the savage pounding of the Warhawk's six fifties. Ten . . . and Anderson wasn't through yet. He caught a 109 low on the water and moved in close, his tracers lacing out in red threads to walk a stitched pattern up the side of the Messerschmitt. A short puff of dirty, black smoke gasped from the belly of the 109, followed by a tongue of flame. Then there was a burst of bright orange and the Gustav came apart in the air. The Squadron's score for the day now stood at eleven.

With the sky full of parachutes "Goose" Gossick and Francis Hennin found eight 109s milling around another hospital plane. Hennin's guns stubbornly refused to fire at a crucial moment (he finally got them working by vigorously rapping on the switch panel; by then his target was out of range) but Gossick, who with his buddies had been celebrating the birth of his first child when the order came to launch the sweep, exploded one of the German fighters for number twelve, and damaged another that hurriedly left the scene pouring coolant.

Then, as abruptly as it had started, the fight was over. One moment the sky had been a wild place echoing to the sound of

The Skeeters were in their "club" at El Houaria on June 10 celebrating the birth of "Goose" Gossick's son when they got the word to make a sweep off Pantelleria. The sweep resulted in their "finest hour" in air-to-air combat. Relaxing in the club are (left to right), standing: Lts. Clinton "Butch" Owen, James Hundley, Ed Fitzgerald, unknown, Johnny Kirsch, Bruce Morrison and Captain Charles Jones the squadron Transportation Officer. Front: unknown, Lts. Morris Watkins and George Lee, Flight Surgeon Captain Stephen Magness, Squadron CO Major Benjamin "Duke" Uhrich, Lt. Charles "Jazz" Jaslow, Captain Frank Huff, unknown, Lt. Paul McArthur, Captain Lee "Goose" Gossick and Lt. Wyman "Porky" Anderson. (Gossick)

chattering guns and the high-pitched whine of over thirty straining engines. Now it was as silent as a cathedral at midnight.

Paul McArthur, who had gotten a MC-202 at the start of the fight, had added another Macchi and two 109s shortly thereafter, and was beating up on another Messerschmitt (claiming a damaged) when his engine started losing coolant. He nursed his bullet-riddled P-40 as close to home as he could, but was eventually forced to give it up some thirty miles off the coast of Tunisia. He bailed out of his damaged X-83, shucked off his chute harness, and clambered aboard a half-inflated dinghy. Overhead orbited "Goose" Gossick and "Ace" Adair until relieved by "Porky" Anderson and Leo Berinati. Gossick and Jesse Jory soon returned in two freshly refueled aircraft to resume the vigil over the downed pilot. The dusk was already deepening to a murky darkness when the air/sea rescue lads of 283 Squadron set down beside McArthur in their sputtering Walrus and hauled him aboard. But if he thought his troubles were over he was mistaken. The Walrus pilot tried every trick in the book in a futile attempt to get off the water, but the ancient flying boat obstinately refused to become airborne. McArthur helped man the plane's bilge pumps and they started taxiing to shore – then the engine quit. In company with his would-be rescuers, Paul McArthur spent an uncomfortable night bobbing about in the Mediterranean. Early the next morning a British corvette tossed them a line and they were towed into Kelibia Bay.

On June 5, and again on June 9, the badly battered garrison on Pantelleria had been given a chance to surrender, but each time the demands were met with silence. The result was a "round-the-clock" bombing campaign on June 10 that left the island "looking like the landscape of the moon."[2] The next morning the bombing attacks reached such an incredible level of violence that Pavesi asked Mussolini for permission to surrender, and a white flag was raised over the island's radio station. The bombing had raised so much dust, however, that the flag couldn't be seen, and at eleven o'clock a British assault team headed for the beaches behind a curtain of naval gunfire.* A little over an hour later the harbor and the city of Porto di Pantelleria were in Allied hands – the only casualty a British rifleman nipped by a local jackass.

At 5:30 p.m. Admiral Pavesi, shaken and unnerved by long days of almost continuous air and naval bombardment, surrendered the island to British General W. E. Clutterbuck in the underground hangar at Marghana airfield. The next day Lampedusa also gave up without a fight. For the first time in history an enemy stronghold had been beaten into submission almost solely by airpower.

With the fall of the Pelagie Islands the way was now clear for the Allied invasion of Sicily.

Following a fight with 79th Warhawks near Pantelleria, this Macchi MC-202 came to an inglorious end on the beach near Cape Bon. (Wright)

If ever there was fought a "clean" war it was probably the one waged in North Africa in 1940-43. There were few innocent civilians to get in the way; no masses of homeless refugees to haunt one's conscience and, because the natives were not related to any of the combatants, there was little hate generated by either side over seeing their homes destroyed or loved ones killed and maimed.

Health was generally good, although hospitals were inconveniently distant and always British. And the ancient British ambulances (lorries with no suspension worthy of the name) frequently broke down. A few cases of malaria were diagnosed shortly after the Group's arrival at LG-174 among pilots who had ferried their planes up from British West Africa where mosquitoes had been prevalent, but the most common health problem was an intestinal ailment the British called "gyppy-tummy." It affected just about everyone at one time or another and consisted of a sudden onset of profuse diarrhea, abdominal pain, malaise, and a two or three degree increase in body temperature. In addition, one soldier in the Group was diagnosed with poliomyelitis shortly after arriving overseas (he had refused to eat anything other than candy and cookies on the voyage across the Atlantic) and was returned to the States.

Morale and spirits were also high, and the constant exposure to new experiences and adventures shared with cherished buddies, plus the nomadic nature of the life itself, made one appreciate the simple pleasures, and created a strong sense of camaraderie among those who toiled and fought in the "blue." The most popular song in the desert for friend and foe alike was *Lil Marlene,* broadcast from behind German lines but universal in its appeal.

The Desert Air Force warrior (and the 79th was by this time more DAF than AAF) was a proud, independent individual, and this was perhaps best reflected by his bearing and in the clothes he wore. Partly by design and partly by necessity, American airmen attached to the DAF wore an odd mixture of British battle-dress and government issue; US insignia; a varied assortment of shoes and boots, and a wide range of official and unofficial headgear. No one wore ties, and the officers generally dressed to suit their own tastes. "These things gave an endless variety to the unvarying dustiness of the desert, but there was nevertheless a certain uniformity . . . the correctly dressed visitor from Cairo or Tripoli appeared wildly unorthodox, and visitors could be picked out at a glance:

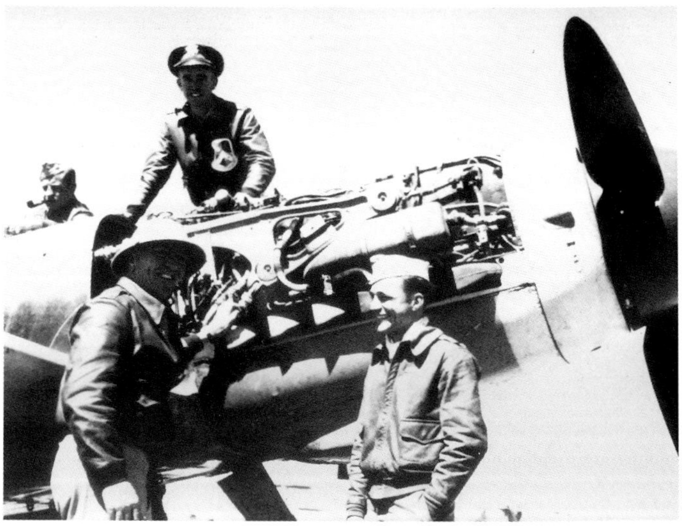

Shortly after the end of the Tunisian campaign, World War I ace Eddie Rickenbacker (pith helmet) visited the Group while on a fact-finding tour for AAF Commanding General H. H. "Hap" Arnold. Here he inspects a captured Me-109 with Colonel Bates (right) and Colonel Art Salisbury, CO of the rival 57th Fighter Group. Salisbury was the inspiration for "Art Solitary" in Milt Caniff's comic strip, Terry and the Pirates. (Hoffman)

* After the surrender, Lt.-General Carl "Tooey" Spaatz, who as commanding general of the Mediterranean Allied Air Forces was in charge of Operation CORKSCREW, apologized to Admiral Pavesi for not seeing his attempt to surrender before the invasion force was landed.[3]

"Alike in the similar dissimilarity of their appearance, the men of the Desert Air Force were alike in other ways: they shared the same rations of bully beef and chlorinated tea; they experienced the same unpleasant conditions, crouched under cover in the same sandstorm, and simmered under the same blazing sun."[4]

The camaraderie and shared experiences notwithstanding, few if any American soldiers shed tears when they learned they were leaving North Africa. Life in the desert was hard, even without the combat. The following poem, penned by an anonymous and obviously jaded soldier pretty well sums it up. It is entitled, "Soldier's Farewell to the Middle East:"

Land of heat, and sweaty socks,
Sun, and sand and tons of rocks.
Streets of sorrow, streets of shame,
Streets for which there is no name.
Streets of flies, and stinking dogs,
Harlots, thieves, and pestering "Wogs."
Clouds of choking dust that blinds,
All "Wog" beer, and wildcat wines.
Aching hearts and aching feet,
Gyppy guts, and camel meat.
An Arab's heaven, and a soldier's hell,
Land of Bastards – "Fare thee well!"

During the North African campaign, including the campaign against Pantelleria (in the strictest sense, the reduction of Pantelleria will go down in history as part of the battle for Sicily, although the Falcons, still based in Tunisia, will always consider it an extension of the North African campaign) the 79th Fighter Group flew 317 combat missions totaling 4,737 sorties (including 886 sorties by attached squadrons of the 324th) since J. Frederick Schoellkopf IV took the first mission aloft on March 14. They were particularly proud of their record of escorting 2,215 light and medium bombers through hostile skies without a single bomber being lost to enemy fighters. Even more impressive, not once during the Tunisian campaign did the Group's pilots attack friendly aircraft, naval vessels or troops, an astounding record considering the incredibly large number of cases of mistaken identity throughout the war that caused thousands of Allied lives; some estimate that "friendly fire" accounted for more than twenty percent of all American battle casualties in World War II.

Falcon pilots also proved that given the opportunity they could acquit themselves well in air-to-air combat against some of the best pilots in the world. With a score of fifty-seven aerial victories, five probably destroyed, and twenty-two damaged as against six of their own killed or missing, their victory ratio was a very respectable nine-to-one and compares favorably with that of the more famous 4th and 56th Fighter Groups with the Eighth Air Force in England, the two highest-scoring Ameri-

Partly by design and partly by necessity, American airmen attached to the Desert Air Force wore an odd assortment of British battledress and government issue, shoes and headgear. Their casual dress is well illustrated here. (Kauffman)

The 79th's medical officers and their staff worked hard to keep the men healthy. Left to right are medical officers Captains Bill Stem, Henry Winsauer and Stephen Magness, and Major Richards H. Hoffman. (Hoffman)

While waiting for the Allied invasion of Sicily, Major Jacob Schoellkopf (right) and Major Bernard "Moon" Mullin, the Skulls' CO and Executive Officer, respectively, find time for relaxation off the Tunisian coast. (Hoffman)

can groups of the war, which had victory-to-loss ratios of six-to-one and eight-to-one, respectively.

In the future, however, the 79th would be assigned almost exclusively to a fighter-bomber role against ground targets, and opportunities for increasing that score would diminish with the decline of Axis airpower in the Mediterranean. Only once again, in the air over the bloody Anzio beachhead in January and February 1944, would the 79th's pilots participate in big aerial brawls reminiscent of those fought over Cape Bon and Pantelleria.

During the period March 14 to June 13 the Group lost nineteen pilots (including two from the 324th) killed or missing in action; one pilot killed in a non-operational flying accident, and two wounded seriously enough to be sent home. Twenty-seven aircraft were lost through hostile action and six more as a result of accidents. It is a credit to the tireless ground crews, who toiled sixteen hours a day under less than ideal conditions, that during the first three months of combat not a single 79th aircraft made a forced landing because of engine failure.

A disturbing portend of the days ahead, however, was the statistic relating to strafing missions. Always the most dangerous of a fighter pilot's chores, the hazards of these low-level attacks were made painfully clear when noted that out of a total of twelve strafing missions flown during this period the Group lost twelve pilots. With over 500 strafing missions still to come, the 79th was, mathematically at least, facing a wholly unacceptable rate of attrition, if not extinction.

seven

The Straits of Messina

"The personal rule of one man has lasted too long, and has brought the nation to the verge of ruin."

– Member of Fascist Grand Council denouncing Mussolini, 7/24/43

In January 1943 Roosevelt and Churchill met at Casablanca in French Morocco. For ten days they talked, the armed camp atmosphere created by barbed wire and heavy security softened somewhat by the setting of "bright skies, palm trees, bougainvillea and orange groves,"[1] as the two leaders of the Free World reviewed the conduct of the war and grappled with the problem of how best to employ Allied forces after the completion of the Tunisian campaign.

The two countries differed substantially in their approach to global warfare. The British, still haunted by the slaughter of a generation of its young men in the First World War, hoped to avoid a head-on confrontation with the full might of German arms. They favored an oblique approach by attacking the "soft underbelly" of *Festung Europa* where British land forces could be used to best advantage.

The Americans wanted to go straight for the jugular. They wanted to build up strength for an attack across the English Channel into northwest Europe, then punch straight to the heart of Germany to bring the war in Europe to a quick, decisive finish. Fearful that further operations in the Mediterranean would be at the expense of the cross-Channel invasion (OVERLORD), they would use excess resources against the Japanese in the Pacific.

As the debate continued, the Soviets were fighting for their very existence in the rubble that was Stalingrad and clamoring loudly for an Anglo-American offensive strong enough to draw at least forty German divisions away from the Russian front.

The Americans gradually gave in. Although they hoped that Sicily would put an end to further excursions in the Mediterranean so they could get on with the big cross-Channel invasion, the build-up of Allied forces in England was not yet sufficient to launch OVERLORD with any reasonable hope of success. Yet some action had to be taken by the Western Allies to take pressure off the Soviets, and an attack on Sicily seemed the surest way to do that. It might also knock Italy out of the war, and open up the Mediterranean to friendly shipping. Therefore, on January 23, General Eisenhower,* who had been picked to command the operation, was directed to launch an attack on Sicily in 1943, D-Day being the date of the favorable July moon – when it would be light enough up to midnight for an airborne invasion force, but dark enough after moonset to allow the approach of naval forces.

Thus, in the hot, dangerous summer of 1943, the armies of the United States, Canada and Great Britain would fight in the hostile mountains of tiny Sicily as the Greeks, Romans and Carthaginians had before them, because *something* had to be done in the European theater in that year, if for no other reason.

The initial plan for HUSKY, as the operation would be called, was developed by a staff planning group in room 141 of the Hotel St. George in Algiers in February and March, 1943. It was immediately recognized that the port city of Messina (located on Sicily's northeast coast just across the Strait of Messina from the toe of Italy) was the key to the entire operation, and success of the Allied invasion hinged on its quick capture. It was through Messina that all supplies and reinforcements for the enemy garrison on Sicily would be channeled, and it would

* Eisenhower's greatest asset was his ability to maintain a smooth relationship between the British and Americans; to soothe the ruffled feathers of the many divergent personalities involved. He once fired an American general, saying: "I don't care if you called him a 'Limey,' and I don't care if you called him a 'son-of-a-bitch,' if that's what he is. But I am damn well not going to have you or anyone else putting the two together. You called him a 'Limey son-of-a-bitch,' and that's why I'm firing you."[2]

One of the hundreds of Sicily's war torn villages during that hot, dangerous summer of 1943. (Kauffman)

also provide them an escape route if they decided to evacuate the island.

But a direct seaborne assault on Messina was out of the question. The Strait, heavily mined and covered by numerous coastal batteries, was closed to Allied shipping. It was also out of reach of Allied fighters based on Malta, Pantelleria and North Africa; out of range of the valuable air cover without which no invasion could succeed.

The planners in Algiers proposed a British landing near Catania on the east coast some 50 miles below Messina, with the Americans going ashore simultaneously near Palermo on the north coast 150 miles to the west. This would almost immediately give the Allies two major ports plus the airfields on the Catania plain. With fighters from the newly-captured airfields providing cover, both armies would then converge on Messina to bring a quick end to the campaign.

Montgomery disagreed with this strategy. He believed that simultaneous landings would disperse the invasion force, courting disaster in the event of a strong enemy counterattack. He argued for a concentrated assault in the southeastern corner of the island by both Allied armies – the British Eighth and the US Seventh – with his Eighth Army spearheading the drive up the east coast, while Patton's Seventh guarded his left flank. Eventually, he sold his plan to Eisenhower.

Not nearly as bold or imaginative as the plan first formulated in Algiers, Montgomery's strategy would result in a protracted thirty-eight day slogging match up the east coast of Sicily. It would also allow the Germans to stage their own "Sicilian Dunkirk." As a result, some 40,000 battle-proven German soldiers would escape across the Strait into Italy to fight again another day. In September, at bloody Salerno, these troops which should have been taken out of the fight in July, would cost the Americans dearly.

After more than 3,000 Axis air raids, Valletta (above) and other Maltese cities were reduced to rubble. (Hoffman)

On the eve of the invasion, Sicily was garrisoned by the Italian Sixth Army commanded by sixty-six-year-old General of the Army Alfredo Guzzoni, who had been called out of retirement and appointed Commander of the Sicilian Armed Forces. His chain of command stretched all the way back to the headquarters of Generalfeldmarschall Albrecht von Kesselring in Italy. Known as "Smiling Albert," Kesselring was sent to Italy in December 1941 as head of *Luftflotte II* (Air Fleet II) and later appointed to head all German troops in Italy.

Kesselring's contact with the Italian Sixth Army was through Generaloberst Fridolin von Senger und Etterlin, who coordinated the employment of German troops under Guzzoni's command. Panzer general Hans Valentine Hube's XIV Corps located in southern Italy, administered and supplied them. A single, unified headquarters known as *Kommandant Messina Strait* was responsible for transportation to and from the mainland, and operated a depot and ferry service. This command, under Oberst (Colonel) Ernst Gunther Baade, would play a key role in the Axis evacuation of Sicily in early August.

For the island's defense, Guzzoni had six divisions of overaged, under-trained Sicilian reservists, plus two German divisions – the 15th Panzer Division and the Hermann Goering Division – a total force of roughly 275,000 men, about one-third of them motorized, and one-eighth of them German. The Sicilian reservists were second-class, but following the invasion approximately 75,000 additional German troops would be fed into the battle at one time or another, including elements of the elite 29th Panzer Grenadier and 1st Parachute divisions, in addition to the units mentioned above.

By contrast, Eisenhower's HUSKY force totaled nearly half a million men. In General Alexander's Fifteenth Army Group were Patton's US Seventh Army and Monty's Eighth. The Seventh, with four infantry divisions, one armored division, three Ranger battalions and the 82nd Airborne, would go ashore at Licata, Gela and Scoglitti. Eighth Army would land on beaches from Syracuse to Pachino, and was composed of the 1st Canadian Division, the 5th, 50th, 51st and 78th Infantry divisions, a regiment of paratroops, a glider-borne brigade, and smaller units.

In the air the Allies held a tremendous advantage. Air Chief Marshal Sir Arthur Tedder had almost 4,000 aircraft available for the operation, while the enemy could muster but less than 1,600 spread throughout the eastern Mediterranean. With six battleships, two heavy cruisers and numerous light cruisers and destroyers, the Italian Navy looked formidable on paper, but would never figure prominently in the battle.

Although the Allies held the edge – on land, at sea and in the air – in both quantity and quality, the great equalizer was Sicily's topography and climate. Roughly the size of the state of Vermont, the triangular-shaped island dominated by towering Mount Etna was harshly patterned, rugged, ridged and sun-baked, and as inhospitable in terrain, climate and primitive communications to the Anglo-American invaders of 1943 as it had been to those who attempted to conquer it hundreds of years earlier. Roads were rarely level and seldom straight, while high summer temperatures and an absence of rain (July was typically the hottest and driest month of the year) resulted in sun-baked hills and fiery valleys. "And the dust! A compound of cattle dung and pulverized chalky rock, it penetrated the throat and made men desperately thirsty. Old desert hands would later swear it was worse than the dust of North Africa."[3] The lowlands were loaded with anopheles mosquitoes, and despite precautions, total Allied casualties from malaria would number over 21,000 – more than would be felled by enemy action.

Ideally suited for defensive warfare, a skillful enemy using the terrain to his best advantage could, with forces inferior in number, fight a prolonged delaying action inflicting heavy casualties upon the attacker. Kesselring's German infantrymen, who had been fighting defensive battles for nearly a year, did just that.

Members of the 79th's advance party at Syracuse, Sicily, listen intently to the war news, courtesy of the BBC. (Hoffman)

When the pilots, planes and B-Party ground echelon moved to El Houaria landing ground on June 2 to take part in the Pantelleria-Lampedusa operations, the 79th's A-Party remained at Hani West near Kairouan until June 6, then proceeded back to Bou Grara to prepare equipment for the Sicilian invasion. On June 14 the entire Group was reunited at Bou Grara but moved back to familiar Causeway the same day to avoid Bou Grara's terrific dust storms.

On June 26, the A-Party ground echelon moved to Tripoli and then sailed via LST for historic, battered Malta. They arrived the next day where they joined other units of the Desert Air Force. The remainder of the Group stayed at Causeway until rejoining A-Party in Sicily four weeks later.

Little Malta was without question the most bombed spot on the face of the earth, having withstood over 3,000 heavy air attacks since the beginning of the war. Now it was jammed

This disabled Tiger tank, its once feared 88-mm gun now useless, serves as a prop for snapshots to be sent to the folks back home. (Kauffman)

with Allied aircraft ready to support the Sicilian invasion. The 79th's A-Party personnel dug in on the rocky ground (tents, dispersed among the rocks, were supported by steel pegs cemented into the solid sandstone) overlooking Gozo Island to the north, and occupied themselves with routine camp duty, waterproofing vehicles, and other maintenance. Their leisure hours were spent exploring the ancient, shattered city of Valletta and swimming in the clear, cool Mediterranean.

On July 7, just seventy-two hours before Sicily's D-Day, ten Falcon P-40s droned out of Causeway, landed later at Malta's Luqa airdrome to arm and refuel, then joined up with a squadron each from the 57th Group and 239 Wing. Meeting their top-cover of three Spitfire squadrons over Filfla Island they proceeded to Sicily on a familiarization flight. There they unloaded six 40-lb. bombs apiece on Biscari landing ground and returned safely. They had encountered only meager anti-aircraft fire and no air opposition. The Luftwaffe had suffered heavy losses since May and its effectiveness was severely reduced.

The 86th Squadron Operations tent. (Kauffman)

Lt. John "Jack" Kelly of the Comanches. Shot down over the desert in January 1943 he made his way back to base with the help of friendly Arabs. Shot down again over Messina Strait in July, he was plucked from the sea by the crew of an Air/Sea Rescue Walrus. (Kelly)

That the Luftwaffe in the Mediterranean was but a shadow of its former self was because during the weeks preceding the invasion of Sicily Allied aircraft had ranged all over the central Mediterranean, hammering targets on the ground and challenging the enemy in the air whenever it came up to fight. Hunted by Allied fighters during the day, their sleep and their airfields shattered with the crump of falling bombs at night, the German fighter pilots were also delivered a staggering blow to their morale in early July when Reichsmarschall Hermann Goering questioned their courage. Individual pilots whose aircraft had not been damaged or who had not themselves been shot down, were threatened with court martial proceedings if they were unable to provide evidence of success in aerial combat,[4] and Goering ordered one pilot chosen at random from each *gruppe* to be tried for cowardice. He followed that up with a blistering Order of the Day to all pilots of *Luftflotte II*:

> "Together with the fighter pilots in France, Norway and Russia, I can only regard you with contempt. If an immediate improvement is not forthcoming, flying personnel from the kommodore downward must expect to be reduced to the ranks and transferred to the Eastern Front to serve on the ground."[5]

Instead of admitting that it was his own bungling that had emasculated the once-powerful Luftwaffe, Goering placed the blame for Allied air supremacy squarely on the shoulders of those who least deserved it – the German fighter pilots. Hounded and harassed by the Allies in the air; their equipment and supplies burning on the ground, and showered with insults from buck-passing leaders in Berlin and Rome, the young German and Italian fliers became easy meat for Spitfire and Lightning pilots prowling Mediterranean skies. For the 79th, however, its planes and pilots still stranded in Tunisia or on Malta, it would be D-plus-seven before a landing ground would be ready for them in Sicily and they joined the battle. By then the Luftwaffe and *Regia Aeronautica* would be all but decimated; there would be little opportunity for aerial combat. Instead, it would be close-support as usual, and near-suicidal runs against enemy shipping in the Strait of Messina – a particularly dangerous place where a man stood an excellent chance of becoming very suddenly dead.

The invasion of Sicily began in the very early hours of July 10, 1943 with airborne landings that met near disaster. British glider troops were to have landed near Syracuse while American paratroopers – those "devils in baggy pants" – were dropped behind Gela. But high winds scattered the airborne force all over southeastern Sicily. Only one-third of the gliders hit the island, most of the rest fell into the turbulent sea, and the American paratroopers were so widely dispersed it would take days before they could assemble and form some kind of an organized fighting force. The next night, when the 82nd Airborne tried to drop reinforcements onto the beachhead they were slashed to ribbons by naval anti-aircraft fire from Allied ships off-shore in one of the worst snafus of the entire war; twenty-three C-47 transport planes were brought down by "friendly fire" and some 300 paratroopers were killed or wounded.

A panoramic view of Sicily, with Palagonia landing ground at right center. When the dust wasn't blowing, Mount Etna could be seen in the distance. But the dust was usually blowing, hampering the takeoffs and landings in addition to spoiling the view. (Kauffman)

On the beaches, the assault went better. The first wave of infantry waded ashore before dawn with little or no opposition, as reports of paratroop landings behind their lines had sent most of the Sicilian reservists manning beach defense guns fleeing their posts in panic. Before the sun set on D-Day all of the assigned beachhead objectives had been secured by the Allies. They dug in, waiting for the counterattack that was sure to come.

They didn't have long to wait. The expected counterattack poured down from the hills shortly after daybreak the next morning, and almost succeeded in pushing the Americans back into the sea. Supported by tanks that rumbled to within a few hundred yards of the beach, the Hermann Goering Division hit the American line at Gela with a savage fury. The great plain around the town became an inferno of fire, smoke, death and destruction as German armor raked the US 1st Division with cruel, deadly fire. The line wavered and buckled, but did not break. With the help of accurate six-inch gunfire from the cruiser *Boise,* and destroyers that moved in close to duel point-blank with Tiger tanks, the doggies, tankers and artillerymen beat back the attack.

Failing in his attempt to drive the invaders off the beaches, the enemy began a slow, fighting withdrawal to the north. By July 15 the two Allied armies had linked up and held a line running across the bottom third of the island from Augusta on the east coast, through Caltagirone to Agrigento.

Alexander ordered Eighth Army to advance north on both sides of Mount Etna, with Messina as the ultimate objective. Patton's Seventh Army would protect Monty's left flank and drive north to the coast, cutting the island in half and mopping up western Sicily. But enemy reinforcements were now coming across the Strait from the Italian mainland, and as Monty moved up the east coast he met increasingly stiffer resistance. By July 17 his advance had all but stalled south of Catania.

That same day, A-Party sailed from Malta and a few hours later moved into an olive grove four miles south of Augusta. With no equipment and no landing ground to operate from, they spent the next twelve days exploring this new land. Behind the lines it was, almost literally, wine and roses. "It was high summer, oranges and lemons were on the trees, wine was plentiful, and the Sicilian girls were disposed to be friendly"[6*] The nights were something else, however. The Luftwaffe, noticeably absent during daylight hours, was over the harbor nightly bombing the ports of Augusta and Syracuse. The 79th's campground was located right between these two targets. With Jerry's nocturnal bomb runs overhead, expended flak raining down, and a delayed action 1,000-lb. bomb that exploded about

* Indeed, they were so friendly that during August 1943 the Group had its highest venereal rate of its overseas tour. Ease of contact with local prostitutes, relaxation following the long sojourn in the desert, and difficulty in securing mechanical prophylactics were all listed as factors.[7]

Captain Stephen "Doc" Magness (left) and "Duke" Uhrich (overseas cap, right) match wits over a friendly game of checkers while Charles Jones, James Hundley, Lee Gossick and Charles Jaslow are the kibitzers. (Jaslow)

200 yards from their noon chow line, there were moments when A-Party would have been willing to forsake the green, lush hills of Sicily for hot and sandy, but safe, North Africa.

On July 19 Mussolini met Hitler in northern Italy to belatedly ask for more armor and aircraft with which to defend Sicily; equipment the Germans could neither produce in time nor afford to withdraw from the Russian front. As they talked, Allied bombers were over Rome for the first time in the war. The morale and psychological shock of this air attack was far greater than the physical destruction caused by the raid. Together with the impending losses in Sicily it meant that the Italian war effort was coming apart at the seams. Instead of a march to glory . . . instead of an empire greater than ancient Rome . . . Mussolini, tired and senile, had led his country to one defeat after another. Now it was the end. The next day he was told by King Victor Emmanuel III that "we cannot go on much longer."[8]

Mussolini acted to gain a vote of confidence, but on July 25 the war-weary Italians staged a palace revolt that overthrew the *Duce* and the Fascist Grand Council. To replace Mussolini the king chose aging, diminutive Marshal Pietro Badoglio. To prevent harsh German reprisals Badoglio openly pledged to continue the fight against the Allies. Secretly he began peace negotiations with members of Eisenhower's staff.

Stunned by the sudden fall of his longtime friend Hitler bowed to the inevitable and ordered the withdrawal of German troops from Sicily. With only a few weak units available for the defense of the mainland he couldn't afford to lose the experienced German divisions now fighting in the Sicilian hills. If the Allies landed in Italy before these troops could be gotten across the Strait, they would be able to advance up southern Italy with little difficulty. Hitler therefore ordered General Hans Valentine "Papa" Hube, a crusty old warhorse who had lost an arm in the First World War,[9] to prepare to withdraw all German forces from Sicily. The German commanders in the field were also directed to stand ready to disarm the Italians should they suddenly surrender to the Anglo-Americans. Quietly, the Germans began moving strong reserve divisions into northern Italy. If an invasion of that boot-shaped peninsula was next on the Allies' list, Hitler meant to have them pay dearly for every yard.

Because it seemed unlikely the British were going to capture a forward airfield for them anytime soon, 79th's A-Party moved south to the vicinity of Syracuse on July 26, to a landing ground hacked out of an almond grove at Cassibile. The planes and pilots landed later in the afternoon. The next day two missions, a fighter-bomber show against shipping off the coast from Catania to Santa Teresa, and a sweep northwest of Mount Etna, and the 79th was back in the war.

On July 28, B-Party caught up with the rest of the Group. They were met by members of the advance echelon who were standing around telling the new arrivals about the "rigors" and "hardships" of the Sicilian campaign when, as if to emphasize their story, a lone Messerschmitt made a couple of low-level strafing passes across the field, forcing everyone to scatter for cover. The 109 did little damage, but from that moment on foxholes were dug a few feet deeper.

Concentrating on enemy shipping off the east coast, the Group's pilots flew seven fighter-bomber missions on the 28th, six on the 29th, and six on the 30th when Lieutenant Jack Kelly of the Comanches was shot down for the second time since arriving overseas the previous November. In January, Kelly came out second best in an encounter with JG 77 *experten* over Libya and parachuted into no-man's land where he was picked up by British infantry. Today, it was flak that would do him in.

Lloyd "Junior" Jonas, the 87th's Communications Officer (left), "Ace" Adair, "Porky" Anderson and Jesse Jory chow down in the Skeeters' mess tent at Palagonia. (Jaslow)

Almost all the comforts of home. Lts. Jim Reutershan (left) and Jack Kauffman of the Comanches on Sicily. (Kauffman)

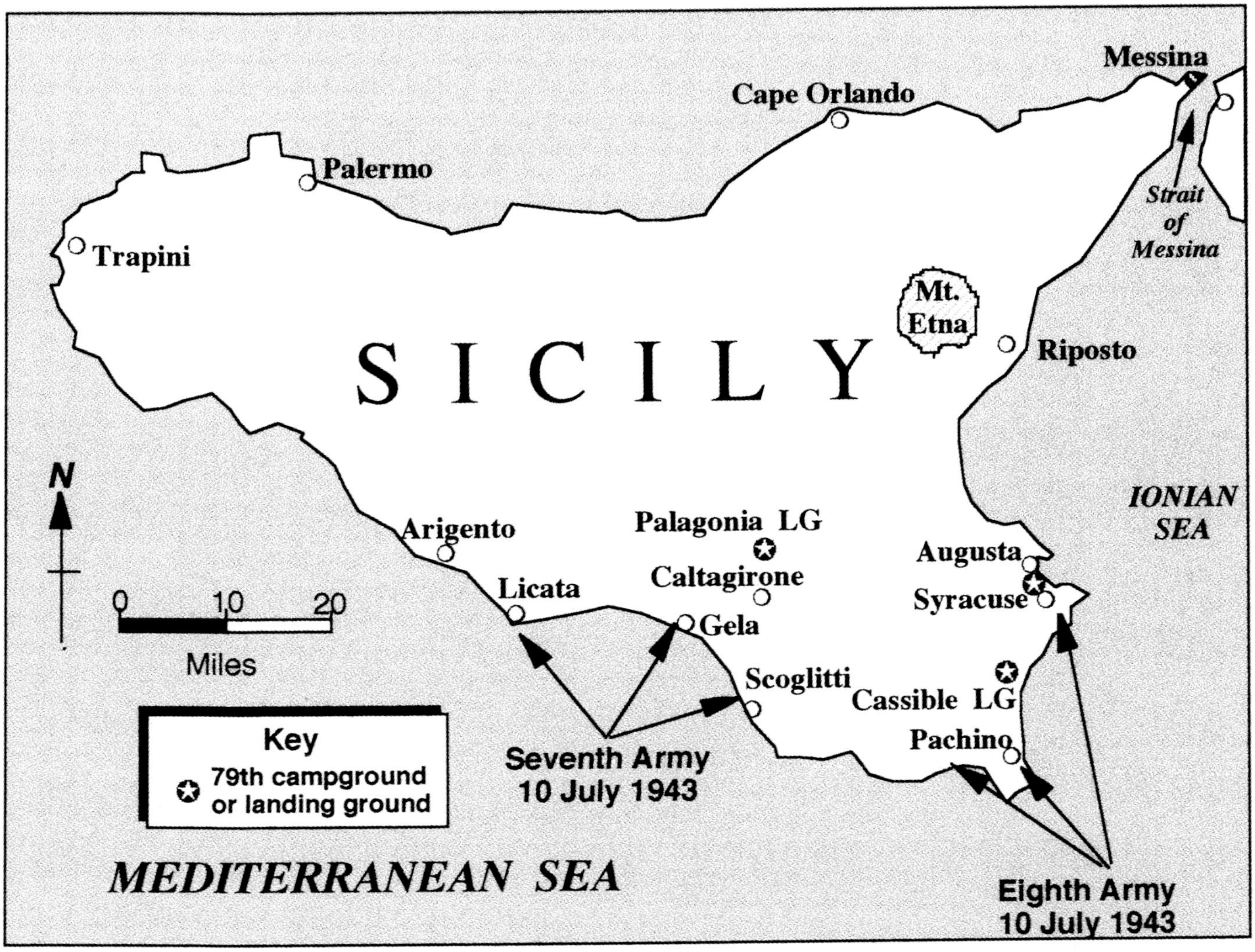

Hit while over the Messina port area dive-bombing shipping, Kelly bailed out a few miles off Cape St. Andrea, and climbed into his one-man life raft. The rest of the flight, led by Captain Wayne "Moldy" Rhynard, circled protectively overhead until forced to head home when they started to run out of both fuel and daylight. Kelly settled in for the night, using the hand-paddles in the raft's survival kit to row away from shore lest he drift into enemy hands. "As night fell it became pitch black and the only sounds I could hear were the engine noises of power boats I presumed were looking for me," Kelly said. "There was a flashlight in my kit, but not knowing whether the people in the boats were friend or foe I decided not to reveal my position." Kelly paddled most of the night, using the silhouette of Mount Etna as a reference, and with first light was "delighted" to see that he had drifted farther out to sea. When the sun came up his buddies were back in the air looking for him. They found him a short time later, "after I remembered to throw out a dye marker," and shortly thereafter he was picked up by a 284 Squadron Walrus flown by Flight Lieutenant R. J. Hayes. Aboard the Walrus was Kelly's squadron mate, Lieutenant Charles Gibson of Detroit, who helped direct it to the spot where Kelly had been seen the night before. The crew (pilot Hayes and RAF Sergeant Cyril Taylor, the radio operator, were later decorated by the Americans for snatching Kelly from under the noses of the enemy.[10]

On the last day of July twelve Comanches, with six 322 Wing Spitfires flying top-cover, were working over two Italian cruisers and a battlewagon that had ventured into the narrow strip of water separating Sicily from Italy's Calabrian peninsula, when two 109s and a pair of Focke-Wulfs made a quick in-again, out-again firing pass at the formation. Lieutenant Frank Newton was missing after this encounter, but whether he was a victim of the fighter attack or fell to shipboard gunners has never been ascertained. He was still unaccounted for at the end of the war.

That same day, using C-47s for the first time to fly crew chiefs and tentage into the new field (the others traveled by truck), the 79th moved to Palagonia landing ground, a dirt strip carved out of a wheat field near Caltagirone. Picturesquely located in a broad, green valley about 40 miles southwest of Catania, Mount Etna could be seen in the distance when the dust wasn't blowing. Unfortunately, the dust was usually blowing, hampering takeoffs and landings, in addition to spoiling the view.

Stubborn enemy resistance and difficult terrain on Sicily's east coast had slowed Montgomery's advance to an agonizing crawl. In that rugged country there was no way he could mass Eighth Army's superiority in artillery and tanks; the few good roads available in that sector were dominated by Mount Etna, and the scores of hilltop villages in the mountain country were turned into miniature fortresses from which a handful of gutsy troops could hold up an advance by a force many times their number. It is sixteen miles up the main coast road from Catania to Riposto – a mere twenty minute drive in peacetime. But this was not a blissful Sunday outing, and the Eighth Army war had now developed into a series of infantry duels fought under the scorching sun. The twenty miles to Riposto would, in July 1943, take seven long, bloody days.

With Monty stalled in the east the main Allied offensive was switched to the west where Patton was beginning to show some of the dash and daring that would later become his hallmark after the 1944 Normandy breakout. With his 3rd Division clearing the way Seventh Army, in a march reminiscent of Stonewall Jackson's "foot cavalry," covered the hundred miles from the landing beaches to Palermo in four days. Once Palermo was secured, he began to advance on Messina from the west. Messina was the prize and "Old Blood and Guts" ("our blood and his guts," one Seventh Army veteran remarked), wanted it badly.

While Patton was closing in on Messina along the north coast road, and Eighth Army was painfully inching forward from the south, the 79th divided its efforts between anti-shipping strikes and close-support over the Eighth Army front.

The Group flew a total of forty-five missions on August 3 and 4, the bulk of them in front of the British and Canadians. As usual, the strafing shows were expensive: seven aircraft and four pilots during the two-day period. Fred Borsodi, who had replaced "Jack" Watkins as the Comanches skipper in June, and Lieutenant Daniel Mayer of the same squadron, were both hit by ground fire on the afternoon of the 3rd while working over an ammo dump northwest of Mount Etna. Borsodi coaxed his faltering Warhawk to a wheels-up landing at Palagonia, but Mayer has never been heard from. He was last seen bailing out near Randazzo.

Captain Leo Berinati of the Skeeters in his "quarters" at Palagonia. He almost met his demise over Sicily when a 57th Group pilot mistakenly thought his P-40 was a Messerschmitt. (Jaslow)

Earlier in the day the Skeeters lost Lieutenant James Pittard of Indianapolis when his P-40 lost coolant while dive-bombing a freighter and he had to bail out off the Italian coast near Reggio. Now, in three separate flights the Skeeters quickly lost three more planes and another pilot. "Ace" Adair was struck by tank fire on the Bronte-Randazzo road and jumped, to be picked up later by British infantry and returned to base. Captain Frank Huff was also knocked down near Randazzo, and "Butch" Owen, strafing in the face of exceptionally heavy Breda (a dual-purpose 20-mm cannon) and light anti-aircraft fire, was shot up badly enough to warrant a deadstick landing. His ship was completely washed out. Pittard and Huff were later reported prisoners of war. As if enemy fire wasn't enough, Captain Leo Berinati became the victim of mistaken identity when a pilot with the 57th Group's Six-Four Squadron stitched several .50-caliber-sized holes across his fuselage and tail section before realizing his error. Skillful airmanship got the veteran Berinati back to Palagonia, shaken but safe.

Later that afternoon four Flying Skull pilots were north of Mount Etna when Johnny "General" Hoagland, returning early with a rough-running engine, sighted a lone 109 that had strayed into the area. He gave the German a good burst from sixty yards and the 109 went into a steep dive trailing a plume of thick, oily smoke. Because of his bad engine, Hoagland didn't follow the Messerschmitt down to learn its fate, and claimed only a probable. His probable victory turned bittersweet however, when he learned after landing that squadron-mate Lieutenant Farrel Yocum of Enid, Oklahoma had died when his P-40 slammed into the side of a mountain while strafing a machine-gun nest.

The next day the Falcons fared slightly better, although Bob Minett of the Comanches was slightly wounded in the leg and shoulder after hit by anti-aircraft fire while strafing a road south of Riposto. His hydraulic system was also shot out, forcing him to belly in at his home drome. Reidy Jones of the same squadron bailed out near Palagonia after hit while strafing a road near Bronte on the west side of Mount Etna. He walked in later suffering minor wounds.

By August 10 Patton was only thirty miles west of Messina, and Montgomery was moving around the slopes of Mount Etna. As Guzzoni's Sixth Army was pushed deeper into the northeastern corner of the island the Germans started to withdraw to the mainland of Italy.

The plan for the evacuation, Operation *Lehrgang Ia,* had been prepared weeks before with characteristic Prussian thoroughness. Taking into account the shipping available, six nights were allowed for the operation, beginning the night of August 11. To buy time for the move, General Hube designated five major lines of resistance around the beachhead perimeter, each line to be occupied on successive nights and held for one day. The first line ran from the north coast near St. Agata, through Bronte, and around the southern slope of Mount Etna to Acireale; the last was just outside the city of Messina. Each night between 8,000 and 10,000 men would be released from the three German divisions still on the island and moved to the debarkation point. On the sixth night the last of the German troops on the island would go directly from the Messina line to the boats.

The Germans had for their use seven *marinefahrprahme* (80-ton ramped barges, each capable of carrying three tanks or five trucks), ten F-boats (a shallow landing craft about 120-feet long), eleven *Siebel* ferries and several pontoon landing craft. No provision was made in *Lehrgang Ia* for the Italians; they would cross over on their own, using the large steam ferry *Villa,* two smaller steamboats, and four motor rafts manned by the Italian Navy. Most of the crossings – both German and Italian – would be made under cover of darkness, and would be protected by a hornet's nest of anti-aircraft defenses.

In August 1943 the airspace over Messina Strait was probably the most heavily defended in the world. More than 500 guns of all sizes, including at least four batteries of giant 280-mm guns; two batteries of Italian 152-mm guns and four batteries of 170-mm guns covered the Strait. There were also doz-

Captain Frank Huff of the Skeeters in his home away from home at Palagonia. Too hot to live in tents, some just set up a cot under a tree so they could swing the mosquito netting down. Huff was shot down and captured shortly after this photo was taken. (Jaslow)

The 79th basked in the title, "Monty's Pets," and General Montgomery was a frequent visitor to his favorite American fighter group. He is shown here with his aide, Major Benson (left) and Colonel Bates. When the 79th was based in Sicily Monty had his personal aircraft crewed by the 85th Squadron's Engineering section. (McGuire)

ens of German "eighty-eights" and Italian 90-mm anti-aircraft pieces, and scores of 40-mm Bofors and 20-mm quads. Searchlights, barrage balloons, motor gunboats and other light craft, all armed to the teeth, supplemented the shore-based batteries and helped guard the Strait with a concentration of fire exceeding that of the Ruhr, "Flak Alley" between Tunis and Bizerte, or the inner artillery of London.

In addition to the 40-mm stuff that looked like puffy white clouds, the biggest threat to fighter-bomber pilots attacking shipping in the Strait was the *Flakvierling* 20-mm Model 38, a four-barreled light anti-aircraft gun with a wide traverse and high rate of fire that made it deadly against fast, low-level aircraft. Pilots soon learned to pull out of their dive-bombing runs before reaching 4,000 feet where the light flak was most effective.

Starting August 12 the 79th went all-out against shipping in the Strait, augmented by fighter-bomber and strafing strikes on the roads leading to Messina. Fourteen missions were flown on the 12th and the harried Luftwaffe made a brief, final appearance over Sicily.

In the middle of the afternoon the Flying Skulls had twelve P-40s low over the Strait working on water traffic when three 109s jumped the lead section as it was leaving the target area. Lieutenant Willis "Harpo" Johnson turned into one, and after giving it a short burst of fire the German went into a steep dive out of control. Johnson claimed a probable. Lieutenant Bob

Skeeter Engineering Officer A. J. "Tony" Cirrito (standing, right) and Squadron Executive Officer Ralph Porter in the 87th Squadron's officers' club at Palagonia. (Jaslow)

Kelley in X-29 fired into the belly of another Messerschmitt from 200 yards. The plane rolled over . . . the landing gear dropped down . . . and the 109 went down out of control. Before he could see the fate of his victim Kelley pulled up and turned into another 109 that he hit in the fuselage with tracers. He claimed a probable and a damaged.

The other two sections were over the Italian side of the Strait when six 109s and 190s hit them from up-sun. Kim Bolack

Dave Vandivort, George Trittipo and Ed Bozzi outside the 87th's orderly room at Palagonia. (Jaslow)

With the fighting in Sicily over, and the long haul up the Italian "boot" still ahead of them, some of the Group's original pilots relax long enough for this informal shot with Colonel Bates (black overseas cap, standing center) at Palagonia. (Lappin)

raked a 109 with a long burst in the fuselage and it fell out of control streaming smoke for a probable. Fred Hale was busy clearing Bolack's tail when he spotted a 190 diving on him from three o'clock out of the sun. Hale hit this one with tracers all the way from the nose to the tail and the Focke-Wulf pulled up sharply and fell off to the left covered with smoke and flames. Hale claimed one destroyed. Lieutenant Harold Burns of Royal Oak, Michigan rounded out the scoring before the Skullmen returned to Palagonia when he fired a long burst of tracers into the belly of a 109 which side-slipped out of control pouring heavy black smoke. Burns petitioned for a probable.

The next day, August 13, it was the Skeeters' turn. Twelve of them were north of Messina with 500-lb. bombs when jumped by ten-plus 109s and 190s. In the running fight that followed Paul McArthur shot a 109 down in flames – his fifth confirmed victory – but Francis Hennin, radioing, "This is number eighty-eight. I'm hit! I'm hit!" bailed out.

A few minutes later the Skeeters got into another scrap with a gaggle of 190s and 109s over the Gulf of Milazzo. Leo Berinati quickly splashed one of the Focke-Wulfs, while "Scotty" Rogers sent a 109 into the water, and shot hunks of debris off another for a probable. Lieutenant Morris "Watty" Watkins got on the tail of a 109 and held the German in his sights as he crept to within a hundred yards of him. Unknown to Watkins, three other 109s had gotten behind him and suddenly Watkins was sprayed with cannon fire. Hit in the shoulder, he managed to squeeze the trigger and the plane in front of him disintegrated in a ball of fire. Watkins then flew back to Palagonia, wounded, and with his controls damaged. Unable to stop his shot-up '40 he rolled off the runway and groundlooped. He climbed down from the smoking Warhawk and put in a claim for a 109 destroyed.

Now the ground crew made a startling discovery. They found that his guns hadn't been fired. The cannon fire from the

109s on his tail had damaged the electrical system and made the guns inoperative; the protective tape was still in place over the gun ports in the wing.

But Watkins had seen the 109 in front of him explode, and this was confirmed by other pilots in the flight. There could be only one answer: the cannon fire from the Germans on Watkins' tail had shot past him and knocked down one of their own planes. The Arkansas pilot petitioned for, and was given, credit for one Messerschmitt destroyed.

Later that same day eight Skeeters led by George Lee picked up a Walrus flying boat off Cape Orlando and went looking for Francis Hennin. They found him a short time later in a half-swamped dinghy firing flares like a man possessed. He was picked up unharmed.

On August 14, when British forces lost contact with the enemy on the ground, General Alexander believed they were crossing over to the mainland in large numbers and suggested that Tedder mount a strong air effort against this shipping. But the bulk of Tedder's air power was already committed to mainland targets as his heavy bombers began softening up Italy in preparation for an invasion, and he could release only a few mediums and light bombers and, of course, the over-worked fighters. Thus, apart from the fighters (from August 8th through the 17th Allied aircraft flew a total of 1,170 sorties against evacuation shipping – 718 by the 79th) a really determined effort was never made to stop the crossings. In fact, on August 13, when the Germans moved 15,000 men, 1,300 vehicles, twenty-one tanks and the same number of assault guns across the Strait, almost three hundred heavy bombers with 135 escorting fighters were hitting targets near Rome because "the land battle [in Sicily] was going so well."[11] The Allies had lost a golden opportunity.

Early on the morning of August 17 American infantrymen probed into the outskirts of Messina. The streets were empty of enemy soldiers. General Hube had finished the evacuation and crossed over to the mainland the night before, reporting to Kesselring that the operation had been completed. Hube's job had been to get the Germans safely out of Sicily, and this he had done despite tremendous Allied air and naval superiority.

Information from German sources after the war show that 39,569 German soldiers, including 4,444 wounded, were ferried across the four-mile-wide Strait. They brought with them forty-seven tanks, ninety-four guns, and more than 17,000 tons of ammunition, fuel and equipment. The Italians, in their own operation, moved 70,000 troops to the mainland along with 500 vehicles, seventy-five to a hundred artillery pieces, and twelve mules. But wars are not won by evacuation, and in spite of the orderly retreat and withdrawal across the Strait, Hube had been forced to abandon large amounts of material and supplies.

The thirty-eight-day Sicilian campaign was over. To the Germans this meant that their positions in Sardinia and Corsica were now in jeopardy. They would also be forced to strengthen their garrisons in southern France and the Balkans, and move still more divisions away from the Eastern Front to shore-up defenses in Italy. The tenacious rearguard action fought in the hot, rugged hill country had given the Germans time to prepare for the Allied invasion of Italy, but it had cost them 12,000 killed, missing or prisoners of war. The Italians lost another 145,000 men, most of them POWs. Allied casualties were 8,375 American, and almost 9,000 by the British and Canadians.

The 79th flew a total of 201 missions (1,791 sorties) during the fight for Sicily, many in the face of the greatest anti-aircraft concentration in the world – over the Strait, flak was once reported 10/10ths over one target – including two occasions when squadrons asked permission to go back and hit targets that weren't clobbered to their satisfaction the first time. In addition to claiming numerous gun positions, bridges, fortified buildings, and other ground and water targets, they destroyed two Fw 190s and three Me 109s in the air; probably destroyed six more, and damaged another. But it had cost them heavily.

Two pilots, Farrel Yocum and Dan Mayer were killed in action and another, Lieutenant Charles Lownders of the Comanches was killed before the flight echelon got to Sicily when his plane spun in during a practice flight at Causeway in Tunisia on July 16. Frank Newton was still listed as missing at the end of the war, while Frank Huff and James Pittard sat behind German wire until VE-Day. Four other pilots – "Ace" Adair, Jack Kelly, Reidy Jones and Francis Hennin were forced to bail out of damaged aircraft but returned to duty; two pilots were wounded, and four more made forced-landings in airplanes that were badly shot-up. In addition, twenty-four other aircraft suffered varying degrees of battle-sustained damage, including six that had to be totally written off. Sicily and the Straits of Messina had been far from peaceful.

eight

Not So Sunny Italy

"All roads led to Rome, but Rome led nowhere strategically."

– Hanson Baldwin, historian

When Eisenhower was directed at Casablanca in January to proceed with plans for the invasion of Sicily no agreement was reached about subsequent strategy or objectives beyond Sicily. Later, at a conference in Washington in May, the British agreed to a cross-Channel attack – but in 1944, not 1943 – and the Americans agreed to additional, limited operations in the Mediterranean with the purpose of knocking Italy out the war. How this was to be accomplished was not spelled out by the Combined Chiefs of Staff (CCS) other than to authorize Eisenhower to "plan such operations in exploitation of HUSKY as are best calculated to eliminate Italy from the war and contain the maximum number of German forces."[1]

Two planning groups were formed – one to study and prepare plans for an invasion of Sardinia and Corsica; the other for an attack on the Italian mainland. The latter held the promise of reaping the greatest reward, but the former was unquestionably the safest. The choice of which road to take was left undecided until the CCS could see the outcome of the Sicilian battle more clearly.

What they saw was encouraging. After watching the dispirited performance of the Italian Sixth Army in Sicily, it was felt that Italy could be invaded with reasonable assurance of success, and Sardinia and Corsica were scratched from the target list.

With the capture of Messina and the fall of Mussolini the basic aim of opening the Mediterranean to Allied shipping had been achieved, but a direct assault on Italy still offered several attractive possibilities. With Italy out of the fight the Germans would be obliged to replace some thirty-five divisions then occupying Greece, Yugoslavia and southern France; the Italian fleet no longer being a threat would free British aircraft carriers for duty against the Japanese in the Pacific; airfields on the Foggia plain of Italy would put German industrial targets presently out of reach of Britain-based bombers within range of the heavies of the new Fifteenth US Air Force, and an Allied occupation of the Italian peninsula would deprive the Third Reich of substantial industrial potential. One other benefit, one that always attracted Churchill, was that success in Italy might induce Turkey to make common cause with the Allies.

With the Allies now in agreement about invading Italy, the only decision left to make was when and where.

Taranto, 'round the heel of the boot, had long been considered as an invasion site as it would give the armies pushing up from the south an excellent naval base and port for supplies. But Naples, on the west coast, was even better, and Lieutenant-General Mark Wayne Clark, whose American Fifth Army had been formed in January, was told to plan for an amphibious landing in the Naples areas, with his primary objectives being Rome and the Foggia airfields.

But, and for Mark Clark it was an important "but," with the build-up for OVERLORD now in full-swing the Mediterranean theater would no longer enjoy top priority of men and material, and he would have to plan his Italian campaign with that in mind. OVERLOARD would be the main arena; Italy would be relegated to a secondary front status – at least to everyone except those who fought there.

Clark initially suggested a landing north of Naples on the coastal plain of the Volturno River, but the Navy was less than enthusiastic about this proposal as the waters there were not well protected. Tedder also objected on the grounds that proper air support couldn't be maintained north of Naples, at least not until airfields were established on the mainland. So Naples was discarded in favor of a landing near Salerno.

The Salerno area provided twenty miles of good shoreline, with direct access to the inland areas, and the underwater gradients were ideal for landing craft to run straight up onto the beaches with no natural obstructions. But there were also several drawbacks.

It was hemmed in all around by mountains and the road exits from the coast to the city of Naples were through ideal defensive terrain. Also, because of a shortage of shipping to put a follow-up force ashore quickly (that "secondary front" status again) a strong enemy counterattack might drive the initial landing force back into the sea. It was conceded that a surprise landing might gain a beachhead, but that the breakout to Naples would be exceptionally difficult.

The key to the entire operation was air cover, as the Salerno beaches were within easy reach of German fighters based on all-weather fields near Naples and Rome. The closest Allied fields in Sicily were those in the Messina area, and they were 180 miles from Salerno. A Spitfire, even with auxiliary tanks, would have only about twenty minutes to patrol over the invasion beaches, while the P-40s had even shorter legs. They could not fly to Salerno, perhaps fight, and still make it back to their home landing grounds in Sicily. And if heavy rains fell in Sicily the primitive airfields there would become unusable. The only bright spot in the whole air cover scenario was the existence of an excellent airfield at Montecorvino, almost adjacent to the landing beaches, and Mark Clark intended to capture it early. He planned to land two corps, one American and one British, at Salerno on September 9, with his immediate objective being the capture of Montecorvino airfield, and the port of Naples, some twenty miles to the north.

Two other landings were planned in conjunction with the one at Salerno. It had been decided to establish Allied forces on the Adriatic side of Italy to seize ports on the east coast, and also to land a force near Reggio on the "toe" of Italy to draw off German troops from the Salerno area. To supply the drive up the Adriatic coast it would be necessary to acquire the Bari-Taranto-Brindisi triangle, so the British 1st Airborne Division would land as straight-leg infantry at Taranto simultaneously with Clark's landing at Salerno, while Montgomery's Eighth Army would cross the Strait from Sicily and land on the Calabrian peninsula. But because of a shortage of assault shipping (landing craft to be used at Salerno would have to serve Eighth Army as well), Monty's army would go ashore a week earlier – on September 3. This landing, code-named BAYTOWN, would seize the nearby airfields then split into two task forces – one sweeping east to link up with the British airborne troops at Taranto; the other heading north to cover Clark's right flank at Salerno. All three invasion forces would then join in a concentrated drive on Rome.

As targets diminished toward the end of the Sicilian campaign there was time to seek a few of the comforts available on the island. Here, several men leave one of the squadron clubs installed in the unoccupied home of a local doctor. (Kauffman)

After the fall of Sicily the Allied air forces, especially the mediums and heavies, had been busy paving the way for the invasion by disrupting enemy lines of communications, upsetting his logistics and post-holing his airfields. By the eve of BAYTOWN the southern part of Italy was virtually isolated. Its network of railroads were shattered beyond immediate repair, airfields were pitted and cratered, and the enemy's coastal batteries had been beaten into silence. During this period most of the Desert Air Force fighter units were regrouping, refitting, reorganizing and resting. The 79th, still based at Palagonia, flew only nineteen missions between August 18 and September 3, all either fighter-bomber attacks against motor transport, troop bivouac areas and other targets around the toe of Italy, or escorting mediums as they hit enemy installations behind the invasion beaches. On one of the latter, on August 30, Lieutenant Milton Clark of the Flying Skulls had engine trouble and was forced to bail out over the sea ten miles north of Cape Spartivento. Fred Hale and Hugh Mathews circled protectively over him as he got in his dinghy, and a rescue operation was organized. Escorted by four Flying Skull P-40s and six Spitfires, a 284 Squadron Walrus picked Clark up about three hours later.[2]

On August 22 Ninth Air Force closed out Mediterranean operations and moved to England. The 57th, 79th and 324th fighter groups stayed behind, transferring to the XII Air Support Command of the Twelfth Air Force, although they were still handled operationally by the Desert Air Force as in the past. A British MORU (Mobile Operations Reporting Unit) took the place of 211 Group for the DAF's forward control.

Toward the end of the Sicilian campaign, and while the 79th was "resting, refitting and reorganizing" at Palagonia prior to the invasion of Italy, the pilots and ground crews tried to make their home away from home a bit more comfortable. The Flying Skulls arranged with a local doctor to use his unoccupied home for an officers' club, and the house was quickly screened in and provided with electric lights. One room was set aside for a bar, complete with the wing of a Me 109 and a brass rail. The Squadron's enlisted men, meanwhile, had their own club, plus a day room built from a pre-fabricated German building. Not to be outdone, the other two squadrons also opened officers' and EM clubs, with the Skeeters' officers taking over a large villa that featured indoor plumbing and a view overlooking the landing ground. All of the 87th's officers lived there.

It was also at Palagonia that the Flying Skulls found a couple of Fw 190s to play with. Before arriving in Sicily, a wealth of discarded German and Italian aircraft had been found on the recently captured airdromes in Tunisia, including Macchi MC-200s, Fiat G-50s, and Me 109s. The "sporty" appearance and forgiving nature of the Italian aircraft appealed to many of the Group's pilots, who claimed them as their personal trophies. One of the 109s, *Irmgard,* was used to teach the 79th's pilots how to fly against it in combat. When the Group went to Sicily *Irmgard* and the other "spoils of war" were left behind. But there were plenty of wrecked Axis aircraft in Sicily, too, and it wasn't long before Johnny Martin and Milt Clark stumbled across a pair of Fw 190s hidden among the weeds on an airfield near Gerbini. The Focke-Wulfs needed major work before they would be airworthy, but with the help of Sergeants Cliff Wallace, Tony Gagliardo, Don Waring and Corporal William Wooten who used parts cannibalized from other damaged aircraft, the instruments and electrical systems were repaired, new props put on, and an engine change was even accomplished on one of the planes. Major Schoellkopf and Johnny Martin then flew the two rejuvenated birds to Palagonia where their flight characteristics were evaluated as pilots took turns taking them for short hops around the field. But alas, like other en-

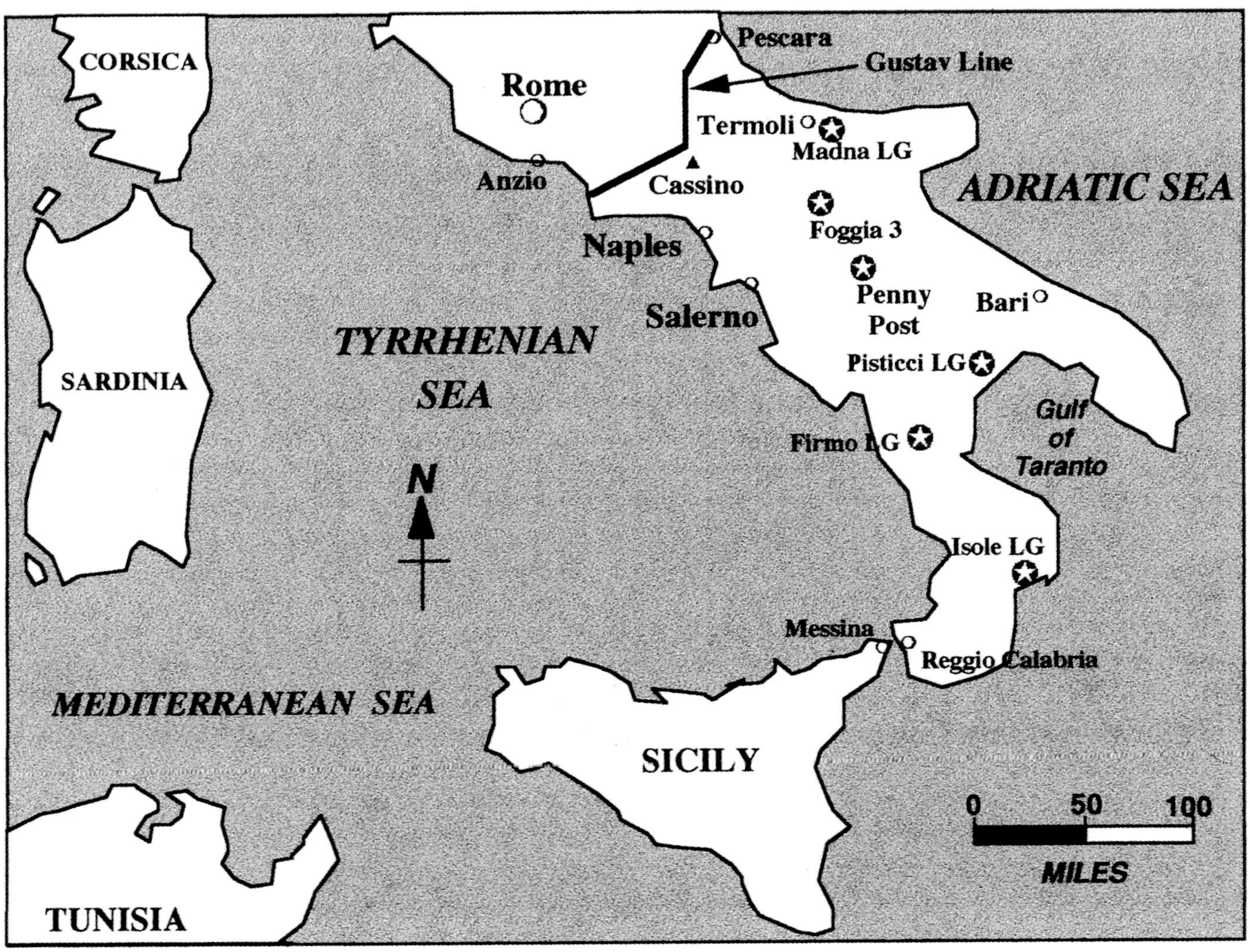

emy aircraft they had repaired and flown, they were soon ordered to turn the two German planes over to higher headquarters. In October, after the 79th had moved to Foggia, Italy, Johnny Martin and Milt Clark flew them to Bari.

One enemy plane that the 79th "captured" on Sicily escaped that fate. An Italian Savoia-Marchetti SM-79 *Sparviero* (Sparrow Hawk) – a tri-motored, wood-and-fabric torpedo bomber and reconnaissance plane with a "humpback" fuselage, somewhat similar in appearance to the Ju 52 *Tanta Ju* – was left behind by the Italians in their haste to get out of Sicily. Lt.-Colonel "Chuck" Grogan, the Group's Ops Officer, found the obsolescent "Eyetee" bomber at Catania Main near Mount Etna, and with the help of his crew chief and a couple of other mechanics got it repaired and back to Palagonia. Grogan planned to use it as a squadron utility vehicle, making beer runs to Alexandria, and the like. Several uneventful flights were made – including once when Grogan and "Duke" Uhrich took "Doc" Magness (Captain Stephen Magness, the 87th's Flight Surgeon) for a ride so Magness could collect his flight pay – until the 79th got ready to move to Italy. That's when the old tri-motored bird ended up on the scrap heap for good, and Grogan "almost bought the farm."

It had been decided to move A-Party to Italy by air, and the old SM-79 (irreverently nicknamed the *The Marcheesi Special*) was loaded with passengers, baggage and crew. Unfortunately, too much weight was placed in the rear of the aircraft, which drastically affected its center of gravity. Grogan got the plane airborne and the gear up with no difficulty, but then his troubles started. The plane started climbing out of control (the trim controls worked just the opposite as they do in American planes, which probably contributed to the problem) and even with Grogan's knee braced against the control column *The Marcheesi Special* went from ground level straight up into a stall at about 1,500 feet. "It was the only time I thought we had 'bought the farm,'" Grogan said. "But fortunately the aircraft was a pussycat. It wallowed over on its side and we were able to get the nose down with the bottom rudder, pick up speed, and get it under control." Grogan eventually got the old bird to the new field, which was full of potholes from 1,000-lb. bombs, and unloaded his passengers without further incident. Unfortunately, everything turned sour again when they started for home. Grogan began taxiing as soon as the flight engineer got the outboard engines running, and in trying to get the center engine going lost air for the brakes. With no brakes the plane drifted left toward a large bomb crater. When he fed in more left throttle the left engine fizzled out and the torque of the right engine pulled the plane into the crater. "End of plane, end of story," Grogan said.[3]

Lts. Jack Kauffman (top) and Jack Kelly tinker with a MC-200 Saetta freshly adorned with Comanche insignia. As was Cape Bon, Sicily was a scrounger's paradise as the retreating enemy left numerous planes and other equipment scattered about. Italian fighters, especially, because of their "sporty" appearance and forgiving nature, appealed to many of the 79th's pilot who claimed them as their personal trophies. (Kauffman)

On September 3, four years to the day since Britain and France had declared war on Germany after Hitler's surprise attack on Poland, Eighth Army became the first major Allied invasion force to land on the continent of Europe since the war began. A thunderous barrage from over 600 heavy guns on the Sicilian side of the narrows was supplemented by covering fire from the Royal Navy's *Nelson, Warspite, Rodney* and *Valiant* as British and Canadian troops landed on the beaches north of Reggio shortly after dawn. The heavy expenditure of ordnance was a needless precaution. The beaches, devoid of even wire and mines, were virtually undefended. "The stiffest resistance of the morning came from a puma that had escaped from the Reggio Zoological Gardens and was seemingly taking a fancy

While scrounging around in Sicily, Johnny Martin and Milt Clark discovered a pair of FW-190s hidden in the weeds near Gerbini. Repairs were made and the 190s flown back to Palagonia, but several weeks later the two enemy aircraft were confiscated by higher headquarters. (Hoffman)

to the Commander, 3rd Canadian Brigade."[4] Meeting only scattered resistance (by the end of the day more than 3,000 Italian prisoners had been taken; some even volunteered to help unload the landing craft) Eighth Army pushed forward in two main task forces. The British headed up the coast along the Tyrrhenian Sea for an eventual link-up with the Americans when they came ashore at Salerno a week later, while the Canadians moved out over the rocky high ground toward Crotone.

The Desert Air Force flew 253 sorties over the beaches on D-Day, mostly Spits from 239, 244 and 7 SAAF Wings. The absence of enemy resistance permitted the DAF to switch to offensive targets by noon, and they began flying against rail traffic, road junctions, and other targets behind the beachhead. The historian of 244 Wing noted that "we should have considered this invasion business a dull performance had not Flight Lieutenant Bolitho of 145 Squadron been forced to bail out owing to engine trouble, for his rescue accounted for the majority of today's sorties."[5]

The 79th did not take part in the D-Day operations until it was reported that German fighters had been seen on the field at Camigliatello east of Cosenza. Then they flew two missions escorting 12th and 340th Bomb Group Mitchells to Camigliatello, and another escorting Bostons to the Crotone-main airdrome, all without incident.

At about the same time that the 79th was over Camigliatello and Crotone-main, Eisenhower's chief-of-staff (General Walter Bedell Smith) was in a tent in an almond grove near Cassibile, Sicily taking the surrender of the Italian Army from Brigadier-General Giuseppe Castellano, a member of the Italian *Comando Supremo.*[*] Because of political considerations (the Italians, who had become dependent on German strength, now sought a way out of the war but were too weak and entangled to escape without German reprisal), the news of the surrender wouldn't be made public until Fifth Army went ashore at Salerno on September 9.

After standing down on September 4 the Falcons were back in the air the following day taking B-25s to Cosenza, and for the first time experienced the vagaries of the Italian weather that was "from then onwards to lead the air forces a perpetual dance."[7] The bombing run was hopelessly fouled up by the low, scudding clouds and the next day all targets within range of the 79th's fighters were completely socked in. The Apennine mountains that split the peninsula produced a Jekyll-and-Hyde condition that could produce every variation of weather known

Irreverently named "The Marcheesi Special," this Italian Savoia-Marchetti SM-79 Sparviero was "liberated" on Sicily and briefly served the 79th well before meeting an ignominious fate when it was taxied into a bomb crater on mainland Italy. (McGuire)

to man in a moment's notice. Time and again, until the end of the war, it would be inclement weather as much as enemy action that frustrated Allied pilots in Italy.

On September 7 the Skeeters escorted Baltimores to the marshaling yards at Catanzaro, while the next day the Flying Skulls and Comanches went hunting for trucks on the coast road south of Marina di Catanzaro. The day's first mission claimed three trucks destroyed and a pillbox shot up, but Lieutenant Gaston Callum of the Flying Skulls turned up missing. His plane was last seen heading southwest smoking badly; it was too late in the day to organize a search.

All three squadrons were up on September 9 shooting up the roads south of Catanzaro, resulting in twenty-six vehicles destroyed and fifty-five damaged or set on fire. They also shot up machine-gun nests, storage dumps and a radio tower. By the end of the day, however, the bomb line had moved out of reach of the 79th's Palagonia-based Warhawks. Another move was in order, this time to the mainland. Before they left, the Group would lose two more pilots. Lieutenant Carl Simpson of the Flying Skulls was killed and Lieutenant Clifford Sachleben of the Comanches was seriously injured when their two planes collided head-on in a landing accident at Palagonia on September 11. Simpson, who was from Lakeport, New Hampshire, had been with the Squadron since it was formed back in Bedford, Massachusetts, and had just completed his 80-mission tour at the time of his death. The only good news that day was that Gaston Callum turned up safe after being reported missing two days earlier.

At 6:30 a.m. on September 8, 1943, General Eisenhower broadcast to the world the news of the Italian surrender that had been negotiated five days before. The next day Fifth Army hit the beaches at Salerno.

The landing was as fiercely contested as any in the war. Only a single panzer division opposed the invaders (wary of another Allied landing elsewhere, Generaloberst Heinrich von Vietinghoff, the German Tenth Army commander responsible

* The complete instrument of surrender was signed by Eisenhower, Alexander and Badoglio on board HMS *Nelson* at Malta on September 29. On October 13, Italy declared war on Germany.[6]

They moved across the narrow Strait from Sicily to Italy via LST without incident. (Hoffman)

for the Salerno section, was reluctant to commit his reserves), but the Germans fought with skill and determination. By nightfall of D-Day Fifth Army had gained only a precarious toehold, and Montecorvino airfield was still German.

Without the airfield, Allied air support was furnished almost exclusively by over-taxed naval pilots operating from four escort carriers off-shore. It was not enough. Tedder's worst fears were realized; the invasion force was nakedly exposed to enemy air attack. During the first three days following the landing the Germans flew almost 600 sorties against the fleet. Using new radio-controlled glide bombs (in addition to conventional bombs) they sank four transports, a Liberty ship, a hospital ship and eight landing craft. They also heavily damaged three cruisers. In all, the Luftwaffe scored a total of eighty-five hits on Allied vessels standing off Salerno. The Navy was in a state of near panic.

The situation on the beaches had also reached a crisis. German reinforcements from the north and other enemy units that had disengaged themselves from Eighth Army's front in the south were rushed to Salerno and thrown into the battle. On September 13 von Vietinghoff discovered a gap in the Allied lines, and shortly after mid-day he struck this soft spot with all the infantry and armor he could scrape together. Throughout the day, into the long night, and until the late afternoon hours of the 14th, American and British troops fought a desperate battle for survival on the dangerously shallow beachhead.

The Germans quickly overran one position after another. They pushed to within a stone's throw of Fifth Army headquarters, and almost reached the sea. For several hours the outcome was in doubt. Clark briefly considered evacuating the beachhead. Vietinghoff proclaimed: "Success has been ours. Once again German soldiers have proved their superiority over the enemy."[8]

But von Vietinghoff's jubilation was premature. Clark reinforced his perimeter with two battalions of paratroopers dropped into the beachhead near Paestum on the night of the 13th; more than five hundred heavy bombers were diverted from strategic targets to hit vital road junctions leading to Salerno; naval gunners stepped up their fire, and artillerymen fired at German tanks from pointblank range until gun barrels were white-hot. Cooks, clerks, truck drivers – anyone who could be spared – were pressed into service as riflemen, and Fifth Army grimly held on. The Germans had shot their bolt. The counterattack slowly ran out of steam and was beaten back. For better or worse, the Allies were in Italy to stay.

On September 15, von Vietinghoff tried once more to break through, but to no avail, and the next day, as patrols from Monty's BAYTOWN force linked up with Fifth Army near Vallo, the German Tenth Army commander asked Kesselring for permission to withdraw.

The landing by the British 1st Airborne Division at Taranto, which had taken place simultaneously with the one at Salerno, had gone much better than the Salerno landing. Meeting little resistance, the British pushed quickly up the Adriatic coast to Bari.

By September 17 Montgomery's Eighth Army held a line running west to east from Sapri to Rotondella, and was beginning to threaten the German divisions behind the Salerno front. Fifty miles to the north was the modern city of Potenza, the main inland center of road communications south of Foggia. At the time, it was held by the German 1st Parachute and 26th Panzer divisions, but if it could be taken by Eighth Army it would be an effective means of persuading the enemy to release his pressure on the Salerno beachhead. Monty gave the job to the Canadian Nova Scotia Battalion, which that same day struck out for the coastal town of Villapiana, turned inland at Rotondella, and followed Highway 92 northwest across mountains and rivers to make contact with the enemy at Potenza.

It was against Potenza that the 79th flew its first mission from Italian soil, a strafing show against targets of opportunity. The day before, September 16, the Group had moved via LST across the narrow Strait from Palagonia to Isole landing ground fifteen miles southwest of Crotone to become one of the first American fighter groups to operate from the mainland. Movie and radio star Jack Benny and his troupe arrived at Isole at about the same time the 79th did, welcoming them with the first USO show to perform in Italy. Isole had been an Italian base before the Americans arrived, and they left half-completed administration buildings, hangars, and new unused barracks that the 79th's enlisted men promptly took over. Most of the pilots, many of whom had lived in the villas they "liberated" in Sicily, went back to living in tents.

On its first day in Italy, the Group flew forty-three sorties in support of the Canadian advance (Potenza was captured September 20), then concentrated on hitting enemy road traffic behind the Fifth Army front, ranging as far north as Benevento. "Butch" Owen of the Skeeters was missing after a strafing show on the 18th, but later turned up safe, as did Lieutenant John Kirsch of the same squadron the next day; engine failure had forced Kirsch to make an emergency landing.

On September 20, while twelve Skeeters were bombing and strafing a road north of Eboli, Charles Cummings, Frank Nicolai and Robert Davis were all hit by ground fire. Cummings and Nicolai made emergency landings at the home of the 33rd Fighter Group at Santa Maria but Davis, his controls and instruments smashed by machine-gun fire, bailed out to begin a five-day adventure behind enemy lines. Fracturing his left arm when it became entangled in the chute's shroud lines, Davis landed about a mile from the machine-gun nest that had shot him down. The first person he saw was an aging Italian farmer who had once worked on a dairy farm in New Jersey and could speak good English. The farmer took him to his nearby house (amidst a swarm of inquisitive townspeople) where he was given food and a place to sleep. The next day the captain of the local *carabinieri* (police) showed up to offer Davis his help, returning later that evening with a doctor. The doctor wanted to turn Davis over to the Germans, but was finally dissuaded from doing so by the farmer and the police captain, and the next day the doctor returned in a friendlier mood to set Davis' arm using the paddles in his seat-pack dinghy for a splint. Davis hid out in the farmer's house for the next three nights, until taken to another farm house about three miles away where he was given civilian clothes. On the night of September 25 he was moved again, this time to the home of an obviously well-to-do farmer where he bathed and shaved and awaited the arrival of friendly troops. The British occupied the town the next morning. After a stay in a hospital at Salerno, Davis rejoined his squadron on October 22.

Meanwhile, on September 21, the day after Davis was shot down, John Dzamba and Jack Maye of the Skeeters both bellied-in at an emergency strip near the beachhead after being shot up while on an armed recce near the bomb line. They had been on the sixth and last mission of the day, which also proved to be the last the Group would fly from Isole. By September 22 they were again out of range of worthwhile targets. It was time to move.

After a harrowing ride over the Calabrian mountains in a motor convoy that looked more like a Gypsy caravan than anything else,* A-Party moved to Firmo landing ground some fifty miles north of Cosenza where British engineers were still blasting stumps to carve out a runway. B-Party, meanwhile, leapfrogged into Pisticci forty miles southwest of Taranto. Firmo possessed a fairly presentable house on the edge of the airdrome which was taken over by the Headquarters officers, while the rest of the party set up camp in an orchard. Pisticci was set in the middle of a wide, flat plain and except for nightly hordes of mosquitoes there were few discomforts. Again, as at Isole, they barely had time to settle in at either field before required to move north in the wake of rapidly advancing Eighth Army.

* The convoy was made up of vehicles of every size, shape, description and nationality — from German motorcycles to British lorries to American Dodge-built trucks. One of the trucks was a two and one-half ton GMC pulling a British trailer that carried belly tanks and vital spare parts. On top of this collection rode the crew chiefs and other ground crew. At one hairpin turn high up in the mountains a half-damaged building blocked the way. The truck was uncoupled and the men pushed the trailer by hand around the bend. They then hitched it to the truck again. That evening the belly tanks and spare parts arrived at the new landing ground on time.

Only six missions were flown from Pisticci and nine from Firmo. Most were armed recces, including a particularly rough one on September 26 in the Avellino area that cost the Comanches Lieutenant Whitman R. Smith. On October 1 the Group moved into a landing ground near Cerignola with the picturesque name of Penny Post.

Located on a flat, treeless plain on the Adriatic side of Italy, Penny Post was one of ten fields that had been part of the Foggia airdrome complex, the enemy's hub of air operations in Italy, until thoroughly worked over by American P-38s and B-17s during the last week of August. It had been heavily mined and booby-trapped when the retreating Germans moved out, and several British soldiers were killed trying to defuse the mines on the day the 79th moved in. The Group ran six missions from Penny Post on October 1, resulting in twenty-eight enemy vehicles destroyed or set on fire and many more damaged, but Captain Melvin J. Nielsen was hit and bailed out while flying with the Skeeters on a strafing show near the bomb line. Nielsen, who would replace Borsodi as the Comanches' skipper at the end of the month, and who would become Group CO in May 1944, was seen to reach the ground safely and eventually walked back from enemy territory. He had nothing but praise for the Italian peasants who hid him from German patrols.

Over the next two days the 79th flew thirteen missions totaling 170 sorties, including three missions on October 3 that destroyed eighteen enemy planes and damaged thirty-three on the ground at Pescara. The next day, four more missions were flown as Falcon pilots shot up a command post and several motor transport, but Lieutenant William Feimer of the Flying Skulls was hit and bailed out – not without some difficulty – while he and his squadron mates were hunting for targets of opportunity near Vinchiaturo. Seriously injuring his back in the bail-out, Feimer was hidden by civilians for eleven days until rescued by a Canadian infantry patrol.

By the first of October Montgomery was knocking at the gates of Termoli, a small port city three miles north of the mouth of the Biferno River. Here, for the first time since landing at Reggio, Eighth Army began encountering serious enemy resistance – it had reached the outposts of the German winter positions.

It had been thought the Germans would withdraw in gradual stages to a line north of Rome and, indeed, that had been Hitler's intention. But so successful had minimal German forces been in hampering Fifth Army's advance from Salerno (Naples was finally taken October 1, but had cost over 11,000 American, British and Canadian casualties) that Kesselring was authorized to form a series of defense lines

USO stage shows provided a welcome diversion to the dreary existence of most forward bases, including this one in southern Italy where the 79th and Comedian Jack Benny arrived at a base near Isole at about the same time. (Kauffman)

some eighty miles *south* of the Eternal City. Termoli and the Biferno River anchored the extreme left flank of those positions.

The British captured Termoli on October 2 with little difficulty. Hanging on to it was another matter. The seizure of this eastern hinge-pin of the German line had caused concern in the enemy camp and the 16th Panzer Division was sent counterattacking down the road to Termoli on October 3. Now the weather turned in favor of the enemy. Heavy rains poured down to send the waters of the Biferno rushing over its banks, and severely hampered Allied efforts in the air. A determined attack by German tanks and infantry drove the British back to the outskirts of Termoli on October 5. A call was sent out for air support.

Despite adverse weather, the 79th responded with six missions. In seventy-one sorties they flamed twenty-seven motor transport and damaged eighteen. They also blew up a locomotive, took out a small bridge with two well-placed bombs, destroyed a trailer and two jeeps, and generally made life miserable for the enemy on the ground.

The next day the weather was still marginal, but nearly 500 DAF Kittyhawks and Warhawks were up from dawn to dusk blasting the roads leading to Termoli. The air effort helped break the German counterattack and the enemy fell back fifteen miles to the north and its next defensive position along the Trigno River. That evening Montgomery radioed Colonel Bates and other DAF commanders: "Many thanks for the terrific effort . . . Jolly good show!"[9] It wasn't without loss, however. Two RAF Kittyhawks and a Spitfire were shot down, Lieutenant Gaston Callum of the Flying Skulls was forced to belly-in because of engine trouble (he was OK), and Lieutenant Henry P. Steele, an original member of the Comanches, was killed.

Steele had volunteered for the late afternoon mission and was killed when his aircraft crashed into the ground at the target. He was posthumously awarded the Distinguished Service Cross, second only to the Medal of Honor.

While Eighth Army built up strength for its assault against the Trigno the 79th moved to Foggia #3 (also called Salsola) eight miles west of Foggia. The field featured a grass landing ground – a far cry from the dusty strips in North Africa and Sicily – but the weather was turning increasingly worse as winter approached and the men lived under canvas in almost a continual downpour. Difficult weather over the backbone of Italy made visibility especially difficult at dawn and last light, the hours when the Germans took to the road, but despite the haze Falcon pilots flew a variety of missions ranging from armed recce to VIP escort. They also had good success against locomotives and railroad rolling stock, and pilots reported that escaping steam from a damaged locomotive is as good a landmark as the red smoke burned by front line troops to mark the bomb line.

Because of the bad weather, combat missions were few and far between during October, and many of the 79th's enlisted men were given five-day passes. Foggia itself was a ghost city – not one building was left untouched by the war – but Bari, with its wide, clean streets and relatively well-stocked stores was a favorite destination along with Sorrento, Manfredonia, and the Isle of Capri. At Capri they discovered Colgate toothpaste, Kodak film and similar items for sale in the shops, plus a hotel with regular beds and clean sheets, and a small bar stocked with neat rows of White Horse scotch and Gilberts gin.[10]

Lt. Henry Steele (right), who later lost his life in a bombing and strafing attack near the Trigno River that won him a posthumous Distinguished Service Cross, chats with Comanche Executive Officer Major Rice Terrill. (Morrissey)

The bad weather also provided an opportunity for some of the officers and men to scrounge for abandoned enemy aircraft, and a partially damaged Ju 88 was found that was put back in flying condition by the Comanches. In just six days, they managed to change engines, props, wheels, brakes, several instruments and repair some sheet metal damage – all accomplished in pouring rain – with visions of converting the twin-engined bomber into a flying "likker lorry" and squadron hack aircraft to ferry non-flying officers and enlisted men on leave. Higher headquarters had different ideas. The brass wanted the Ju 88 sent to Wright Field in Dayton, Ohio for evaluation and research.

Fred Borsodi, who had been CO of the 86th Squadron since replacing Jack Watkins the previous July and was due to rotate home, persuaded the powers that be – including 12th Air Force Commander Lieutenant-General Jimmy Doolittle, who got a ride in the restored bird when he visited the Group in mid-October – that he should fly it back to Dayton. With Pete Bedford in the right-hand seat and accompanied by two P-40s for escort, Borsodi flew the Ju 88 (now named *Comanche* and sporting US insignia) to Tunis, where newsreel cameras filmed them being handed a large German flag by Doolittle and General "Tooey" Spaatz to be delivered to AAF chief "Hap" Arnold in Washington. At Tunis they picked up a navigator and flew to Marrakech, Algiers and eventually Dakar (where they were joined by a B-24 for navigational purposes), and after 51 hours of flying time reached Miami on November 6, but not before an air raid warden recognized the plane as a Ju 88 when it passed over the Florida coast and reported it as "hostile." After flight evaluations at Wright Field, the Ju 88 was flown to several US cities and displayed for war bond drives. In Los Angeles it was damaged by a streetcar, but subsequently repaired and flown to Freeman Field, Indiana. Later it was flown to a base in Arizona where it was scrapped.[11]

Meanwhile, on October 16 the 99th Fighter Squadron was attached to the 79th to gain combat experience. The 99th was the AAF's first all-black fighter squadron. They were then commanded by Major George S. "Spanky" Roberts, and had been overseas since May with the 33rd and 324th fighter groups. The squadron had seen limited action over Pantelleria and Sicily, but their performance up to this point had been disappointing; so much so that at the very moment the 99th was joining the 79th its former commanding officer, Colonel Benjamin O. Davis, Jr., was appearing before a Senate Advisory Committee in Washington to answer charges concerning the 99th's poor combat record. The squadron's morale had sunk to a new low and they were under the gun from many sources, but all this would change in January and February when, as a component of the 79th, the "Tuskegee Airmen" (name given to black airmen who trained at Tuskegee Army Air Field in Alabama) would come into their own over the beaches of Anzio-Nettuno.

Toward the end of month, the Desert Air Force began experimenting with a new method of coordinating fighter-bomber strikes in support of ground operations. The system was called "Rover David cab-rank" and featured a forward controller (Rover David) with the infantry on the ground who selected specific targets and called down air strikes from aircraft patrolling overhead (cab-rank). Theoretically, targets could be attacked only minutes following a request from ground forces, instead of having to be first approved by Eighth Army Headquarters and then relayed through DAF Headquarters and the MORU to the various wings and groups as in the past. "Rover David" got its name from Wing Commander David Heysham of DAF Headquarters, who organized the first "Rover party,"[12] but the Americans usually called the guy on the ground "Rover Joe." The Germans soon wised up. On October 23, the Skeeters were being controlled by a Rover while bombing troops and gun positions near Spinete when another Rover with an obvious German accent broke in on the radio to tell "Tadpole Leader" (the Skeeter flight leader) to bomb a different target. Tadpole Leader made a suitable reply. Similar incidents were reported throughout the course of the war.

On October 29, in addition to shooting up ammo dumps, troop concentrations and gun positions on the Eighth Army front, the Falcons also went after enemy shipping in the harbor at Pescara and other ports on the Adriatic coast. On one mission, a weather front almost spelled disaster for eight Skeeter pilots, including Charles Jaslow, one of the original members of the squadron who was leading the show. He was on his 80th mission, the magic number needed to go home. On his wing was Dave Vandivort, on his very first combat mission. As the flight turned for home after bombing two small freighters and fishing boats in the harbor at Torino, it ran into a towering thunderhead and was swallowed up by the rain and darkness. Hugging the waves the pilots followed the coast southward until reaching the checkpoint to make the turn to Foggia thirty miles inland. There they ran into a solid wall of rain and visibility dropped to zero. With fuel gauges dropping steadily, and mountains lurking in the stormy clouds, they were ready to put their planes down on the beach wheels-up when John "Lydia" Pinkham remembered seeing a small British strip near Termoli on their way to the target. Following his lead, the flight found the strip, which Jaslow circled to check out, and then said he would land first and, "if I don't make it, head for the beach and belly-in there." Jaslow got down safely although the strip was so short and slippery he had to lock his brakes as soon as the wheels touched down, sliding all the way to the end. The others did the same, and all got down without further incident. Because of the mud, it was two days before they'd be able to fly the planes out.[13]

This refurbished Ju-88 was flown back to the States by Fred Borsodi and Pete Bedford, startling an air raid spotter on the Florida coast who identified the plane as "hostile." (Hoffman)

Lt. Charles "Jazz" Jaslow of the Skeeters. One of the squadron's original "Desert Rats," his last mission was Dave Vandivort's first and made a lasting impression on both of them. (Jaslow)

For Jaslow, it was perhaps a fitting way to end a combat career that had seen enough excitement to last a lifetime. For Dave Vandivort it was a rude introduction to the war in the air as it was fought on the Italian front.

Montgomery had resumed his offensive on the east coast on October 27. Continuous rains had turned Italy's roads into a quagmire, however, and the advance was soon halted. On the night of October 29/30 he attacked again after moving up more reinforcements. After several initial setbacks the British 78th Division crossed the Trigno and seized the town of San Salvo. The Germans were now obliged to pull back to the Sangro River, part of the main German winter positions, where it would take a major Allied effort to dislodge them.

It was about this time that Churchill abandoned any hope of the Allies reaching Rome before the end of the year.

nine

Stalemate

"No one who had not seen that mud, those dark skies, those forbidding ridges and ghostlike clouds that unveiled and then quickly hid the enemy, had the right to be impatient with the progress along the road to Rome."

– Ernie Pyle

Convinced they could stave off the Allied advance well south of Rome the Germans began a slow, methodical withdrawal in September and October that followed a definite, prearranged pattern. Gradually they yielded less important transpeninsular positions – the Volturno, Biferno and Trigno rivers – until by early November they moved in behind the well-established fortifications of their Winter (Gustav) Line.

This line ran across the width of the Italian peninsula from Gaeta to Ortona. It was anchored in the east by the flooded banks of the river Sangro; in the west by the Garigliano. The center of the line was dominated by some of the highest peaks in the entire Apennines mountain range – peaks that provided a natural impregnability surpassing even that of the river barriers on the flanks. There were few roads through the rugged mountains, and all were unsuited for heavy military traffic under the best of conditions. With heavy autumn rains heralding the onset of a harsh Italian winter these roads became virtually impassable.

The Germans took advantage of the natural terrain by conscripting thousands of Italian laborers to transform the Gustav Line into a truly formidable defensive belt almost twenty miles in depth. Many of its fortifications were underground, while above ground the line was studded with pill boxes, hidden machine-gun nests, reinforced farmhouses and thick minefields (by November 1 over 75,000 mines had been sown in the coastal areas alone). This was "no mere check line, but the inner doors of the fortress of Italy, locked and barred."[1]

If the Gustav Line had a weak link it was near the western end where the Liri Valley offered a flat corridor straight to the heart of Rome. But even here this seemingly inviting avenue was deceiving as it had to be entered through a narrow defile between the Matese and Aurunci mountains, and was well covered by artillery dug into the side of the hills.

Facing the Allies from behind these positions Kesselring, who assumed command of all German forces in Italy on November 21, had two armies: von Vietinghoff's Tenth, and the Fourteenth commanded by Generaloberst Eberhard von Mackensen.

While the German decision to make a stand south of Rome affected somewhat the timing of the Allied offensive in Italy, it did not greatly alter their general strategy. The CCS had embarked on the invasion of Italy with the intention of forcing the Italian Fascists out of the fight while tying up as many German divisions as possible. When the Badoglio regime toppled in September the first part of that strategy was realized. What happened next was up to the enemy. If the Germans decided to withdraw all the way up the Italian peninsula to defensive positions in the vicinity of the Alps or on one of the major rivers of northern Italy, the administrative and logistical difficulties imposed on the Allies would be tremendous. The enemy would then be able to contain a sizable number of American and British troops for an indefinite period with a force of relatively modest strength. Instead of the Allies containing the Germans, it would be the other way around. Thus, Hitler's decision to hold south of the Eternal City was welcomed by Alexander and other Allied commanders as it offered them the opportunity to fulfill the second part of the CCS directive.

The immediate objective for the Allies was, of course, still Rome, a city with both strategic and political importance. The all-weather airfields in the Rome area would put Allied heavy bombers over two hundred miles closer to the industrial heart of Germany than those based on the Foggia plain, while politically the city held all the significance to the Allies as it did to the enemy. And above all, the enemy's obvious determination to dispute the possession of Rome presented the Allies with the opportunity they had continually sought – to draw the enemy into battle and destroy him.

Before a drive on Rome could be undertaken, however, the problem of shipping had to be resolved. The buildup for OVERLORD was continuing steadily on the other side of Europe, and shipping available for Alexander to build up strength on the Italian mainland would necessarily have to be that not needed for the cross-Channel attack. He was also hindered by the establishment of the new US Fifteenth Air Force near Foggia, as the transport required to move this force was equal to that required in moving two divisions, and its maintenance gobbled up almost the same amount of resources needed by Eighth Army. The heavy bomber force in Italy, although vital to the overall war effort against Germany, was a positive detriment to Alexander's campaign.

Continuously plagued by a lack of shipping Alexander had only two choices: call a halt to the offensive and consolidate the gains already made, or fight on to Rome with the resources at hand. Because the political significance of Rome far outweighed its strategic importance; and because Rome – and its all-weather airfields – in enemy hands threatened the Foggia airfields and the port of Naples, the CCS agreed with Alexander's proposal to maintain the initiative and plan to capture the Italian capital. With that strategic decision there still remained the task of formulating a tactical plan.

By early November Clark's Fifth Army was in front of Cassino and along the Garigliano River some 90 miles south of Rome. On the east coast, Montgomery's Eighth Army was up against the banks of the flooded Sangro. Montgomery's plan called for an attack against the main German positions on the other side of the Sangro, hoping to capture Chieti and gain the main Rome-Pescara road. He could then move westward down that road and threaten the enemy's line of communications in Fifth Army's rear.

Monty's attack started on November 20, but persistent rains and increasingly bad weather hampered his advance and he had to wait until November 27, and a break in the weather, before trying again. With the Desert Air Force finally able to get off its soggy fields, Eighth Army moved slowly forward, and by mid-December was in the outskirts of Ortona. But again the weather turned against them and by the end of the year Eighth Army was stalled in front of a line running from Ortona to Orsogna. Monty had crossed the Sangro, but his plan to rush into Chieti and down the road to Rome was spoiled. Unfavorable terrain, a determined enemy, and weather that bogged down tanks, made re-supply difficult, and grounded the DAF – or at least reduced its effectiveness – had proved too much of an obstacle to overcome.

Engine mechanics work on a 79th Warhawk. (USAF)

Fifth Army's advance also fared badly. The attack began on December 1, but made only limited gains, and finally petered out. Throughout the width of the Italian peninsula both sides dug in for the winter.

Still at Foggia #3, the 79th flew forty-seven missions in support of Eighth Army during the first three weeks of November. Most were uneventful – if being shot at, and risking collision with unseen mountains ("cumulous granite") while climbing out and letting down through the thick clouds and heavy weather can be considered "uneventful" – but another move soon became necessary and on November 19 A-Party left Salsola for muddy Madna, a coastal field hacked out of the lowlands just south of Termoli. B-Party joined them four days later.

As they moved into their new quarters the rains came! Trucks bogged down, clothes became crusted with layers of mud, and the tent area was surrounded by water – "it was a lousy place, the worst yet encountered. Everyone sort of came apart. By the end of the year morale would be the worst since leaving for overseas; men rarely washed – it was too cold – and most of the food was canned and dreary".[2] They traded their British desert tents for larger (but colder and draftier) American pyramidal tents and scrounged up small iron stoves to heat them. The stoves had a habit of blowing up.

The airfield itself was crowded with planes, bombs, gasoline and people (in addition to the 79th's four squadrons, there were two RAF squadrons and the 358th Service Squadron at Madna) and was a disaster waiting to happen. Fortunately, it never did. The runway, which ran uphill (takeoffs were downhill, landings uphill, regardless of wind direction) had been covered with a narrow strip of PSP (pierced steel planking) matting that buckled and rattled whenever a plane landed on it, but dispersal areas were still knee-deep in a sea of sticky gumbo. As the weather grew colder five-day passes to Naples and Sorrento were given but the hassle with MPs in both cities almost outweighed the short respite from Madna's muddy miseries.

With the almost incessant rain it was a rare day when the 79th could get its P-40s off the ground. So when the weather broke slightly near the end of November everything that could fly was put in the air to support Monty's attack across the Sangro. Only seven missions were flown on the 28th when Lieutenant Herman Leuther of the Comanches bailed out after being hit by ground fire (he was soon back with the squadron), but twenty missions were run on the 29th and twenty-seven on the 30th – the latter being a new record – and during the last four days of the month over eighty-five tons of bombs were dropped by the Group on enemy gun positions between Orsogna and Ortona. The clearing skies also brought out the Luftwaffe.

On November 30 the Skeeters had a flight over the bomb line when they spotted ten Focke-Wulfs low on the deck strafing British motor transport. With George Lee leading the charge one section jettisoned its bombs and dove into the enemy formation. Lee, who had replaced "Duke" Uhrich as the 87th's skipper on November 19, got behind a 190 and chased it over the mountains half-way to Rome before he got in close enough for a hit that sent it crashing into a ravine. While Lee was badgering the 190 two more had gotten on his tail. Lieutenant Jack Wainwright took care of one with several short bursts that knocked it into the sea, and Lee turned into the other, firing until he ran out of ammunition, leaving the 190 smoking badly. Lee claimed one destroyed and one damaged, while Wainwright's victory brought the Group total to sixty-four confirmed. Meanwhile, Lieutenant Edwin Joh was hit by British anti-aircraft fire and bailed out, successfully, from less than five hundred feet. On the way home Canadian Spitfires made a firing pass at George Lee's flight – no damage was done – and, on another mission later in the day members of the same squadron had another narrow escape from "friendly" action when a flight of Bostons dropped their entire bomb load through a formation of Skeeter P-40s that were strafing down on the deck. Again, no damage was done, but it pointed out yet another hazard faced by fighter-bomber pilots.

The record number of missions flown by the Group those last few days of November could not have been possible without an all-out effort by the ground crews. With missions taking off and landing every few minutes it meant a constant schedule of bomb loading, gun cleaning and refueling. Damaged aircraft were repaired, props changed, and instruments adjusted practically on the spot. Not only did the crew chiefs sit on the wing as the planes taxied to the runway (the P-40 was nose-high on the ground so pilots were guided down the narrow taxi strip by men sitting on the wings) but also the armorers and mechanics, who did their work right up to the last minute before takeoff. It was an all-out effort by everyone, which did not go unappreciated by the troops on the ground. The Commander of the 8th Indian Division sent a message thanking them for the fine air support and a job well-done.

Operations for December picked up where they had left off the month before. Six fighter-bomber and strafing missions

Skeeter armament personnel manhandle a 500-pound bomb into position as they ready a Squadron P-40 for another fighter-bomber show. (USAF)

Lt. Basil Blair of the Comanches was wounded slightly on December 9 when a 40-mm cannon shell shattered his cockpit while on a dive-bombing run. Later, in February, Blair and Lt. Wayne Sherer would have a hot time at an emergency landing strip near Nettuno when they escorted a medical plane into the short strip, landing with the brakes on all the way, then helped unload medical supplies as artillery shells exploded around them. (Blair)

were flown to the Chieti-Orsogna area on December 1, and twelve the next day. Lieutenant Ernest Kellerman, a Skull pilot from Weehawken, New Jersey, was killed on December 2 while strafing along the coast road near Ancona. His aircraft was hit by flak and exploded seventy-five feet off the ground. On the same mission Lieutenant William Glasgow came back to Madna with the leading edge of his wing chewed up from running through a grove of trees. Later that afternoon Lieutenant Charles DeFoor, also of the Flying Skulls, hit a high-tension line with his wing that left wires burning and flashing on the ground and the entire electrical system north of Pescara cut. In the desert, carrying away communications wire was a good show as the supporting poles were usually made of light wood; European cables were erected on steel towers, and were another story. DeFoor returned uninjured but his vertical stabilizer, prop and wing were badly damaged.

On December 4 operations were halted when the rains came pouring down again. The weather remained unfavorable the next few days and only an occasional mission got off the ground until December 8 when another maximum effort was directed against gun positions near Orsogna and Ortona. Lieutenant Charles Kehr, a Comanche pilot from Westville, New Jersey was killed when his Warhawk exploded after taking a direct flak hit at the beginning of his bomb run, and William Glasgow, also a victim of anti-aircraft fire, bailed out of his burning P-40 and was taken prisoner. Thirteen days later he would make his way back through the lines after an incredible escape from the enemy.

The next day, December 9, Lieutenant Basil Blair of the Comanches was wounded slightly in the face by flying glass when a 40-mm cannon shell hit the cockpit of his '40 just as he pushed over from 8,000 feet to begin his dive-bombing run. The shell shattered the armor-thickness windscreen and was deflected out the top of the canopy. Blair jettisoned his bombs into the sea and headed home where he landed safely. On December 12 the Skeeters lost Lieutenant Burke Allen, a sixty-five mission vet from Falconer, New York, and Lieutenant Howard A. Smith of the Skulls was missing (last seen at 400 feet with his belly tank on fire), but later reported a prisoner of war.

The Hawks went in under a solid overcast to tackle more gun positions on December 18, and it was another costly day for the 79th. Lieutenant Ralph Specht mushed into the ground during his bomb run; Lieutenant Wendell Simmons' Warhawk exploded before he could bail out, and Lieutenant William B. Marshall bailed out over the water after his '40 took a fatal flak hit. Lieutenant William Mathesius saw Marshall having trouble with his dinghy, inflated his own and dropped it. Then, after radioing Marshall's position to air/sea rescue, the flight returned to Madna to refuel. With a fresh load of fuel on board they took off immediately and searched for their missing comrade. He was never found.

A Red Cross worker serves up steaming hot coffee to two GIs. (Hoffman)

The 79th flew missions on the 19th, 20th and 22nd, then stood down until the 29th when four aircraft searched for survivors of a ditched B-24 off Rimini. Twelve missions on the 30th and eight more on the 31st rounded out the year's activities. Lieutenant Albert Kettenbrink bailed out over the bomb line on December 30 (turning up safe later with minor head injuries), but Lieutenant William Martin of Selina, Alabama was killed the same day when hit while strafing near the mouth of the Sangro River.

Flying under the most adverse weather conditions, the Group averaged thirty-six to forty-eight sorties a day during December, and exacted a heavy toll on the enemy. But Kellerman, Kehr, Allen, Specht, Simmons, Marshall, Martin and others had paid the price.

Perhaps the Group's activities for the month of December can best be described from excerpts of Major Richards H. Hoffman's diary. Hoffman was the Group's Flight Surgeon:

> **December 1:** Weather bad and got off only six missions today. Only one, the 87th's, was effective – they got twelve flamers. Weather increasingly worse and windy as hell. Raining pitchforks tonight so it's back in the gumbo again. Rumors still thick about the war ending soon – Mac and Jimmy from 21 Mobile Field Hospital say in a fortnight. Don Turner says one of his Docs definitely saw FDR at El Houaria. Oh, well, I'll save my celebration until I see which way the ship is sailing.

Twelfth Air Force boss, Major-General John K. "Uncle Joe" Cannon in the "front office" of his personal A-36. Colonel Bates is standing on the port wing. (Kauffman)

December 2: Plenty of missions today, but still not close to the record of November 30.

December 3: Down to Ops today and took some pictures of operations in the mud. Twelve-plane shows going out on close-support. Think we must be doing most of the ground support for the whole Eighth Army. Saw a few dozen medium bombers, the first in three or four days. They're telling over the radio that FDR, Churchill, et al, are in Persia. Guess it wasn't a rumor after all. Hope much comes of it.

December 4: Very few missions today, weather lousy. Heard Bari got bombed plenty night before last.

December 6: Overcast, dull, poor visibility and a fine drizzling rain – no flying at all. A Red Warning in the afternoon and heard some bombs going off but never found out where.

December 7: This, two years ago, was Pearl Harbor. And it's our fifteenth month overseas. The radio is blaring with news of the declaration following the conference of FDR, Winston, and Joe Stalin [at Teheran]. A little activity this afternoon, even bombers. Supposed to be a big push on.

December 8: Fine visibility. Saw the flak over the lines this morning. Big day today, fourteen 12-plane missions. One pilot gone for good [Kehr] and Glasgow missing. Word is that a lot of big shots will be here tomorrow: Alexander, Tedder, Conningham, Monty and others – big show!

December 9: The show began after breakfast. More clean-shaven faces and clean clothes than I've seen since Cairo. The "doings" were to begin at ten o'clock, and did – only at 244 Wing. A lot of the lesser lights ate lunch at our Headquarters mess. Then, news that at three o'clock a VIP would arrive. Bets were on Stalin,.FDR, Churchill, etc. Finally, just as a 99th plane pooped out on takeoff and crashed into an 85th ship, bombs and all – no one got hurt and missed all the visiting firemen – two DC-3s flew in loaded to the gills with cameramen and reporters and an-

Group Captain Lance Wade, better known as "The Arizona Wildcat," was the top-scoring American ace with the RAF with twenty-five victories. Two days after visiting the 79th he was killed in a flying accident over Termoli. (Kauffman)

Lt. Alva Temple walked away from this one. A pilot with the 99th Fighter Squadron, Temple damaged his landing gear while taking off on a mission. With one gear partially retracted, and fully aware of his plight, he completed the mission then returned to make a safe landing at muddy Madna. (McDowell)

nounced the big shot would arrive soon. They did – in two B-25s. Four-star General "Hap" Arnold, three-star General Spaatz, two-star General Cannon, and other ranks galore. Lots of flash bulbs went off, a short review, a few exchanges, and finally all left and everyone breathed a sigh of relief.

December 10: Not so clear today. Not so many missions. We've flown 945 sorties in the first fourteen days at this field. The pilots are flying too much, averaging three sorties per pilot per day on busy days. Need more pilots! We've lost three for good, two probably dead, one probably a POW, two more bailed out and came back, one still in the hospital. One bunch got in a good – very good – strafe yesterday afternoon.

December 12: Cloudy and rainy in the a.m. but a few missions this afternoon. Wrote a Care-of-Fliers Report. Wrote an extra letter regarding pilots being overworked. Haven't heard anything lately about the war ending before January 1. Johnny Martin told me tonight that each squadron flew one mission today. Flying Skulls lost Smith – a flamer at 400 feet. The 87th lost Allen – disappeared at 6,000 feet with his bombs still on. Rough! We're losing too many lately. That makes five, with three sure goners. Glasgow and Allen may be OK. They say the flak is very thick.

December 13: Amazed by the number of aircraft in the vicinity. There are five or six groups on Foggia Main, including the old 325th; a Spitty outfit; the 12th Bomb Group; a Fortress group, and others. A P-38 group between Foggia and San Severo, and out near Manfredonia the 321st Bomb Group, 2nd Bomb Group, and the 57th Fighter Group. What airpower!

December 15: Getting whiskey requisitions ready for the squadrons. Got thirty-three, twenty-eight and twenty-eight quarts apiece for the 99th, 85th and 87th squadrons. Schenley and Gibson six-year-old. Their eyes did some poppin' when they saw that.

December 17: Overcast, not much flying today. A P-47 [from the 325th Fighter Group] landed here this afternoon.

December 18: Tough day for pilots – we lost three. One definitely gone, his ship blew up [Wendell Simmons], Marshall from the 85th in the drink. Another [Specht] of the 87th hit a mountain. Rough! Weather piss-poor but they flew anyway; had to go in under the overcast.

December 19: Very cloudy. We got ten new pilots this morning, no new rumors. Everything pretty quiet.

December 21: Over to the 325th Group today, they have P-47s. My old Bradley Field buddy, Captain Gershon Silver, wasn't there. He was out picking up the results of a chute that didn't open – two P-47s collided, one got out.

December 22: At 2:30 p.m. went over to the 87th for tea. Imagine, the 87th having tea! The pilots blew in all hot because they pranged a train and gun positions. Someone broke out a bottle of Old Schenley. S-sh-sh! Was that good. They're liquidating Ortona today. Lots of fighter-bombers, twenty-four Baltimores and twelve Bostons went up. The mountains visible all day. The first for quite a while. The campaign would be shorter with more weather like this.

This RAF Kittyhawk became an instant pile of junk after a bad landing accident at Capodichino. (McDowell)

December 23: Another dull day with ground fog, low ceiling and rain. Best news is that Glasgow is OK and due back. Chow lousy. Hear a lot of very good cognac came in.

December 24: Shaved again, and had just shaved yesterday. Going sissy I guess. Big celebration tonight. Lots of drinks and we joined the Headquarters enlisted mens' party. Started to visit all the squadrons but only got as far as the 87th. What an evening, everyone pranged. Trying to forget that we aren't home I guess. They say Glasgow has a great story to tell.

December 25: Awoke at nine o'clock and what a hangover. Lousy weather last night and today, which made everyone happy as there would be no flying. Had a fine turkey dinner with huckleberry pie – good show, the Army crashed through OK. Heard a bunch of bombers going over and soon eleven P-38s [from the 1st Fighter Group] came in low on gas. Frank Wagner (Group Operations; and the Skulls CO until replaced by Melvin Nielsen on December 24) said he couldn't find an enlisted man fit to drive the gas bowser so the P-38 pilots stayed all night. Then an A-36 came in and out jumped good ol' "Uncle Joe" [General] Cannon just to wish us Merry Christmas and to make sure we got the turkey, drinks, etc. The weather was lousy too. It was a fine gesture, and one that few of the Big Boys would have done. Lots of radio news regarding FDR's speech last night. Eisenhower and Monty will go to England, I guess. Spaatz is the Big Boss of the bombers. General Cannon said we're next on the list for P-47s. Not many cheers, but few bitchin'.

December 26: The weather gets worse and worse. Cold as the devil, windy, and lots of rain. The P-38s [that had been scheduled to escort B-17s over the Brenner Pass] couldn't leave. I got up dirty and stayed that way all day.

December 27: Left for Naples full of pep, pilots and patients. Got there in six hours. The Group apartment is swell – except for the two missing window panes, no heat and the gas shut off.

The new year for the 79th started off with a howling gale-force wind that blew down tents, and a driving, slashing rain that canceled all operations for the day. On January 2 nine tough missions were gotten off, all fighter-bomber and strafing shows near the Eighth Army bomb line. Lieutenant John L. Beck of the Skeeters bellied-in after his engine quit, and Lieutenant George Greer of the Comanches bailed out over the water after being hit by anti-aircraft fire while bombing and strafing a huge warehouse at St. Benedetto. He was seen to free himself from his chute harness and it was believed he would be taken prisoner, but the Bonners Ferry, Idaho pilot was still listed as missing at the end of the war. Lieutenant Powell Scheumack of the Flying Skulls also had to bail out, being hit by ground fire near Ururi, but was soon back with his squadron. It was the second time in his career he had been forced to hit the silk – the first was over Panama five months earlier – but it wouldn't be his last.

Nine more missions on the 3rd, and three on the 4th, then bad weather forced a three-day stand down. They were in the air again with two missions on January 8 and six on the 9th when Lieutenant Lawrence Varner of Johnstown, Pennsylvania was killed by tank fire while strafing snowbound tanks with the Skulls on the mountain roads near Pescocostanzo. The next day Randy Silsbee of the Comanches had a close call over Popoli when his Warhawk was hit by flak just behind the cockpit, blowing away his radio equipment – the plane bucked and swayed, and Silsbee almost lost it, but managed to hang on and bring it home – and the Skeeters lost Captain Richard Wiener of Highland Falls, New York. He was last seen strafing four tanks in the same area where Varner went down the day before. A rescue recce made up of George Lee and Dave Vandivort immediately searched for Wiener, but he was never found.

Twenty-three missions were flown between January 11 and 17 – including a Skeeter show on the 13th when a new type of anti-aircraft fire was observed for the first time; the shells burst in three consecutive explosions, each at a higher succeeding level – then the Group moved in under the shadow of Mount Vesuvius at Capodichino airfield near Naples. Again, the first seventeen day of January 1944 as recorded by "Doc" Hoffman:

> **January 1:** New Year's Day, and what a day! I awoke at five o'clock with a veritable machine-gun nest in my ears. A gale was blowing and driving rain into the tent, and the tents were flapping and fluttering so loudly that sleep was impossible. Kept it up all day and by nightfall half the tents were blown down or torn to shreds.
>
> **January 2:** Big Ops today. Skeeters on the late mission caught a large column of Jerry motor transport snowbound – they got twelve flamers and fifty damaged. Greer bailed out into the sea. Two others also bailed out or bellied-in. Three runway crack-ups. "Butch" Owen forgot to lock his gear down and a 99th pilot, Lieutenant John Morgan, cracked up and received a frontal skull fracture. He died on the way to 21st Mobile Field Hospital.* As "Duke" Uhrich would say, "A lot of 'em augered in today."
>
> **January 3:** The war news is good. Russians really going to town, and terrific bombing of Germany by Eighth Air Force. Our boys flew a lot today – nine 12-plane missions.
>
> **January 4**: A wonder, a clear, sunny day! Quite a bit of flying and lots of Eighth Army stuff – artillery, tanks, etc. – going toward the rear. There is something cooking, I can feel it in the air. Don't know what, but I smell a boat ride; maybe to Africa and new type planes, who knows?
>
> **January 5:** Knew the weather couldn't last. About midnight it began to blow and rain like the devil. Kept it up and still going strong this afternoon. No flying at all – in fact, no nothing. Few got up for chow; just huddled around fires and tried to keep warm.
>
> **January 7:** Wind blew hard all day, but mostly sunny. Existence is largely a matter of keeping as warm as possible. Plenty of banging going on up the line in spite of the masses of artillery we have seen coming back for nearly a week now.
>
> **January 9:** We got eighteen new pilots today, and a B-25. Sweat out the Colonel landing it as he brought it in

* Ninety percent of all pilot injuries were from crash landings, with skull fractures and scalp lacerations leading the list. Hard helmets would undoubtedly have saved countless lives but didn't come into use until the jet age.

The Empress, a P-40 flown by Lt. Bill West of the Comanches, sits on the grassy runway at Capodichino. (McDowell)

plenty hot (The B-25 would be used to ferry men on leave and to obtain fresh fruit, eggs and liquor. Mission whiskey, scarce or non-existent until the 79th moved to the Naples area, helped keyed-up pilots from "re-flying the show" on the ground and let them get some sleep).

January 14: A-Party pulling out soon for Capodichino. Something going on, maybe Rome. Group Captain Lance Wade, an American pilot with the RAF, was buried today at Termoli. He fell out of a roll near the ground over the 57th's drome. (With twenty-five victories, Wade was the top-scoring American ace with the RAF. He had just visited the 79th two days before his death).

Indeed, as "Doc" Hoffman observed,* something *was* in the wind. With the Allies still stalled in front of the Gustav Line they planned to break the stalemate by "hurling a wildcat" ashore at Anzio. Unfortunately, the "wildcat" soon turned into a "stranded whale."

---

* Major Hoffman left the Group on January 17 for reassignment as Command Surgeon for XII Air Support Command Headquarters in Caserta. Major Jack Doughtie took over his old duties in the 79th until June when he was replaced by Captain Stephen Magness, who had been the 87th's chief medic. Magness returned home in April 1945 and his place was taken by Major James Blair.

ten

The Stranded Whale

"I thought we had flung a wildcat into the [Alban] Hills, but instead got a whale floundering on the beach."

– *Winston Churchill*

It was soon obvious to even the most optimistic Allied commander that the much vaunted November offensive against the Gustav Line was going nowhere. Kesselring's forces were being steadily reinforced – von Vietinghoff's Tenth Army now numbered ten divisions; Mackensen's Fourteenth Army eight. True, many of those divisions, especially those dug in across central Italy, were weakened and exhausted, but the unyielding terrain and the onset of one of the harshest Italian winters in years were advantages only the enemy could enjoy. Flooded rivers, washed-out mountain passes, and roads that were hubcap deep in a quagmire of mud made foot and vehicular travel difficult. Low, overcast skies kept Allied aircraft on the ground or, at best, severely hindered their effectiveness, and offset the superiority the Anglo-Americans held in the air. The campaign had bogged down to trench warfare reminiscent of the Western Front during the First World War. The attendant political and military advantages of such a stalemate were all in Kesselring's favor.

It was imperative the Allies maintain a steady, unrelenting pressure against the enemy on the ground. If not kept occupied and continuously off-balance he could strengthen his positions across central Italy to where the Allies would be tied up indefinitely, thus making possible the transfer of German divisions to other fronts.

But this meant a winter campaign in increasingly deteriorating weather. It meant tackling head-on a seemingly unending series of strong defensive positions anchored in rugged terrain that limited the maneuver and massing of tanks and artillery, negating the superiority the Allies held in such weapons. Something had to be done by the Allies in Italy in the winter of 1943-44, but a direct frontal attack against the meat of Kesselring's defenses was not the answer.

A natural solution pointed toward an amphibious end-run behind the Gustav Line. A landing close to Rome coinciding with a renewed Fifth Army offensive along the Garigliano and Rapido rivers might lever the Germans out of their winter positions and break the deadlock. But where to strike and how to launch such an assault with the limited shipping available remained questions with no easy answers.

Most of the landing craft still in the theater in November was scheduled to go to England by the end of the year; the assault shipping that remained for use in the Mediterranean was meager, having the capability of lifting one combat division at most. A series of small landings of one-division strength immediately behind the Gustav Line was briefly considered, and promptly rejected as the tactical value of a landing that close behind the front would be practically nil. Only a direct threat against Rome with a force strong enough to make it believable would stimulate Kesselring to withdraw his units from the south.

But Rome was a hundred miles above the Gustav Line. A landing force of only one division would be pushed back into the sea long before a link-up with Fifth Army could be made. Moreover, one division, no matter how close to Rome it landed, would not panic the enemy into disengaging along the Fifth Army front. Only by retaining enough landing craft in the Mediterranean long enough to disembark and support a sizable force near the capital could the Allies realize any possibility of success and hope to break the stalemate. And although it had been agreed at Casablanca that the campaign in Italy would be subsidiary to the cross-Channel attack (OVERLORD), a stalemate in Italy would not only jeopardize Allied aims in the Mediterranean, it would jeopardize the success of OVERLORD as well. In addition, Churchill still clung to his hope of pro-

Returning from a successful patrol, four Warhawks of the 79th Fighter Group buzz the field at Capodichino and peel off for a landing. (USAF)

voking a decisive action in southern Europe, and considered the stagnation of the peninsular campaign as nothing short of scandalous.

Under his insistent prodding and cajoling it was soon unanimously agreed that a landing in January of at least two divisions near Rome was a vital necessity. A site had already been chosen – the beaches of Anzio-Nettuno some thirty-five miles south of the Eternal City. It remained only to find the shipping to lift two divisions to the invasion beaches.

The British Prime Minister brought into play all of his famous persuasive powers in appealing to President Roosevelt to postpone taking landing craft from the Mediterranean to send to England, explaining: "Otherwise . . . the Italian battle [will] stagnate and fester on for another three months."[1] He also cautioned the American president that "if this opportunity (the Anzio landing) is not grasped we must expect the ruin of the Mediterranean campaign in 1944."[2]

On December 28 Roosevelt acquiesced to Churchill's convincing argument and agreed to delay the departure of fifty-six LSTs to England until early February. The Anzio end-run (Operation SHINGLE) was on. D-Day was set for January 22, 1944. It now fell upon those who had in one way or another become convinced of its feasibility to prove that it would work.

From a small flanking maneuver as first envisioned before the shipping problem was resolved, the Anzio landing soon developed into a major operation planned as a giant pincers movement. The invasion would be preceded by a strong feint against Pescara on the Adriatic coast, while at the same time Fifth Army would launch a series of attacks along the Rapido and Garigliano rivers on January 12 in an attempt to pierce the Gustav Line and break into the Liri Valley. Ten days later Major-General John P. Lucas would lead US VI Corps ashore at Anzio. It was hoped that as soon as Kesselring realized the magnitude of the VI Corps landing and its threat to Rome, he would withdraw from the Gustav Line, thus bringing an end to the stalemate across central Italy. It remained to be seen if the distance of seventy miles between the two main fronts was too great for the action of one to influence the other. Nevertheless, it was a risk that could not be avoided.

The beaches chosen for the landing seemed ideal. The harbor at Anzio, although not large, was suitable for putting follow-up forces ashore, and was reasonably well protected by a mole. The planners felt sure they had picked the right spot to "hurl a wildcat ashore."

Roughly an hour's drive south from Rome, the low masonry buildings that constitute the twin fishing villages of Anzio and Nettuno hug the western Italian coastline as it juts slightly into the waters of the Tyrrhenian Sea. Long, empty beaches of fine, white sand reach out from either side of the two pre-war bathing resorts until blocked by the Moletta River ten miles above Anzio, and the man-made 36-foot-wide Mussolini Canal almost an equal distance south of Nettuno. Behind the two towns, after about twenty miles of flat, level ground, the vine-covered slopes of the Alban Hills rise gracefully upward some 3,000 feet and completely dominate the open area between the hills and the sea. From Rome the historic Appian Way (Highway 7) flows south between the Alban Hills and the beaches as it winds through Velletri and Cisterna before reaching Naples two hundred miles down the coast. Further inland the Via Casilina (Highway 6) skirts the eastern side of the hills as it passes through Valmontone, Frosinone, and numerous smaller villages, before it joins the Appian Way as it nears Naples. These were the two military roads to Rome, and the military commanders in Italy in 1944 knew, as did countless field generals for hundreds of years before them, that whoever controlled the broad paved avenues now known as Routes Six and Seven controlled the southern approaches to the gates of the ancient capital.

For the Allies, the road to Rome was not going to be easy. Two months after the landings, after some of the bloodiest and most furious fighting of the war, they were still hung up on the exposed beaches at Anzio. The "wildcat" that Churchill had hoped to "hurl ashore" had turned into an expensive, vulnerable "stranded whale."

For Operation SHINGLE the US XII Air Support Command (ASC) of Major-General Edwin J. House was being steadily reinforced in January by units of the Desert Air Force as they left the Eighth Army front to move to the west. The Spitfires of 244 Wing had already left Termoli and moved into Marcianise, while 324 Wing was installed at Lago near the mouth of the Volturno River by the time the 79th joined XII ASC on January 18.

Changing their radio call-signs so Jerry would think they were still active over the Eighth Army front, and briefly leaving behind fifteen aircraft and pilots to complete the deception, A-Party left the mud and slush of Madna by truck on January 15. Two days later, after the convoy had wound its way over ice-covered roads through the treacherous, mountainous spine of Italy, it reached Capodichino airfield on the outskirts of Naples. Waiting from them when they arrived was a complete sound photo outfit taking newsreel pictures.

Accustomed to the primitive facilities of North Africa, Sicily and the "other side" of Italy, the 79th's enlisted men luxuriated in the large modern (but unheated) apartment that served as crew quarters and looked forward to being back in the civilized world again – at least until they ran into the Naples Military Police that marked their return to the United States military establishment.

The officers were housed five to a room in a large apartment building with real toilets and bathrooms (but no hot water) on a hill overlooking Naples. They slept on canvas cots, "and could get complete laundry and dry cleaning service for about a dollar, but stoves and electric lights were promised 'tomorrow.'"[3] The food was reasonably good, especially compared with the chow at Madna where as often as not it was C-rations supplemented with bread and jam, and occasionally spam. At Capodichino, cauliflower and chile con carne were big ticket items on the menu, along with meat (sometimes of questionable taste and origin), dehydrated potatoes, bread, and a few vegetables, with canned fruit for desert. A typical breakfast would be hot cakes, syrup and coffee (real butter would be an unexpected treat), while noon chow might consist of Vienna sausage, sauerkraut, fruit, bread, apple butter and grapefruit juice.

There were also Red Cross clubs, a well-stocked post exchange, and real entertainment in the form of movie houses, "leg" shows, or a good symphony. But Naples itself was drab and dirty, and long unused neckties and Class "A" uniforms were required as MPs of all grades patrolled the streets asking officers and men alike to show their AGO cards and dogtags, and "saluting" and "non-saluting" areas kept everyone on their toes.

Boasting wide, flat, grassy runways that quickly absorbed the near continuous rain, Capodichino – or "Capo," as it was called – was filled to capacity with Allied aircraft of every description, all poised for the Anzio invasion. In addition to the 79th's Warhawks, the field was crowded with the Bostons of a medium bomb group, another P-40 outfit, three squadrons of B-25s, an ATC (air transport) squadron and an air/sea rescue unit. On the eve of Anzio's D-Day more than 2,500 Allied aircraft sat on Mediterranean hardstands ready to take part in the invasion, including over 850 in the Naples area alone.

Flying out of Capodichino for the first time on the afternoon of January 18 the Group escorted ships moving through the Gulf of Gaeta. Lieutenant Dale DeHay of the Flying Skulls bailed out over the water after his engine seized, but was promptly picked up from the icy sea by a friendly cruiser steaming nearby. An orientation sweep by all four squadrons up the coast to Rome and back two days later, and the 79th was ready for yet another invasion.

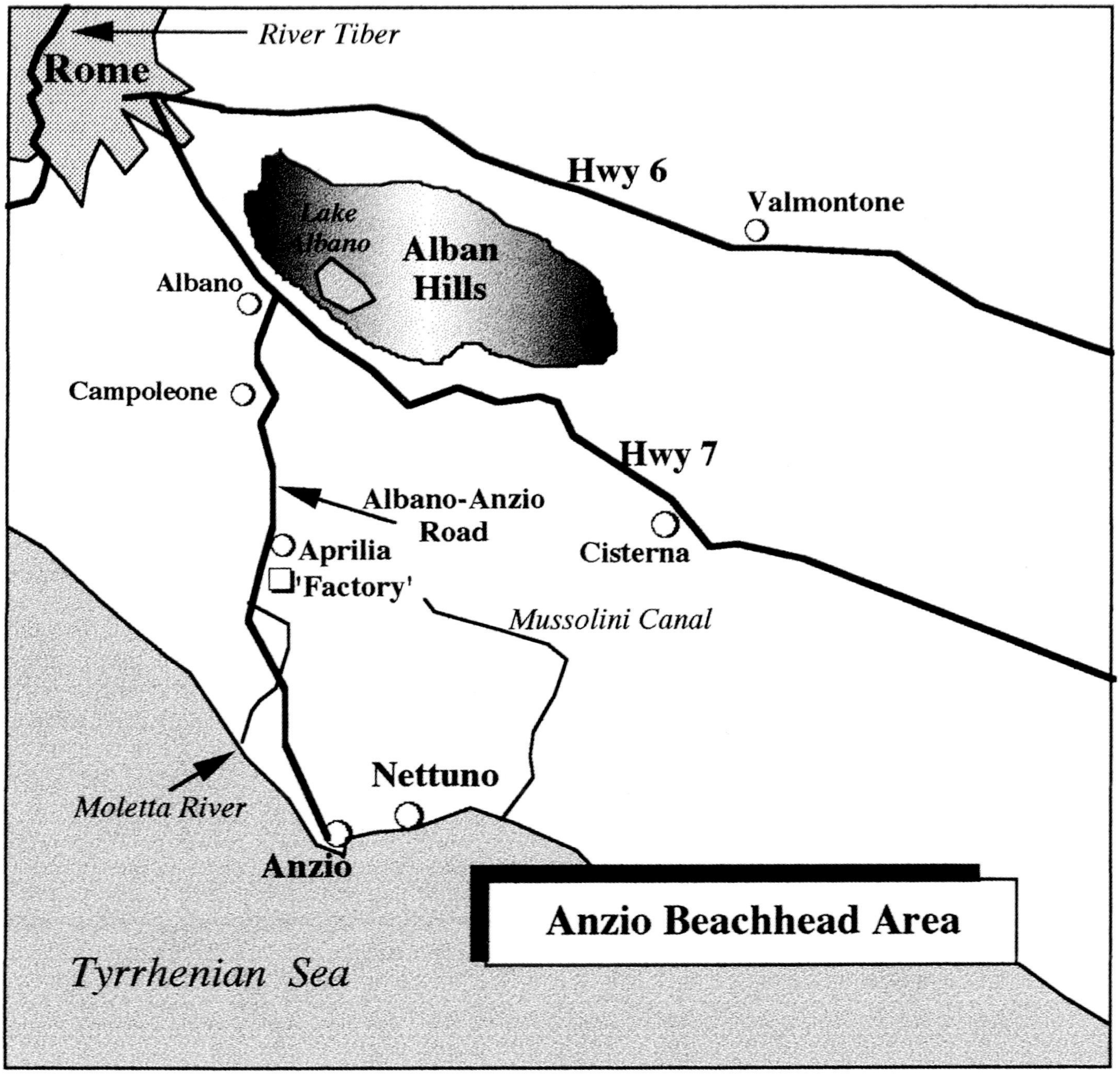

After a disastrous dress rehearsal on January 19 that tragically wasted men and material, the heterogeneous collection of more than 240 ships comprising the SHINGLE invasion armada dropped anchor four miles southwest of Anzio a few minutes after midnight on January 22. Assault craft were lowered into the calm waters and two hours later a five-minute rocket barrage against harbor installations preceded the first wave as it went ashore. Miraculously there was no answering fire from the beaches. Was it possible they had taken the enemy by surprise, or was it a clever trap?

British Intelligence had estimated there were at least 310 enemy fighters within striking distance of the beachhead, with 110 of these being stationed near Rome and immediately available. Consequently, beginning before dawn on the 22nd, General House kept continuous standing patrols of Warhawks and Spitfires over the beaches and convoy lanes. Spits from 244 Wing and the American 31st Fighter Group patrolled between 12,000 and 25,000 feet, while the P-40s of the 33rd, 79th and 324th groups cruised at the lower altitudes. The radar of the 64th Fighter Wing's signal air warning battalions collected and displayed information concerning Allied and enemy air activity within its range, while combat air patrols (CAP) were vectored to incoming hostile targets by the 82nd and 328th fighter control squadrons.

Their vigilance was soon rewarded. Shortly after 6:30 a.m. four bomb-toting Focke-Wulf 190s of SKG 10 (*Schnellkampfgeschwader*, or fast bomber wing)[4] attempted to penetrate the fighter screen. One was picked off by a 244 Wing Spitfire and the others driven away. Five hours later eight more of the Rome-based 190s tried to get at the fleet, and again they were turned away. It wasn't until noon that the Luftwaffe reacted to the presence of the Allied invasion force with any appreciable strength – and this time they ran into the Skeeters.

George Lee had sixteen P-40Ls on patrol when GRUBSTAKE (call-sign of the 82nd Fighter Control Squadron) reported twenty 190s north of Anzio and seven Me 109s a few miles to the east. Short minutes later the two enemy formations had an unwelcome "escort" of American P-40s. "Butch" Owen took out a 190 with a fifty-degree deflection shot to start the action, and a few minutes later added another. David Vandivort, who was covering "Butch" Owen's tail, fired several short bursts into a 190 that was closing in on Owen . . . the mortally wounded Focke-Wulf pulled up sharply . . . stalled . . . and the pilot bailed out. Walt Peterman turned into another head-on . . . out-shot the other guy with his six fifties . . . the 190's gear dropped awkwardly out of the wells . . . the canopy flew off . . . and the German went over the side grabbing silk. Frank Nicolai got two. One went into a spin and slid into Lake Albano on its back; the other he picked off as it was hugging the deck near Guidonia. William Dean shot part of a wing off a 109 for a probable, while Jack Wainwright damaged a Focke-Wulf. Their ranks depleted by at least six, the Germans headed north and disappeared in the haze.

The Skeeters had one Warhawk damaged by cannon fire and lost Lieutenant Jack Maye, last seen when his flight was chasing four 190s north of Ciampino. Two parachutes were observed in the area where Maye was last seen, with one being definitely German. Maye, from Milwaukee, Wisconsin, was later reported a prisoner of war and returned to the States in 1945.

The 79th flew a total of eleven D-Day missions, numbering 133 sorties, and accounted for six of the seven enemy planes definitely shot down over the beachhead by the fighter patrols that day. The Spitfire pilots, stooging around at a higher altitude than the P-40 drivers, bitterly lamented: "We are being made to fly too high for effective interception . . . [we] will never have any joy."[5]

Instead of a trap as General Lucas had first feared, the landing had indeed caught the enemy by surprise. Almost inconceivably the invasion convoy had sailed into the assault area unmolested. What Lucas did not know, of course, was that the German radar system had failed at a critical moment. Also, a large attack by 449th Bomb Group B-24s against Perugia on January 19 had taken out many of the enemy's long-range reconnaissance aircraft on the ground, while Allied air action over the German dromes on D-Day rendered the rest of their reconnaissance force ineffective. In addition, a naval demonstration off Civitavecchia and Leghorn had completely fooled the enemy as to Allied intentions. By nightfall of the first day VI Corps had over 3,000 vehicles and most of the assault force ashore. Total Allied casualties had been thirteen killed, forty-four missing and ninety-seven wounded – most attributable to mines.

The road to Rome was now wide open. An audacious attack straight up the Appian Way would probably have punched easily through the thin enemy defenses and penetrated to the city. Kesselring would then have been forced to withdraw from the Gustav Line. But Fifth Army commanders from Mark Clark on down had expected the landing to be as bitterly opposed as the one at Salerno in September. With vivid memories of that near disaster still etched firmly in their minds, Clark, Lucas, and even Alexander were inhibited by a "Salerno complex." Instead of striking boldly north in a move that would almost certainly have gotten him Rome, Lucas, with Clark's blessing, was content to consolidate his forces and build up his beachhead perimeter (now extending inland some eight miles), expecting a German counterattack to come rushing down from the hills at any moment.

Ironically, while every effort had been aimed toward catching the enemy unaware, no one had really expected to gain complete, total surprise. Lucas had based his plans on a contested landing and the need to dig in immediately. Caught off guard by the lack of opposition on the beaches, he was unable to adjust to the situation and dug in just the same. The Allies had missed a golden opportunity. By the time they recovered, Kesselring had slammed shut the door to Rome.

The main Fifth Army offensive along the Gustav Line, the first phase of what was to have been a giant pincers to ensnare von Vietinghoff's Tenth Army, had opened on schedule on January 12, ten days before the Anzio landing.

In atrocious weather that alternated between blinding snowstorms and freezing, slashing rain, the Free French Expeditionary Corps started the attack. With a fierce, burning desire to regain their national pride they fought like men possessed amid the tangled mass of mountain peaks and along the upper reaches of the Rapido River. They quickly punched ten miles through the German lines, overran numerous enemy positions, and gathered up more than a thousand prisoners. On January 15 the US II Corps took Monte Trocchio in the center of the line and was moving up to the Rapido. Two days later the British X Corps attacked across the rain-swollen Garigliano to capture the town of Minturno on the extreme left flank of the Gustav Line. Then, enemy resistance suddenly stiffened all along the front and no further progress could be made.

When it started January 13, the Fifth Army offensive had appeared to Kesselring to be his greatest crisis. Anticipating a major assault against his winter positions, yet fully cognizant of the fact that his long sea flanks were exposed to amphibious operations – with a landing near Rome to be a *most* serious threat – Kesselring was faced with a dilemma.

Believing in the basic military principle that a commander without a reserve could do little to influence the outcome of a battle, Kesselring had kept two divisions in reserve near Rome, and was building up a third. But now, on January 17, with Allied pressure all along the line, von Vietinghoff requested Kesselring's two reserve divisions to help stabilize his front. Kesselring had to make a difficult choice: was the situation in the south as critical as his Tenth Army commander painted it and, even if it was, did it warrant denuding the defenses around Rome. For the answer, he turned to Admiral Wilhelm Canaris, chief of German Intelligence.

Canaris reported that although there had been rumors of an imminent Allied landing somewhere along the Italian coast, he believed a large-scale amphibious operation by the Anglo-Americans was out of the question for at least six weeks.

Kesselring put his faith in the intelligence estimate. Believing that the fate of Tenth Army rested on his decision to release his reserves, he sent two divisions plus the headquarters of a parachute corps south on January 18. It was the arrival of these fresh troops in the Gustav Line that halted Fifth Army's advance four days before VI Corps went ashore at Anzio.

It was also the reason, if Lucas had but known, why the door to Rome was wide open.

Kesselring's reshuffling of his forces on January 22, 1944 has to be considered one of the more remarkable feats of courageous, decisive generalship in modern military history. Had he made the wrong decision the entire German strategy for the Italian campaign would have been jeopardized. A more pessimistic man might have panicked into pulling out of the Gustav Line when confronted by the massive array of Allied military might pouring onto the beaches of Anzio-Nettuno. But

Major John McEwen, Group Operations Officer, looks out the window of the Ops trailer as the Group's aircraft return to Capodichino after a mission. (USAF)

Generalfeldmarschall Albrecht von Kesselring was not called "Smiling Albert" because of his pessimism.

As soon as he heard of the landing below Rome he drove to the hills overlooking the beaches to determine for himself if it was a diversionary feint or a major, large-scale offensive. "The spectacle of Allied power was awesome: hundreds of ships, with barrage balloons above them glistening in the sunlight; countless landing craft plying back and forth; everywhere troops, vehicles, bulldozers, artillery, tanks; overhead a bristling curtain of aircraft."[6] This was no mere raiding party behind his lines, this was a bona fide amphibious assault of major proportions. The only bright spot appeared to be that the Allies were in no hurry to strike out from their beachhead to exploit the unopposed landing; all indications pointed to Lucas first wanting to build up sufficient strength ashore. That hesitation, Kesselring thought, might give him the time he needed to block the inland routes.

His first move was to gather up whatever forces were in the area, including troops from rest camps and on garrison duty, plus whatever artillery could be found, and move them into positions to block the roads from Anzio to the Alban Hills. He then ordered Mackensen to get his Fourteenth Army on the road to the beachhead at once, and rang up Berlin requesting reinforcements. He was given two divisions – one from southern France, the other from the Balkans – and all the miscellaneous units that could be spared from Germany proper, including additional Luftwaffe squadrons.

Next came Kesselring's most critical decision. At the risk of fatally weakening the positions along the Rapido and Garigliano rivers, he directed von Vietinghoff to release all the troops he could spare. That evening (January 22) the parachute corps headquarters just recently sent to Tenth Army, plus part of three divisions, began moving north to support the makeshift forces ringing the Anzio-Nettuno beachhead. Satisfied he had done all he could for the moment, Kesselring waited for Lucas to make the next move.

From January 23 until the end of the month 79th pilots followed the same air cover routine used on D-Day – with one exception. Now, as they left Capo they first bombed targets on the perimeter, then resumed their patrol over the area until relieved by another flight. On the way home they would go down low to strafe targets of opportunity. In this way they were able to provide air cover over the beachhead while at the same time supporting the troops on the ground. On a typical mission pilots wore helmet and goggles, oxygen mask, gloves, shirt, sweater, trousers, leather jacket (for protection against fire as well as cold), and they were advised to wear shoes "they would want to walk home in." A Mae West with a dye marker was worn over the jacket, and they sat on a parachute pack that contained a dinghy, paddle, water bottle, emergency rations for three days, first aid kit with a packet of morphine, and either a flare pistol or smoke grenade. Many also strapped on a holstered .45-cal. pistol, and after someone's life raft accidentally inflated in his cockpit most also carried a hunting knife for just such an emergency. Within a month they would also be issued fur-lined "escape boots" designed especially for bailouts. The boots extended high on the leg for protection against scratches or injury, and contained a small knife. When the user was safe on the ground the upper portion of the boot was cut away with the knife, providing him with comfortable, low-cut walking shoes. Mission briefings were just that, brief, and at the post-mission debriefing pilots were usually given the customary shot of bourbon before their coffee and donuts.

Sixteen Comanches were on patrol over the beachhead on January 23 when two Me 109s dropped through a 3,000-ft. overcast and flicked through the flight waggling their wings violently in an apparent attempt to appear "friendly." The ruse didn't work. Lieutenants Bob Skotnicky and "Randy" Silsbee teamed up on one and sent it into a fatal split-s from an altitude of less than 1,500 feet. Then, with Lieutenant Alan Austin, Skotnicky and Silsbee chased the other Messerschmitt – all the while hammering it with machine-gun fire – until it disappeared in the haze just south of Rome. As a result of using war-boost emergency power in pursing the fleeing 109, Silsbee

Lts. E. R. "Randy" Silsbee, Robert Crawford and Herman Leuther in front of the Comanches' Operations tent at Capodichino. (Silsbee)

sweat out a two hour and ten minute patrol the next day with a rough-running engine.

Late on the afternoon of January 24 Flight Officer Ed Bozzi – one of several "blue bar" flight officers, some of them former enlisted pilots who, by virtue of their experience, filled key leadership positions within the squadron when the original flight leaders went home in the fall of 1943 – was leading eight Skeeters over Anzio when they were bounced by more than thirty enemy aircraft southwest of the Alban Hills. Bozzi and his wingman, Lieutenant Charles Trumbo, went into a wicked right-hand turn to get at a 190. Bozzi got in a couple of bursts and the Focke-Wulf's wheels dropped down out of the wells. He chased it a bit farther and got in two more bursts. With the Focke-Wulf now on fire, the pilot bailed out. Lieutenant Bill Colgan saw the chute, thought it was Trumbo, and followed it down to pick him up. He already had his gear down and locked and was on his final approach to land when he identified the guy on the ground as German. As he pulled up to rejoin the formation two 109s dove on him and Lieutenant Jack Wainwright from out of a wisp of cloud. The Jerry was on Wainwright's tail and, in turn, Colgan was banging away at the German. 'Round and 'round they went, Wainwright . . . the German . . . and Colgan. When they were down to 2,500 feet Colgan got in a good burst that knocked pieces of metal fabric off the 109 and sent it into a tight spin. But by this time GRUBSTAKE was calling out more bandits over Anzio and they broke off the attack. As they waded into this new gaggle of enemy fighters Colgan damaged a 109 before momentarily falling out of control, and Lieutenant Albert Lincicome damaged another that had been picking on Lieutenant Gordon AcMoody. Then, with red warning lights reminding them of fuel shortages, the flight returned to Capo.

The next day, January 25, six Skeeters were again over the shipping lanes when they ran into ten 109s and 190s. While two P-40s stayed high to protect against any surprises, Captain John L. Beck and the others started down after the Germans. Beck glued himself to a Fw that he quickly shot into the sea, and damaged a 109 with a thirty-degree deflection shot. Herb Anderson also shot up a 109, getting in a long burst behind the canopy, before the German executed a snap roll and got away.

Later in the morning the Skulls added to their score when they tangled with fifteen bandits that were diving through a hole in the overcast to bomb shipping in the Anzio port area. Gaston Callum put a long ninety degree deflection shot into one of five 190s coming down in a string in front of him, and the Focke-Wulf fell off on one wing wrapped in flames. Bob Duffield, on his 63rd mission and flying a '40 he called *Speedy Ede* hit another – a 109 – from dead astern at 300 yards, and that one also became enveloped in a sheet of fire. Bob Proctor followed four 109s into a cloud, saw one come out, and gave it a squirt from dead astern. Proctor claimed a damaged, as did Bill Mathesius who raked a 109 from stem to stern but didn't see it go down. The January 25, 1944 issue of the Mediterranean *Stars and Stripes* commented:

> "The 79th Fighter Group continued its own private war with the enemy at the beachhead today by shooting down three more German aircraft and damaging four others. Today's bag brought the total score for the veteran Warhawk group to eleven destroyed, and another ten probably destroyed or damaged, during the first four days of patrolling over the assault area."

The Group's pilots were beginning to enjoy some of their finest success against the enemy in the air since Pantelleria.* As additional Luftwaffe units arrived in Italy the volume of enemy sorties against the beachhead increased daily. Falcon pilots, most of whom had gone weeks without even seeing a German plane in the air, now began to consider it a rarity if a day went by that didn't involve at least one squadron in a fight. One scrap, on January 27, pitted the Luftwaffe against the 99th Fighter Squadron. When it was over the latter's spirits were soaring.

The 99th, the AAF's first all-black fighter squadron, had been attached to the 79th Group since October. It had arrived overseas in May 1943 and sent into combat over Pantelleria as a component of the 33rd Fighter Group. Its pilots achieved no spectacular success at first, and when that campaign ended could claim only one Fw 190 probably destroyed. In the last week of June they were attached to the 324th Group and began escorting medium bombers over Sicily. On July 2, 1943 Lieutenant Charlie Hall of Brazil, Indiana made history when he became the first Negro pilot to shoot down an enemy plane in World War II, nailing a Focke-Wulf over Castelvetrano, Sicily.*

But then aerial targets began to diminish rapidly; the 99th was assigned almost exclusively to a ground-support role. It was the beginning of a long drought for the squadron – a drought that soon brought highly-placed officials in the States to question the unit's courage to fight. The protest against the black pilots reached national attention on September 20 when *Time* magazine ran an article suggesting that because of its poor record overseas the unit should be disbanded. Major George S. "Spanky" Roberts, the 99th's Commanding Officer and one of the first five Negro pilots accepted by the Air Corps for pilot training, recalled that "people assumed we were not producing because we were black. It was remarkable the men kept their morale, being under such a strain . . . We went for months without even seeing an enemy aircraft, not to mention shooting one down."[7]

Then came memorable January 27.

Roberts was leading fifteen P-40s over the beaches in an early-morning patrol when they sighted sixteen Focke-Wulfs pulling out of a bomb run over Anzio harbor. This was the opportunity they had been waiting for. Desperate to gain victories – or die trying – they fell upon the German fighters with a vengeance. As quickly as it had started, the fight was over, but they had at long last broken their dry spell. Willie Ashley, Leon Roberts, Ed Toppins and Bob Dietz each had a confirmed 190, while Clarence Allen and Howard Baugh shared in the destruction of another. John Rogers and Elwood Driver teamed up to probably destroy another 190, while Roberts, Baugh, Henry Perry and George McCrumby damaged one each.

The German fighters hadn't touched them. "Spanky" Roberts had his electrical system shot out by ground fire while strafing a machine-gun nest on the way home, and Hank Perry was sporting an 88-mm hole in his port wing, but the flight had nevertheless been an unqualified success. In less than four minutes they had downed five enemy planes, probably de-

* An aircraft was classified as "destroyed" when it was seen to crash, catch fire, lose a wing or some other integral part of its construction, or when the pilot bailed out. A "probable" was harder to determine but was usually based on the type and amount of damage inflicted and the aircraft's position relative to the ground. A plane was classified as "damaged" when pieces were observed flying off of it. Just seeing tracers going into the wings or fuselage were not sufficient evidence.

* Jim Peck, a black aerial soldier of fortune, had flown with the Loyalists in the Spanish Civil War where he became the first American since World War I to destroy a German plane in the air. He became an ace in Spanish skies with two German and three Italian aircraft to his credit.

stroyed another, and damaged four more. It was the biggest day in the squadron's history; their morale was at an all-time high.

After lunch the 99th's pilots again caught the Luftwaffe over the beachhead and again they drew blood. Lemuel Custis, Wilson Eagleson and Charles Bailey each claimed a 190, and Bob Lawrence a probable. But this time they lost two pilots. Lieutenant Allen Lane was hit by flak and bailed out, to return a short while later, and Lieutenant Samuel "Lizzard" Bruce of Seattle, Washington was last seen chasing two Focke-Wulfs toward Rome. His death was later confirmed, and Bruce thus became the first black pilot to be killed in air-to-air combat in any war.[8]

As part of this same mission the Flying Skulls interrupted twenty Focke-Wulfs and Messerschmitts bombing the harbor, and waded into the enemy formation through a fierce hail of "friendly" anti-aircraft fire. Albert Benz picked a 190 off Gaston Callum's tail, and the German pilot bailed out just seconds before the Fw turned into a fireball. With his six o'clock position now clear, Callum chased another Fw half-way to Rome, firing some 1,200 rounds of ammo at it before his guns jammed. Pieces of cowling flew off the Focke-Wulf, and when last seen it was streaming black smoke, losing speed, and looked like it was about to crash. Callum petitioned for a probable. Carl Stewart got another probable, a Fw that he caught near the deck and hit with a long, 90-degree burst, and Powell Scheumack and his wingman spoiled the bomb run of a flight of Fws but were unable to concentrate their fire and the Fws got away unscathed.

Except for the loss of "Lizzard" Bruce, January 27 had been a pretty good day for the 79th with nine enemy aircraft destroyed, four probably destroyed, and four damaged. January 28 would see a repeat performance by the 79th, and the day would prove to be one of the best air combat days for Allied aircraft in the entire Italian campaign. Defending fighters over the Anzio beachhead would knock twenty-one German aircraft out of the sky while Flying Forts raiding the south of France would destroy fourteen more.

After its landing gear was shot away during a fight over Lake Albano, this 79th Group P-40 was set down on its belly at Capodichino and hauled away by maintenance personnel. (USAF)

Sixteen Skeeters were on station at 4,500 feet early in the morning when they spotted twenty-plus bomb-carrying Fw 190s coming down over the harbor area from 9,000 feet. The Skeeters went down with them, wading through thick, black puffs of anti-aircraft fire from the ships below. As the Fws pulled out of their dive-bombing run, the Skeeters struck. Bill Colgan, who was leading the flight, hit them first as he poured tracers into a Fw and shot pieces of its wing off until the 190 headed for the deck and home. Colgan then got behind another 190 – this one didn't get away – and the German kite crashed in a gully. Gordon AcMoody, flying Colgan's wing, got in a few bursts at another Fw . . . its gear dropped down (hardly a peaceful gesture as it was usually meant to slow the craft down, forcing the pursuer to overshoot) . . . and the German went into a shallow turn. This was the opening AcMoody was waiting for. He quickly turned inside the 190 . . . gave it another squirt . . . the Fw began to pour smoke and lose altitude apparently out of control. Forced to turn away at 500 feet, AcMoody didn't see the fate of the 190, but was given credit for a probable. AcMoody then turned sharply into another Fw with its gear down and a Spitfire on its tail, and got in one quick burst before breaking off the attack for fear of hitting the British plane. "Butch" Owen dived on a 190, but lost it in the ground haze, then crossed over to hit another that was pulling out of a dive . . . put a long burst of machine-gun fire into it . . . and the enemy plane flipped over and dove straight into the ground, exploding as it crashed. William Dean took on a pair of Focke-Wulfs. He turned them north then dove to 1,000 feet to get behind the closest one. The German went for the tree tops with Dean right behind him, firing furiously. A few seconds later the 190 plunged straight into the frozen earth. Walt Peterman, Leo Joh, Al Lincicome, Gordon Bell and Don Sirman each damaged a Focke-Wulf to round out the scoring, but Sirman was hit by ground fire and had to belly-in at an emergency strip at Anzio. He returned to Capo in a Piper Cub later that same day.

Skeeter Intelligence Officer Captain Elliott K. Shapira debriefs 87th pilots after their big show over the Anzio beachhead on SHINGLE's D-Day. The Skeeters claimed six of the seven enemy aircraft shot down over the beachhead by the fighter patrols that day, but lost Lt. Jack Maye. (Church)

While the Skeeters were mixing it up with the Luftwaffe, a hurry-up call was put in to the Comanches for an escort of three PT boats that were taking General Clark and members of his staff from the mouth of the Volturno River to the beachhead for a conference with the corps commander. Most of the squadron was already airborne on another mission, so the job was left up to Lieutenant F. R. "Randy" Silsbee and two other Comanche pilots. One of the P-40s developed engine trouble before it got off the ground and was scratched from the mission, while the second was late getting off and didn't join up with Silsbee until later. When Silsbee located the PT boats a dogfight between Focke-Wulfs and Spitfires was going on overhead. The fight drifted slowly to the north, but one of the Spitfire pilots bailed out near Gaeta Point. Silsbee guided a PT boat to the downed pilot, who was taken aboard and then, with Silsbee hovering protectively overhead, the little flotilla headed for Anzio. As they drew close to the assault area, several destroyers fired on the three patrol boats – there was always someone who didn't get the word – and it wasn't until Silsbee got their attention with a frantic, wing-waggling buzz job at masthead height that they finally realized the PT boats were friendly. By that time the second P-40 had arrived on the scene, and General Clark and his party proceeded to the beachhead without further incident.[9]

Later that same morning the Comanches and the 99th (eight from each squadron) were patrolling over the beaches when they spotted ten 109s and 190s. Risden Wall of the Comanches, who had learned to fly with the RCAF in Canada, caught a 190 from dead astern at close range and watched as it plowed into the ground, while Herman Leuther and Leonard Penar ganged up on two more. One of the 190s got away, but the combined fire of Leuther and Penar spelled doom for the other; it started smoking, then dove into the ground and crashed. The 99th pilots, meanwhile, shot down four more. Charlie Hall, who had gotten the squadron's first kill in July 1943, got two – one with a 15 degree deflection shot from 300 yards, the other from dead astern at close range – and Robert Dietz and Lewis Smith bagged one apiece. In two days the 79th's four squadrons had shot down eighteen enemy aircraft, probably shot down five more, and damaged ten. Said Twelfth Air Force General John K. "Uncle Joe" Cannon, "It's a grand show. You are doing a magnificent job."[10]

General Lucas continued to build up his beachhead perimeter. By the end of January VI Corps had swelled to the equivalent of four divisions. He had 70,000 men, 508 guns, 237 tanks, and 27,000 tons of supplies ashore, with more coming in each day. It was time to break out of the ring.

Two roads ran from the beachhead across a vast expanse of rolling farm land to the Alban Hills. The main route was in the north near the Moletta River and ran up a gradual slope from Anzio to Highway 7 and the town of Albano. In the south, a dirt road led to Cisterna, Velletri, and eventually Valmontone. Valmontone was behind the hills to the east and straddled Highway 6. If Lucas could reach both Albano and Valmontone he would then have severed the main line of communications between Rome and the German Tenth Army; Tenth Army would be cut off and the road to Rome would be wide open to the Allies.

After extensive artillery, naval and aerial preparation, Lucas planned to send the British 1st Division down the Albano road to clear the high ground along Highway 7 between the Alban Hills and Rome. The US 3rd Division spearheaded by the Ranger Force would advance on Cisterna, cut Highway 7 at that point, then move around the southern edge of the hills to Valmontone.

The attack began at ninety minutes after midnight on January 30 as two battalions of US Rangers crept silently down a water-filled irrigation ditch toward Cisterna in a daring plan to capture that town in a surprise attack that would pave the way for 3rd Division's advance. They had only a few hundred feet to go when disaster struck; they were hit by rifle, machine-gun and mortar fire from all sides as they walked into a well-prepared ambush. Equipped with only small arms the Rangers split into small groups, fighting from the edge of the ditch, in a vain effort to hold on long enough for 3rd Division to join them.

The 3rd Division never got there. Even if it had it would have been too late for the Rangers. By mid-morning German tanks and self-propelled guns had moved to the edge of the ditch and mercilessly cut them to pieces from point-blank range. By noon the lop-sided fight was over. Of the 767 men who had started down the irrigation canal less than twelve hours earlier, only six returned.

The 3rd Division never reached the Rangers because it had run into a buzz saw of its own. Making steady progress at first, the 3rd Division had been stopped cold by German tanks and infantry a mile short of Cisterna. After a thirty-hour fight, the Americans were forced to back down the road, giving up most of the ground they had gained.

On the northern edge of the beachhead the British 1st Infantry and US 1st Armored divisions had attacked toward Albano. The British made good progress, pierced Kesselring's main line of resistance, and reached Campoleone. The 1st Armored Division, however, ran into serious trouble. It floundered in impossible terrain not shown on maps or aerial photos, and as its tanks bogged down in the marshy ground so did the Allied offensive.

With 1st Armored's advance stalled, the British flank was now dangerously exposed. On the other side of the beachhead the Rangers had been annihilated and 3rd Division beaten back with heavy casualties. It was also expected that the Germans would counterattack at any moment. After a hasty conference, Alexander and Clark agreed that the beachhead should go over on the defensive.

Unknown to the Allies their offensive had come within an eyelash of succeeding. One more determined effort might have broken them out of the stagnated beachhead. On the surface VI Corps had been stopped by what appeared to be overwhelming German strength. In reality that "strength" was a hastily thrown together hodge-podge – a "higgledy-piggledy jumble"[11] – of many different confused and disorganized units or parts of units. Only by desperately juggling his forces and feeding them into the battle piecemeal had Kesselring managed to hold on.

When the Allies decided to go on the defensive they not only lost the initiative, and another golden opportunity to capture Rome, they also gave Kesselring the breather he needed to build up for a strong counteroffensive. When that counterattack came – not imminently as Alexander and Clark had feared, but almost two weeks later – VI Corps would indeed be up against overwhelming strength; it would be involved in a fight every bit as desperate as that at Salerno the September before.

During the first ten days following the landings at Anzio the Luftwaffe put up an average of 100 sorties per day against the beachhead and the fleet. While these attacks never posed a threat serious enough to decide the outcome of the battle, they were a definite nuisance. Coupled with the almost constant and indiscriminate shelling from German artillery looking down on them from the Alban Hills – including a huge 280-mm railway gun nicknamed "Anzio Annie" by the Allies, *Schlanke Bertha* by the Germans, that could drop a 560-pound shell on the beachhead from thirty-eight miles away – the air attacks continued to harass the SHINGLE force daily. By the end of January the aerial attacks alone had succeeded in sinking four Allied ships and damaging two others. But the cost to the Luftwaffe had been high.

Allied day fighters of the 31st, 33rd, 79th, and 324th groups and 244 Wing were flying more than 450 defensive sorties a day over the immediate battle area. Since D-Day they had claimed the destruction of fifty enemy fighters, while night fighters destroyed another fifteen German intruders. Fleet gunfire and shore-based anti-aircraft fire shot down almost a hundred more.[12] The 79th led all day fighter groups with twenty-nine destroyed, seven probably destroyed, and eighteen damaged, while losing two of its own (Jack Maye and "Lizzard" Bruce) to enemy fighter action, and another, Lieutenant Mike Mauritz of the Comanches, to an overheated engine. Mauritz ditched in the sea off the coast on January 31, and was taken prisoner. He later escaped and rejoined his squadron in July. In 1998, his aircraft was recovered from the sea where it had gone down fifty-four years earlier.

But then almost a week of bad weather set in, hampering air operations on both sides. Allied pilots saw little of the Luftwaffe over the beachhead during the first few days of February. There were plenty of rumors, however, including one that the 79th was going to go to India or Burma. Unfortunately for the Germans, nothing ever came of it.

The morning of February 5 dawned bright and clear. With the advent of better weather the tempo of air activity picked up noticeably.

Shortly after a cold breakfast Captain Clarence Jamison was leading seven P-40s of the 99th Squadron over Anzio when they were vectored by GRUBSTAKE onto an incoming raid of ten Focke-Wulfs. A few minutes later they were sighted visually and the black pilots closed in for the kill. Almost at once everything started to go wrong for Jamison. First his guns jammed. Then a particularly persistent German glued himself to his tail. As cannon shells whizzed past his canopy Jamison hedge-hopped across the Italian countryside for twenty or thirty miles before he managed to shake the 190. Then his engine began sputtering and Clarence Jamison knew he was flogging a dying horse; it was time to get out. He tried to reach bail-out altitude but the old Warhawk would have none of it. Instead, he set it down wheels-up in a small clearing and the P-40 threw up dirt like a runaway plow before sluing to a stop in the middle of no-man's land. Beckoned by three American paratroopers, he scampered across the open stretch of land to safety.

George McCrumby, meanwhile, had his controls shot away by flak. After a few frantic seconds battling a stubborn slipstream he managed to bail out and startled a herd of cows as he floated gently down into a pasture. The 99th had two pilots down, but Lieutenant Elwood Driver evened the score somewhat when he shot up a Focke-Wulf that briefly trailed a bright plume of fire before crashing in a grove of trees.

The perverse weather remained good for the next few days and the Luftwaffe took advantage of it by striking regularly at the beachhead with about 120 sorties a day. Just as regularly the Warhawks and Spitfires struck back.

On February 7 eight P-40s of the 99th had been on patrol for forty-five uneventful minutes when, at ten minutes after eight in the morning, ground controllers called out twelve Focke-Wulfs coming in at 16,000 feet. The Fws were picked up visually as they were pulling out of their bomb run over the VI Corps command post at Nettuno, where they succeeded in blowing up three ammo trucks, destroyed several above-ground structures, killed or wounded a dozen men, and persuaded General Lucas to move his CP into an underground wine cellar.[13] As the 190s struggled for altitude they ran into the hard-charging P-40s.

One four-ship section consisting of Lieutenants Wilson Eagleson, James Knighten, Clinton Mills and Leonard Jackson whipped around in a tight turn and the Jerries broke away to the left. Jackson closed to within 150 yards of one . . . hit it with a long burst from dead astern . . . and the 190 tumbled earthward out of control. At 1,500 feet the German pilot somersaulted free of his plunging death trap. Eagleson and Mills each bagged a 190 to raise the squadron's score to seventeen before red warning lights winked at them to remind them of fuel shortages and the flight returned to Capo.

Shortly before noon another enemy raid hit the harbor area. This time the Skulls had an eight-ship patrol in the vicinity that was bounced by eight 109s running interference for twenty bomb-carrying Focke-Wulfs.* Lieutenants George Bolte and John Keene took on two of the "delousing" Messerschmitts, chasing them twenty miles up the road to Velletri before Bolte exploded one with a 30-degree deflection shot. Seconds later he got on the tail of another 190 and banged away at it, scoring some hits, before the Fw pulled away in a sudden burst of speed. Keene, meanwhile, was going 'round and 'round with a Focke-Wulf, hammering enough metal fabric off the 190 to persuade its pilot to break off combat and head back north.

At the same time, Lieutenants George Nashold and Raymond Higgins, who had been mixing it up with two different formations of Fws without success, turned into another large gaggle of bandits. Higgins latched on to a 109 and the fight slowly drifted east. The 109 pilot was good, but Higgins took advantage of a brief opening and soon a dirty, gray-colored German parachute blossomed in the air.

Lieutenants Bob Duffield, Bob Bartlett, William McLane and Don Gravenstine had ignored the Messerschmitts and gone straight for the enemy *Jabos*. Duffield fired a short burst into a 190 and the plane began to emit puffs of black smoke. He hit it again, then watched as the 190 lost glycol and fuel, and gained

* Many of the sorties flown by German fighter units over the beachhead were intended to draw off Allied fighters so *jabos* (fighter-bombers) of SKG-10 would have a clear shot at ground targets.[14]

Lt. Gordon AcMoody inspects a close one. AcMoody claimed a probable in a fight over Anzio on January 28, and six months later would lead the Skeeters in a successful strike against an aircraft carrier found hiding in the harbor at Genoa. (Church)

scarlet fire. Before the pilot could bail out the 190 dove straight into the ground. Duffield and Bartlett then chased another Fw up the Appian Way and got in several good hits that left the Focke-Wulf trailing smoke. Duffield turned away to let Bartlett close in, and watched as the 190 ran into the side of a stone building and blew up. McLane, meanwhile, picked a Focke-Wulf off Bartlett's tail and the 190, with an apparent dead man in the cockpit, went down out of control and plowed into the ground. Before turning for home, Don Gravenstine caught a straggling 190 with a good deflection shot and the Fw rolled completely over on its back, hit a row of trees, and skidded into an open field where it became an instant fireball.

The eight Skullmen had taken on almost thirty enemy aircraft, and had knocked down six and damaged two without loss to themselves. Yet enough of the hostile raiders had gotten through the defenses to hurt the fleet; two small ships had been damaged and thirty men killed.[15]

At a quarter after three in the afternoon another incoming raid of ten Focke-Wulfs, each carrying a full warload, was picked up 12,000 feet over Nettuno. Again it was the Flying Skulls who were in position to intercept.

Lieutenant Carl Stewart went for a Focke-Wulf head-on, guns firing, then tacked onto its tail as it passed and continued hosing steel-jacketed shells into the Fw from dead astern. With the engine shattered by Stewart's fire the 190 assumed all the flying qualities of the proverbial brick. The German had few options left; it was time to get out. He jettisoned his canopy, kicked the stick far forward with his feet, and flipped out into the air just moments before the 190 exploded like a ripe plum.

Lieutenant Martin Granberg picked out the tail-end Charlie of three Fws going down in a string over the harbor. He closed in until the Focke-Wulf filled his windscreen, then raked it from the wing root to the cowling. The Fw went into a steep dive and the pilot bailed out. Lieutenant Robert Proctor got in several bursts on another Fw, which began smoking, and followed it down until his guns jammed and three other Fws drove him off.

The high-flying Spitfires had also been busy. One was hit by friendly anti-aircraft fire and the pilot never got out, while another latched onto a Focke-Wulf. In an effort to gain altitude the German pilot jettisoned his bombs. Several fell on the 95th Evacuation Hospital, killing twenty-eight patients and medical personnel, and seriously wounding sixty-four.[16] The front was relatively quiet this bright February day, but the troops in the rear areas – if any part of the Anzio beachhead could be called a rear area – were taking a beating. A decision by Lieutenant Alan Austin of the Comanches a few days later undoubtedly saved lives on the beachhead when he elected to crash-land his sputtering P-40 in a clump of trees (where his chance of survival was almost nil) rather than in an open clearing when, at the last moment, he discovered the clearing was occupied by a hospital. Miraculously, he survived, and was awarded the Silver Star for his unselfish act.

Jack Wainwright of the Skeeters picked off another 190 later in the afternoon, while a strafing show to Cisterna by the 85th netted a personnel carrier, an armored car and two staff cars. John Keene bailed out near the Mussolini Canal after his engine caught fire but was picked up by British infantry and returned safely to Capodichino.

The beachhead defenders had done a creditable day's work this February 7. Seventeen enemy aircraft had been destroyed and twelve more probably destroyed by the fighter patrols, while anti-aircraft gunners shot down seven (not including the Spitfire) plus six probables. Out of this total the 79th tallied twelve confirmed kills and sent three more back to Rome with varying degrees of battle damage. But the German raids were still causing considerable destruction and men were dying. The high brass – especially the Navy brass – expressed concern and more effective countermeasures were explored. One such measure included retaliatory strikes against German airfields. After the enemy raids over the beachhead on February 7, Fifteenth Air Force sent three groups of B-24s (100 of the slab-side bombers in all) to hit airfields near Viterbo, Tarquinia and Orvieto. The bombing was apparently effective because for several days afterwards enemy air activity over Anzio was reduced to just a few hit-and-run raids by Rome-based Focke-Wulfs.

General House had also originally intended to base a large number of fighters in the beachhead perimeter immediately after the landings. A shortage of shipping, the confinement of the bridgehead by the German Fourteenth Army, and the close proximity of Naples-based fighters to Anzio (fifteen minutes flying time) curtailed his initial plan, but a squadron of 31st Group Spitfires began providing on-the-spot cover from a short strip near Nettuno on February 1. Almost immediately the airstrip became a prime target for long-ranging artillery, as Lieutenants Wayne Sherer and Basil Blair of the Comanches soon found out. On February 7 Sherer volunteered to escort a medical plane to the beachhead, and was told to pick a pilot he had confidence in to accompany him, so he picked Blair. They were also told the runway was very short, and to lay on the brakes all the way, and if they didn't touch down within the first fifty feet to go around and try it again. "They weren't fooling," Sherer said. "We both had to brake one wheel and spin the planes to a stop, and we still ended up between the buildings at the end of the runway. I'm glad I had Blair behind me."[17] Both pilots then helped unload medical supplies from the hospital plane while artillery shells exploded all around them. They got off again without incident, but five days later, after losing five Spits on the ground, the strip was abandoned for all except emergency purposes.

After its success in the air on February 7, the 79th enjoyed three more days of ideal flying weather and averaged eleven missions a day – divided between area patrol, fighter-bomber, strafing, and riding shotgun to bridge-busting Bostons and VIP-carrying C-47s – before being grounded by the weather on February 11 and 12.

On February 10 the weather wasn't yet bad enough to keep the 79th on the ground, and the Skeeters were up in squadron strength dodging snow and rain squalls between Lake Albano and the coast. Shortly after noon eight Focke-Wulfs were sighted a thousand feet below them dive-bombing British positions along the northern edge of the beachhead perimeter. Shoving the power to the big Packard-built Merlin engines eight of the Skeeters flicked over as one, giving each other the aerial elbow to be the first to get to where the action was. Frank Nicolai and Jack Wainwright won the race. Wainwright knocked the rudder off one Fw as it circled back at him and the 190 dove into the ground, hit on its nose in an empty field, then shredded its wings as it skidded along for another hundred yards before coming to a rest in a clump of trees. Nicolai chased another over the tree tops toward Rome for several miles, raking the Fw with several good bursts before he lost sight of the camouflaged 190 against the foliage.

After a two-day stand-down the Group was up early on February 13 running fighter-bomber shows against enemy troop concentrations and gun positions. Returning from one mission Lieutenants Pepper, Saverio Martino, Bill West, Robert Grier and Major Melvin Nielsen of the Comanches damaged several Fws after encountering thirty bandits working over the Anzio-Nettuno area, but none were seen to crash.

For the next few days the Group devoted its time almost exclusively to interdiction missions against enemy communications and, when the expected German counterattack against the beachhead finally materialized, supported the troops on the ground.

Kesselring had originally hoped to launch Mackensen's Fourteenth Army in a decisive blow against the beachhead on February 1, but the ill-fated VI Corps offensive on January 30 had upset his plans. Further, although Lucas' attack on the 30th did not achieve the desired results, it had succeeded in capturing a complex of red brick buildings near Aprilia. These buildings were located on high ground commanding the immediate area, and were considered by Mackensen as an indispensable springboard for his own attack. Because of their fortress-like appearance this cluster of two- and three-story farm settlements was known to the Allies simply as the "factory."

Beginning February 7, Mackensen hit the beachhead with small local blows designed to regain the "factory" and other key terrain, while a series of artillery duels and small, but fiercely fought patrol actions flared up all along the line as each side struggled to improve its tactical situation. Finally, on February 9, the Germans wrested the "factory" from the British; three days later they had improved and consolidated their positions based on this strategic strongpoint.

With the "factory" secured, a reinforced Luftwaffe standing ready to give him the needed air support (Luftwaffe fighter units supporting German ground operations at Anzio included JGs 4, 51 and 53) and with ten divisions now gathered under his command, Mackensen was at last ready to launch the counterattack he hoped would push the Allies back into the Tyrrhenian Sea and once and for all eliminate the threat to the German rear. In Berlin Hitler, who placed great political significance on the outcome of the battle, and believing a German victory at Anzio would postpone indefinitely the Allied invasion of Northwest Europe in the spring, watched closely the final preparations of Fourteenth Army.

In his main attack, Mackensen planned to send five divisions spearheaded by the Infantry Lehr Regiment (an elite unit of hand-picked men who had been Hitler's personal bodyguard, but had never seen combat) in two waves down the east side of the Albano-Anzio road at dawn on February 16. On his right flank two divisions would conduct a subsidiary effort, while small-scale attacks along the length of the entire front would, he hoped, conceal his primary intentions. Beginning at first light German fighter-bombers would also conduct nuisance raids over British and American forward positions. And in an effort to gain some measure of local surprise no unusual patrol or artillery activity would be undertaken until just before the attack began. If all went as planned, Mackensen's counter-offensive would split VI Corps down the middle, reach the sea within three days, and remove what Hitler termed that beachhead "abscess" on the Italian coast.

Simultaneous with an enemy artillery barrage of a density and volume never before experienced at the bridgehead, German infantrymen began moving ghostlike out of the haze and ground fog shortly after daybreak on February 16. This was Mackensen's diversionary effort preceding his main attack. The enemy riflemen pushed and probed against Allied outposts on the outer fringes of the VI Corps defense line. Near Cisterna, in the 3rd Division's sector, the Americans quickly recognized the feint for what it was and all but annihilated two inexperienced rifle companies of the Hermann Goering Division with a devastating artillery barrage.* Elsewhere, however, the attack took the defenders by surprise and the Germans plunged forward to penetrate as much as two miles in many sectors.

Then, behind a curtain of smoke and shellfire, and with supporting armor moving easily across the frozen ground, the main German attack exploded against the six-mile front held by the US 45th Infantry (Thunderbird) Division in the critical center of the line.

Sheer weight of numbers at first carried the assault as forward outposts and companies were overrun; entire squads and platoons swallowed up without a trace. Heavy casualties mounted on both sides at an alarming rate as the battlefield churned and boiled under the pounding of hundreds of large-caliber guns. The Americans committed many of their reserves, and although the line buckled and wavered it did not break. Gradually the German rush slowed. The Anzio plain became soft and muddy as the frost went out of the ground with rising daytime temperatures, making tank maneuver impossible. German armor was soon confined to the narrow roads where it was vulnerable to Allied air and artillery. Coming under fire for the first time the elite Infantry Lehr Regiment (Hitler's favorite) broke and ran, robbing the attack of its momentum.

The British and American infantrymen, artillerymen and tankers – fatigued and bloodied, their ranks seriously depleted – had held. By nightfall the Allied front was still basically intact.

As the cool February sun faded in the western sky the enemy renewed his assault along the shell-cratered Albano-Anzio road with refreshed vigor. Under the cover of darkness he succeeded in doing what he had failed to do in daylight. Testing and probing throughout the long winter night for soft spots in the Allied line a small gap was eventually forced between two regiments of the 45th Division. This was what Mackensen had been looking for. He quickly brought up his reserves and by dawn was ready to exploit this new-found opportunity.

Shortly after eight o'clock on the morning of February 17 thirty-five German fighter-bombers whistled low over the forward Allied positions showering the exhausted troops with a cascade of high-explosives and a hail of cannon and machine-gun fire. A few minutes later three divisions of Mackensen's panzer grenadiers followed over three-score Tiger and Panther tanks into the breach.

---

* In trying to explain their poor showing, captured members of these units "pointed to an exceptionally high rate of dysentery that had swept their ranks just before the attack. American soldiers recognized the symptoms well as it afflicted many soldiers of all nationalities who came under fire for the first time.[18]

The Americans reeled and staggered, and finally fell back before the onslaught, retiring in full daylight across open country, taking enormous casualties. By noon, after another attack by forty-eight Focke-Wulfs, the Germans had driven a wedge two miles wide and a mile deep into the 45th Division. They were almost back to Lucas' final, last-ditch defense line; the Allies at Anzio were on the brink of disaster. "All hung in the balance. No further retreat was possible . . . it was life or death,"[19] said Winston Churchill.

Lucas poured more reserves into the battle, including two tank battalions he had husbanded for just such an emergency, and sent out an urgent plea for all available aircraft to rush to his aid.

The Mediterranean Allied Air Force (MAAF) responded with over 800 sorties that afternoon. Aircraft of every conceivable description heeded the call for help and came tearing in from all over southern Italy to unload nearly 1,000 tons of bombs on German positions – most of it on the road between Carroceto and Campoleone. Warhawks, Spitfires and A-36 Invaders (P-51 Mustangs converted to dive-bombers) roared in over the road to bomb and strafe, as tiny L-4 Cubs flitted sparrow-like through the dangerous skies spotting targets. Desert Air Force Baltimores crossed the Apennines from the other side of Italy to lend their weight to the attack, and RAF and AAF mediums and heavies, diverted from their customary roles, came down low to bomb as close as 400 yards in front of the American positions.

The blistering air strikes represented the heaviest weight of bombs in support of ground forces in a single day ever recorded. Together with the reckless expenditure of artillery, tank and mortar fire, the effect was devastating . . . "a volcano in full eruption – flaming, roaring, shuddering, the shrapnel raining down far out to sea."[20] Once again the German assault had been slowed – pulverized to an agonizing crawl, but not yet completely halted.

Mackensen continued to hit the Allied line throughout the night, but his attacks were weak and did little more than harass Lucas' weary troops. Like the Americans, the Germans were also battered and exhausted. Regiments had been reduced to the size of battalions; battalions to companies, companies to platoons.

The weather on February 18 turned horrendously bad, grounding all Allied air except for a few sorties by A-36s and P-40s. Mackensen took advantage of it by massing a large concentration of troops and tanks near Campoleone, and the column moved down the road headed once more for the Thunderbirds of the 45th Division.

Within minutes most of VI Corps artillery was falling on the advancing column. Four times the Germans attacked. Four times they were halted by the massive volume of shells dropping on them. That afternoon they struck the 45th Division again in the heaviest attack of the day. The Thunderbirds refused to budge. After four frantic hours of desperate, confused fighting, this last serious bid by the Germans to punch through to the sea was beaten back. A few, feeble attempts were made during the next two days, but gained little. Mackensen's five-day counteroffensive had cost him over 5,000 men killed, wounded or missing, and had failed to dislodge VI Corps from the beachhead. The crisis at Anzio was over.*

Lts. Leonard Penar (above) and Herman Leuther ganged up on two Me-109s. One got away, but their combined fire spelled doom for the other. (Horn)

The 79th had gone all-out against Mackensen's counter-offensive from the beginning. Lugging 1,000-pound bombs from the wide, grassy runways of Capodichino, Falcon pilots struck hard and repeatedly against the on-rushing German tide. When Mackensen threatened to overrun the Thunderbirds on February 17 the Group flew 103 of the 813 sorties mounted by MAAF that day in response to Lucas' cry of "Hey, Rube!" All but two of their thirteen missions were over the beleaguered 45th Division, and all were heavily opposed. The Skeeters lost Lieutenant Paul Hartman during that hectic afternoon. Hit by ground fire, the Union City, Michigan pilot crashed and was killed before he could bail out of his burning plane.

The next day, when bad weather grounded most of MAAF – the Allied air effort over the beachhead dwindled to a mere 127 effective sorties; fifty by the 79th – the Group was up dodging local snowstorms, rain squalls, and 20-mm cannon shells.

* General Lucas was relieved of command of VI Corps on February 22 and replaced by Major-General Lucian K. Truscott, Jr. Truscott, who had led the 3rd Infantry Division since Sicily, would replace Mark Clark as Fifth Army commander in December 1944 in a major reorganization of Allied forces in Italy. Lucas spent the rest of the war in Texas training troops.

Before the day was over they left a railway station burning fiercely, took out an 88-mm gun position that disappeared in a blinding flash, silenced three machine-gun nests, destroyed a brace of armored cars, and shot up six Mark VI tanks and two platoons of infantry. In return, the Comanches lost Lieutenant Albert Mace when he took a 20-mm round in the belly tank over Anzio. Advised by the rest of the flight to jump, he never got the chance as his P-40 plunged through the overcast and into the ground wrapped in a sheet of flames. It was his first combat mission, and his last.

As the ground attack began to slow down the 79th was released from its almost 100 percent ground-support role, and on February 19 Falcon pilots once again began dividing their time between fighter-bomber strikes and defensive patrols over the beachhead.

The Flying Skulls had just finished an early-morning bomb run on an ammo dump when they spotted fifteen Focke-Wulfs (including new long-nosed Fw 190Ds, arguably the best fighter of World War II) bombing British positions in the same general area. The Skull pilots waded into them as ground gunners from both sides threw up a curtain of anti-aircraft fire. Lieutenant Carl Stewart got on the tail of one Fw and fired at it for several long seconds before the 190 flipped over and exploded against the side of a small hill. Before the rest of the Germans pulled out of the fight with their superior speed, Lieutenants Ray Wadja, George Bolte, Albert Benz and Powell Scheumack damaged one apiece. For Scheumack, the Skulls Ops Officer, the day was far from over.

He had been banging away at a Fw from about 300 yards when a burst of flak slapped his Warhawk aside, knocked out his aileron controls, and put a large, gaping hole in his starboard wing from which spilled about eight feet of belted .50-caliber ammunition. With the belted ammo trailing behind him, Scheumack broke off his attack and headed for the emergency strip at Nettuno.

As he bounced to a rough landing on the deserted runway the Germans started lobbing artillery shells his way – the Texas pilot had to make a quick decision: either abandon the shot-up P-40 and try to slip out by boat after dark, or make an effort to repair the damaged plane. The thought of spending the day on the exposed strip didn't appeal to him, so he set about getting his kite back in flying condition. With no tools and no material aside from some bits of safety wire, he repaired the damage and took off to the thundering applause of exploding artillery shells. Safely back at Capo he remarked, "I'd rather be upstairs than on the beach, it's a helluva lot safer."[21]

Those sentiments were echoed by Lieutenant Don Sirman of the Skeeters later in the day after he also made a forced landing at the Nettuno strip. He came in wheels-up however, and was forced to wait for a boat ride back to Naples. It was his second visit to the strip, having also crash-landed there on January 28 after being hit by ground fire.

The emergency strip had proved to be a godsend for Scheumack and Sirman, as it would for several other 79th pilots during the remainder of the campaign, but it wasn't lucky for Lieutenant Alwayne Dunlap. Dunlap, from Fort Wayne, Texas and a pilot with the 99th Squadron, was killed while attempting a wheels-up landing there on February 21. With his P-40 spewing smoke, Dunlap overshot the runway, stalled out in a turn at 500 feet, and crashed and burned. Eight days later the 99th would lose another pilot when George McCrumby pulled out of his formation near Gaeta Point, radioing that he had engine trouble and was heading for home. When he didn't show up, Colonel Bates personally led a search mission, but McCrumby was never seen or heard from again.

Because of the great political significance he attached to the elimination of the Anzio beachhead, Hitler urged Kesselring to try another counterattack. Kesselring had misgivings, but grudgingly gave in, and ordered Mackensen to strike at Cisterna, the only area of the beachhead where the line had remained virtually unchanged since the beginning of the February 16 offensive.

On February 29 four German divisions pushed down the Cisterna road in a blinding rainstorm to smash once again at the battered and weary warriors of the US 3rd Division. Again, it was touch and go until the enemy advance began to crumble under the pounding of 3rd Division artillery. On March 2 Mackensen was compelled to halt his drive. Four days later Kesselring explained to Hitler that a continued assault would needlessly waste manpower and material; that it was better to consolidate what they had and prepare for the big Allied push that was sure to come in the spring. Disappointed, *der Führer* agreed, and allowed Kesselring to go over on the defensive. Five divisions were left to hold the ring around the beachhead, while the rest withdrew to prepare for another day.

Both sides exhausted, and each with twenty-two divisions in Italy, now settled down to wait for dry weather. Although there was constant patrolling action, and men died each day, there were no major ground operations on the Italian peninsula – with the exception of Fifth Army's assault on Cassino in mid-March – for the next two months. The enemy worked to strengthen his fortifications along the Gustav Line, while at Anzio the Allies continued to pour material and supplies ashore in an unloading operation that would make that port the fourth largest in the world by the end of March.

eleven

Cassino, Strangle and Rome

"The little fellows (the fighter-bombers) were remarkably successful against bridges . . ."

– Lt.-General Ira Eaker

The three corps of the main Allied Fifth Army – British X, US II, and the French Expeditionary Corps – had been hammering away in a gallant but futile effort to crack the Gustav Line since early January. Their objective was to draw German reserves away from the Anzio beachhead (which they did, at least during the initial hours of the invasion), open up the Liri Valley and link up with Lucas' seaborne force. That they were frustrated in their attempt to pierce the Gustav Line was due in part to horrendous weather, but mainly because of the skillful use the enemy made of terrain features behind the town of Cassino.

Cassino, and the historic, centuries-old Benedictine Abbey on the massive heights of Monte Cassino a few miles to the north, was the very heart of the German defense line across central Italy. The Abbey especially, thought to be filled with irreplaceable art treasures and valuable artifacts, commanded the entrance to the Liri Valley and dominated the approaches to the Rapido River. German units manning these heavily-fortified positions were the elite troops of Generalleutnant Frido von Senger und Etterlin's XIV Panzer Corps, tough, hard-nosed veterans who didn't panic or crack easily, and who were among the best in the entire German army. Utilizing the rugged terrain and "German weather" to their best advantage they proved true with painful clarity the old military axiom that "whoever is master of the hill is also master of the valley."

When the Fifth Army offensive against the Gustav Line began on January 12, small gains were made on both sides of the Cassino sector – by the French through the mountains on the right flank; the British near the coast on the left. But although some local success was achieved, casualties were heavy and the arrival of German reinforcements from Rome blunted the drive. When II Corps failed to bridge the rain-swollen Rapido River after three days of extremely savage fighting that all but decimated the 36th (Texas) Infantry Division,* the Allied offensive was stopped dead in its tracks. For the next three weeks the main Fifth Army front stagnated into a series of artillery duels and small unit skirmishes in the shadow of Monte Cassino.

On February 11 General Freyberg's New Zealand Corps, consisting of the 2nd New Zealand Division, 4th Indian Division, and the British 78th Infantry Division, began to relieve US II Corps in the center of the line. A few days later these fresh troops would attempt a renewed assault straight up the steep slopes in front of the Benedictine Abbey. First, however, Freyberg insisted the historic buildings be bombed.

Freyberg believed the Abbey was being used by the enemy as a fortress and observation post. Whether or not he was correct in this assumption has never been ascertained and is still a matter of controversy; the Germans insisted they never occupied the building, and investigation by the Vatican afterwards seemed to bear this out. In any event, Freyberg had his way and the bombing caused considerable anti-Allied feelings throughout Italy and made fine grist for the German propaganda mill.

Precisely at nine o'clock on the morning of February 15 the first wave swept in over the Abbey to herald the beginning of an aerial onslaught that would continue throughout the remainder of the day. Altogether a total of 254 medium and heavy

* The 36th Division was a Texas National Guard division, and in the eyes of many Texans the battle of the Rapido, which cost the division 1,681 casualties in three days, is an event as memorable as the stand at the Alamo. The Rapido debacle created much controversy, and "it is almost indisputable that Mark Clark failed to become chief of staff of the American Army [after the war] because so many Texans were slaughtered on the banks of that obscure river."[1]

bombers unloaded 576 tons of high-explosives over the target. Between air raids Allied artillery fired into the rubble, further churning up the ruins. Then the NZeds and the Indian Division attacked.

The assault was beaten back with comparative ease. German paratroopers discovered that the ruins made an excellent defensive base and used the rubble to their best advantage. The next day medium bombers again pounded the Abbey, and again Freyberg's foot-sloggers attacked, this time with fighters strafing and dive-bombing in front of them. Again the attack was repulsed. After four days only a small bridgehead had been gained over the Rapido and about a third of Cassino town. The German was still master of the hill. For the next few weeks ground activity along the Gustav Line was limited as both sides regrouped and planned for future operations.

Ancient and historic Monte Cassino erupts with great gouts of smoke as it is heavily pounded by Allied airpower. (National Archives)

The failure of the Allied armies in Italy to break the stalemate greatly worried London and Washington. The possibility that the enemy might wipe out the Anzio salient was far from remote, and the stalemate might even affect long-range strategy by forcing the postponement of OVERLORD scheduled for May or June. Further, because the troops now fighting at Anzio had been earmarked for an invasion of southern France in conjunction with OVERLORD, and because there were not enough landing craft in the Mediterranean to support both VI Corps south of Rome and a landing on the French Riviera, the assault on the south of France might have to be canceled entirely.

Field Marshal Sir Henry "Jumbo" Wilson, the Supreme Allied Commander in the Mediterranean, wanted to scratch the southern France invasion in favor of extensive operations on the Italian mainland designed to contain the maximum number of enemy divisions with the resources available. He wanted to keep the pressure on the German Fourteenth Army at Anzio and use his airpower to disrupt the enemy's lines of communications, thereby making the maintenance of a German line south of Rome impossible.

General Henry "Hap" Arnold, the Commanding General USAAF, had other ideas. He believed that up to now Allied airpower in Italy had not been used to its full potential – had been thrown into battle in a sporadic and piecemeal fashion on behalf of the ground campaign – and he favored a true mass air assault; a "blitz" in the manner of El Hamma, only many times larger. Arnold urged Lt.-General Ira Eaker, who had succeeded Tedder in January as head of MAAF, to use every heavy and medium bomber in the theater to break the stalemate by blasting a path at Cassino through which the ground forces could exploit.

Among those who disagreed with Arnold's plan was Brigadier-General Gordon P. Saville, the fiery and outspoken head of XII Air Support Command whose planes would be involved in the operation. He doubted it would work, adding that it had been tried before on February 15 with unsatisfactory results. Saville asked to be relieved of his command, "refusing to be associated with a plan that was so mind-boggling stupid."[2] His criticisms were rejected (Eaker sent him on leave to Algiers) and "Jumbo" Wilson was ordered by the Combined Chiefs of Staff to proceed with a new offensive involving a mass air attack as soon as weather permitted. It was left up to Wilson to decide whether to apply the air strike at Anzio or at Cassino. Wilson chose Cassino.

New Zealand infantrymen wait in the rubble of Cassino town before moving up the slopes of Monastery Hill. (National Archives)

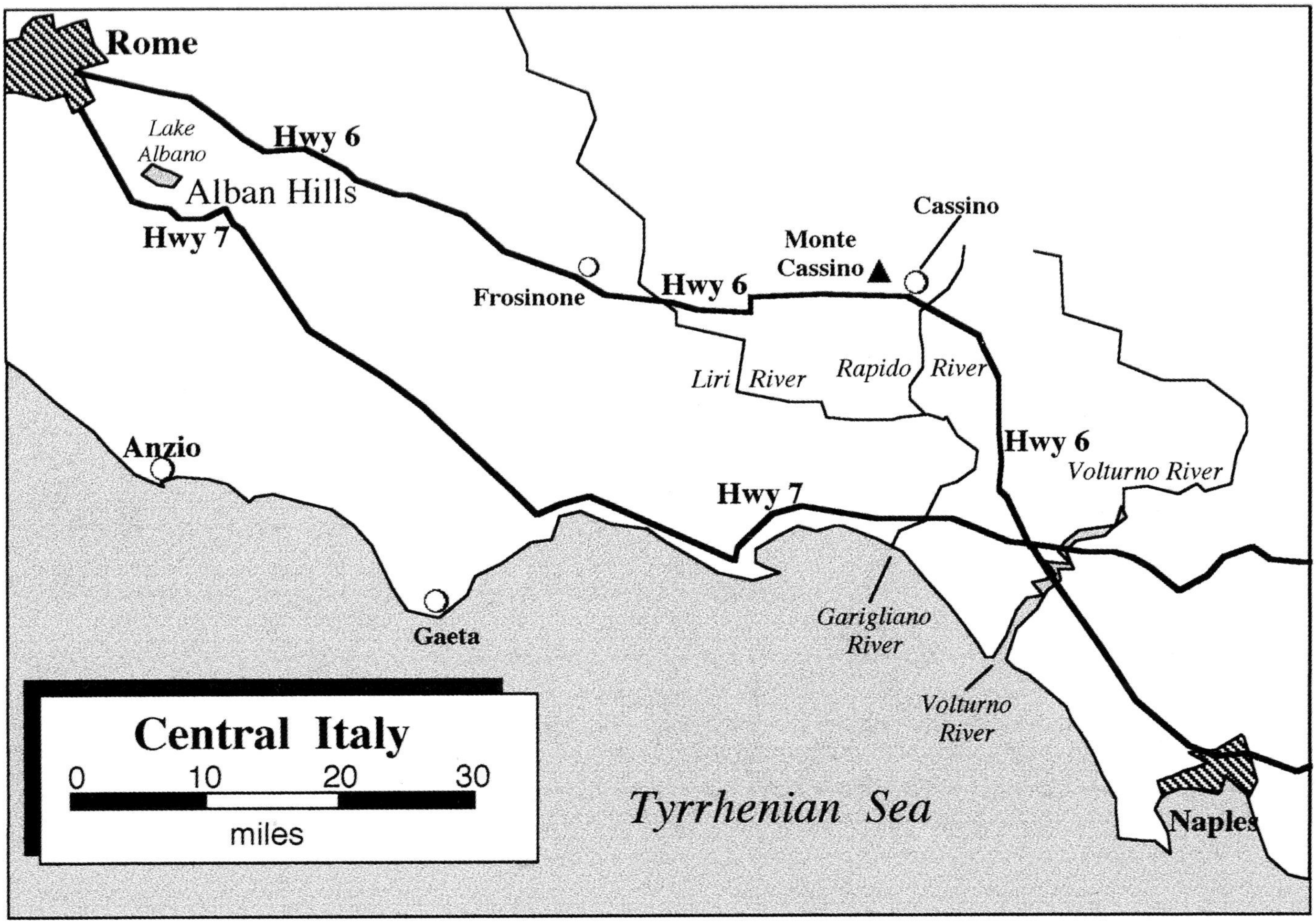

For this second battle of Cassino five groups of medium bombers and eleven heavy bomb groups would flatten the town of Cassino in one overwhelming air assault lasting from early morning until noon. As soon as the last bomber passed overhead the NZeds would move in on the town from the north, seize Cassino and the nearby high ground, and set up a bridgehead over the Rapido River. The 4th Indian Division would capture the Monastery and cut Highway 6, while the remainder of Fifth Army poured through the gap into the Liri Valley. All that remained to start the operation was the right set of weather conditions: the ground had to be dry enough to support tanks, and the skies clear over both the target and the bomber bases near Foggia, Naples, and in Sardinia.

On March 15 the overcast skies broke. The first bombers appeared over the Cassino front on schedule, and for the next three and a half hours spilled more than 1,000 tons of explosives over the already shattered Abbey and the town of Cassino. As soon as the last bomber wheeled away from the target 748 guns opened up with a tremendous barrage, firing no less than 195,969 shells against the enemy strongpoint over the next seven hours.

As the artillery barrage began to creep forward the NZeds moved out behind their armor. They promptly ran into trouble. As Saville had predicted, the bombing had filled the narrow streets of Cassino with rubble, and the tank force was stopped. The infantry hardly fared better. As was the case on February 15, they were again slow to exploit the air attack and this hesitation gave the German defenders time to recover from the initial shock and take up positions amid the ruins.

By mid-afternoon the skies again closed in, canceling a scheduled air attack by the mediums and heavies that would have kept the enemy pinned down as the NZeds attacked. A few fighters and fighter-bombers – including a few from the 79th – did, however, manage to slip in under the overcast to blast the railway station at Cassino and work over the slopes of Monastery Hill, and with their help the NZeds were able to make small gains despite strong resistance. By nightfall they were into the northern outskirts of Cassino.

That night the rains came, turning every bomb and shell crater into a miniature lake. Again the advance was stopped. For over a week the New Zealanders battled stubbornly to reach the top of Monastery Hill, and each time the enemy just as

Their war was one of repetition and boredom; dull, monotonous work that required a special kind of courage. Group armament men loading P-47 machine-gun belts. (USAF)

Captain Risden Wall led eight Comanche Thunderbolts on an uneventful patrol over Anzio on March 9. It was the Group's first mission with the "Jug." (Church)

stubbornly pushed them back. By March 23 the Allies held most of the town of Cassino and some of the high ground around it, but had not reached the Abbey. The attack was called off. The breaching of the Gustav Line would have to wait for drier weather.

Eaker's Mediterranean Allied Air Forces had done its job well. In fact, it had done it too well. Large craters blocked the roads and the rubble offered numerous positions for enemy strongpoints. Allied commanders were hopeful in the beginning that the bombing might achieve a breakthrough as it had at El Hamma. But Cassino was not El Hamma, and it was vividly demonstrated that against certain types of targets air attacks on such a large scale actually helped the defenders.

When the German counterattack at Anzio ground to a halt in late February, the tempo of air activity over the salient diminished to some extent. The 79th continued to fly defensive patrols over the beachhead – bombing and strafing ground targets as the entered and left the sector – but the front was nevertheless relatively quiet. German flak and ground fire, however, plus the normal hazards of flying over mountainous terrain in weather that was less than ideal, kept the pilots from becoming bored.

The Skeeters lost an airplane but not the pilot on March 6 when a flak-crippled Warhawk crashed at Capodichino, and Robert Laird of the Flying Skulls pranged his bird the next day when forced to make an emergency landing at San Severo, home-drome of the Spitfire-flying 31st Fighter Group. That same day, Glenn Lyans, a Comanche pilot from Madison, Wisconsin with over ninety missions in a P-40 dubbed *The Guinea Barber,* was seriously injured while on a P-47 transition flight – his engine conked out on takeoff and he went in from 200 feet. That was also the day General Cannon put on a one-man "show" when he made a spectacular landing at Capo in a smoking A-36. Crash crews raced to the scene, but didn't know who the pilot was until the general stepped off the wing.

On March 8, in what would prove to be the last mission for the Flying Skulls in the P-40, Bob Duffield of Cleveland Heights, Ohio got shot up while strafing a truck convoy on the Appian Way. He and his wingman had just made three successful passes over the trucks when he took hits in the engine, canopy, instrument panel and rudder controls. Nursing the faltering '40 up to 2,000 feet Duffield jumped – just seconds before it exploded – "landing in the only briar patch in Italy."[3] He was immediately picked up by three British Tommies in a jeep who delivered him to the American fighter base at San Severo.

Aside from the adventures of Laird, Duffield, Lyans and "Uncle Joe" Cannon, the big new for the Group during the first week of March was the arrival of P-47 Thunderbolts to replace their old and weary Warhawks. For the pilots and ground crews, the change was viewed with mixed emotion.

The P-40 had served well, but old age was catching up with it. At the time of Pearl Harbor the Curtiss P-40 and the Bell P-39 Airacobra were the Army Air Force's first-line fighters, but both were fast approaching obsolescence even as the carrier planes of Vice-Admiral Chuichi Nagumo's strike force swept over Battleship Row.

The Airacobra, plagued by an unreliable engine, a slow rate of climb, and utterly useless over 15,000 feet, was never popular with Air Corps pilots, and equipped only a handful of American squadrons; more than half of all P-39s produced were sent to the Soviet Union under the lend-lease program.

The Curtiss P-40, on the other hand, continued in service with American and Allied units throughout the war, fighting in every major theater of war under every possible weather condition, and it was employed in a diversity of roles. It couldn't climb and it couldn't run, and over 16,000 feet its performance fell off sharply. It was limited in range, the guns spewed oil, the cockpit was cluttered and noisy, and the ship required constant application of rudder to keep it straight and level. As one P-40 pilot remarked: "You couldn't outrun a Messerschmitt and you couldn't outclimb one. You had to shoot it down to get home, it was as simple as that."[4]

Yet, despite many shortcomings, including a tendency to ground loop, it also had virtues that made it a favorite with the pilots. It could absorb a great amount of battle damage and still get home, and it had good visibility. It could also turn with a 109, and more than hold its own in a dive. It provided a very stable gun platform, and its six .50-caliber machine-guns were generally more effective than the firepower of its opponents in the air. More importantly, it was the AAF's best fighter available during the critical early months of the war, and until Mustangs, Lightnings and Thunderbolts began rolling off American production lines it was the much-maligned P-40 that held the enemy at bay.

But now the P-40 was gradually being retired as second-generation fighters began arriving overseas for duty with front-line units. The Republic P-47 Thunderbolt was of this new breed.

In the summer of 1940, based on the air war then raging over Europe, the Army had asked aircraft manufacturers for an interceptor with a speed close to 400 mph, a ceiling of 40,000 feet, and heavier armed than the fighters (pursuits) then in production. Alexander Kartveli, an engineer with the Republic Aviation Corporation came up with a design for an eight-gun, 11,500-pound single-seat fighter powered by a turbo-supercharged Pratt & Whitney R-2800 Double Wasp radial engine. A contract was signed with the Army Air Corps on September 6, 1940 and eight months later the first prototype lifted off Republic's runway at Farmingdale, New York. The Army nodded approval, and the Thunderbolt was born.

As the bugs were gradually worked out of the experimental versions the first production models rolled off the assembly lines and were sent to Europe. There, as they entered the air battles over the continent during the winter of 1942-43, it was discovered that this brutish fighter originally designed to fight eight miles above the earth could survive on the deck as well. Stories of the P-47's ruggedness and durability – "she can fly through a brick outhouse and come out smelling like a rose" – became commonplace. Its ability to absorb and shake off battle damage that would prove fatal to a lesser plane, plus the tremendous firepower of its eight .50-caliber guns and the capability to carry everything, including the kitchen sink, made it a natural for low-level bombing and strafing missions.

Altogether more than 15,000 P-47s, the bulk of them "D" models, were produced during the war, coming off assembly lines at the rate of twenty a day during 1944. With the addition of paddle-bladed props and water/methanol injection systems the Thunderbolt became the first American fighter superior to any of its piston-engined adversaries. Weighing almost seven tons (three tons more than a fully-loaded Fw 190A) it could roll with amazing agility, was faster at all altitudes than either the 190 or the Me 109, and had no peer when it plunged into a dive. It was easy to fly in formation, and easy to land. It provided a stable gun platform and, unlike most of its contemporaries, the front office was roomy and comfortable, prompting some wag to comment that "evasive action in the P-47 was when the pilot got up and walked around inside the cockpit." It was truly the Cadillac of fighters. When going somewhere in a hurry it also guzzled gas at the rate of 350 gallons per hour, which explains why civilians back home were limited to just four gallons a week.

Awed at first by its enormous size, pilots liked the punishment it could give (and, more importantly, take) and were soon affectionately calling it many names: the Repulsive Scatterbolt, Thunder Mug, Bucket of Bolts, Big Ugly, the Cast Iron Beast, the Big Iron Bird, the Seven-ton Milk Bottle and perhaps more than anything else, the Jug (for juggernaut). The company that produced this behemoth was referred to with tongue-in-cheek as the Republic Locomotive Works and Iron Foundry.

By the end of January 1944 more than forty percent of all AAF fighter groups overseas were equipped with P-47s. The 325th Fighter Group became the first to do so in the Mediterranean when it phased out its checkertailed Warhawks in November 1943. The 57th followed suit two months later, and when two P-47s were assigned to the 79th in February everyone knew their relationship with the faithful P-40 was also drawing to a close.

On February 13 Colonel Bates and George Lee became the first to check out the hand-me-down T-bolts (the first ships assigned were D-6 and D-10 models inherited from the 57th and 325th) and for the next six weeks the Group began a difficult transition period necessitating long hours of training for both pilots and ground crews as the P-40s were gradually phased out and replaced by the massive Thunderbolts. The changeover from the P-40 to the P-47 was hard on both planes and pilots – "one guy dropped in so hard on landing that he drove the landing struts up through the wings"[5] – and cost the Group two pilots killed, in addition to seriously injuring Glenn Lyans, when Lieutenant Raymond Higgins, a Skull pilot from Gladwyne, Pennsylvania, spun in near Naples on March 11 during a transition flight, and Flight Officer Vincent Wall from West Haven, Connecticut was killed the same day in a landing accident at Venosa, Italy. Even without fatal consequences, the Thunderbolt could scare the hell out of pilots unfamiliar with its idiosyncratic ways. "While checking out in the '47 I ran out of gas in one tank while buzzing the field at 350 miles per hour," Louis Rouleau of the Comanches wrote his brother Dave. "The P-40 quits cold, but the Thunderbolt just kept backfiring and making a heckuva racket in general. There is a little window in the canopy which can be opened to let in air, but I didn't know it was there and it startled me when it opened by itself; especially since I was upside down at the time. It sounded like a subway train suddenly coming into the station."[6]

The Group's first mission with the new aircraft was on March 9 when Captain Risden Wall led eight Comanche Thunderbolts on an uneventful early-morning patrol over Anzio. Wall, who had transferred to the AAF from the RCAF in May 1942, said the T-bolt was easier to handle than the '40, but grumbled slightly that because it could stay in the air for a greater length of time missions were longer and more fatiguing. Ground crews also liked the P-47 because it was easier to maintain than the P-40.

The Skulls had ended their long association with the P-40 the day before, on the strafing show that saw Bob Duffield shot down, but wouldn't fly the Jug in combat until March 14, while the Skeeters were the last squadron to make the change (the 99th never flew the P-47 while attached to the 79th) and continued using both types until late April. *Ha-Gaa,* an ancient P-40L (X-86) was the last Warhawk to leave the Group. Crewed by Sergeant Pete Melonakis and last assigned to Lieutenant John L. Balega, it had an impressive record of 462 hours in the air.

On March 9, one plane from the 99th Squadron crash-landed at the Nettuno strip, the pilot was OK, and Lieutenant Hamilton of the same squadron was wounded in the leg. March 9 was also the day Lieutenant David Shuttleworth of the 87th was saved from an embarrassing wound when a shell fragment the size of an egg pierced the bottom of the seat he was sitting on and lodged in his parachute pack.

A new endurance record was set by the Comanches in their new P-47s on March 10 when they stayed over the target area for three hours and ten minutes. The mission was a routine patrol, flown without incident.

The Group celebrated one year (1,400 missions and 15,000 sorties) of combat operations with six fighter-bomber shows on March 14. The Luftwaffe joined in the festivities by bombing the Naples area that night. "At two a.m. the sirens blew and almost immediately the flak opened up. Tracers rolled lazily into the sky that was already lighted by a full moon and Kraut flares. The heavy stuff shook the house and rattled the window panes. Then the whistle of a falling bomb, endless,

Mount Vesuvius blows its top, and threatens nearby airfields with the same fate as Pompeii. (Lapin)

until the gratifying KRRUMPH and the realization the bomb missed. At night the whistle is lazier than by day, and you can't tell direction, size or amount. It's best to stay in bed because the shelter is crowded with civilians and it's not worth the false security that is promised."[7] Nuisance night raids over Naples were a fairly common occurrence. This particular one was carried out by seven German aircraft, and lasted three-quarters of an hour. Two bombs fell on the Vesuvius side of the field, destroying a P-39 and damaging another before the intruders were driven off by anti-aircraft fire.

The morning after the raid the 79th joined in the massive aerial assault on Monte Cassino, and also flew four beachhead patrols. Lieutenant George Bolte was leading a flight of twelve Skull Thunderbolts over Anzio when a British artillery shell tore the wing off his Jug. After a frantic struggle with a stubborn canopy he cleared the plane and his chute opened at 200 feet. British ground troops who witnessed the incident reported that Bolte made a definite thud when he hit the ground. The Cranford, New Jersey pilot survived the fall and had nothing but praise for the excellent spiked tea served up by the Brits.

Two days later Falcon pilots had a chance to see for themselves the P-47's worth in air-to-air combat when the Flying Skulls bounced a gaggle of dive-bombing Messerschmitts near Roccasecca. Captain Carl Stewart brought down one of the 109s – his third confirmed victory – while Charles DeFoor destroyed another, and Earl Maxwell damaged a third. All three pilots praised the P-47's combat performance, and particularly favored its great speed and firepower.

On March 23 Stewart and Johnny Martin made Group history when they each carried aloft a pair of thousand-pound bombs on a test flight, the largest load ever carried by a Falcon fighter. The experiment proved a two-thousand-pound bomb load was practical, but bad weather prevented Martin and Stewart from reaching the target and the bombs were jettisoned into the sea. That same day five Free French pilots of the Lafayette Squadron were assigned to the 79th to check out in the T-bolt, which they had never flown before.

During the Salerno days someone had jokingly suggested dropping a large bomb in the crater of Mount Vesuvius with the hope of inspiring an eruption. Now they had a chance to see what the fabled volcano could do without human help when Vesuvius belched mightily during the third week of March. The eruption, the first in thirty-eight years, lasted for four days before Vesuvius briefly quieted down, only to misbehave again on March 25, and sent smoke towering 20,000 feet in the air and great fingers of red-hot lava splaying down the slopes, while burning cinders fell like thick snow. Several small villages were crushed by the molten fire and nearby airfields were threatened. One airdrome, nestling against the side of the volcano, suffered the same fate as Pompeii as hot ash flowed down in ever-thickening layers to burn every bit of fabric off eighty aircraft before they could be moved. Other endangered fields were evacuated and the planes flown to Marcianise airdrome. As these squadrons bunched together on that already overcrowded drome they would have made an inviting target for the Luftwaffe. But a massive Allied air attack on March 18 by 373 heavies against enemy airfields at the head of the Adriatic claimed fifty-six aircraft destroyed on the ground, plus twenty-three downed by bomber gunners and seventeen by escorting fighters, and all but emasculated the Luftwaffe in Italy. The only area where enemy fighters challenged with any consistency was in the sector between Rome and Orvieto. And when the Luftwaffe mustered its strength it could still be a highly dangerous foe, as the Flying Skulls found out March 24.

Twelve Skull Thunderbolts were escorting a squadron of B-26s to Orvieto when a dozen 109s tried to lure the escort away from the bombers. The Messerschmitts pecked at them all the way to the coast, making only long distance firing passes, then moving out of range when the Skulls turned into them. High in the wings sat eight Focke-Wulfs ready to pounce on the bombers should the P-47s take the bait. But the Skull pilots were battlewise and stuck close to their charges. Finally, out of apparent frustration, the Fws made one desperate sweep through the Thunderbolt formation and headed for home. They didn't get to the bombers, but the Skulls were hurt. One Thunderbolt limped home shot full of holes; another had its radio smashed by a 20-mm cannon shell, and Lieutenant Ward Pringle of Chicago, Illinois was missing. Pringle, in X-15, and on only his

Captain Carl Stewart and his "shootin'-arn." After notching his third confirmed victory he had nothing but praise for the Thunderbolt's great speed and firepower. (Church)

third mission, was last seen going down from 16,000 feet trailing smoke and with two Jerry fighters on his tail.

On March 27 Lieutenant Herbert Anderson of Dixon, Missouri was killed when an 88-mm shell exploded in his cockpit as the Skeeters were returning from an otherwise uneventful Anzio patrol. The next day the same squadron lost Lieutenant William H. Rueschoff, and the 99th lost Lieutenant Edgar Jones. Jones, from New York City, was killed in a takeoff accident, while Rueschoff was killed when his Jug lost power in the landing circuit over Capodichino. He bailed out at low altitude and hit the ground with his partially-opened chute trailing behind him, and died on the way to the 70th Station Hospital. He was from St. Louis, Missouri. Two days later Rueschoff was buried in the Naples American Military Cemetery. "Standing bareheaded in the cold drizzle with the roar of A-20s overhead, the dreariness of war was felt by everyone. Italian workers were digging fresh graves – uniform slits in easily cut soil, the dirt piled high in even rows – as Lieutenant Rueschoff's flowers lay neatly on the ground beside his grave, interrupting the monotony of dirt and death."[8]

Captain Edward Byron polished off two Me-109s when the Skullmen were bounced on a bomber escort mission to Orvieto. (Church)

Orvieto continued to be one of the few targets in Italy that could still provoke enemy fighter reaction. On March 30 the Skullmen were riding shotgun to a squadron of B-25s when twelve pale-gray Focke-Wulfs with black spinners jumped the bombers over that city. Captain Carl Stewart, leading the Skulls in a P-47 named *West by Gawd Virginia,* quickly dampened the Germans' enthusiasm when he turned the 190 leader into a blazing ball of fire. Flying on Stewart's wing was Pierre Gouachon, one of the Free French pilots who had joined the Group a few days earlier. He got on the tail of another Fw, fired a long burst from dead astern, and the 190 went into a half-roll and fell down out of control streaming black and white smoke. The remaining Fws left as quickly as they had arrived.

No sooner had the Fws been driven off than a flight of Messerschmitts tried their luck. Gouachon damaged one while Captain Edward Byron, Jr., the Group Ops Officer, polished off two more; he turned the first one into a torch with a head-on firing pass, and shot the tail off the second from directly behind it.

Meanwhile, another Messerschmitt had come up unannounced behind Milo Klear and his wingman, Merlin "Elzy" Eltzroth, with all guns blazing. The Messerschmitt driver missed, overran the two American pilots, and suddenly found himself sitting in front of their combined sixteen guns. Eltzroth was handicapped by an empty belly tank that he couldn't shake loose, but Klear hosed off a few rounds and the German split-essed and was last seen going straight down through the cloud deck. Whether he made it home or not is anyone's guess, but because the clouds were full of large rocks (the Apennines) his odds weren't good.

As the last enemy fighter disappeared from view, and the bombers bid farewell and wheeled for home, the weather closed in with a solid undercast as far as the eye could see. With gas running low, the flight soon broke up into sections and it was every man for himself.

Stewart and another pilot made it back to Capo, and still another landed at nearby Pomigliano. Four more (including Ed Byron, Harold Land and James Scofield) flew all the way south to Taranto before finding a place to set down, and Pierre Gouachon wiped out his Jug when forced to belly-land in the mountains; he was shaken up, but safe. That left four pilots unaccounted for – Klear, Eltzroth, Matthew Purchla and Powell Scheumack. Over the next few days Klear, Eltzroth and Purchla eventually made it back to Capo after first putting down at emergency strips or landing grounds all over central Italy. Scheumack bailed out. He had two shells explode in his cockpit during the fight with the Fws, injuring his leg, and on the way home counted at least five holes in each wing. Low on fuel and with his plane badly damaged and starting to smoke, he decided to get out. "I'll see you guys in the funny papers,"[9] he said, rolled the Thunderbolt over on its back and dropped free. He landed safely and was picked up by two Tommies. The next morning, after having his leg treated by the British, he caught a ride back to Capodichino. This marked the third time Scheumack had had to jump out of a damaged or faltering aircraft. The first was in August 1943 while with the 16th Fighter Group in Panama when his engine quit while on patrol (he spent a couple of uncomfortable hours in his dinghy in shark-infested waters until picked up by a Navy PT boat); the second was in January 1944 shortly after joining the Group at Madna when he was knocked down by anti-aircraft fire near Ururi.*

The next day, March 31, Lieutenant Charles DeFoor from Ft. Meyers, Florida failed to return from his ninety-first combat mission. The Skulls were enroute to the Anzio patrol area in weather that was 10/10ths at sea level when DeFoor's Thunderbolt inexplicably rolled over onto its back and plunged into the water. Only an oil slick and a water-soaked map marked the spot where he went in.

It was also on March 31 that the 99th Squadron was released from operations with the 79th and rejoined the 324th Fighter Group at Cercola. Although the 99th had been promised Thunderbolts and bomber escort duty (which didn't happen until weeks later when it joined the Fifteenth Air Force's all-black 332nd Fighter Group), the black pilots were genuinely disappointed to leave. To a man, they felt that Colonel Bates was "conscientious, fair, and highly competent,"[10] treating them as equals by mixing squadrons on missions and giving all four squadrons identical assignments. When NAACP Secretary Walter White visited the Group on a fact-finding tour he noted the "total obliteration of consciousness of differences in skin color among both white and Negro fliers of the 79th Group . . . and evidence is strong that Colonel Bates avoided the pitfalls of the white liberal of the 1940s, the urge 'to do something for the Negro,' which could often be translated by blacks as doing something *to* them."[11] To make their parting a little less painful, the 99th threw a farewell party in downtown Naples attended by Colonel Bates and top officers of all four squadrons.

Following the failure of Fifth Army to breach the Gustav Line, and thus break the stalemate in Italy, Allied commanders began to consider using their superiority in the air to disrupt the enemy's lines of communications to the extent that it would deny him the means to resist a major ground effort. Air officers had been advocating such an operation for months, pointing to the successful interdiction campaigns in Tunisia, Sicily and southern Italy where only a fraction of the total Allied air effort in the theater had been utilized in that role. Agreeing that the Mediterranean Allied Air Forces should be used to its fullest capability the only difference of opinion among planning officers was over target selection. One faction wanted to concentrate on rail centers and marshaling yards; the other wished to strike against bridges, viaducts and other choke points in a quick, simultaneous cutting of all rail lines leading from northern Italy to the front.

Proponents of the latter argued that because of the mountainous topography, bridges, tunnels and viaducts were highly vulnerable to air attack, could not be easily by-passed, and were difficult to repair. They noted that studies also showed that bridge targets were more economical than rail centers, as it took almost three times the weight in bombs to block a marshaling yard effectively as it did to destroy a railroad bridge. Desert Air Force and XII TAC fighters averaged one hit for every nineteen sorties against bridges, while the mediums and heavies averaged one hit per thirty-one sorties.[12]

Those in favor of hitting major railheads insisted that locomotives, rolling stock, repair sheds and warehouses were conveniently concentrated, and that bridges were difficult targets to hit and not worth attacking.

A compromise was reached. Medium and heavy bombers would concentrate primarily on marshaling yards and repair facilities, while light bombers, fighters and fighter-bombers hit the rail lines leading south from the Po Valley. The entire effort, named Operation STRANGLE and scheduled to begin March 19, would be coordinated to strike the German rail transportation system simultaneously – yards, repair depots, bridges, tunnels and open stretches of track – forcing them to turn to the roads where they would become prime targets for Allied airmen.

During April the weather, although marginal much of the time, permitted the Group to fly on all but three days for a total of 168 missions – eighty-nine of them fighter-bomber shows, and about half of that number in support of Operation STRANGLE.

The Comanches had a particularly successful mission to Itri on April 4 when Lieutenant Herman Leuther led a flight of twelve P-47s through heavy flak and small arms fire to plant twenty-two of twenty-four 500-pound bombs squarely on target. That same day Louis Rouleau of the same squadron survived a freakish takeoff accident that had the potential for disaster when his P-47 struck the tail of a parked B-17, crashed into the bomber's cockpit, then slid on its belly to a crunching, grinding halt while its wheels and two five-hundred-pound bombs sailed menacingly through the air. The bombs landed near a cache of gasoline, but didn't explode, and Rouleau walked away unscathed.

In addition to the April 4 mission to Itri, the Group had other shows during the month that were equally impressive. Two stand out in particular: the Germans found themselves minus a railroad (electric engine, 20-plus railway cars, four

* Scheumack finished his tour in September 1944 after 113 missions. He stayed on active duty until November 1945, and on September 21 of that year (just one day short of his twenty-fourth birthday) he bailed out for the fourth time when the engine of his F-6D photo Mustang failed over Pine Bluff, Arkansas.

rail cuts and a power plant) after a visit by twelve Comanche Thunderbolts on April 14, and ninety-eight sorties in a Group effort against harbor installations at San Stefano and the marshaling yards at Orbetellow on April 28 effectively disrupted enemy traffic destined for southern Italy.

The Skeeters lost Lieutenant Robert Paul of Brooklyn, New York on April 6. The squadron was on a routine patrol off Gaeta Point when Paul dropped out of formation and was never seen again. The only hint of disaster was a green oil slick on the water. Another Skeeter pilot, Lieutenant Berning T. Edds of Freeport, New York, was killed April 21 when he spun in just north of Naples on a P-47 transition flight, and Lieutenant James Scofield of Susanville, California, a pilot with the 85th, died at the base infirmary of injuries received when he attempted to land with a hung bomb. The bomb release mechanism on a P-47 was simply a cable hooked to clamps on the bomb shackles under each wing. When activated by the pilot (a T-handle left of his seat), the cable not only released the bombs it also pulled the safety pins on the nose and spinner, thus arming them so they would explode on impact. A hung bomb was bad enough; Scofield's situation was made worse because the bomb stayed on but the safety pins pulled out and the bomb was live. Advised by the rest of his flight to bail out, Scofield elected to land. When he touched down, the bomb exploded.

On April 15 the 79th set a new world record when three Comanche Thunderbolts each hauled a pair of 1,000-pound bombs and a 500-pounder to targets in the Cassino area. A check with AAF officials and Republic Aviation representatives revealed that although the big aircraft had carried loads of equal weight in trial flights, this was the first time a P-47 had taken a 2,500-pound ordnance load on a combat mission.

On April 18 Captain Saverio Martino was leading a flight of twelve Comanches against a railroad bridge when eight Fws were sighted over Lake Bolsena. Six of the 190s immediately fled north while the remaining two turned into the Comanches. Risden Wall sent one crashing in flames, while Lieutenants Bill West and Ray Hagler teamed up to finish off the other. The two victories brought the Group's total to 115 enemy aircraft destroyed in the air, but the victories were bittersweet. While the Focke-Wulfs were being dealt with, the rest of the flight had continued in its bomb run and Lieutenant Don Mulkey caught a burst of flak over the target that set his plane afire. It went into a split-s from 4,000 feet and crashed before the St. Louis pilot could get out. Six days later, on April 24, Lieutenant Frank Burch of the same squadron was injured in a takeoff accident when his plane crashed into an A-20 parked alongside the runway. Yet another pilot was injured in an accident on April 28 when Lieutenant Peickert of the Skeeters lost power on takeoff and crashed, suffering second degree burns. A few moments later a B-24 attempting to land at Capodichino spun in, killing all on board.

Eighteen times during April the 79th's pilots were called upon to escort medium bombers hitting STRANGLE targets near Orvieto, Perugia and Viterbo. Three times they were challenged by the Luftwaffe as they shepherded their charges over hostile territory. Again, as in the past, not a single bomber under their protection fell victim to enemy fighters.

In addition to the bomber escort shows, the Group also continued its daily support of STRANGLE during April by working on the railroads and hitting other transportation targets. Bridges and tunnels especially, were prime targets. Learning from experience, the pilots soon discovered that instead of a miss being as good as a mile, against bridges with concrete foundations a near miss was not only as good as a hit, it was usually better. A direct hit, even with a thousand-pounder, would do little permanent damage, but a near miss buckled the foundation the same as a near miss buckles the plates on a ship. Dive-bombing procedure was simple: dive on the target at a fairly steep angle (using the gun sight to aim), beginning a smooth pull-out when passing through 1,500 feet. When the target disappears under the nose, toggle the bombs. To discourage ground gunners it was standard procedure to hose them down with .50-cal. machine-gun fire during the latter stages of the dive. "If you pulled up steeply into a somewhat inverted position you could usually see the bombs hit and explode."[13]

A near miss also worked well against tunnels, causing them to collapse, or sealing the entrance. But tunnels weren't easy targets because they were located in very difficult, mountainous terrain. They could also bite back, as would sometimes happen when a bomb with a delayed fuse hit the face of the mountain a glancing blow and bounced back up into the path of the aircraft, or exploded beneath it.

Against road targets, missions would take off at dawn and dusk to catch the truck convoys as they were pulling off the roads to hide during the day, or forming up to travel by night.

On May 1 the Group moved eight miles across town to Pomigliano airdrome at the base of Mount Vesuvius. Once the home of the Alfa-Roma aircraft factory, Pomig was much like Capodichino in that it was an established, permanent base. It differed, however, by featuring better crew quarters (apartments again, but pilots lived two to a room) and an exceptionally long concrete runway.

It was while preparing to move to Pomigliano that Colonel Bates left for the States for a short leave before returning to Italy to take command of the 86th Fighter Group. He had been with the 79th from the beginning, assuming command after

Peter McGoldrick was killed in Egypt in November 1942. Not content to fly a desk, Bates had ninety missions at the time he left the 79th on April 24. His place was taken by Colonel Charles W. Stark of Orlando, Florida who had been flying with the 79th since early April.

Stark was a veteran career officer and graduate of West Point Class of '37 who had previously been with Headquarters, XII Air Support Command. An aggressive commander who ran a tight ship, he was not universally loved by his pilots. Many felt they were being treated like cadets because he soon had them scrubbing the walls of their rooms and performing other housekeeping chores. Even more unpopular was Stark's view on bombing. "To improve our accuracy, he thought it would be a good idea to lower the bomb-release altitude to 1,000 feet, then 500 feet," Merlin Eltzroth said. "This scared hell out of nearly everybody, including me, since those big [thousand-pounders] could fling shrapnel and debris a lot higher than that."[14]

Stark's theories about bombing notwithstanding, the 79th's ground crews were working eighteen hours a day to keep their planes in the air as the long awaited Allied spring offensive drew near. Pilots were airborne over enemy targets thirty out of thirty-one days during May, and racked up an enviable record. As a result of the heavy schedule, however, losses were the highest for any month to date, and one of the highest for any month during the 79th's entire wartime tour. During the first eleven days of May, as Operation STRANGLE was winding down, the Group lost five pilots.

Colonel Stark and Lieutenant Merle E. Stafford of the Comanches both got into serious trouble on the same fighter-bomber show to Fabro on May 7, and both ended up prisoners of war. Stafford's woes were caused when he dropped his belly tank and instead of falling clear it hit the tail of his P-47, causing it to tumble out of control. Stafford bailed out and was captured.

Stark's troubles began when his Thunderbolt was hit by flak, although some believe (wishful thinking, perhaps) that his own bomb blast may have done him in. When his "lead sled" quit flying he put it down in the surf north of Lido di Roma near Anzio. He managed to evade capture for two days before taken prisoner by an Italian bicycle patrol and turned over to the Germans. After being thrown in the cooler (solitary confinement) for a couple of weeks he was questioned at length by Hanns Scharff, a master interrogator who had a reputation for making prisoners talk without resorting to threats or violence. Stark was one of only a handful of American fighter group commanders captured during the war and eventually became the senior Allied officer at Dulag Luft, the transient

Lt. Louis Rouleau of the Comanches survived a freakish takeoff accident on April 4 when his P-47 struck the tail of this parked B-17, crashed into the bomber's cockpit, then slid on its belly to a grinding halt as its wheels and two 500-pound bombs sailed menacingly through the air to land near a cache of gasoline. (Rouleau)

POW camp for Allied airmen at Wetzler, Germany established specifically for the interrogation of downed airmen. The idea was to bring in the POWs, interrogate them, and send them to permanent camps elsewhere.*

After Stark was shot down, command of the 79th went to Major Melvin Nielsen who had been Deputy Group CO since mid-March. Before that, he was 86th Squadron commander, having taken over from Fred Borsodi in October. When Nielsen was appointed Deputy Group CO, his spot in the 86th was filled by Captain George W. Ewing. Nielsen was from Idaho Falls, Idaho and had attended Stanford University before being commissioned in 1941. His older brother, Lt.-Colonel Ariel Nielsen, commanded the 350th Fighter Group on Corsica.

On May 9 Lieutenant Lawrence Borsheim was shot down and taken prisoner after he and the Skulls encountered eight enemy fighters over Rome, and Lieutenant Maurice Wilson, a Comanche pilot from Kansas, was killed attempting a crash landing. The next day Lieutenant Frank J. Seres was also killed near Rome after being hit by ground fire.

By the first week of May preparations for renewing the Allied offensive against Rome were almost complete. While Mediterranean Allied Air Forces had been hammering German rail and road targets steadily during the six weeks of STRANGLE

* According to Scharff, Stark was picked for the job because of his manners, straight-forwardness, military bearing and personality. Because of Stark's rank he was given "ever-so-slightly" preferential treatment which resulted in a 1948 investigation of his conduct. Scharff testified that during his imprisonment Stark "behaved as would be expected of a West Point colonel," and no charges were ever filed. Stark never found out who pointed the finger at him, or why. During the Korean War he commanded the 6131st Tactical Support Wing, and the 8th Fighter Bomber Wing in Korea, and later the 43rd Air Division in Japan. He retired in 1961.[15]

– flying 50,000 effective sorties and dropping some 26,000 tons of bombs – Army ground planners had not been idle as there were a myriad of planning details to attend to before the big push could get underway.

Allied Intelligence had identified twenty-four German divisions in Italy. Five were under Generalleutnant Gustav Adolph von Zangen garrisoning the northern cities; seven under Mackensen surrounding the Anzio beachhead; and the rest belonging to von Vietinghoff's Tenth Army along the Gustav Line.

Alexander had three options: 1.) hit both fronts – Anzio and Cassino – simultaneously, 2.) break out of the beachhead first, followed with an attack against the Gustav Line, 3.) make his primary effort near Cassino with the beachhead breakout a secondary operation.

The first option was turned down because a simultaneous assault on both fronts would split and weaken Allied airpower, and the second plan was rejected because it was doubtful if an offensive near Anzio could induce von Vietinghoff to move troops out the south. Alexander therefore chose to make his major effort at Cassino.

He moved Eighth Army (leaving only one corps to defend the quiet Adriatic sector) across the Apennines where it took over from Fifth Army at Cassino. This would be his main striking force, with the primary objective to break through the Gustav Line at Cassino and advance up the Liri Valley toward Rome as quickly as possible. At the same time, Clark's Fifth Army would mount an attack along the southern side of the Gustav Line, and both attacks would then continue to advance with heavy air support until seriously checked or forced to pause to regroup. It was hoped this would force Kesselring to withdraw troops from the Anzio sector to reinforce von Vietinghoff. Then Truscott's VI Corps could strike out from the beachhead and sever the principal German lines of communication leading south from Rome.

The operation was named DIADEM. D-Day was set for May 11, a date arrived at by figuring the time it would take to move the assault divisions into place, and a time when the moon would be favorable for moving troops and supplies at night just prior to the attack. The breakout at Anzio would come some time after D+4.

An hour before midnight on May 11, the more than 1,500 heavy Allied guns that were dug into the mud from the Tyrrhenian to Cassino began belching smoke, flame and destruction as the combined artillery of Fifth and Eighth armies heralded the spring offensive in Italy with a massive 40-minute barrage. Crouching beneath the continuous rumble of "outgoing mail" more than 100,000 shock troops – Britons, Poles, Frenchmen, Indians, NZeds, Canadians and Americans – fidg-

Colonel Charles W. Stark (the Falcon)

Lt.-Colonel Melvin J. Nielsen (the Falcon)

eted nervously, adjusting and readjusting personal combat gear as they counted the slow minutes to H-Hour.

May 12 was exactly one hour old when these troops lunged out of their soggy positions and struck at the heart of the enemy's main defensive position in Italy. Right from the start everything went wrong.

The Polish Corps had been assigned to take the vital Cassino massif and abbey, but it ran into much heavier resistance than expected; ninety minutes into the battle the Polish battalions had one man in five either dead or wounded, victims of extremely accurate automatic weapons fire that continued to reap a deadly harvest throughout the long night. By dawn the situation in front of Cassino was completely muddled. Twelve hours later the Poles, badly mauled and far short of their objective, were pulled out of the fight to rest and reorganize.

The lack of initial Allied success elsewhere along the front was equally disappointing. The divisions of Lt-General Sir Sidney Kirkman's XIII Corps had painfully gained a precarious toehold on the north side of the Rapido, but only after much British and Indian blood had been spilled, while in the low coastal area that was the American sector the battle swirled indecisively for almost seventy-two hours. By May 15, after three days and nights of savage combat, Alexander was no closer to breaching the Gustav Line than he had been before the offensive began; the entrance to the Liri Valley and the road to Rome was still effectively blocked.

Then suddenly, and for no apparent reason at first, the Germans began to pull out of their positions in front of Cassino.

During the first three days of DIADEM Mediterranean Allied Air Forces swarmed all over northern and central Italy. The heavies went for rail yards and ports in the north, while the mediums and fighters hit targets in front of the ground troops. The fighters were directed by jeep-borne spotters on the ground (Rover Joes and Davids) who coordinated air/ground operations, and were especially effective as they blasted bridges, gun emplacements, troop concentrations, supply dumps and other enemy strongpoints. In addition, they so thoroughly worked over German supply routes leading south from Rome that von Vietinghoff's Tenth Army could only be supplied at night.

On the afternoon of May 13 Lieutenant Sam Rospo of Akron, Ohio was having his troubles. He was one of sixteen Comanche pilots cutting rail lines north of Cassino and he had an armed 500-pound bomb glued to his port wing that stubbornly refused to budge. Only a few minutes earlier he had watched in despair as squadron-mate Don Richer of Manchester New Hampshire went straight in with a hung bomb and now it was his moment of truth. He could bail out, and almost certainly spend the rest of the war behind German wire, or he could attempt a landing with the fickle 500-pounder still stuck to his wing – a form of aerial Russian roulette he didn't particularly relish.

In a last desperate attempt to dislodge the deadly missile Sam Rospo put the olive-drab Thunderbolt through every violent maneuver he had learned in 400 hours of flying – all to no avail. Then wingman Ed Lemmon moved in close, surveyed the situation, and decided to try to pry the bomb loose with his wing.

Rospo throttled back until he was mushing along just a fraction above stalling speed. Lemmon, flying what would prove to be a virtually indestructible P-47 called *Lucifer's Ghost*, inched in closer and closer, then warily jabbed his wingtip into the troublesome bomb shackle. Once . . . twice . . . three times he stabbed, then the bomb tumbled harmlessly away.

On the way back to Pomigliano Rospo, Lemmon and the rest of the Comanche flight were bounced by fourteen 109s and 190s. In the melee that followed two Messerschmitts and a Focke-Wulf were shot down, and three more 109s shot up, but Lieutenant Michael J. Slater of Cohoes, New York was killed and Lieutenant Robert Pepper was wounded in the shoulder. Captain Roger Files got one of the 109s and damaged another, while Lieutenants Robert Crawford and Malcolm "Pappy" Hayles bagged a 190 and 109, respectively. Robert Patin and Stu Bartlett, neither of whom would survive the war, each damaged a Messerschmitt.

Two days later, on May 15, it was the Skeeter's turn to tangle with the Luftwaffe. A flight led by Lieutenant David Shuttleworth was preparing to bomb a target north of Anzio when twenty enemy aircraft roared down on them from out of heavy cloud cover. The Skeeters quickly jettisoned their bombs and screamed to the challenge. When the short fight was over Lieutenants Damon Adkins and Walter Peterman, and Flight Officer Wilton Thompson each had a confirmed kill, while Adkins also added a probable to bring the Group total to 121 destroyed, twenty probably destroyed, and more than four dozen damaged.

Earlier that same day the Skeeters also ran a highly successful armed recce, surprising a truck convoy that netted them seventeen "flamers" and eleven damaged. Lieutenant John Winslow got all shot up, however, and while attempting to land at Pomig his Jug stalled, landed tail first, and nosed over on its back. Winslow was shaken up, but unharmed.

The reason behind von Vietinghoff's sudden withdrawal from the Gustav Line on May 15 was not as inexplicable as it first seemed. While the Polish Corps had been sent reeling back from its first rush against Cassino, and the Americans and British floundered under heavy fire along the banks of the lower Rapido, General Alphonse Juin's French Expeditionary Corps had been fighting like men possessed since the first hours of the offensive.

One of the factors that had long hindered Allied success on this bitterly contested front had been the lack of trained mountain troops. Now they had them in the form of the Moroccan and Algerian divisions under Juin's command. These men were seasoned mountain fighters who viewed the rugged terrain as an advantage rather than a handicap. They took to the mountains easily and their experience and élan, plus the natural desire of the French to wipe out the humiliation of four years of German rule, broke the back of the Gustav Line.

Within the first twenty-four hours of DIADEM Juin's Frenchmen, spearheaded by gourmiers (Moroccan irregulars), had vaulted quickly into the hills over ground the enemy thought impassable and had not fortified extensively. They overran everything in their path and by nightfall of the 13th had reduced the German division guarding that sector to a mere handful of effectives and gained the lofty peaks of towering Monte Maiola. Before them stretched the wide, broad expanse of the Liri Valley.

As Kesselring rushed reinforcements to plug the gaps in his line created by the French, other sectors were correspondingly weakened. The Americans, British and Poles began to advance once again, and slowly the Gustav Line crumbled. On May 15 Kesselring ordered Tenth Army to make a fighting withdrawal back to the Hitler Line* some eight miles north of the Gustav Line, and three days later the Polish standard flapped in the wind atop the churned-up ruins of the Cassino monastery. A few hours later, when British foot patrols linked up with the Polish Corps in the open country north of Cassino, the defensive network that had frustrated Allied commanders for better than four months was finally breached.

Now it was time to break out of the Anzio beachhead. Shortly after dawn on May 23 three divisions of Truscott's VI Corps moved through a drizzling ran to hit Mackensen's Fourteenth Army near Cisterna. After heavy Allied losses, especially in the US 3rd Division, a wedge was driven between Mackensen's troops and those in the south. Once again

Flying Skull pilots take a breather at Pomig. Standing (left to right) are Lts. Len Beckermen, Richard Long and Delmar Estes. Sitting: Jack Beeks, Bernard Mullin, Jay Gruver, Merlin Eltzroth, Harry Odle and Ed Evans with their mascot, "Jerri," sitting in front. (Odle)

Kesselring was forced to pull back, this time to the Caesar Line – a third defensive belt south of Rome that stretched from the Tyrrhenian coast north of the Anzio beachhead to the Alban Hills, and then wound its way through the Apennine Mountains to Pescara on the Adriatic. The Caesar Line is where Kesselring prepared to make a final stand below Rome. His "final" stand didn't last long. Truscott had Cisterna by May 25, and when the beachhead force joined up with elements of US II Corps above Terracina later that same day, VI Corps was once again part of the main Fifth Army. Five days later, with German forces disintegrating, the Texans of the 36th Division, punched through the Caesar Line.

Kesselring had done his best to deny Rome to the Allies, but when the Caesar Line was cracked he reluctantly asked Berlin for permission to give up the city. Three days later that request was granted and he began a masterful withdrawal that would continue for 150 miles up the Italian peninsula.

On the afternoon of June 4, 1944, just two days before world attention would suddenly shift to the cross-Channel invasion of northern France, Mark Clark's Fifth Army entered Rome amid throngs of cheering Italians. The first of the three Axis capitals had fallen. A few weeks later, in a special ceremony marking the occasion, the flag that had been flying over the White House on December 7, 1941 would be raised in front of Rome's equestrian monument to Victor Emmanuel II.

The spring offensive had cost the Allies over 40,000 casualties, but it succeeded in driving the Germans from southern Italy; forced the resignation of Marshal Pietro Badoglio (Ivan Bonomi, a prominent anti-Fascist politician would form a new government June 9), and had contributed heavily toward final Allied victory in Europe by tying down large formations of enemy troops that would otherwise have been used against Eisenhower's army coming ashore at Normandy.

* When the Allies threatened to break through the Hitler Line a few days later, it was renamed the "Dora Line" by the Germans to disassociate *der Führer's* name from certain defeat.[16]

But for overwhelming Allied air superiority the Italian campaign would probably have stalemated in front of Cassino indefinitely. In the final analysis, of course, it was the intrepid men-in-the-mud who took Rome, for airpower could not, and did not, achieve singular victory. Airpower did, however, so severely maul Kesselring's forces that the German soldier was close to complete moral and physical exhaustion. Moreover, airpower prohibited the enemy from massing his reserves or coordinating an effective counterattack – both of which were vital to any hope Kesselring entertained of halting the Allied offensive once it was unleashed. The contribution of the 79th Fighter Group to this end was considerable, but the price had been high.

The Comanches lost Lieutenant Louis Rouleau in a non-operational flying accident on May 16. A few weeks earlier the Brooklyn, New York pilot sliced through a parked B-17 while taking off and lived to tell about it. Now, on the 16th, he was killed when he unaccountably dived into the ground near Marigliano while slow-timing a P-47. Rouleau, whose father was a Navy flier in World War I, had sixty-five missions to his credit.

The next day the Skeeters lost two pilots – one for the duration, one for eternity. Captain Clarence Stevens was shot down on his twenty-first mission and spent the rest of the war in a German stalag, while Lieutenant Ray Ermis, an eighty-two mission vet from Fort Worth, Texas was killed.

On May 22 Lieutenant Edward Letzkus, a Comanche pilot, was on a fighter-bomber strike near Rome when his target suddenly blew up in his face. With his aircraft enveloped in flames from the bomb blast, Letzkus bailed out. He was seen to reach the ground safely, but was then dragged across a plowed field by his chute. When the rest of the flight swooped down low they saw his motionless body lying against a rail fence. At the end of the war he was still listed on the Group's records as missing in action.

The next day the Skeeters lost Lieutenant Robert Biting when a flight of P-40s whipped through his formation without warning, forcing the Quincy, Florida pilot to swerve suddenly to avoid them. He struck the wing of his element leader, Lieutenant Charles Logel, and bailed out at 200 feet. His chute never had a chance to open. Logel was killed less than twenty-four hours later when he attempted to leave his flak-damaged P-47 and struck the craft's tail surface. Three pilots gone in three days: one by bomb blast, one by mid-air collision, and another in an attempted bail-out. Proving once again there were a thousand and one ways for a fighter pilot to die.

By May 24 German rail lines in central Italy were so badly mauled the enemy was forced to rely almost solely on motor or horse-drawn transport to supply and reinforce his front line troops. Horses and mules were pressed into service to tow vehicles immobilized for lack of fuel, and even native carts were used to haul men and equipment. With his tactical situation deteriorating rapidly, and his harried troops being squeezed into an ever-narrowing pocket just south of Rome, Kesselring could not wait for the cover of darkness to haul his supplies – he had to take to the roads during daylight hours. As a result, Allied fighter-bombers had a field day during the last week of DIADEM. They created road blocks that forced traffic jams, which in turn were blasted to pieces in heavy bombing and strafing attacks. So great was the destruction of enemy road traffic that pilots' claims were at first thought to be greatly exaggerated; they probably would have been discredited if not later confirmed by advancing ground forces.

Setting the pace in number of sorties flown and bomb tonnage dropped were the three squadrons of the 79th. The period May 24 through June 10 proved to be one of the most fruitful in the unit's history.

The Group celebrated its 20,000th combat sortie on May 24 by setting an all-time, single-day record for any one fighter group by toggling 306,000 pounds of high-explosives on enemy targets. The ground crews worked feverishly re-arming and re-fueling to keep the Thunderbolts airborne as most pilots flew two or even three missions. Pomigliano was a beehive of activity. Runways and taxi-strips were clogged with arriving and departing aircraft – not only 79th aircraft, but those from other units based at Pomig, as well as air-evacuation C-47 transports that landed every thirty minutes bringing wounded ground troops to Naples – and numerous emergency landings by light and medium bombers unable to reach their own fields, or with wounded or dying crewmen on board, contributed to the general confusion. Late in the day a British Warwick almost curtailed base operations when it attempted a landing with one dead engine and crashed into the weather hut at the south end of the runway. The wreckage was quickly pushed aside, and the fast pace continued.

On May 25 the Skeeters fared well against both ground and air targets – on one mission they accounted for twenty-nine motor transport flamers and another forty damaged – but lost Lieutenants Robert Swenson and Garth Thornton while bombing and strafing in the Viterbo-Civita Castellana-Borghetto area. Swenson, from Hillsdale, New York, was on his twenty-third mission, while Thornton was on his fifty-third. He was from Shaker Heights, Ohio. Both pilots were still listed as missing when the war ended. Wilton Thompson, who had

Lt. Raymond Nystrum and crew chief at Pomig. Nystrum was an eventual one hundred mission man from New Jersey. He flew with the Flying Skulls. (Odle)

bagged a 109 ten days before, was wounded on the same mission that saw Thornton and Swenson go down.

A later mission that day attracted twenty aggressive Me 109s as the Skeeters were pulling out of a bomb run north of Rome. William Fuestal twisted and turned with four of them before he blasted one into a water-filled ditch; James Blassingham got another by using repeated head-on firing passes; Ferdinand Tichenor shot the wing off a third; Robert Noell turned another into a blazing torch, and Walter Peterman and Walt Favorite dueled with a flight of 109s for several minutes before the Jerries broke off and headed for home – not, however, before Peterman shot one up badly enough to make it doubtful the German ever got there. On landing, Blassingham discovered he had no brakes and ran off the runway into several barrels of gasoline. Fortunately, there was no explosion or fire, and he wasn't hurt.

The next day the Comanches had an outstanding fighter-bomber show south of Rome when they shattered a supply-laden train with sixteen direct hits, then wreaked havoc with a large truck convoy in two separate attacks. In one attack they left only seven German vehicles unscathed out of a convoy of sixty-five. Returning pilots reported during the post-mission debriefing that all of the trucks must have been loaded with fuel and ammo as everything they hit blew sky high, forcing them to swerve sharply to avoid exploding debris. They also got a bigger bang for their buck than expected when they hit the train. The partially camouflaged train was twenty cars long, and all twenty cars and the locomotive went up with an ear-shattering roar just as Lieutenants Romie Royse and George Huntsberger were directly over it. "Train parts were flying all around, but we both came through without a scratch,"[17] Royse said.

The Skeeters got into a fight with fifteen "bandits" while working on the railroads on May 27 – David Shuttleworth turned one into a cripple with a ninety-degree deflection shot, which discouraged the others who fled the scene – and two or three times during the latter part of the month "friendly" Spitfires made menacing moves toward flights of 79th Group Thunderbolts, forcing them to jettison their bombs. It was suspected they may have been captured aircraft flown by German pilots, but no one knew for sure, and no shots were ever fired. All it did was waste bombs, which may have been the point if the Spits were indeed being flown by Luftwaffe pilots.

On June 4 the Comanches shattered all records for a single squadron when they left 114 German trucks and armored vehicles smoldering on the roads north of Rome, while the Group's total score that day included 275 motor transport riddled by bullets, 154 of which went up in flames or were otherwise thoroughly destroyed. They also sliced rail lines, blew up an ammo dump, knocked out a tank, and destroyed a 20-mm gun position. They left the area north of Rome a mass of flames, which returning pilots described as a "huge forest fire."[18] On the negative side of the ledger, a Comanche pilot was missing but would turn up safe later, and Lieutenant Matthew Purchla of the Flying Skulls was seriously injured when his Thunderbolt, which had been damaged by flying debris over the target, struck a tree while he was attempting an emergency landing at Nettuno.

During the next six days the Group put up forty-three missions, all of them against road or rail targets. On one mission, on June 6, twelve Skeeter aircraft carried a ton of bombs each to "post-hole" the roads between Valentano and Gradoli. They scored sixteen direct hits, cutting the road in at least four places. Post-holing missions were not as spectacular as busting trains or strafing truck convoys, but it harassed the enemy and bottled up his motor transport, and forced him to use vehicles to haul dirt instead of men and supplies; it took up to forty truck loads of dirt to repair the damage caused to a road by one 1,000-pound bomb.[19]

It was also on June 6 that Lieutenant Charles Landers of the 87th was knocked down by flak near Tarquinia and captured, and Gordon Bell went into the sea thirty miles north of the Tiber estuary, where he was rescued by the crew of a 284 Squadron Walrus. Four other aircraft on the mission were damaged severely enough to relegate them to the boneyard. The next day Romie Royse of the Comanches was strafing northeast of Rome when he caught a 20-mm round in the engine. With two cylinders shot away, and losing oil, he nursed his Jug (*The Spook*) back to a safe landing at Pomig where the engine froze up just as he put it down on the runway. That same day another Comanche pilot, Ed Walsh, was knocked out of the air by ground fire but turned up safe twenty-four hours later dressed as an Italian peasant and brandishing a long rifle he had "liber-

Lt. James Blassingham of the Skeeters bagged a 109 on May 25, but almost "bought it" on landing when he discovered he had no brakes and ran off the runway into several barrels of gasoline. (Blassingham)

ated" while making his way back through the lines. Lieutenant Robert Richmond of the same squadron had a similar experience. He was shot down June 8, hidden by partisans for several days, then picked up by the British. He would rejoin his squadron on June 18.

On June 9 Lieutenant Stuart Bartlett, a Comanche pilot from Lapeer, Michigan, was killed when his P-47 struck a house while strafing near Foligno, and the next day the same squadron lost Lieutenant Bill West when he was seriously injured in a takeoff accident, and Lieutenants Damon Adkins and John Winslow of the Skeeters were killed. Adkins, from Oak Hill, West Virginia, was strafing at deck level in a valley north of Rome when he failed to pull up in time and slammed into the side of a mountain. Winslow was killed on a fighter-bomber mission to Orvieto when hit by flak. He was from Kansas City.

By the second week of June the rapidly advancing bomb line threatened to place all targets out of range of the Pomigliano-based P-47s and a move was imminent. Orders were cut sending the Group to an airdrome just south of Rome, and then canceled. It finally developed that Corsica would be the 79th's next operational base.

twelve

Corsican Summer

"God help your ass if you were a tail-end Charlie in the last wave. By then, those ack-ack guns were ready."

– General Chuck Yeager on strafing airfields[1]

During the Allied advance on Rome the main striking power of Fifth and Eighth armies (one Eighth Army corps had continued to fight alone on the Adriatic coast) drove up the Italian peninsula along a comparatively narrow front that stretched from the Tyrrhenian Sea to roughly as far inland as Highway 6. Now, as the Allies pursued Kesselring north toward the Gothic Line – a series of German fortifications running roughly from Pisa to Rimini that defended the Po Valley and the major industrial centers of northern Italy – the front began to expand laterally. Fifth Army moved up the west coast from Rome toward Siena, taking the vital port of Civitavecchia on June 7 and the airfield complex at Viterbo two days later. Eighth Army advanced northeast to Terni, Foligno and Perugia, with its primary objective the city of Florence. V Corps continued up the east coast and eventually rejoined main Fifth Army.

As the front widened the operational areas of the two Allied armies became more separate and distinct. It then became practical to divide operational control of tactical air units between two commanders, each responsible for air operations in support of a separate army. XII Tactical Air Command (of which the 79th was now a part) would support Clark's Fifth Army in the west, while the Desert Air Force covered Eighth Army in the east. But by now Fifth Army's bomb line was out of reach of Naples-based fighters and only a few airfields recently captured near Rome met the operational requirements of XII TAC. Consequently, it was decided to move the 79th to Corsica.

Only sixty miles off the Italian coast and a little over a hundred miles from southern France, the French island of Corsica had come under Vichy control early in the war and was garrisoned by German troops until they were driven out by a local revolt and regiments of the *Armee d'Afrique* (Africa's Army) commanded by General Henri Giraud in October 1943. Corsica, whose chief claim to fame was that it was the birthplace of Napoleon Bonaparte, was a beautifully rugged island, practically untouched by the advancing hand of civilization. It was composed of jagged mountain peaks, narrow, twisting roads, sandy beaches, and an unfriendly population. Being French, and traditional allies, one would have expected the civilians to be hospitable and friendly. Quite the contrary. They were coldly independent, sometimes openly hostile, and seemed to regard the presence of American airmen as even more disagreeable than the recent German occupation.

Aviation engineer battalions had begun repairing and improving the four existing airfields on the island immediately after the Allies gained control, and during the winter of 1943-44 several new fields were hacked out of the rough terrain. By the middle of April all three of Twelfth Air Force's B-25 groups, and the 57th and 350th fighter groups were nestled on Corsican hardstands. Now, in the second week of June, the 79th prepared to join them.

Early on the morning of June 11 a dozen olive-drab C-47 Skytrains thundered out of busy Pomigliano for the short over-water hop to Corsica. On board were some 300 men (ground officers, enlisted men and a few pilots) of the 79th's advance echelon. Two hours later they set down on a 5,000-foot slash of dirt on Corsica's east coast. This was Serragia airdrome, a crude fighter strip the engineers had recently carved out of a valley on the coastal plain some twenty miles south of the island's second largest city of Bastia. Within weeks it would become one of the largest fields the Group would operate from, and feature an extensive set of taxiways and revetments.* Planes and pilots arrived later in the day, just ahead of a violent rain squall that precluded any late afternoon missions, and the Group officially became part of XII TAC's 87th Fighter Wing. The 87th Wing controlled three groups – the 57th and 79th on Corsica, and the 86th in Italy – and was commanded by Brigadier General Thomas C. Darcey from his headquarters at nearby Vescovato.

Until the remainder of the 79th's personnel joined A-Party nine days later, living and operating conditions at Serragia were far from ideal. Short of personnel, short of equipment, short of supplies, and on short rations (the chow line was literally the traditional mile long) the entire party was uncomfortably quartered in a congested tent area among a grove of cork-oak trees about a mile from Serragia's north-south – and only – runway.

Uncomfortable they might have been, but once again they were in excellent position to lend their awesome firepower to Fifth Army's drive above Rome. Their deep-bellied Thunderbolts could now range over all of northern Italy as far as Milan and, if the on-again, off-again invasion of southern France ever became reality, they could easily support that operation as well. Early the next morning the 79th Fighter Group hung out its shingle and opened shop from its new base.

Starting June 12, and for the next five days, the Group ran thirty-three highly-successful fighter-bomber strikes against road, rail and bridge targets ahead of Mark Clark's advancing foot-sloggers – thirty-three 12-ship missions that thoroughly chewed up a large portion of Kesselring's transport system north of Rome, but marred by a pair of operational accidents that cost the Skeeters two good men.

Lieutenant William F. Pritchard, a Wilmington, North Carolina pilot just recently assigned to the squadron, was killed June 13 when his P-47 swerved off the runway on takeoff and struck a tree. One of the 500-pounders he was carrying exploded, killing Pritchard instantly and knocking personnel in the Ops tent off their feet by the blast that sent bomb fragments whip-sawing through the early morning air. Four hours later Lieutenant David Moss, a sixty-six mission veteran from Van Buren, Arkansas, died when he attempted an emergency landing with a hung bomb while landing at Alto, home of the 57th Fighter Group. At a critical moment on his approach the usually reliable four-bladed prop on his massive Thunderbolt failed. With a 500-pound bomb stuck to his wing,** and a useless propeller windmilling in front of him, Moss didn't stand a chance. The heavily-laden Jug sank like a rock, smacked into the ground, and disintegrated in a pillar of smoke. Moss died at once in the crumpled wreckage, and another P-47 parked nearby was blown into smoking chunks of torn and twisted metal by the fiery blast.

This sign mysteriously burned down one warm summer night. Those suspicious by nature pointed the finger at the 57th Fighter Group. (Lappin)

Falcon operations from Corsica had gotten off to a tragic start.

Of six missions flown against railway bridges and tunnels on June 14, three turned out to be "milk runs" (no flak, no fighters), two drew scattered, ineffectual anti-aircraft fire, but one not only put two direct hits on the approach to a bridge, but also shot up three patrol boats. The latter was an early-morning mission by the Skulls against a bridge at Pisa. Pilots were admonished not to hit the fabled Leaning Tower only a few hundred yards away – "don't bother coming back if you do, because you'll probably be court-martialed."[3] – but coming up on the target they spotted three fast-moving patrol boats heading south from Spezia, apparently trying to make Leghorn before full daylight. The pilots "very carefully" dive-

* Airfields on Corsica were named after rivers, fields, villages, a hill or a forest, etc. Serragia, which was located in the district of Castellare di Casinca, was named after a field. Today (1999) there is no trace that a large airbase once existed there, and of the seventeen airfields on Corsica used by the Allies in 1944, only five remain in service.[2]

** Until the bomb release was redesigned by a sergeant in the 16th Service Squadron (S/Sgt. Robert Perdue of Cedartown, Georgia), hung bombs were a major concern and caused the death of several pilots. The old release was located to the rear of the pilots' seat close to the floor. While dive-bombing the pilot had to grope for the release handle which was far below him while at the same time keeping his eyes on the target, one hand on the trim tabs, and the other on the control stick. If he didn't pull hard enough on the release a hung bomb was often the result. After the release was redesigned hung bomb were less frequent, but still occurred. Al Hearne of the Comanches had a hung thousand-pounder around the first of August that was pried loose by Fred Zilly in the same fashion that Ed Lemmon had pried a bomb off Sam Rospo's wing back in May.

bombed the bridge and then streaked for the boats. One got off a few 20-mm rounds before it was sunk, and despite a hastily-laid smokescreen that was too little, too-late, and anti-aircraft fire from batteries ashore, the other two were left burning brightly as the Skulls wheeled for home. Upon landing, one pilot found an armor piercing 50-caliber bullet lodged in the cowling of his P-47, obviously a water richocet from his own guns, or the guns of the guy behind him. Although the boats had been hugging the shore well north of the lines, at least one pilot on the mission afterwards had nagging doubts as to their identity – he feared they may have been "friendly" – but a check of records after the war reveal nothing to indicate that they were. The best guess is that they belonged to Mussolini's exiled fascist forces.[4]

All regularly scheduled missions were abruptly canceled on the morning of June 17 when operations were hastily diverted to cover the French landing on the nearby island of Elba. Only thirty-five miles from Serragia and eight miles off the Italian coast below Leghorn, tiny Elba was originally to have been seized by the Allies in a shore-to-shore assault during the last week of May. But Fifth Army's preoccupation with getting to Rome, plus command difficulties with the French (who would supply the landing force) caused the project to be temporarily postponed.

The island was garrisoned with over 3,000 German grenadiers under orders from Hitler to "hold to the last man and cartridge"[5] (probably because he associated the island with his hero Napoleon), but became untenable for the Germans, and held little tactical or strategic value for the Allies after the fall of Rome. Alexander wanted to cancel the entire operation, arguing that an invasion could serve no useful purpose. The French forces under Giraud insisted on taking Elba, ostensibly to secure a base for small naval craft and to install a landing strip and radar station on the island, but their underlying motive was to employ French troops against the enemy to prove their value to the Allies and help boost French morale.

On June 17, 12,000 French, North African and Senegalese assault troops waded ashore from landing craft towed to the beaches by motor launches. Overhead, Thunderbolts from the three groups of 87th Fighter Wing weaved a protective umbrella and swooped low to attack shipping, docks, harbor installations and gun emplacements. With the exception of a couple of wet, uncomfortable hours spent by Lieutenant Noel Sonnichsen bobbing around in a dinghy after his engine cut out on the 18th, the eighty sorties put up by the 79th during the three-day operation went off without a hitch. The Luftwaffe, much to every pilot's disappointment, failed to put in an appearance; anti-aircraft fire was almost non-existent (no one minded *that*) and by the afternoon of June 18, eighty-five-thousand-dollar Thunderbolts were being squandered in strafing runs against twenty-dollar rowboats. The next day the entire island was in French hands.

With Elba reduced and B-Party back in the fold, having rejoined the forward party earlier in the day after a stormy trip by LST and an equally rocky ride from the docks at Porto Vecchio to Serragia over primitive roads, the Group resumed its efforts over the Italian mainland on June 20.

Shortly after lunch Lieutenant Gordon AcMoody was taxiing out with a flight of twelve Skeeters to hit a road bridge when 87th Wing suddenly flashed a hot target. Reconnaissance aircraft had spotted the 20,000-ton *Aquila,* an Italian aircraft carrier now flying the German ensign, anchored in the harbor at Genoa. The carrier had been converted from the luxury liner *Roma* and was one of two flattops the Italians had been work-

Missions took off from Serragia from dawn to dusk bound for targets north of Rome. (Church)

ing on at the time of the September armistice. It had been swiftly commandeered by the German Navy, and when the sharp eyes of the reconnaissance crew found it beneath a heavy layer of camouflage netting at Genoa it was almost completely refitted and ready for service.[6]

The bridge-busting mission was quickly scrubbed and pilots re-briefed. Thirty minutes later, as every gun in the harbor came alive to fill the sky over Genoa with deadly shards of white-hot metal, AcMoody and company swept over the vessel at masthead height. They raked the carrier with .50-caliber machine-gun fire and showered it with a hail of 500-pound bombs. Two direct hits on the starboard bow; two more amidships, and another on the stern rent huge, gaping holes in the hull that spewed out black, oily pools of diesel fuel. Another bomb shattered the dock, and the *Aquila* rocked and bucked from many near misses that sent up great gouts of water.

Finally, their ammunition exhausted and bomb racks empty, the Skeeters sighed high and away for home. Behind them the ship shuddered violently from an explosion somewhere deep in her bowels. Eighteen hours later the *Aquila* was still burning fiercely, sending up a column of black smoke visible fifty miles out to sea.

At a cost of one shot-up but flyable P-47 and a seriously wounded pilot (Lieutenant Tom Hawk) the *Aquila* was out of the war. During the next several months the Germans worked to raise her battered hull from Genoa's mud, and by April 1945 they had succeeded in getting the carrier afloat and were preparing to tow it from the dock area to block the harbor entrance when word of their intentions leaked out. On the night of April 19, 1945 several Italian motor torpedo boats stole quietly into Genoa harbor in a daring surprise raid and sank the ship before it could be moved away from its berth.[7]

After the arrival of the remainder of the Group, camp life on Corsica began to improve. New squadron tent areas were situated three or four miles from the airstrip, and tents with canvas cots and mosquito netting were pitched in a converted vineyard. Some of the more innovative men constructed elaborate shelters from packing crates, belly tank containers and other discarded material. Washstands and showers were constructed; slit trenches dug (never used and invariably filled with water every time it rained); a public address system hooked up to broadcast news and music, and a baseball diamond leveled. A clear, cool mountain stream offered a place for relaxing and skinny-dipping (pilots could be picked out at a glance because their posteriors were red from many hours of sitting on hard parachute packs), and clubs were built for the officers and enlisted men. Opening a club, whether it be in a tent in the desert or an Italian villa in Sicily, was always the first order of business every time they moved to a new landing ground, and the Flying Skulls built an O-Club at Serragia that stands as the high point in constructive ingenuity for the unit's entire overseas tour. Fashioned from logs and bamboo, screened in and provided with tables and other furnishings, it also included a sofa and two easy chairs that someone had scrounged up. The club's interior was decorated with a parachute suspended from the ceiling, and featured indirect lighting achieved by placing light bulbs inside partially opened tin cans; electricity came from a large generator. A bar at one end was complete with running water from a propped-up 150-gallon wing tank, and a hack B-25 made periodic trips to Naples to keep it well-stocked.

Lt. Harry Odle of the Flying Skulls with S/Sgt. Ed Campbell, his crew chief, and armorer Sgt. Orion Jones. Odle flew ninety-six missions without a scratch, then got a 20-mm hole in his port wing on his ninety-seventh mission, and a similar-sized one in his right wing the following day. (Odle)

Lt. Ben Cassiday shows fellow Skeeters how he bagged a Me-109 on his first mission. Cassiday would finish the war with 116 missions and was the Skeeters' last wartime CO. His postwar career would include a stint as an exchange pilot with the Navy during the Korean War where he flew forty-three missions in F9F Panthers off the USS Philippine Sea. He retired in 1972 as a brigadier general. (Church)

Skeeter pilots in downtown Bastia where coffee, sandwiches and ice cream were available at a Red Cross club, and "it was an education in itself watching the girls operate in the bars." Back row (left to right) are Lts. Donald Aldrich, Frank Milstead, John Kittrell, Keith Croskery and John Balega, while Lts. Richard Cross, Ben Cassiday and John Cochran are kneeling in front. (Cochran)

The club attracted visitors from all over the island. When a P-47 taking off on a mission hit and demolished the B-25 as it sat empty on the far end of the runway, a Thunderbolt took over the liquor run, using special drop tanks to haul the precious cargo. An opening with hinged doors was cut in the side of each tank, and bottles were placed inside and packed with straw. A uniquely modified wing tank was also used to fly in fresh fruit and vegetables from Naples.

In Bastia the Red Cross opened a club that served coffee, sandwiches and ice cream to those able to get away from the base for a few hours. Officers also bought their rations in town, and idled away their free time ogling the local girls in the bars. "They understand English too well for us to talk behind their backs, but we sure have a good time watching them operate," Herb Woerpel wrote his brother shortly after joining the Skeeters in late July. "Since I've been going bareheaded my hair is getting more blond, and the other day some gal came up to me and ran her hand through my hair and called my 'blondie.' Then she spoiled it all by telling me that I looked like a German. I don't know if she meant it as a slander or a compliment."[8] Woerpel, a "blue-bar" flight officer from Marshall, Wisconsin, would later be killed over southern France.

Missions over the mainland of Italy continued daily. Squadrons conducted operations from tents near the runway, where pilots got a fast mission briefing and a quick look at the flak map before being taken by jeep to their assigned planes dispersed among the cork-oak trees. Chutes were issued and returned after each mission to a trailer for safe-keeping, and planes taxied to the south end of the runway and took off north regardless of wind direction.

After each mission pilots were greeted by Helen Ellor of South Orange, New Jersey, and Adele Davis of Washington, DC, who served coffee and donuts from a Red Cross mobile canteen.

On June 26 the Comanches were jumped by six 109s and a Focke-Wulf over Imola and claimed one probable and three damaged, but lost Lieutenant John H. Bothe. Bothe was killed when he tried to nurse his malfunctioning Thunderbolt back to Serragia, stuck with the plane a few seconds too long, and spun in too low to bail out.

Four days later, on June 30, twelve Skeeters were bounced by an equal number of 109s over Bazzano. While two of the Skeeters continued in their bomb run (scoring a pair of direct hits on a section of railroad track) the remaining ten shook off their payloads and belly tanks and turned into the Germans. In the short fight that followed Lieutenants Benjamin B. Cassiday, Jr. and David H. Shuttleworth each destroyed a Messerschmitt. Cassiday had just graduated from West Point the year before and was on his first operational flight. He was flying wing to Shuttleworth, a 116-mission vet who was leading the show. Shuttleworth shot one of the Germans off Cassiday's tail, and the novice returned the favor by prying a 109 off his leader's back. The rest of the Germans had seen enough fancy shooting for one day and scooted back up north.

The months of May and June had been two of the most productive in the history of the 79th. Flying over 4,000 sorties during that period they created havoc with the enemy's transportation network, sank an aircraft carrier, and knocked twelve enemy aircraft out of the sky. But it was not without loss. Thirteen pilots were known dead; four were missing, and four were known to be prisoners of war.

July witnessed more of the smooth-working cooperation and close-support for which the Falcons were noted, and on occasion they met the Luftwaffe in the air. One such encounter took place on July 1 when four 109s challenged a Flying Skull fighter-bomber show. Two of the bandits got nicked for their troubles when Lieutenants Richard Long and Cecil Bush ganged up on them, and Captain Eugene Kleiderer shot up another.

Bad weather plagued operations for the remainder of the week, resulting in spotty success, but missions were flown out of Serragia from dawn to dusk just the same. Independence Day was hardly noticed; chicken for supper that night caused more comment than patriotic discussion.

One July 5 the Comanches and Skeeters bombed and strafed a German headquarters building and bivouac area at Castelnovo at the request of Italian partisans with very good results – all bombs were in the target area and numerous fires were started – but Lieutenant Thomas Baker, a newly assigned Skeeter pilot, was shot up by flak over northern Italy the next day and forced to ditch at sea. He was promptly rescued by the Walrus crew.

Lieutenants Sam Rospo, Robert Ryan and Robert L. Patin were not so lucky. One of the most popular pilots in the 86th Squadron, Rospo was killed on July 11 practicing night flying. Two days later Ryan was shot down in a fight with five Me 109s west of Occhiobello, and Patin was killed when he crashed into a mountain on a routine flight. Rospo, Ryan and Patin were tent mates and had been inseparable buddies. Now, in less than forty-eight hours, all three were down. Rospo and Patin were dead, but Ryan would later make his way safely back through the lines. In the fight with the 109s, Major George W. Ewing, Jr. of San Antonio, Texas evened the score somewhat when he shot down one of the Messerschmitts.

During the next ten days the Group continued to run missions to Italy, and Serragia was a beehive of activity. A French-flown P-47 started a large grass fire when it crashed off the runway on July 14 (the pilot escaped unhurt); Lieutenant Elroy Roehrdanz was wounded in the arm while on a Comanche fighter-bomber show on the 17th and made a successful crash landing at an Italian drome; Lieutenants Martin Granberg and Bill "Red" Stalter (plus an unidentified pilot) each damaged a Focke-Wulf when the Skulls were jumped by five 190s while escorting B-25s to Ostiglia on July 19, and Don Urquhart of Medford, Wisconsin, a pilot with the 27th Fighter Group stationed on the other side of the field, was killed in a takeoff accident on July 20.

Lieutenant J. C. Beeks of the Skulls almost suffered a similar fate the next day when his engine cut out on takeoff. With his heavy Jug moving down the runway at close to 100 miles an hour Beeks quickly released both bombs safe on the runway, gingerly applied the brakes, and managed to keep the Thunderbolt right side up and in one piece in the ground loop that followed.* He finished his combat tour in October after eighty-nine missions and later flew DC-8s for United Airlines out of Chicago.

In December 1943 when Roosevelt, Churchill and the Combined Chiefs of Staff met in the shadow of Egypt's ancient pyramids on their way back from a summit meeting with Stalin at Teheran, it was agreed that the major Anglo-American effort in 1944 would be the invasion of Northwest Europe through Normandy in May or June, with a simultaneous landing on the resort beaches of southern France (Operation ANVIL) as a diversion.

ANVIL's assault battalions would come from Alexander's Fifteenth Army Group (Fifth and Eighth armies) then engaged in Italy. It was assumed that by D-Day his infantry and armored units would be pressing against the Pisa-Rimini (Gothic) Line where they would contain a maximum number of Wehrmacht divisions with a minimal force. Alexander should, it was thought, have little difficulty releasing the manpower required for the Riviera landing.

* In a ground loop one side of the plane would drop and the other wing and wheel would go up, and the plane would do a fast spin around (like a pivot) in one spot. Sometimes the plane would spin a half circle, sometimes a whole circle, and severe damage to it was almost certain.

But the Cairo planners hadn't reckoned with the iron will and military genius of "Smiling Albert" Kesselring. His stubborn resistance to the Allied advance up the mountainous boot; his tenacious stand among the scabrous peaks and behind the swollen rivers below Cassino, and his intimidation of VI Corps at Anzio-Nettuno quickly dashed whatever hope the CCS had of launching ANVIL concurrently with OVERLORD. With their timetable upset by the bitter Italian fighting, the British and Americans held another conference in late March. Again, they could not agree on strategy.

The Americans, thinking only of the fastest way to end the war, considered ANVIL a logical adjunct to the overall grand strategy of the Allies whose ultimate aim was the absolute defeat of Nazi Germany. The British, closer to the political pulse of the Slavic nations, and seeing clearly the problems that could arise from a Communist-dominated post-war Europe, wished to scrap ANVIL completely and advance from Greece, Albania or northeastern Italy into the Balkans to reach Budapest and Vienna ahead of the Russians. The Americans considered the problem purely a military one; the British had political as well as military objectives in mind. Unable to reach an agreement, and with the Italian front stalemated, the CCS temporarily shelved plans for Operation ANVIL.

After Fifth Army swept through Rome, and with Eisenhower now ashore in Normandy, these plans were once again dusted off. This time both sides agreed that a triphibious operation should be initiated somewhere in the theater to assist OVERLORD, but again they were divided over the specific objective.

"Jumbo" Wilson wanted to go ashore at Trieste. In his view only a landing at the head of the Adriatic, plus a continued vigorous prosecution of the Italian campaign, would draw German divisions away from the hedgerow country of northern France.

Ike wanted ANVIL. He desperately needed another port to sustain his drive to the German frontier. Cherbourg was already straining under the weight of material coming ashore; the Brittany ports were sure to be stubbornly defended and thoroughly destroyed, and Antwerp wouldn't be in Allied hands until 1945. The quick capture of Marseille which ANVIL would provide would open up a relatively undamaged port outside of Normandy through which he could pour men and supplies. ANVIL's forces moving up from the south would also screen the right flank of Eisenhower's armies fighting their way to the German border.

With the two theater commanders each unshakable in his beliefs, and the CCS adopting a "hands-off" policy concerning decisions by their field commanders, the matter was dropped squarely into the laps of Churchill and FDR. By July the two heads of state had hammered out an agreement. Churchill still voiced misgivings, but reluctantly ordered "Jumbo" Wilson on July 2 to prepare to land an invasion force on the south coast of France no later than August 15. In case the enemy had learned the meaning of the original code-word, ANVIL was changed to DRAGOON, a word the Prime Minister supposedly personally selected for the operation because "I was dragooned into it."[9]

Lts. Bill "Red" Stalter, Don Gravenstine and Dick Sanderson of the Flying Skulls. Stalter got a piece of a Focke-Wulf on July 19, and Gravenstine led the Skulls in the strafe of an airfield at Valence a few days later that caught the enemy flat-footed on the ground. (Sanderson)

The softening up of German airfields and other enemy installations in the south of France was to have begun at least thirty days prior to the invasion – or about July 15. Mediterranean Allied Air Forces mediums and fighters had been so busy with Italian targets, however, and the heavies similarly engaged in an all-out campaign against Rumanian oil, that MAAF's aircraft appeared over the Riviera only infrequently during that period; Fifteenth Air Force Fortresses and Liberators went to southern France only five times during July, XII TAC mediums never got there at all, and the only fighters other than those escorting the bombers to penetrate French airspace before August were the Thunderbolts of the 79th when they worked over an airfield north of Marseille on July 25 and 26.

In mid-afternoon of July 25, as the Skulls stayed high to watch for enemy fighters, the Skeeters swooped down over the German airdrome at Valence, some 130 miles up the Rhone River valley from Marseille. Valence was the home of two Ju 88 units (KGs 26 and 100) but on this hot summer day the twin-engined Junkers weren't home; the Skeeters had to be content with chewing up ground installations, and three E-boats that Captain George Vaccaro strafed and burned in the harbor at Nice as he returned early with a malfunctioning belly tank.

The next day the same two squadrons went to Valence again. This time they found what they were looking for when they caught over thirty German aircraft of all types flat-footed on the ground. They caught the enemy completely unawares. "Trucks were making their rounds delivering bombs and fuel to the planes on the ground; one plane was leisurely taxiing into takeoff position; a mechanic had the cowling off another and was working on the engine; while one guy was standing on the wing of a plane taking a leak."[10] After a textbook example of inter-squadron teamwork that left the drome littered with burning Junkers, Heinkels and Dorniers, they raced for home. Behind them, dead in the wreckage of his mangled P-47, lay George Vaccaro, one of the Skeeters' premier fighter pilots.

Vaccaro, a 130-mission veteran from Roxbury, Massachusetts, was leading the Skeeters this July afternoon while Lieutenant Don Gravenstine was leading the Skulls. Over Valence each squadron took its turn orbiting overhead alert for the 109s and 190s while the other roared in low over the drome. Because of the skillful use the enemy made in dispersing his aircraft the strafing pilots were compelled to make as many as four complete circuits of the field (flying over the outskirts of Valence, where French civilians cheered them on),[11] all the while being peppered by a barrage of wicked flak and small arms fire. Vaccaro's guns had already chewed up three Junkers and he was swinging around to begin his fourth pass when he was hit. Too low to bail out he crashed in a nearby field – the first of a dozen Falcon pilots to find his grave in France.

While the Skulls and Skeeters were desperately dodging cannon shells near Valence, the Comanches were in a hassle of a different sort over the rugged mountains of northern Italy. Earlier in the day twelve of the squadron's P-47s had been providing area cover for 310th Bomb Group Mitchells near Ostiglia

Sgt. Charles Lankford and friend. Lankford was a sergeant in the 87th's Communications section, while his "friend" answered to the name of "Skeeter Monk." (Church)

when a brace of Focke-Wulfs and a lone 109 made a high-side swipe at the bombers. Major George Ewing turned one of the Focke-Wulfs into an instant fireball while Lieutenant Eugene Gilmore probably destroyed the Messerschmitt. The other 190 driver, finding himself suddenly friendless and hip-deep in Thunderbolts, scampered to safety as Lieutenant Edwin Walsh raked him with .50-caliber machine-gun fire.

Now the Comanches were at it again. They had just finished busting a railroad bridge northwest of Brescia when eleven aggressive, blue-nosed 109s pounced on them from out of a wisp of cloud – angry, eager, and spoiling for a fight.

The American pilots couldn't know it of course, but within the next few seconds they would be in their last big aerial scrap of the war. In September, when the 79th probed into German airspace below Stuttgart, and again over Udine in March, they would skirmish briefly with enemy pilots in a couple of chance encounters, but today would be the last time they would meet any willing to mix it up in a fashion reminiscent of the brawls over Tunisia, Anzio and Rome. They did know, however, that such opportunities were becoming increasingly rare. Luftflotte

II had pulled most of its Jagdgeschwader units out of Italy the month before to help defend the Reich against the massive bomber streams thundering across northern Europe; many Allied fighter pilots in the south would now fly their entire overseas tours without once spotting a hostile plane in the air. With the hope of notching a personal victory evaporating with each passing day, here was an unexpected stroke of good fortune – an opportunity they could ill-afford to miss. If the Hun wanted a fight, he was damned well going to get one.*

With a high-pitched whine the two formations clashed. Messerschmitts and Thunderbolts zoomed in and out from all points on the compass, guns sparkling, as tracers and debris flew in all directions. The fight quickly disintegrated into a disorganized jumble of individual duels. Slashes of oily black smoke violated the clear Itàlian sky as the Americans' wing guns began to tear the German planes to wreckage. A parachute, dirty gray and belching little puffs of talcum opened. Then another . . . and then two more. The battle seemed to go on endlessly.

Suddenly it was over! Only a few vertical columns of smoke coiling up from the hard-packed earth below testified to the violent collision of the two forces moments earlier. Separated and widely scattered, but with everyone safe and spirits soaring, the Comanches regrouped and headed for Corsica.

Dick Hilgard was the last one home. Flying a '47 he called *Deacon Dandy*, and on his thirteenth mission, he figured he was in trouble because he had lost his element leader, a grizzled veteran who had told him to stick close to his wing. But Hilgard had a 109 to his credit that his gun camera would verify, and he celebrated his return to Serragia with a victory roll over the field.

Bob Steiner in his *Blitz Buggy* also had a 109, while Billy Head and Charlie Hancock each had a pair of victories, plus Hancock had turned another 109 into a cripple. Warren Tallent petitioned for a probable. The tally for the two shows: six confirmed kills, a probable and a damaged. All without loss to themselves. In fact, no one had received a scratch. It was the squadron's finest hour in air-to-air combat.**

Lt. Bob Steiner had a 109 to his credit in the big brawl the Comanches got into over Brescia, Italy on July 26. (Church)

It had been decided during the early planning of ANVIL/DRAGOON that special attention would be given enemy airfields near Toulon, Udine, and in the Po Valley. The heavies would take out the first two, while the mediums and fighters had the responsibility for neutralizing those in the valley of the Po.

After a three-day breather, standing down while Serragia's runway was lengthened and resurfaced with steel matting (making the takeoff roll a little less hairy, especially when struggling aloft with a 2,000-pound payload), the 79th joined other XII TAC fighters in hitting German airfields in the Po Valley.

At least once a day during the first four days of August Falcon pilots sandwiched an airfield strike in between their regular fare of rail-cutting and bridge-busting missions. Never completely easing up on the interdiction campaign, they usually struck one of the communications targets first with 500-pounders, then moved on to strafe an airdrome until their ammunition was exhausted. As expected, the dromes were fat with anti-aircraft batteries and fiercely defended. In their first five trips to airfield targets they lost two pilots to airfield defenders and another while strafing a bridge.

Lieutenant Noel Sonnichsen, the Skeeter pilot from Willimantic, Connecticut who had been plucked from a watery grave during the Elba operation six weeks earlier, was slapped down by flak near Verona on August 1, crashing on the edge of that city's Villafranca airdrome; the Skulls lost Lieutenant Vincent Millican, a fifty-five mission vet from Dillsboro, Indiana over Bergamo-Seriate the next day, and Lieutenant James Green on August 3. From Cleveland, Ohio, Green was killed strafing a railroad bridge near Verona on his very first mission.

---

* The Messerschmitt pilots were not German, but Italians of 2° *Gruppo Caccia* (2° *Gr.C*), one of two fighter groups of the *Aeronautica Nazionale Repubblicana* (Northern Italy Fascist Air Force) that fought against the Allies in Italy from April 1944 to the end of the war.[12]

**According to Ferdinando D'Amico, an Italian journalist who researched the history of 2° *Gr.C*, victory claims by both sides were wildly exaggerated. He notes that although American pilots claimed six Me-109s destroyed, 2° *Gruppo Caccio* actually lost only one plane that day. Likewise, the Italian pilots claimed three P-47s shot down when in fact actual losses for the Comanches were nil.[13]

Despite the heartfelt loss of Sonnichsen, Millican and Green the counter-air program proved highly successful. Airfields at Gallarate and Dolceaqua, in addition to the ones at Verona and Bergamo-Seriate, were thoroughly worked over. The 79th accounted for thirteen enemy aircraft destroyed on the ground, another twelve probably destroyed, and thirty-nine damaged. They also gutted hangars and repair shops, blasted revetments, and shot up a host of other ground installations. By August 4, when a weather front moved in to close down operations, enemy airpower in the Po Valley had been neutralized.

A persistent rain curtailed all combat operations on August 5. Cross-country and other training flights were scheduled however, and while taking off on a non-operational hop Lieutenant George W. Beers, a Skull pilot from Fort Wayne, Indiana, was killed when his P-47 swerved off the runway and crashed. The next day the skies cleared. After an absence of more than a week the 79th returned to France.

The Skeeters took Marauders of the 320th Bomb Group to Beaucaire twice during the day, including a three hour and fifty minute show (the squadron's longest to date), as the B-26s methodically worked over a railway bridge. The Skulls escorted 340th Bomb Group Mitchells over a road bridge near Avignon on two separate missions that day, while the Comanches ran an afternoon fighter-bomber strike to Puget Theniers in France and a pair of similar missions over Italy, all without incident.

The next day, August 7, two more runs were made to France before early afternoon showers washed out operations: a fighter-bomber show to Nice harbor by the Comanches that left the German's short one 500-foot cargo ship, and a combined escort and strafing show by the Skeeters as they shepherded ninety B-25s up the Rhone River to the airfield at Orange Plan de Dieu. After the Mitchells dropped their loads, the Skeeters swooped low over the field in a strafing attack that left one Heinkel He 111 burning and a Ju 52 damaged, but Lieutenant William "Doug" Brittian, a "sprog" who had just joined the squadron in late July, was injured. New pilots were called "sprogs." After a dozen or so missions they were "sports." After twenty or thirty missions – if they survived that long – they became "old sports."

As Brittian came in over the fence at 400-plus, he not only saw 20-mm "golf balls" floating toward him and tracers zipping all about, but also noticed that the defenders were firing 88-mm flak guns into the ground in front of the strafers,* sending up showers of dirt and debris. Some of that debris hit his *Tennessee Tom* in the engine, and his canopy was immediately covered with oil. The oil soon seeped into the cockpit, and with his airspeed down to 160 (the last reading he noted before oil obscured the instruments) he was flying but gaining no altitude. As he headed out over the sea Brittian thought seriously about ditching. But the old R2800 kept going, although laboring badly, and when two Spits joined up alongside to keep him company he decided to try for a dirt emergency strip the RAF had on the north coast of Corsica. He made landfall and touched down on his one good landing gear (the wheel came off the other when he tried to lower it), and after a long, rough slide down the runway *Tennessee Tom* ended up on its nose. Brittian, who had been flying around loose in the cockpit, was cut and bruised and dislocated his shoulder. He was pulled from the wreck by the British, who sedated him and patched him up.

"They treated me great," Brittian said. "They had gotten all the oil out of me and had put my arm back in its socket, and patched up the other cuts and bruises. But my right leg was hurting so I raised the blanket from my naked body to see what was what. The female British nurse said, 'Don't worry Sonny, all the parts are still there.'"[15] He was back on Ops within a week.

August 8 operations were mixed between Italian bridgework and bomber-escorts to France. All missions were scrubbed on the 9th – not unwelcome news as that was the day when American brands of liquor were available for the first time in several months to supplement their beer ration – and starting August 10 and continuing for three days, seventeen missions totaling 139 sorties were flown against coastal defense guns and radar stations between Marseille and Genoa.

Because of the overwhelming air superiority enjoyed by the Allies as they counted down to DRAGOON, Luftwaffe opposition to the landing was not considered a serious threat. Enemy bombers and fighters based within striking distance of the assault area numbered less than 200, while the Allies had the combined weight of the entire Mediterranean Allied Air Forces at their disposal. In addition, shipborne Seafires and F6F Hellcats from nine carriers of Task Force 88 operating in offshore waters would help cover the invasion until D+14.

Despite this awesome array of friendly airpower Allied planners were taking no chances. To forestall any chance of enemy planes attacking the invasion force, Fifteenth Air Force P-38s and XII TAC Thunderbolts (211 aircraft in all) were ordered into the air on August 13 to beat up seven airdromes in

* Another pilot with the Skeeters, Lieutenant John Cochran, was also "very much impressed" with the "eighty-eights" that fired at them as they came across the airfield. Cochran had joined the 87th in Naples in late April, and had 78 missions by war's end. On a long train trip across North Africa enroute to the war, Cochran relieved the boredom by firing his pistol at telephone poles and water tanks along the way, and trading cigarettes for blood red oranges that tasted "terrific."[14]

the Rhone River delta and in northern Italy. This decision would cost the 79th Lieutenant Robert H. Williams and Flight Officer Herbert H. Woerpel.

For their targets this sultry Sunday evening the Group drew La Jasse, Istres-Le Tube and Le Vallon airfields, all sited on the flat lowlands between the mouth of the Rhone River and Berre Lagoon, forty miles northwest of Marseille. Of these La Jasse, a grass field just southwest of Eyguieres, would prove the most expensive.

The Skulls were first into the area, arriving over their first target at about 6:30 p.m. They made a quick strafing pass over two dromes in the Le Vallon area, shooting up six Ju 88s and a 109 on the ground, plus hangars, boxcars and storage tanks, then struck at La Jasse. Almost immediately Lieutenant Archibald McIlwaine was hit. Suffering flesh wounds and nursing a shot-up Thunderbolt his luck held, and he miraculously weaved safely through the maelstrom of ground fire.

For Lieutenant Bob Williams, who had been to the well eighty-two times before, luck ran out. He didn't make it. Apparently hit as he was leaving the target, he crashed into the sea off Cape Couronne. Jay Gruver and Bill Ogden circled overhead for about ten minutes but found only what looked to be a seat cushion floating in the water. Nine months later, after the Germans quit the war in a schoolhouse at Reims, France, the Olyphant, Pennsylvania native was still unaccounted for.

With all hope of a peaceful Sunday evening now shattered, the La Jasse ground gunners were alert, ready and waiting when the Skeeters showed up twenty minutes later. After flying past the field for about ten miles, the Skeeters suddenly wheeled about and came screaming down from 10,000 feet to tree-top level at full war emergency power. The field was empty of enemy planes, but was vigorously defended, and in just a scant few seconds five of the twelve pilots were flying battle-damaged aircraft, and a sixth was down and burning. Lieutenant Al Bratt remembers the reception they got. "Flak was coming from both sides and from directly ahead. One shell passed just inches in front of my canopy and there were tracers all over the place. I managed to get off a short burst at a barracks building before turning my guns on the winking lights of anti-aircraft fire coming from the far edge of the airdrome."

Just after passing over those guns Bratt saw a fireball traveling through the trees to his left – "I knew one of us had bought it, but didn't know who it was" – then headed for the coast. Passing over the north shore of Berre Lagoon the flight strafed a massive shipping crane, and a three-stack passenger liner, which Bratt almost ran into, just skimming over it by a whisker. "It was one of those 'I almost bought the farm' incidents you tend to remember," he said.[16]

Flight Officer Herb Woerpel was killed August 13 strafing dangerous La Jasse. He is shown here with P-40 while stationed at Florida's Dale Mabry Field in April 1944. (Author's photo)

The fireball Bratt had seen in the trees was Herb Woerpel's funeral pyre. Like Doug Brittian, Woerpel was another "sprog," having joined the squadron just two weeks earlier. Apparently hit by the intense ground fire, his plane skimmed over a small rise and crashed in a rock-strewn field five miles south of La Jasse. The impact tore the engine loose, which slid through a vineyard before ending up in a heap on the railroad tracks about 100 meters west of the station at Calissanne.

Vincent Remble, who lived a short distance from the station worked at the nearby Saint Chamas powder plant – "I was coming back from my work when the air raid siren yelled and flak shot everywhere" – and that night, after it was safe to do so without getting hit by exploding ammunition from the burning plane, he inspected the wreckage. "The pilot was burned in his cockpit; I couldn't do anything for that poor guy," he said. The next morning when the Germans came, one told Remble: "You see, your American friends, they only devastate your vines."[17] Woerpel was a twenty-four-year-old Wisconsin farm boy on only his sixth mission. He was buried by French civilians the next day in the cemetery at Berre-L' Etang.

The Comanches had fared better. Half an hour after the last of the Skeeters roared away from dangerous La Jasse they were churning up the enemy drome at Istre-Le Tube, "where the flak towers were like Christmas trees."[18] By nine o'clock that evening the last of their squadron's aircraft was safely down at Serragia, their only casualty one flak-damaged P-47.

Behind them, in addition to Williams and Woerpel, the three squadrons left behind a pair of Ju 88s burning on the ground, two more probably destroyed, and five more plus a lone 109 damaged. They also shot up hangars, storage tanks, railway boxcars and flak batteries on the airfields, and the 400-foot three-stacker in Berre Lagoon that almost got Al Bratt.

At first glance the August 13 airdrome sweep by marauding MAAF fighters showed a virtual standoff in the losses and claims columns. Lightning and Thunderbolt pilots destroyed eleven aircraft on the ground, probably destroyed four, and damaged twenty-three. Losses to the raiders numbered ten planes, plus twenty-three others in varying degrees of battle damage. The true yardstick in determining the success of the operation was not readily apparent however. The strafing attacks pointed out to the Germans the vulnerability of their bases in the Rhone delta and northern Italy, and many units were quickly withdrawn to the relative safety of the German frontier. As a result, during the critical early hours of the DRAGOON invasion, the skies over southern France would be completely devoid of enemy aircraft.

Apparently hit by groundfire, Woerpel's Thunderbolt skimmed over the hills in the background and crashed in this field near the spot where Messieurs Claude DeLuy (left) and Vincent Remble are standing in this 1999 photograph. (Besson)

thirteen

Rhone Valley Massacre

"Among the wrecked vehicles were some 1,500 horses, burned and twisted in gruesome shapes, bloating in the sun."

– Ralph Colmer, 86th Fighter Squadron

August 15,1944! Serragia's pre-dawn darkness was shattered by the deep-throated rumble of over a hundred Pratt & Whitney aircraft engines coughing and sputtering to life. Smoke and flame boiled out of P-47 exhaust stacks casting an eerie glow over the airdrome and illuminating the shadowy, ghost-like figures of hundreds of men as they readied the Group's striking power for the early morning missions. On fields all over the island similar scenes were being enacted. DRAGOON's air cover was poised and ready.

At 0430 Double Daylight Saving Time (two hours later than Greenwich Mean Time) Captain Eugene Kleiderer, Jr., the newly appointed Skull skipper from Montgomery, Alabama, led a four-plane flight off Serragia's steel-matted runway and headed for France. One hour and forty minutes later Kleiderer's pilots were toggling 500-pound general purpose bombs over German positions at St. Maxime, sixty-five miles up the coast from Toulon. They had beaten the rival 57th Group to France by a matter of minutes to become the first Allied fighters over the invasion beaches on D-Day.

For the next hour and a half Falcon Thunderbolts shuttled endlessly back and forth between Corsica and the assault area in a nearly constant stream. Approximately every ten minutes a four-ship mission was airborne out of Serragia bound for the Riviera. As they approached the French coast they were given vectors to gun emplacements and other targets by members of the 2nd Air Combat Control Squadron (Amphibious) aboard the USS *Catoctin.* Steaming in a race track pattern a few miles offshore, the *Catoctin* furnished incoming air strikes with up-to-the-minute target information gleaned from reconnaissance flights, homeward-bound missions and, later, liaison officers on the ground. The *Catoctin* would direct all offensive fighter-bomber strikes until D+4 when XII TAC Advance established a fighter direction center ashore.

By 0715, a full forty-five minutes before the first assault troops hit the beaches near St. Raphael, the 79th had already flown off fourteen missions. From then until noon, with coastal targets diminishing, they would fly only four more against gun positions, then switch to road and rail targets behind the lines in an attempt to isolate the battlefield.

Despite being conceived amid a bitter storm of controversy, hastily planned, and eventually becoming one of the most hurried pieces of maneuvering in modern military history, the Riviera landings were flawlessly executed; initial D-Day gains far surpassed all expectations. This was due in part to the effectiveness of the pre-invasion softening-up program carried out by MAAF, and partly because the overall military situation in Europe that had been very much in doubt at the time Churchill relented to the invasion in July, had now shifted in favor of the Allies. It had only been six weeks since "Jumbo" Wilson was given the green light for ANVIL/DRAGOON, but much had happened in those six weeks: the Russians were across the Vistula and probing through the streets of Warsaw; Eisenhower's armor had broken out of Normandy's hedgerow country near St. Lo and was stampeding toward Paris, and Fifth Army was at the outer defenses of the Pisa-Rimini line in northern Italy.

With pressure mounting against him on three separate fronts, Hitler was obliged to weaken his defenses in southern France. By August 15 more than 75,000 German troops had been moved out of the south, leaving only the six understrength divisions of Nineteenth Army guarding the "soft underbelly" of Europe between the Spanish and Italian frontiers. Another division was garrisoned near Lyon but was already heavily engaged with French Resistance forces and would be of little help in repelling the invasion.

D-Day broke fair and calm. Commando units and small bands of French Maquis were already roving behind the beachhead, and the first of DRAGOON's assault troops were pouring onto French soil long before the heat of the late summer day burned away a lingering, misty haze.

Even as Captain Kleiderer was gathering his flight to race the early morning sun to France, more than 5,000 American and British paratroopers of the 1st Airborne Task Force were spilling out of troop carrier aircraft near Le Muy. These advance troops would create roadblocks and hold other key objectives until a link-up could be effected with the seaborne invaders. The airborne assault of southern France went much better than the tragic fiasco over Sicily more than a year before, yet some paratroopers were dropped up to thirty miles off target, with many falling with full packs into the sea, where they drowned.

At 0730 aerial bombing of beach defenses ceased to allow the Navy to move in close. For the next twenty-five minutes destroyers and rocket-firing LCTs punished the beaches with a drenching rain of fire. Then all was quiet save the throbbing of landing craft engines as troop-laden LCVPs sped down boat lanes toward the beaches. While Winston Churchill surveyed the scene from a British corvette steaming several miles off the coast, Major-General Alexander M. "Sandy" Patch (whose Americal Division had relieved Guadalcanal Marines in December 1942, and who had now inherited Patton's Seventh Army) put Lucian Truscott's VI Corps ashore along a broad, thirty mile front. Precisely at 0800 Truscott landed three divisions of American infantry and a French armored task force on the sandy beaches between St. Tropez and Cannes. An hour later nine serials of glider-borne infantry joined the fight when they cut free of tow-planes and slued to rough, bumpy landings behind the German lines.

The Flying Skulls were the first fighter pilots over the southern France invasion beaches on D-Day, and some of those "early birds" are shown here on the steps of the old stone building that served as the Squadron Ops building on Corsica. They include (left to right) Don Gravenstine, Frank Harlocker, Leonard Charpentier (an 86th pilot), Johnny Martin, William Ramsdell, Joseph Lansing, Jack Slatton and Carl Cronk. (Charpentier)

Men died and others were wounded, and fully one-third of the airborne force were casualties, but enemy resistance was comparatively light. Only near St. Raphael did VI Corps encounter serious opposition, and this was quickly squashed by fighter-bomber strikes and pinpoint naval gunfire. By the end of the day contact had been made with the paratroopers and 86,000 Allied soldiers were firmly ashore in southern France along with large stores of equipment and supplies. The next day the French II Corps of General Jean de Lattre de Tassigny made a follow-up landing near Toulon and quickly set out to invest that city, and the major prize of Marseille, while Truscott pursued the retreating enemy up the Rhone Valley.

The Allies advanced rapidly. Operating under friendly skies and meeting only limited opposition on the ground, Seventh Army rolled up fantastic gains; twice in the first three days after coming ashore they outdistanced their supplies and had to be replenished by drops from cargo aircraft. With the exception of small, stubborn pockets of enemy resistance near Toulon and Marseille that were not reduced until August 28, the German Nineteenth Army quickly fell apart. By August 20, five days after the landings, Allied ground forces were already 135 miles inland.

With eighteen D-Day missions already behind them by noon, 79th pilots spent the remainder of August 15 flying against road and rail targets just behind the immediate battlefield. Results were excellent – they took out several bridges, cut a score of railroad tracks, and escorted B-26s on two successful bridge-busting shows – but the Skeeters lost Lieutenant James P. Williams. From Holcomb Rock, Virginia and on only his second operational flight, Williams was hit by flak southwest of Cannes and crashed at sea.

A Comanche Thunderbolt kicks up a cloud of dust at Serragia as it heads for the French Riviera on D-Day. (Church)

Two separate operational accidents the next day cost the life of one Skull pilot and seriously injured another. Lieutenant William M. Ramsdell of Buffalo, New York was heading out for a fighter-bomber mission to Cannes shortly after noon when he failed to negotiate the takeoff and was killed. Three hours later a similar mishap injured Lieutenant William E. Hodge of Mineral Springs, Arkansas. Both were newly-arrived, inexperienced pilots with three and two missions, respectively. At this stage of the war, many fighter RTUs (Replacement Training Units) in the States still used P-40s to train replacement pilots, and some "sprogs" joined the Group with no time in the P-47. Many times they were just handed a copy of the pilots' manual for the Thunderbolt, checked out in the layout of the cockpit, and after a familiarization hop they were turned loose. One pilot, with only four hours in the P-47, was "appalled" to be told he was scheduled for a mission,[1] while another credited his squadron commander (Earl Maxwell) for "probably saving my life" after Maxwell talked him down to his first-ever landing in a Thunderbolt.[2]

Back from a raid over southern France, a flight of B-25 Mitchells line up in front of Serragia's tower. (Church)

Because of the almost unbelievable progress being made by the Allies on the ground, by August 19 the 79th was hard-pressed to locate worthwhile targets within range, and a new move was imminent.

On August 20, as Falcon pilots once again hit Italian as well as French targets, members of the 79th's advance party left Serragia by truck and wound their way across the mountainous backbone of Corsica to their staging area at Calvi. There they boarded LSTs for France. Late the next afternoon they beached near San Raphael and moved into a grassy orchard a mile east of Le Muy, site of the paratroopers' D-Day drop zone. While they waited for the new landing ground to be ready they acquainted themselves with the nearby towns of Le Muy, Frejus and Draguignan. Some, despite signs near the beach proclaiming *Achtung minen* and the presence of small bands of armed Germans still roaming the rear areas, strayed as far as Toulon, Cannes, and even Marseilles. The local French, free at last of German rule, welcomed them with typical Gallic fervor, and were wonderfully hospitable.

On Corsica, meanwhile, it was business as usual. Missions were flown from first to last light each day, and during its last week of operations from that rugged little island the Group put up 377 effective sorties over hostile territory. They ranged up the Rhone Valley and into northern Italy as far as their fuel-hungry P-47s would take them, harassing the fleeing enemy at every opportunity. They bombed and strafed roads choked with German vehicles; knocked out gun positions; escorted B-25s and A-20s as the bombers postholed roads and burned ammo and fuel dumps, and they swarmed all over the enemy's rail transportation system in blistering fighter-bomber attacks. A particularly successful dive-bombing show over Italy on August 21 left the marshaling yards at Alessandria a shambles, and two days later they blasted the docks at San Remo into useless kindling. Opposition to the 79th's efforts as the Group terminated its Corsican tour was sporadic and generally ineffectual – only five aircraft were slightly damaged by anti-aircraft fire – but Lieutenant Harry Mitchell, who had just recently been assigned to the 85th Squadron, was killed in a landing accident on August 25. That same afternoon, Lieutenant Don Lawless of the same squadron almost suffered a similar fate while struggling to get airborne in a war-weary Thunderbolt that had seen better days. His clunker had been shot-up and bellied into the dirt alongside the landing strip by another pilot several days earlier, but had been repaired and given the OK after a short test hop. The test flight didn't include bombs and ammo, of course, and the extra weight just about did the plane (and Lawless) in. When he couldn't get it into the air after hitting 110 mph on the takeoff roll – and too late in the game to abort – Lawless released his bombs safe on the runway and retracted his gear; the '47 struggled off the ground, its bombs tumbling along on either side of it. Barely above stalling speed the P-47 mushed through the branches of a row of trees at the end of the runway, and disappeared from view. Those watching waited for the sound of a crash and the telltale fireball and column of black smoke. But the Wichita, Kansas pilot nursed the Jug up to a hundred feet, made a gentle turn over the beach, and slipped back in over the tree tops to put it down in once piece on the runway behind them. Because he didn't cross the bomb line into enemy territory, his hair-raising experience was just another routine flight as far as Lawless was concerned, and didn't count as a mission.[3]

Squadron Intelligence Officer Captain Robert S. Brown briefs Comanche pilots for another mission up the Rhone River Valley. Major Fred Zilly is at bottom left, while Lt. Tom O'Brien is at upper left. Others are unidentified. (Church)

By August 25 range had become a definite, critical factor. Worthwhile targets in France were no longer within reach of XII TAC's Corsican-based fighters, and the island's usefulness as an "unsinkable aircraft carrier" (except for bombers and cargo aircraft) was over. Two days later, on August 27, the 79th ended its eleven week stay on that inhospitable island. Three C-47s, two hack B-25s and an A-20 made two or three trips each to southern France transporting equipment and pilots not scheduled for a mission, while other pilots wrestled their deep-bellied Thunderbolts off Serragia's runway for the last time, scooted low up the Rhone Valley hunting for targets of opportunity, then set down at dusty St. Raphael. B-Party followed the next day, arriving at Ile Russe (code-named IVAN) on Corsica's west coast that same afternoon, where they boarded two British landing craft for the six-hour run to the French coast.

The Group's stay at St. Raphael would be short, fruitful, and expensive. Five days after touching down in France the rapidly changing bomb line dictated yet another move. When they left they would leave behind the results of some of the most successful and devastating strafing conducted by any fighter group during the war. They would also leave behind two more pilots.

As the enemy hurried north in a confused, disorganized rout he was unmercifully slaughtered from the air. Particularly along Highway 7, that winding, twisting, north-south arterial that hugs the banks of the Rhone from Marseille to Lyon, was he especially vulnerable to air attack. An early morning mission by the Comanches on August 28 left over thirty German vehicles destroyed or burning on the clogged road. Another fifty were badly damaged. The Skulls also enjoyed success against road targets and, in addition, set a long string of railway cars on fire and sank a pair of river barges. But the highlight of the day occurred when seven Skeeters caught over 500 vehicles on the road fifteen miles south of Lyon. The column was spotted after a hurry-up call for a late-afternoon mission "to go take a look north of the bomb line"[4] put Captain Bill Colgan, Lieutenant Phil Bagian and Flight Officer Russell Jennings over Highway 7. They found a solid mass of enemy men, vehicles, and equipment that covered the road for some thirty miles south of Montélimar; the column was so large there was fleeting concern that perhaps Allied ground forces had gotten ahead of the bomb line.[5] When a closer look proved otherwise, Colgan led his "Red Flight" in a strafing attack against the trucks and tanks at the head of the column, while radioing the flight behind him (Lieutenant John Boone's "White Flight") to hit the column's tail. With burning vehicles blocking the road at both ends, the Skeeters then made pass after pass over the stalled column, firing until their ammunition was exhausted. Forty-seven trucks, trailers and other vehicles shuddered under the impact of their guns and were utterly destroyed. Another sixty-four were damaged. Returning pilots reported the destruction of equipment and loss of life surpassed anything yet encountered in their experience.

But the enemy had not sat idly by while being pounded to pieces. He fought back with a savage fury. In some places the hail of automatic weapons and small arms fire nearly rivaled that of El Hamma seventeen months earlier. The German gunners took a deadly toll. Bagian and Jennings were knocked down, and three of the five remaining aircraft were thoroughly chewed up by the large volume of Krupp steel hurtling skyward.

Bagian, a gutsy pilot-warrior from Philadelphia, had his engine freeze up after hit by ground fire, and with what little airspeed he had left dove on the guns that had hit him and blew them up. He then skimmed over a large hill and made a dead-

A strafing Thunderbolt faintly visible in the upper middle of this photograph works over a road in southern France. (USAF)

As the enemy hurried north in a confused, disorganized rout he was unmercilessly slaughtered by the low-flying Falcons. Highway 7 near Montélimar. (Murto)

stick belly landing in a small field, breaking his ankle in the process. Hobbling away from his smoking and appropriately named *Balls Out,* Bagian hid in a nearby vineyard, which German soldiers randomly sprayed with burp-gun fire when looking for him some twenty minutes later. Fortunately they missed, and failed to find him hiding among the vines. Bagian soon hooked up with French partisans and was back with his squadron within a week.[6]

August 28 was a bad day for pilots, but Captain Roger Files was one of the lucky ones. Hit while strafing, he put his Thunderbolt down wheels-up and walked away unscathed. He would later command the Flying Skulls. (Church)

Jennings was a replacement pilot from St. Charles, Illinois with eight missions under his belt. He had no sooner seen Bagian crash than he radioed Colgan that he had problems of his own. He died moments later when his crippled Thunderbolt slammed into a hillside a few hundred yards off Highway 7.

Colgan joined up with Boone's flight and made it home in one piece, but his P-47 was shot so full of holes (more than a hundred when he quit counting) and a smoldering engine fire had burned through the firewall, that it was scraped on the spot.[7]

Earlier in the day Percy Brown, the Comanche pilot from Hanson, Mississippi who had flown the Group's 25,000th sortie ten days earlier, was down and missing after another spectacular strafing attack, as was Lieutenant William Ogden of the Skulls. Captain Roger Files was also hit, had his hydraulic system shot away, and put his T-bolt down wheels-up. Files walked away unscathed, and Ogden walked in twenty-four hours later (after being shot at by "friendly" infantry), but Brown was still listed as missing at the end of the war.

During the next four days the Group continued to hammer the bumper-to-bumper road jam that Colgan and company had created. "It was an unbelievable sight, with trucks, cars, motorcycles, artillery caissons, half-tracks, tanks, horse-drawn wagons and countless other vehicles stretching back as far as the eye could see," said Don Lawless. "We'd fire all of our ammunition, then go back to get more. Some vehicles tried to get around the road block by taking to the fields on either side, but most became mired in the mud and were easy targets for our guns."[8]

After nearly four years of harsh Nazi occupation, the French welcomed the Americans with typical Gallic fervor. Valence Airdrome looks like "old home week" as civilians swarm over the field. (Church)

The French, understandably, were in a festive mood. A French girl shares a bottle of wine with Comanche ground personnel. (Church)

Lt. Harold Hall sweat out the long ride home on September 4 after hit by the same burst of flak that knocked Don Claycomb out of the sky. Hall is shown here later in the war, after air-to-ground rockets had been added to the Group's arsenal. (Horn)

Seventy-one motor transport were destroyed on the road that day, and another ninety-three damaged, bringing the Group's total for its six-day stay at St. Raphael to 143 destroyed and 216 damaged, not including an untold number of horse-drawn vehicles shot up, or other claims against bridges, rail targets and river traffic.

But not everything went their way. Lieutenant Leonard Charpentier was on his 29th mission on August 29 as part of a flight of eight Comanches making a sweep up Highway 7 between Valence and Montélimar when they spotted an armored column and dove down to attack. Coming in at tree-top level with ground fire "all over the place," Charpentier was hit in the back of the head. His Jug hit the ground at over 300 mph and cartwheel across a field, scattering P-47 parts all over the French countryside and throwing the Caldwell, New Jersey pilot out of his cockpit. He woke up in a German field hospital three or four days later where some "physician-first, soldier-later surgeon" had pieced him back together. Because of the Allies' fast advance, the Germans soon abandoned the hospital, leaving Charpentier and other litter cases behind to be cared for by the French. A few days later American troops moved into the area and Charpentier was flown to a hospital in Naples where the only additional surgery needed was a skin graft to his left ankle. He was back in the States by Thanksgiving.[9]

On September 1, just two days after B-Party had finally caught up with the rest of the Group, an advanced party moved into Valence airdrome 140 miles (as the crow flies; 200-plus by truck) north of St. Raphael.

Alexander Patch's original plan had been to capture the two large ports of Toulon and Marseille as quickly as possible after D-Day. Then, using these ports as a supply base, he would drive the Germans up the Rhone Valley. But the enemy had left only a small rearguard holding the two cities, while the remainder of Nineteenth Army hurried north to escape being trapped. This, and the welcome but unexpected disintegration of the enemy, altered "Sandy" Patch's strategy.

Leaving the French Corps to deal with the enemy rearguard, Patch sent one American division hot on the heels of the retreating Germans while a small armored task force and two other infantry divisions worked their way though the mountains east of the landing beaches in an attempt to cut off the German retreat.

On August 21 this encircling force collided with the main body of Nineteenth Army near Montélimar. For six days both sides fought for control of the Rhone Valley. Although dominating the skies, the Allies were handicapped by being at the end of a long supply line and were constantly short of ammunition, fuel, rations, motor transport and artillery. The enemy enjoyed a much more favorable logistical position but was being pounded unceasingly from the air and, more importantly, had been caught in headlong retreat; once in motion a retreat is one of the most difficult military maneuvers to reverse and the negative thinking that accompanies such a move has a debilitating effect on morale. As a result, the enemy's spirits were sagging, he was disorganized, and almost totally unprepared both mentally and militarily to do battle.

By the evening of August 28, the battle for southern France was, for all practical purposes, over. The French had cleared Toulon and Marseille earlier in the day, and a final effort by Seventh Army had completely closed the Rhone Valley. Although almost half of the encircled Germans managed to escape through the Montélimar bottleneck (and slipped from Seventh Army's grasp again a week later near Belfort), the enemy had suffered heavy casualties, including more than 100,000 taken prisoner. Marseille and Toulon had been captured in less than half the time expected – the Allies began unloading cargo ships there on September 3 and 4, respectively – and by the end of the war in Europe more than 900,000 Allied troops and over four million tons of cargo would be put ashore at Marseille, Toulon and nearby Port de Bouc in addition to the men and supplies that had gone ashore over the invasion beaches in the six weeks following the landings.[10]

By September 3 Lyon was abandoned, and eight days later Seventh Army, now under General Eisenhower's operational control as part of Lieutenant-General Jacob L. Dever's Sixth Army Group, established contact near Dijon with Patton's Third Army armor from the Normandy front. The Allies now held a continuous line stretching across western Europe from Switzerland to the North Sea.

Once again out of fighter range, the Group's advance party had left St. Raphael on the morning of September 1 and coaxed their battered, war-weary vehicles up Highway 7 to Valence. As they neared Montélimar the awesome effect of tactical airpower became apparent with grim clarity. Here, along one thirty mile stretch of road that Falcon pilots had worked over only a few days before was a shambles that may well have had no equal in the war. The wreckage of over 2,200 German vehicles littered both sides of the road. There were bullet-riddled staff cars, trucks and trailers; great diesel buses that had once carried peacetime passengers through the streets of Berlin lay smoldering in the ditches; there were the blackened hulks of knocked-out tanks and half-tracks; twisted and torn artillery pieces, motorcycles and fuel bowsers, and hundreds of horse-drawn carts and wagons. Everything on wheels that could move had been used by the retreating Wehrmacht in its hasty flight north, and now lay abandoned and useless, all victims of Allied airpower. The sweet, sickening odor of rotting and decaying flesh was everywhere. Bulldozers had scooped out hollow graves alongside the road, partly succeeding in covering up

Lt. Robert Steiner and "fans" at Valence. Steiner and his Blitz Buggy flew with the Comanches. (Church)

Plucked German Storch at Valence. (Church)

some of the mangled corpses, but the stench from the bodies of men and animals bloating in the late summer sun was almost unbearable. The convoy quickened its pace, anxious to escape this scene of almost unbelievable carnage.

They rolled into Valence surrounded by throngs of deliriously happy civilians. The last of the German garrison had left just eighteen hours earlier, and the entire population had turned out to greet the liberators. Expecting the infantry, they met instead a weary, sweaty advance party of the 79th Fighter Group. The men were showered with wine, flowers, and kisses from beautiful French girls as they moved slowly through the streets of Valence, savoring every minute of the hero reception that mitigated a great deal their past two years of toil and tribulation.

Finally, three miles northeast of town, they reached their destination – a huge, sprawling airdrome still littered with the wreckage of over thirty German aircraft, mute testimony to the accurate bombing and strafing performed by Falcon pilots in July. Here the enlisted men settled down in tents while the officers located an abandoned farm house for their quarters. Four days later the remainder of the Group's ground echelon motored up from St. Raphael to join the advance party, missing by only a few hours a wild, unforgettable celebration and street dance thrown by the local population on September 4 to commemorate their country's Independence Day. After four long years under Nazi rule the French, understandably, were in a festive mood.

Socially, Valence was an unqualified success, a vastly marked improvement over any of the more than two dozen bases they had inhabited since being put ashore at Port Tewfik nearly two years before. The skies, however, were as dangerous as ever, as they quickly found out.

Lts. Robert Bartlett (left) and Leonard Beckerman of the Flying Skulls in Lyon, France. (Payne)

The Comanches lost Lieutenant Donald Claycomb on September 4 when his flight, which had just finished busting a bridge across the Doubs River near Dole, spotted a truck convoy a few miles upstream. Claycomb was swinging around for his fifth low-level pass when his engine stopped a 20-mm round from a half-track, and quit. He pointed his powerless bird towards a nearby field to belly it in when he noticed his ailerons dangling impotently beneath his wings. With no aileron control he hit the ground with one wing lower than the other and went into a flat cartwheel which tore up his airplane and knocked him unconscious. Luckily the plane smoldered and smoked but didn't burn, and when Claycomb woke up he was still in the cockpit, but with a fractured back, ankle, and shoulder, plus the traditional fighter pilot "gunsight gash" across his forehead. Lapsing into unconsciousness once more, when he awoke again he had German soldiers for company. They piled him into a horse-drawn hay wagon and hauled him off to a hospital and captivity.[11]

Meanwhile, Lieutenant Harold Hall, a twenty-three-year-old farm boy from Garfield, Kansas, was struck by the same burst of flak that knocked down Don Claycomb. It hit the $C0_2$ bottle in the life raft stowed in the seat pack attached to his parachute harness, demolished his radio, and tore up his hip and elbow. Flying with his left hand, Hall got himself and his *Farmer's Friend* home battered but safe, and he was still around to celebrate the end of the war eight months and some seventy missions later.[12]

The next day Lieutenant Arthur Palmer of the Flying Skulls was seriously injured attempting to land his flak-stricken Jug after a strafing show to Belfort and, on September 9, on the Group's 2,462nd combat mission of the war, the 79th became the first Twelfth Air Force fighter group to penetrate German airspace when eight Skeeter and four Comanche Thunderbolts strafed the airdrome at Freiburg.* The Skeeters were first over the target and caught several Heinkels, Junkers and Focke-Wulfs on the ground, setting a Heinkel on fire and damaging twelve other aircraft, adding to the seven enemy planes they destroyed or damaged on the ground at Mulhouse earlier in the day. A few minutes later the Comanches showed up, wasting their ammo on several dummy aircraft before working over two troop trains northeast of Freiburg. They also scared off a lone 109 that had timidly poked around the edge of their formation before the Messerschmitt driver took off for parts unknown. The Skulls, meanwhile, had been working on the roads between Belfort and Mulhouse where they destroyed fourteen motor transport and damaged ten in exchange for three shot-up but flyable P-47s.

That night the Comanches threw a party at Valence that attracted a large number of French civilians, and a group of French FFI (French Forces of the Interior, the military arm of the French Resistance) officers with insatiable appetites and a fondness for American whiskey.

The Comanches may have celebrated too soon because on September 11 the squadron sustained one of its worst blows of its overseas tour when two pilots were killed, and two others injured in a series of tragic mishaps. Two flights of four had taken off late in the afternoon and flown 200 miles north to scour the roads between Lure and Mulhouse. After an uneventful forty-five minute patrol that yielded only a few horse-drawn carts they turned south for home. By the time they were over Valence it was already dark and they were critically short of fuel.

With tanks almost bone dry four of the eight pilots put their planes down safely on the runway on their first attempt. Two others were forced to bail out when their fuel-starved engines began sputtering and both were slightly injured. Captain Jack Fortune from Augusta, Georgia, and Lieutenant John Winschell, an Etna, Pennsylvania native, were the last to come in. As they groped for the runway in the dark both pilots crashed and were instantly killed.

By the middle of September the bomb line had taken another crazy jump north. The 79th's flight echelon jumped with it. While B-Party remained at Valence until September 22 and then moved back to a staging area near Marseille, the air echelon occupied Bron Airfield just outside Lyon on September 15. The enlisted men pitched tents in the city park where they lived a goldfish bowl existence under the continual, curious stares of the local citizenry, while the officers acquired as their billet a beautiful villa recently vacated by the Germans. With beer and liquor easily obtainable from nearby Lyon, little time was wasted in opening a club and bar that was to gain local renown. Bad weather kept flying to a minimum during their two-week stay, but their social life soared to an all-time high as they fought the "champagne campaign."

Lts. Don Lawless (left) and Eugene T. Van Houten of the Flying Skulls "shoot the parley-vous" over a glass of beer in downtown Valence. (Lawless)

For those lucky enough to be there, Lyon was the highlight of their overseas tour. It was the first large European city they had been in since leaving bombed and battered Naples, but unlike the Italian metropolis, Lyon had hardly been touched by the war. Cafes and theaters were open; the French were friendly to the extreme, and Americans were still considered a

* The first (unofficial) penetration of German airspace by the 79th occurred on August 23 when Earl Maxwell led seven Flying Skull pilots on an armed recce of the Belfort Gap and the flight ventured into Germany for about fifty miles looking for targets of opportunity.[13]

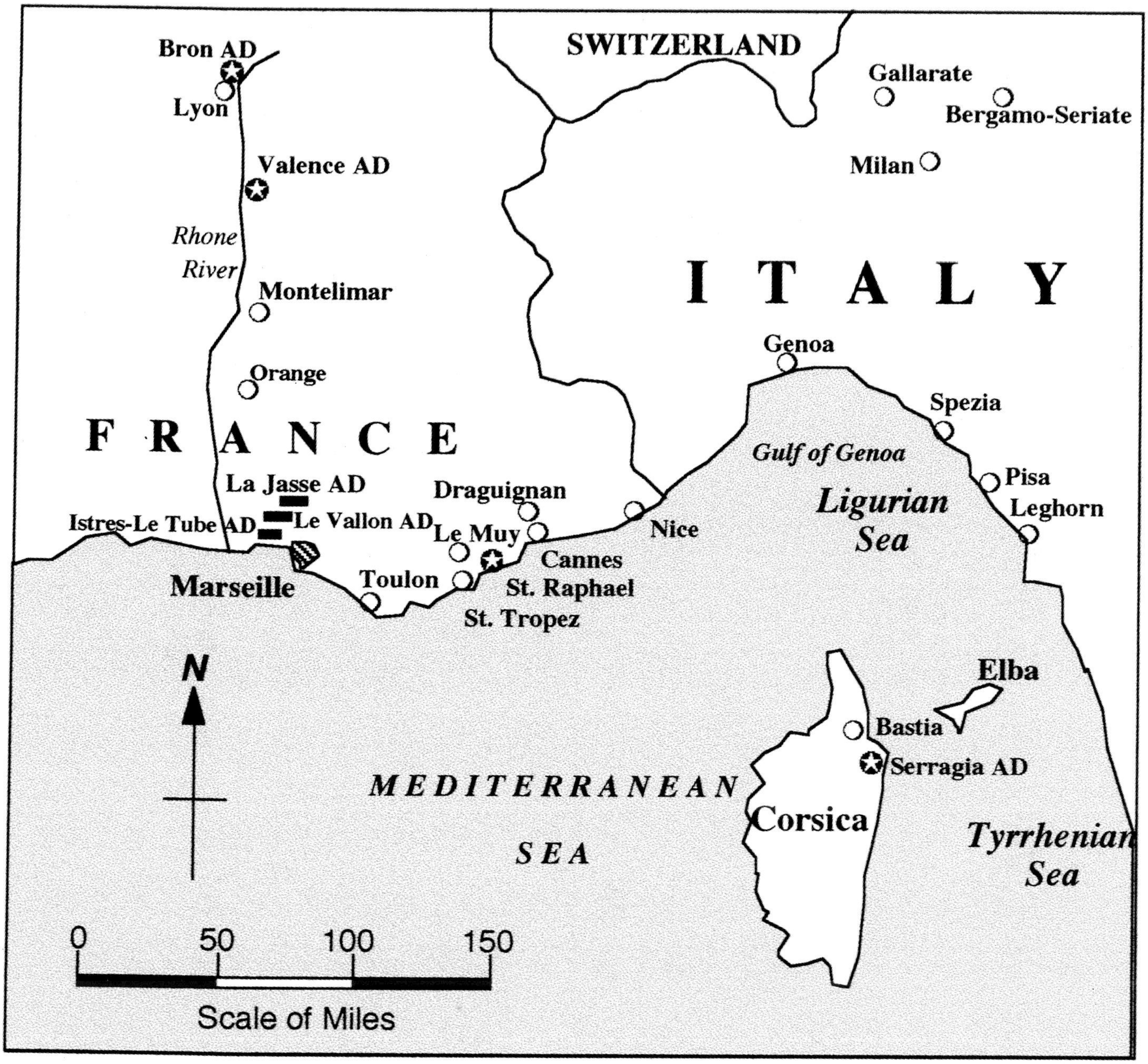

novelty by the native population. What more could a homesick GI ask for. If not for the loss of a Comanche pilot a few days later, it would have been the ideal way to fight a war.

Although no one really minded (except possibly the brass and some poor rifleman in the mud who considered it a luxury if he owned a pair of dry socks) operations were continually plagued by foul weather. On six of sixteen days missions were canceled altogether, and the remainder of the month they were severely curtailed.

On the rare days when skies were clear they flew armed recce patrols over the Mulhouse-Freiburg-Strasbourg triangle, but suitable targets were becoming increasingly harder to find. On September 20 the Skulls shot up a small convoy of vehicles between Mulhouse and Belfort; two days later they and the Skeeters worked over another column of trucks and also exploded a locomotive, while on September 24 the Skeeters bagged another loco, and Lieutenants Ronald Faison and William Waller notched the Group's last aerial victories of the war when they picked off two of three Me 109s encountered over Mulhouse.

On September 28, the last day the Group would operate in French skies, Lieutenant Marion M. Zipperer, a Comanche pilot from Savannah, Georgia, was killed when he spun in and crashed on a weather recce to Belfort.

Rumors had been circulating for days that the 79th was soon to move back to Italy. All hope that they were false were quickly dashed on October 1 when they found themselves strung out in familiar convoy fashion heading south on Highway 7. That same day they rejoined B-Party at Septemes, a staging area near Marseille.

B-Party had never gotten to Lyon, but was ordered back from Valence to Le Vallon on September 22, and then to Septemes on the 29th. There they spent several tiresome days loading and preparing equipment for a return trip to Italy. On October 3, A-Party and the air echelon flew back to the Italian peninsula while B-Party left by LST two days later. After a three-day trip they docked at Leghorn, and on October 9 left by truck for the trip over the Apennines. On October 11 they rejoined A-Party and the Desert Air Force at Jesi airdrome, fifteen miles from the Adriatic port city of Ancona.

fourteen

Back in the Gumbo Again

"On the German side of the lines the roads were deserted, rail lines empty. Nothing moved. The shadow of airpower lay over it all."

– Anonymous war correspondent in Italy

Italy is a country almost completely dominated by its mountains and rivers, with fully four-fifths of that nation's topography consisting of undulating hills and lofty, craggy peaks. Far to the north near the Italian-Swiss frontier tower the majestic, snow-covered Alps, but it is not the Alps but the Apennines that truly determines the country's internal geography and accounts for the bulk of her mountainous terrain. Curving downward from the Italian Riviera southeast to Rimini before turning more directly south toward the Calabrian toe, the Apennines divide the southern two-thirds of the peninsula into eastern and western slopes from which a number of swift-flowing rivers course their way to the Adriatic and Tyrrhenian seas. It was over those rivers and mountains that the Allies had fought, suffered and bled since September 1943. Now, in the summer of 1944, they faced the dreary prospect of crossing the foreboding, fog-shrouded mountains of the northern Apennines.

Fifty miles deep and rising to nearly 7,000 feet in many places, the northern Apennines slash diagonally across Italy's thigh from Spezia to Rimini, guarding the entrance to the broad Po River Valley as they form an almost unbroken barrier of flinty rock and scabrous, razor-backed slopes from the Ligurian Sea to the Adriatic. From the German point of view there was nowhere in Italy (and probably nowhere in all of Europe) that afforded them better natural terrain from which to defend the Reich. And it was here in these cruel, rugged crests and deep gorges of the northern Apennines, where often the only arteries of communications were cliff-hanging trails that rose high in the cold, thin mountain air, that the enemy had begun construction of the last in a seemingly endless series of fortified belts running across the width of the peninsula – the Pisa-Rimini, or Gothic Line. Although a misnomer, for it neither started at Pisa nor ended at Rimini, it featured linked strongpoints dug into the mountains from Carrara to Pesaro. It was labeled the Pisa-Rimini Line by the Allies for the sake of convenience until a captured enemy document revealed its true German code name. Later, on Hitler's orders, it was renamed the Green Line, but on Allied situation maps, and in the minds of those who fought there, it will always be known as the Gothic Line.

The Germans had been fortifying the Gothic Line for almost a year. Fifteen thousand conscripted Italian laborers supervised by engineers of the Todt Organization (the company that had constructed Germany's pre-war autobahn and the vaunted Siegfried Line) were working on a defense line 200 miles long and twelve to fourteen miles in depth. Thirty 75-mm gun turrets from Panther tanks embedded in steel and concrete bases, over 2,000 machine-gun pits, hundreds of other dug-in gun emplacements, acres of minefields, and mile after mile of wire and anti-tank ditches were just a few of the surprises the Germans were preparing for the Allies in northern Italy.

The hearts of the Italian workers were not in the project, however, and numerous acts of subtle sabotage and delaying tactics had slowed construction considerably; the fortifications were still far from complete when the Allies swept through Rome in the first week of June.

Because of this Kesselring, who for many months had masterfully faced one continuing crisis after another, was confronted with one more once again. Somehow, despite absolute Allied aerial supremacy that would dog him every step of the way, he would have to conduct the northward withdrawal from Rome in such a manner as to delay the Allied advance as long as possible; he would have to trade lives for time until the Gothic

Line defenses were completed. To some extent he succeeded. That he did was due in large part to the Allied decision to invade southern France.

When Fifth Army captured Rome on June 4 the liberators did not pause long to savor their victory. Instead, Alexander immediately pushed them north hard on the heels of the battered remnants of the German Tenth and Fourteenth armies. The Allies now had the momentum. Well supplied, led by capable commanders, owning the skies over Italy and the seas around it, their spirits were high, the sweet smell of victory still lingered in their nostrils, and they had the enemy on the run. Alexander was confident he could punch through the unfinished Gothic Line and break into the Po Valley within two months. Once on that broad, fertile plain he could then exploit his gains by attacking westward into southern France or east into Austria.

With Eighth Army (which had been under the command of Lt.-General Sir Oliver Leese since December when Monty went to England) on the east coast of Italy, and Mark Clark's American Fifth on the west, the Allies ground steadily north during the first three weeks of June. Less than fourteen days after clearing Rome they held a continuous front seventy-five miles above the Eternal City. From where Alexander now stood, his chances of reaching the Po Valley by August seemed excellent.

Suddenly, German resistance stiffened. The heady, northward rush slowed once again to that familiar agonizing crawl. The reason was the shifting of large troop formations on both sides of the line.

Almost coincident with the transfer of seven of Alexander's best divisions (including his only experienced mountain troops) for the forthcoming invasion of southern France, Kesselring was reinforced with eight divisions originally earmarked for Normandy or the Eastern Front. The departure of Allied bomber and fighter units for southern France also stripped the Italian front of air strength, forcing the Desert Air Force to provide most of the tactical support for both Eighth *and* Fifth armies until those units returned to Italy in September and October.

The wily, experienced Kesselring would make the most of this division of Allied strength. Using the terrain to his advantage as always, and ruthlessly sacrificing units of second-rate quality to allow his elite divisions time to reorganize and consolidate, he again waged a brilliant holding action. The Allies continued to slowly inch ahead – Eighth Army took Ancona on July 18, and Leghorn fell to Fifth Army a day later – but casualties were high and for each day spent battling Kesselring's rearguard the Germans were one day closer to finishing their elaborate defense line in the northern Apennines.

Major Earl Maxwell, a 130-mission man and 85th Squadron CO in the fall of 1944. Don Lawless said that flying with Maxwell "was always an adventure," including the time Maxwell's flight strafed railroad rolling stock in the Belfort Gap and Lawless came home with twenty-six holes in his P-47. Everyone else in the flight had at least one hole in his aircraft, and Maxwell counted forty in his. (Tobin)

By August 4 the Allies were up against the outer fortifications of this stronghold. They held a line along the Arno River from Pisa to Ancona, and were just a few miles south of Florence. Here Alexander halted. His forces were already weakened by the transfer of many units to DRAGOON and his troops were exhausted from sixty-four days of continuous fighting. He would have to rest, regroup and replenish before tackling the Gothic Line.

By August 25 Alexander was ready. He had secretly shifted most of his weight to the east coast while carrying out overt preparations in the middle of the line to convince Kesselring the main attack would be along the Florence-Bologna axis. When Eighth Army jumped off it caught the enemy by complete surprise and the weight of the assault carried them through the eastern portion of the Gothic Line with comparative ease. When Kesselring rushed reinforcements from other sectors to help shore up his sagging positions along the Adriatic coast, Fifth Army struck in the center of the line north of Florence. By September 18 both Allied armies had pierced the vaunted Gothic fortifications in several places; Rimini fell on September 21, and by the first of October Clark was only nine miles from Bologna. There, however, he was checked when Kesselring shifted his reserves to meet this new threat.

Alexander's troops were now totally exhausted. They were at the end of a long supply line, the weather was rapidly deteriorating, and the Germans had begun to fight with renewed vigor. Eighth Army managed to get a few miles beyond Ravenna during the next several weeks, but Fifth Army was stopped cold in the mountains below Bologna. The autumn battles that had held such great promise in the beginning had failed to dislodge the enemy. By the end of the year Alexander halted his offensive to spend another winter of recuperation and build-up, bitterly aware that victory in Italy had eluded him once more.

The Thunderbolt, such as the one being gassed up here, was the plane best suited for the air war on the Eighth Army front. (Church)

They weren't asked for their opinion, of course, but given a choice most members of the 79th Fighter Group would have been content to finish their tours from French bases. No one looked forward to another winter in the Italian mud. Had it not been for their popularity with Eighth Army and the Desert Air Force they might have done just that.

In the summer of 1944 some of the top American brass wanted to pull Clark's Fifth Army out of Italy and attach it to General Dever's Sixth Army Group in France. To them, it seemed apparent no decisive action was forthcoming in Italy and Fifth Army could be more economically utilized elsewhere. If Fifth Army went, Twelfth Air Force would go with it. But after the initial success against the Gothic Line in late August and early September the ground situation in Italy seemed more optimistic. It was then decided that Clark's troops would remain under Alexander's control, at least until the battle in northern Italy was clarified. Twelfth Air Force, of course, would stay with them.

But this didn't solve the air support needs of the ground forces in southern France. Until Ninth Air Force from northern Europe was in a position to assume that responsibility, the Twelfth would have to divide its forces to cover both fronts. At a conference in September attended by air commanders from both the ETO (European Theater of Operations) and the MTO (Mediterranean Theater of Operations), details of the split were hammered out. Twelfth Air Force fighter and reconnaissance squadrons; Headquarters, XII TAC, and fourteen service units would remain in France to support Seventh Army. The remainder of Twelfth's units would return to Italy no later than October 10 and be redesignated XXII Tactical Air Command.

The 79th had not even been in the running for one of the units to stay in France. It would return to Italy – not as part of XXII TAC, but as the sole American unit to rejoin the Desert Air Force. The 79th had long been DAF's favorite American fighter group,[1] and during the time when Montgomery commanded Eighth Army they were often referred to as "Monty's Pets." In addition, their Thunderbolts were badly needed over the Eighth Army front. Most DAF squadrons were at the time equipped with Spitfires, a few had Mustangs or Kittyhawks, but none flew the barrel-chested P-47 which, because of its coolant system and large, radial engine was less vulnerable to ground fire. The seven-ton Jug could also carry a heavier war load than its lightweight cousins.

Because of the 79th's excellent rapport with the British, and because the P-47 was the aircraft best suited to support Eighth Army's war in the mountains, the Desert Air Force immediately requested the return of the Falcons to its operational control.

When the 79th's air echelon touched down at Jesi on October 3 the reception they received from their British friends of

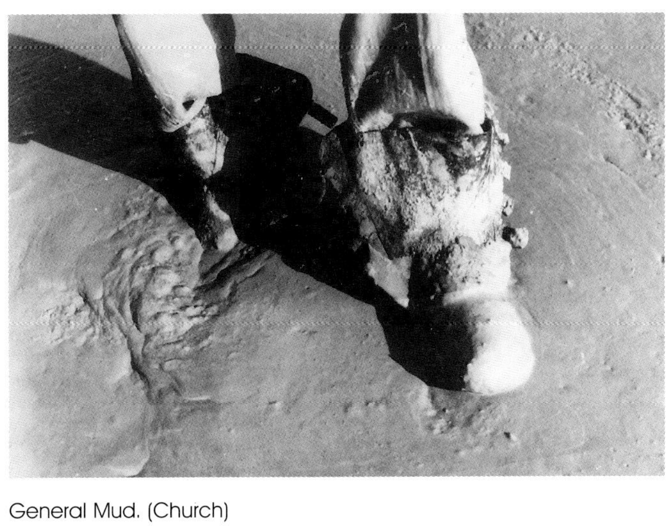

General Mud. (Church)

Their stay at Jesi was a constant, losing battle with the harsh Italian elements. (Church)

Jesi chow line. (Church)

the Desert Air Force was hearty and heartwarming. Their reunion with the harsh Italian elements, however, was just what they had feared the most: cold . . . rain . . . and acres and acres of mud. They had arrived at the beginning of the rainy season and for the next two months mud would be their daily diet. Intermittent rains kept the goo constantly gooey in the dispersal areas, while the campsite was located in a swampy quagmire that became increasingly worse with each passing day.

The grass runway was short, and slick when wet, and the field was packed with aircraft. In addition to the Group's P-47s, all six squadrons of 239 Wing were there, plus anti-malarial Fairchilds, drogue-towing Bostons, and RAF 167 Maintenance Unit which shuttled Spitfires from Jesi to DAF's Spitty wings at such a rapid pace as to almost give them operational status.[2] A few weeks later 3 South African Wing brought its Marauders into Jesi as well. Crowded and cramped, the muddy airdrome bustled with activity.

During the sixty days they were at Jesi, the 79th was continually frustrated by the abominable weather. On seventeen days they were socked in completely, and many other times missions got airborne but were soon aborted. Nevertheless, they still managed 2,099 effective sorties during that period, most of them against German lines of communications. And just as steady as the unceasing rains, they continued to lose planes and pilots.

After a layoff of more than a week the Group returned to the combat arena on October 7 when Captain Fred Zilly, who six days later would replace Major Ed Byron as commander of 86th Squadron, led a flight of Comanches on a bridge-busting show to Cesena. Zilly's flight had been in the air less than an hour when German flak gunners welcomed them back to the Italian campaign by knocking Lieutenant Calvin Arnold out of the sky. Arnold, on his twenty-eighth mission, was flying a P-47 borrowed from Lieutenant Allen Gilbert (his was mired in the mud) and was also wearing Gilbert's chute. "It fit very snugly," he recalled many years later, "and the crew chief offered to adjust it for me. I declined, thinking a tight fit would be good in case I had to jump – which of course I did thirty minutes later."[3] The Southwick, Massachusetts pilot was captured by the Germans soon after he hit the ground and spent the remainder of the war in Stalag Luft III near Sagan, Germany.

Two days later, on October 9, two separate fighter-bomber strikes against road bridges near Rimini cost the Comanches Lieutenant Robert Stahl and James Menifee when both pilots crashed and were killed after being hit by flak over the target, and the Skeeters lost Captain Victor Phelps on October 11, and Captain Gordon A. Bell on the 12th. Both Bell and Phelps had accumulated more than enough combat hours to have qualified them for rotation home, but both had elected to stay with the Group. Phelps, a 116-mission vet from Welsh, Louisiana, was shot down by light anti-aircraft fire near Imola and soon joined Calvin Arnold at Stalag Luft III. Bell, from Tacoma, Washington, was killed making an emergency landing after his plane lost a prop; the landing was good, but the wing of his plane cut down a tree which fell across his open canopy. He had 153 combat sorties to his credit.*

Friday the 13th was an unforgettable day at Jesi. To begin with, Lieutenant Bob Sweeney of the Flying Skulls, returning from his 13th mission, had to make a "blind" landing at Jesi after his Jug blew a jug (cylinder) that drenched his canopy with a thick layer of oil. He groped his way down the runway by lining up with another P-47 flying alongside, but came in too hot the first time and had to do it again, His engine froze as soon as the wheels touched down. His X-81 (which he had planned to name either *Dr. Rat* or *Sweet Lorraine,* but never did) had to be towed off the runway.[4]

Sweeney had no sooner landed than all base operations were halted for the day by returning Fifteenth Air Force bombers. The big birds had been cut up badly over Vienna and were

Captain Fred Zilly led a Comanche bridge-busting show to Cesena on October 7 to mark the Group's return to the Desert Air Force. They were soon welcomed back to the Italian campaign by German ground gunners. (Church)

* At the time, it was generally recognized that a pilot's combat tour would be over after he completed eighty missions. As Harold Land recalls, there was some serious sweating going on when a pilot got close to that magic number. "On my eightieth I was overly alert and extremely observant, and kept thinking how horrible it would be to get shot down on my last mission," he said. "I returned to base unharmed, but we were told at debriefing that there were no replacements and that we would have to continue flying. I was finally replaced after ninety-six missions." Land joined the Flying Skulls in March 1944 and finished his tour the following October.

Friday the 13th was an unforgettable day for Lt. Robert Sweeney of the Flying Skulls. Returning from his thirteenth mission, his Jug blew a jug and drenched his canopy with oil. He made it back to Jesi and put his Thunderbolt down on the runway in one piece on his second attempt, but the plane's engine froze as soon as the wheels touched down. (Sweeney)

now struggling to reach their home bases on the Foggia plain. For many – those with feathered or fuel-starved engines, control surfaces shot away, or with wounded aboard – their only hope lay in reaching the first friendly runway they could find behind Allied lines. Jesi's runway was short, but it was friendly, and it offered the bomber crews just such a haven. The shot-up but still majestic Fortresses and slab-sided Liberators began limping in just as flights of fighters were also returning home. Some of these, too, showed the scars of battle, and all were critically low on fuel. The resulting chaos was a tower operator's nightmare.

A B-24 lay squashed like some prehistoric bug in the middle of the runway. Another, landing close behind it, somehow avoided the wreck and slid to a halt in the mud where two Forts had also bogged down. In the circuit were four more Libs, while overhead circled more of the big bombers, plus dozens of Mustangs, Kittyhawks and Thunderbolts, many firing distress signals, and all clamoring loudly for landing instructions.

A Fifteenth Air Force B-24, unable to make its home field after a raid on Vienna, comes to grief at Jesi. (Church)

With Hollis Merrill, Al Fetters (above) hovered protectively over Bob Bell when Bell went into the drink following a bridge-busting show. A rescue attempt failed when the PBY "Dumbo" was driven off by an enemy shore battery. Fetters would later become the Comanches' last wartime commanding officer. (Fetters)

"Ambulances and cranes scurried from wreck to wreck. Men were impounded to act as messengers from the control tower to the relief parties. In the tower itself, radio on two separate frequencies issued and countermanded orders; red Very lights shot upward in clusters; signal lamps flashed toward aircraft out of radio contact. And in the midst of . . . [all this confusion] operations continued until the sheer pressure of events led to their cancellation."[5] Weeks later crews were still busy freeing Forts and Libs from Jesi's mud and flying them out.

Three days after the Friday the 13th "show" Group operations at Jesi had just about returned to normal. Lieutenant Jack Slatton, a Skull pilot from Anderson, South Carolina, was hit by flak over Ravenna on October 16 and ditched in the Adriatic. While Lieutenants John Rhodes and Ed Payne hovered protectively overhead, Slatton was plucked from the icy water by an air/sea rescue Walrus of 293 Squadron. It was a close call, as Slatton wasn't in a dinghy, he had only his Mae West to keep him afloat, and survival time in that part of the Adriatic at that time of the year was measured in minutes.[6]

Lieutenant Delmar Estes, another Skull pilot, also had a narrow escape over Ostiglia on October 25 when a 20-mm cannon shell whizzed through his cockpit, shattered his goggles, and exploded just outside the airplane.

A lone German snooper appeared over Rimini on October 27, and another over Ancona the next day, providing a brief flurry of excitement and visions of an "easy" victory. But both interceptions were hindered by the soupy weather and the snooping Germans escaped. On October 29 the Skulls lost Lieutenant Robert B. Bell, and two days later the Skeeters lost Captain Keith Croskery.

Bell, who had flown air-sea rescue PBYs and C-47 cargo planes before joining the 79th on Corsica, was hit while bombing a 300-year-old bridge near Argenta. He nursed his shot-up Thunderbolt half-way home before losing power completely and was forced to ditch. After a few frantic moments struggling to open the canopy, which had slammed shut on impact,

Left: Bad news for the enemy was the tube-mounted HVAR (High-Velocity Aircraft Rocket) first introduced on the Eighth Army front by the 79th. It was usually referred to by its designation, pronounced "havar," or by its nickname, "Holy Moses." (Church) Right: Cleaning rocket tubes. (Church)

Bell popped to the surface and inflated his small life raft. As he climbed into his dinghy Al Fetters and Hollis Merrill circled overhead until relieved by a flight of Spitfires. A short time later a PBY from his old outfit landed to pick him up, but the crew was driven off by an enemy shore battery which bracketed the PBY with two artillery shells. Before another rescue attempt could be organized it was dark. When British Spitfires and a PBY searched the area the next morning there was no sign of Bell, although he watched the failed rescue from afar, his dinghy having drifted miles away from where he had gone down the day before. He eventually made it to shore, where he was captured by the Germans, thus ending his 13th and last combat mission.[7]

Croskery "bought it" on his 59th mission. Armed with rockets his flight had been patrolling between Venice and Udine when they spotted several enemy vessels just off the coast. The targets turned out to be deadly flak barges and the flight was badly cut up by the intense barrage of anti-aircraft fire that greeted them: two aircraft were severely damaged and Croskery was killed. He was from Scarsdale, New York.

The Group had added air-to-ground rockets to its ordnance inventory (becoming the first fighter group on the Eighth Army front to do so) on October 19 when Colonel Nielsen led a Comanche armed recce mission up Italy's east coast. Although the tube-mounted projectiles (three tubes under each wing) were estimated at having the hitting power of a 105-mm howitzer, they were unreliable at first and not very accurate. The folding fins did not always deploy properly with the result that the missiles sometimes went into wild gyrations. In addition, the high explosive warheads were virtually useless against tanks and other thick-skinned vehicles. Brought to bear against motor vehicles, light shipping, railway rolling stock, gun positions, and as a flak suppression weapon, they proved reasonably effective. On occasion, when close support with the new airborne artillery was carried out in plain view of the forward troops, the foot soldiers were stimulated to no ordinary degree by the rocket's destructive power and requested more and more missions with them. "Please accept our grateful thanks and genuine admiration for the brilliant attacks by your rocket-firing Thunderbolts," an infantry brigade commander signaled

Lt. Robert Norman, shown here on Corsica, was hit by ground fire while bombing a bridge with the Skeeters on November 6, and ended up a prisoner of war. (Norman)

Lts. James Phelan (left) and Don Lawless of the Flying Skulls with 500-pound bomb. (Lawless)

Near continuous rains left the dispersal area at Jesi a sea of mud. Number "79" has 57th Group rudder markings. (USAF)

the 79th after a flight of Falcon P-47s had battered an enemy stronghold in front of his positions with air-to-ground rockets. "Come up and see us again sometime."[8]

Although the demand for more rocket missions involved another major training program – the tubes greatly affected the Thunderbolt's flight characteristics – the 79th willingly obliged. During the remainder of the month 444 rockets were loosed at enemy targets (with 97 direct hits observed; many targets were obscured and results were unknown), and from then until the end of the war they were employed with increasing regularity.

November started out with the weather going from bad to worse. Living conditions became near impossible as some tents had six to ten inches of water on the floor, and half the Group's ground transportation was continuously engaged in pulling the other half out of the muck and mud. They were completely weathered in for ten days during the month, and missions were aborted regularly because of low overcast skies shrouding the target. Two days of continuous rain at the beginning of November left the entire bivouac area under water and, to further add to their discomfort, mail was slow and hot food was the exception rather than the rule.

On November 4 straggling Fifteenth Air Force heavies and their escort, unable to make their home fields after raids on Germany and Austria, once again sought out Jesi's runway. This time they didn't inundate the airdrome as they had October 13, and all of the cripples set down safely with the exception of a P-38 coming in with one engine out. The pilot overshot the runway on his first approach, then made the fatal mistake of turning into his dead engine while low and slow. The Lightning hung in the air for a few brief seconds, then disappeared in a blinding flash of fire. The pilot didn't get out.

That same day the Falcons flew what would prove to be their first of many missions to Yugoslavia (or Jugland, as it was called by the pilots) when a pair of Comanches reconnoitered the Kocevje area without incident. With the enemy in the Balkans retreating before a heavy Russian offensive, the Desert Air Force began to fly an ever-increasing number of missions to that area to harass and block his escape. Although the hunting was good, and would get much better, Yugoslavia did not prove to be a popular target with the pilots. Mission routes took them across the choppy Adriatic which at that time of the year was "a mighty frosty place to sail a dinghy."

The skies cleared sufficiently on November 6 to allow missions against an airdrome at Rivolta; a highway bridge near Ravenna; an ammo dump outside of Padova; targets of opportunity near the Eighth Army bomb line, and an electrical transformer station a few miles southwest of Verona.

The Skulls fired the dump, blowing it sky high with an ear-shattering roar, and also flew the airfield strike where they damaged a lone Me 109 caught on the ground, and several railway boxcars found in a nearby marshaling yard. They also had six out of twelve P-47s damaged by flak and ground fire during the airdrome strafe – vividly demonstrating once again the enemy's determination to defend his forward airfields.

At Ravenna, the Skeeters took out the bridge with eight 500-pound bombs planted squarely on target, but lost Lieutenant Robert Norman to ground fire over the target – he bailed out and was captured – and Lieutenant William Peters was killed at the start of a Comanche armed recce mission when he spun in shortly after take-off. When Norman hit the ground he landed right into the waiting arms of several enemy soldiers with rifles leveled at him. *"No pistola! No pistola!"* they shouted, thinking he was going for a gun as he reached around behind him to unhook his chute. Cold and soaking wet from the soggy landing in the swampy terrain, he was bundled into a motorcycle sidecar and "almost literally froze to death" as the driver sped off at high speed to start him on his way to captivity.[9] Norman was from Norfolk, Virginia; Peters from Marion, Wisconsin.

The big show of the day however, was against the transformer station, the 79th's contribution to Operation BINGO, a plan conceived to reduce enemy rail traffic through the Brenner Pass.

The Brenner Line ran from Innsbruck, Austria to Verona and was the main supply artery into northern Italy. When operating at full capacity 24,000 tons of supplies sped down it daily bound for Kesselring's army in the Po Valley. Previous attempts to interdict the Brenner had met with little success as the perverse autumn weather precluded a strict bombing regimen, thus affording the enemy a respite from daily air attacks. As a result he was able to restore damaged bridges and repair rail cuts almost as fast as the damage was effected.

Unable to shut down, or even temporarily block the Brenner Line with a conventional interdiction program, Allied tacticians sought to force the enemy to switch from electrical to steam power. Steam locomotion, especially in the mountainous terrain of Austria and northern Italy, was far less efficient than electrical, and by denying him the use of electrical power it was estimated the enemy would have to keep the line open at least fifty percent of the time just to maintain minimum daily tonnage requirements. Under those conditions, even taking into account extended periods of non-operational weather, they would have to run their trains during days when skies were clear, thereby exposing the system to marauding Allied airpower.

The targets for BINGO were seven transformer stations: four between Verona and Trento, and three near the entrance to the Brenner Pass. Mediterranean Allied Strategic Air Force B-24s would hit the northern end of the line; three groups of B-25s and 57th Group Thunderbolts would strike at targets at Domegliara, Ala, and Trento in the south, while the Comanches and Skeeters – armed with rockets – joined two squadrons of bomb-toting 239 Wing Kittyhawks in a blitz against the station near Verona.

The heavy bombers fared badly. Bombing from altitude, most missed their mark and the enemy was able to continue using electrical power at that end of the line. In the south however, the four stations assigned to XXII TAC and the Desert Air Force were rendered completely useless. At Verona, Falcon and 239 Wing pilots scored eighteen direct hits on the main buildings of the complex and twenty-three against the transformers. When they left, the sky was filled with vivid blue flashes of crackling electricity, and a dense pall of oily smoke hung over the area. Never again would the enemy regain use of electrical power on the line between Verona and Trento. Although anti-aircraft defenses were heavy, only one plane, a Skeeter P-47, was slightly damaged.

After a rough mission over northern Italy, Lt. Robert Peters of the Comanches inspects his flak-damaged P-47. (Church)

After the BINGO blitz the 79th returned to more conventional targets. When weather permitted they roamed the battlefield in front of Eighth Army clobbering a hapless but still dangerous opponent. Sometimes they got clobbered in return.

While the Skulls were bombing a marshaling yard near Imola on November 7, Lieutenant Eugene T. Van Houten took a crippling flak hit and was last seen gliding north with a dead engine. He was later reported to be a POW, but in fact Van Houten managed to evade the Germans for the remainder of the war, hiding out much of the time in a church where he "never missed a meal," and because the water was bad drank one-year-old wine during the day, and the "good stuff" (three-year-old vino) at night.[10]

Two days later Lieutenant James Anderson, Jr., a Comanche pilot from Houston, Texas, was killed in a freak mishap southwest of Forli. The 4th British Infantry Division was making a strong bid for Forli that day but their advance was being held up by a stone building the Germans had fortified and made into a stronghold. Six Comanches and a flight of Skeeters answered the Britisher's call for help and were making rocket attacks against the enemy position. Down on the deck, where there was little room for either mental or mechanical error, Anderson's rocket tubes became entangled with his ailerons. The sudden loss of control flipped his heavy Thunderbolt over on its back and it dove into the ground. Anderson died instantly, but twenty-six rocket hits had completely demolished the enemy strongpoint, and Forli fell to the British later that day.

There were still many "bugs" to be worked out of the new weapons system – as Anderson and others were finding out the hard way – but the rocket attacks served as a great morale booster for the men-in-the-mud who were visibly impressed with their effectiveness against fortified positions. A similar attack November 13 near San Tome earned the Group a congratulatory message from the British brigade commander in charge of the ground assault: "Attack most successful. Our casualties lightest (only just reached double figures) sustained in any similar operation. We took 106 prisoners."[11]

The weather remained bad – not bad enough, apparently, for an "extremely intoxicated"[12] mechanic at 239 Wing to attempt a takeoff in a Spitfire (he crashed at the end of the runway) on November 11 – but following two days of steady rain and snow that grounded all aircraft the weather broke on November 16 (the day a RAF Mustang collided with a gas bowser and narrowly missed crashing into the Comanche's tent area) and remained favorable for a week. The Group took advantage of the clear skies to put up seventy-seven missions during that period.

Many of the sorties were directed to help Eighth Army advance on Faenza, where the British hoped to capture that city and gain the high ground around it to launch an offensive against Bologna and Ravenna, as they took out bridges behind the lines and blasted tanks and enemy strongpoints in support of the infantry. They also returned to Jugland November 18, rocketing rail lines and rolling stock near Ljubljana and, for the first time in several weeks, were called upon to provide fighter escort for XXII TAC Mitchells and bomb-carrying Desert Air Force Kittybombers (P-40s) as they ranged over Austria and Yugoslavia.

Preceded by an armed recce sweep that flushed only a gaggle of Russian Yaks south of Karlovac, the Skulls took 239 Wing Kittybombers across the Adriatic twice on the 18th and once again the next day, as the Kittybombers worked over rail lines between Ljubljana, Yugoslavia and Villach, Austria. All three missions were unopposed by enemy fighters, as was yet another on the 18th when the same squadron shepherded eighteen B-25s of Colonel Pete Remington's 310th Bomb Group to Borkurpa, Yugoslavia. Although unchallenged by the Luftwaffe there was still valid reasoning behind the order to resume escort service for DAF's and XXII TAC's less-maneuverable aircraft.

By this stage of the war the battle for air superiority in the Mediterranean had obviously long been won by the Allies. Since mid-September, when enemy air strength in Italy was estimated to be only the twenty or thirty 109s based near the Swiss frontier at Ghedi, it had become standard operating procedure for medium bomber crews to fly unescorted. A month later they began encountering small formations of Me 109Gs and Ks flown by pilots of the new Fascist *Republica Sociale Italiana* (RSI) Air Force.

The shadow of a strafing Thunderbolt looms large over enemy motor transport being worked over near Verona. (USAF)

The RSI was a shadow government set up by Mussolini on the shores of Italy's Lake Garda shortly after he was overthrown in 1943. Ground forces loyal to Mussolini waged a bitter "civil war" against partisans in the hill country, and fascist pilots were absorbed into the Luftwaffe and sent to Germany to train and receive new equipment. By the early fall of 1944 many of these airmen returned to their homeland as 2° *Gruppo*, Jagdgeschwader 1 (*Italien*), under the operational control of Luftflotte II and the Jadgfuhrer *Italien*, Oberst (Colonel) Eduard Neumann. It was also about this time that fighter units of Luftflotte IV and the Hungarian Air Force, having been pushed back into Hungary by the advancing Russians, started challenging Allied bombers over the Balkans.

More of a nuisance than a serious threat at first – the RSI pilots especially, seemed content to fly little more than standing patrols over the Brenner Pass – their formations grew larger and more aggressive in early November. Allied intelligence now counted more than a hundred hostile fighters in northern Italy alone, most of them sitting on hardstands at Aviano, Vicenza, Villafranca and Udine. After three B-26s were shot down and six others damaged by twenty Me 109s over Rovereto

Their work was never done. A mechanic inspects the propeller of a P-47 for nicks and dents as it sits in the mud at Jesi. (Church)

Lts. Jack Tobin (left) and Bob Sweeney of the Flying Skulls. (Tobin)

November 5, Allied air commanders ordered close escort for the bombers on all missions where they were likely to meet opposition. As an added precaution Fifteenth Air Force Liberators and Fortresses carried out a series of devastating attacks against these airfields on November 17 and 18. After this visit by the heavies enemy aircraft, whether flown by German or Italian pilots, were noticeably absent from Mediterranean skies.

The 79th's main enemy however, was weather, mud and flak, not fighters. After a mission over Yugoslavia November 19 where the Skulls exchanged two P-47s and Lieutenant Fred J. Moschberger (later a POW) for four locomotives, and three days of rocketing German defenses south of Faenza, they were once again grounded by the weather. The weather may also have contributed to an accident on November 25 when a B-17 crashed just off Jesi's runway, killing seven of the eleven men on board.

The skies cleared momentarily on December 2 to allow the Group to fly nine missions, including three against a particularly obstinate observation post the Germans had set up in a church steeple at Russi, and two days later they got off thirteen close-support missions to mark their last day at Jesi.

As had happened on their first day of operations from the muddy field, when the Comanches lost Calvin Arnold, the Group also lost a pilot on its last day at Jesi. Lieutenant Ronald Faison, who had a 109 to his credit in a fight over Mulhouse, France in September was shot down while the Skeeters were rocketing a German divisional headquarters building near Cotignale. Like Arnold, he too, would spend the rest of the war behind German wire.

The next day the 79th left Jesi and moved twenty-five miles up the coast to Fano.

fifteen

Italian Finalé

"The effectiveness of fighter-bombers lay in that their [mere] presence over the battlefield paralyzed every movement."

– Generaloberst Heinrich von Vietinghoff

Fano was a one hundred percent improvement over Jesi. Weather continued to hamper flight operations, but the men were at least out of the mud. Officers quickly commandeered living quarters in the middle of town, while the enlisted men were billeted in a cluster of pink stucco bungalows built before the war as part of Mussolini's better housing program. Devoid of plumbing or heating, except for improvised gas stoves that had a tendency to blow up, and far from luxurious by American standards, Yankee ingenuity soon had them in creditable shape.

Off-duty diversion was also more plentiful. A warehouse was converted into a USO and movie theater; the Desert Air Force also ran a theater in downtown Fano where, in addition to nightly movies, popular British dance bands were featured; a Special Services gymnasium was opened, and a Red Cross club run by matronly Miss Lillian Seller in a two-story residence at #17 Viale Margherita offered a quiet place to relax, with coffee and pastry in abundance.

Colonel Gladwyn E. Pinkston, who had previously been with the 87th Fighter Wing, took command of the 79th from Lt.-Colonel Melvin J. Nielsen on November 28, and after he tested the runway by taking off and landing with two 1,000-pound bombs the 79th was back in business.

Unlike Jesi, Fano had a steel-mat runway. Like Jesi, it was slippery when wet or mud-covered and also 1,500 feet shorter than required for a safe takeoff with a full ordnance load. Most of the Group's missions were now being run with either 1,000-pounders and belly tanks, or wing tanks, rockets, and belly tanks. The latter combination allowed them to hit rail transport and other targets many miles beyond normal bombing range, but both loads tested and strained the efficiency of pilots and ground crews. Aircraft had to be in perfect flying condition and handled with consummate skill, as any defect or pilot error would almost certainly result in disaster. "The first time off with a 1,000-pound bomb under each wing, most of the pilots used water injection for added boost, but still some of the clunkers struggled. After that, 1,000-pound bombs were routine."[1]

Routine or not, aircraft accidents were frequent during the first weeks at Fano, although not all could be attributed to the heavy bomb load, and not all were by 79th aircraft. A RAF fighter wing also shared the field, so both British and American crash crews were on duty. American ambulances, being more durable in the muddy, uneven terrain, were usually first on the scene of a crash. During one takeoff a British P-51 plowed into one of the ambulances on line duty. Fortunately, no one was injured, but the ambulance was a total wreck. Another accident a few days later had more tragic results.

That was on December 17, when a bomb-carry Australian P-51 failed to negotiate the takeoff and ended up in the Comanches' dispersal area where one of its bombs exploded. The pilot, and Sergeant Gerald V. Ervin, a crew chief from Detroit, Michigan, were killed and seven others injured in the explosion, which also demolished three Comanche Thunderbolts and damaged teǹ more.

Because of the fickle weather, combat operations were sporadic for the remainder of December. Long hours of alert and standby duty were required of pilots and ground personnel, however, as every daylight hour was spent in watchful waiting for the skies to clear. They did on December 31, the day the Skeeters lost Lieutenants Richard Gorsuch and Albert V. Bratt, Jr. to enemy action. Gorsuch, from Orlando, Florida, was still listed as missing at the end of the war, while Bratt ended up as an enforced guest of Hitler's Third Reich.

Bratt was shot down over Yugoslavia while on a two-ship weather recce led by Harry "The Horse" Bartley that turned into a train-busting show. Bratt usually flew a "razorback" Jug (X-84) that he had inherited from Ferdinand Tichenor when Tichenor left for the States the previous October, but X-84 was being repaired for flak damage, so he was flying someone else's "bubble-job" today. He was also wearing flying boots over his shoes for the first time ever, and almost "lost it" on takeoff when the wide boots prevented him from toeing the brake pedals properly. Flying in the soup all the way, Bratt and Bartley crossed the Adriatic, making landfall west of Zagreb, then turned north until breaking into the clear just south of Ljubljana. They radioed their weather info back to base, then went looking for targets of opportunity. Almost immediately they spotted a train in a valley between two mountains. With Bartley in the lead they went down to strafe. Bartley's pass failed to "blow" the locomotive, but Bratt's did, although he almost mushed into the mountain as he pulled out of his dive. They soon spotted another train, and attacked this one head-on. The train crew fired back, hitting Bratt's Thunderbolt in the engine, which promptly caught fire. He struggled to reach bail-out altitude (there was no hope of setting it down wheels-up in the rugged

Colonel Gladwyn E. Pinkston. (Church)

Flying Skull pilots celebrate Christmas in the Officers' Club at Fano. Note the parachute draped from the ceiling. (Odle)

terrain), jettisoned the canopy, and prepared to jump. "The PIF (Pilots' Information File) said to dive for the right wingtip so you'd slide off the trailing edge of the wing, minimizing the chance of hitting the horizontal stabilizer, but whoever wrote that never tried it," Bratt said. "I tried it but only got halfway out of the cockpit; my upper torso was plastered against the side of the fuselage by the slipstream, while my legs were still back inside." That was the last thing Bratt remembered until he woke up lying on the ground with at least a dozen of the local inhabitants staring at him. Twenty minutes later he was taken prisoner and spent the remainder of the war in a prison camp.[2] Harry Bartley, meanwhile, had a lonely ride back to Fano. Four days later he would be dead.

As the war entered its fifth and final year an uneasy quiet fell over the battlefield in northern Italy – quiet only in the sense that there was no mass maneuvering of troops as men on both sides of the line continued to daily flirt with death as they sniped at each other with artillery, mortar and small arms fire, patrolled and probed, and fought isolated actions designed to improve their positions – and despite four months of bitter fighting in the mountains north of Florence, by New Year's Day Fifth Army was still nine miles short of Bologna. In the eastern sector Eighth Army* was also hopelessly bogged down. Worn out by weeks of struggling to cross an endless succession of rain-swollen rivers, they had made it to the banks of the Senio above Ravenna, but could go no farther.

Exhausted, short of artillery ammunition, and with three long months of winter still facing them, the Allies halted their autumn offensive. Both sides dug in to await yet another spring.

With the front stalemated, Allied tactical airpower was freed from close-support chores and turned almost exclusively to an interdiction campaign aimed at isolating the battlefield. Indeed, by January 20, instead of the normal one-to-one ratio they had been flying, DAF squadrons were putting up only one sortie in support of the ground troops for every seven against communications targets. This policy change was also reflected in the 79th's mission lists as it too began devoting more time to Italy's complex rail system north of the Po, and less against gun positions and fortified buildings near the bomb line. The Group also ventured into central and northern Yugoslavia more and more as the month wore on, harassing the enemy as he made a slow, torturous withdrawal through the Balkans. While

It was a sad day for the Comanches when an Australian P-51 crashed into the Squadron's dispersal area, killing Sgt. Gerald Ervin. A crew chief, Ervin was one of the Squadron's original members. The three photos on this page show the damage that resulted when one of the Mustang's bombs exploded. (Colmer)

the hunting was generally good, enemy flak and the hazards of normal combat operations continued to take its toll.

Lieutenants William Harding and Harry Bartley became the Group's first casualties for 1945 when both were killed January 4. Harding, from Omaha, Nebraska and on his seventh mission, was with the Skulls over Yugoslavia rocketing motor transport and rail traffic near Sarajevo when ground gunners knocked him down. Bartley had logged more combat time – eighty-two missions – but the flak was impartial and he was hit while bombing a railroad bridge near Stenghella, Italy with the Skeeters. From Sarver, Pennsylvania, his P-47 plunged into an irrigation canal before he could bail out. A week later, on January 11, Lieutenant Richard Menger was wounded while over another Italian rail bridge near Sacile, and Lieutenant Archibald McIlwaine, a Skull pilot from Meyers Hills, South

* In November, command of Eighth Army passed to Lt.-General Sir Richard McCreery who replaced Oliver Leese, while Mark Clark replaced Alexander as commander of Fifteenth Army Group and Lucian Truscott moved up from VI Corps to take over Fifth Army. Alexander was then elevated to the position of Supreme Allied Commander in the Mediterranean.

Left: Lt. James Hannon of the Comanches, killed while working on the railroads south of Giorgio. (Church) Right: Lt.-Colonel Johnny Martin (left) and Republic Tech Rep Tom Drummond with 10 Grand, the 10,000th Thunderbolt produced by Republic Aviation. WASP Pilot Teresa James started 10 Grand on its journey to Fano, where Martin used it to fly the Group's 30,000 sortie. (Lappin)

Carolina, was killed in a takeoff accident as his squadron was leaving Fano to hit the same target.

Sandwiching fighter-bomber and armed recce missions in between periods of bad weather, the Group lost three more pilots during the last half of January. Lieutenant Robert F. Hewitt unaccountably dropped out of a Comanche formation and crashed on January 21; Flight Officer Wesley Stage was shot down while over Padova with the Skulls on January 23 and taken prisoner, and Lieutenant James F. Hannon was killed when he flew through a flight-mates bomb blast while the Comanches were cutting railroad tracks south of Giorgio, Italy on January 27.

Lieutenant John C. Kittrell almost became another casualty on January 15 while taking off with the Skeeters on his 60th mission. As he was barreling down the runway trying to get airborne his engine quit just as he passed the point of no-return. He crashed into the opposite bank of a small creek, and the two 1,000-pound bombs he was carrying flew off without exploding. The plane was on fire, however, and the force of the impact had slammed shut his canopy, giving Kittrell several anxious moments before he was able to force it open. "Well, that's the end of Kitt," the guys in the Ops tent thought when they saw smoke rising from the area where his plane had augured in. But Kittrell had named his plane *Zozo,* an African nut which supposedly connotes "good luck" or "good fortune," and good luck was riding with him this day. He got out of the wreck unscathed, and bought drinks all around at the officers club that night.[3]

It was also in January that Deputy Group Commander Lt.-Colonel Johnny Martin flew the Group's 30,000 combat sortie. To honor the occasion he flew *10 Grand*, the 10,000th Thunderbolt produced by Republic Aviation. The plane had been christened at Republic's Long Island, New York plant on September 20, 1944, by aviatrix Jacqueline Cochran, who had flow its prototype, the Seversky P-35, to victory in the 1938 Bendix Race. As newsreel cameras whirred and hundreds of Republic factory workers cheered, Cochran smashed a bottle of champagne against the plane's cowling. WASP (Women's Airforce Service Pilot) Teresa James then climbed into the cockpit and flew *10 Grand* to the docks at Newark, New Jersey, where it was later loaded aboard ship for the trip to Italy. James left a note in the cockpit: "To the pilot of the *10 Grand*, you hit the jackpot. May every mission be a grand one and every chance a winner. Good hunting."[4] Martin's sortie with *10 Grand* was uneventful, and the plane itself had a rather unspectacular combat career.

Fano was covered with a heavy blanket of snow on January 28 – a rare sight to the natives in that part of Italy – and the field was still being shoveled out the next day. But flight operations resumed on January 30, and four train-hunting expeditions to Austria were mounted, the first of many armed recce missions the Group would run to Austria over the next several

Officers' billet at Fano. (Kelly)

weeks. It was a roundtrip ride from Fano of over 400 miles – most of it over the icy Adriatic where a downed pilot's survival time was measured in minutes, or the fog-shrouded Alps – but the area between Villach and Klagenfurt was packed with enemy rail traffic and was an excellent hunting ground for trains.

Don Lawless led five Skull Thunderbolts on the day's first mission to the Villach area – to get there they had to crest the Austrian Alps and drop down into the narrow Drau Valley – and they found a happy hunting ground as they swooped down on the unsuspecting Germans. Using rockets, bombs and machine-guns they blew up five locomotives and 20 railway cars, and damaged three more engines and thirty more box cars. Lawless and his wingman hit one loco with a head-on rocket attack, blowing it clean off the tracks. It disintegrated in a tremendous explosion, sending large chunks of debris flying through the air. Lawless ducked instinctively as he flew through the debris, narrowly missing the engine's front guide-wheel and axle which had been hurled into the air.[5] Two more missions were flown to Austria that day, all with the same good results.

As January gave way to a new month all hands were anxious for the skies to clear so they could turn that particular part of Austria into a graveyard of Axis trains. But the weather steadfastly refused to cooperate. Fano or the target area were either completely socked in, or operations severely restricted, for sixteen of the first eighteen days in February. Even on clear days Austrian and Yugoslva skies were deceptive and dangerous. The mountainous terrain was covered with snow and offered few check points, and missions were usually against targets situated in haze-covered valleys between mountain peaks from which the enemy poured anti-aircraft fire *down* on them.

In addition, the 79th had to provide its own weather reconnaissance. Previously, during the time lapse between a favorable weather report over the target and the arrival of the Group's striking power, the area would often be totally blan-

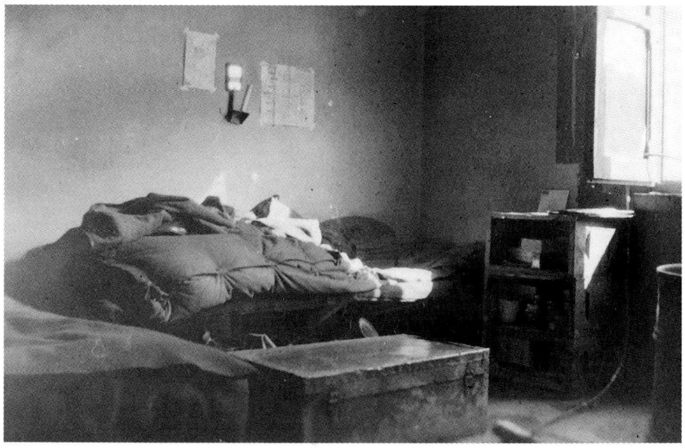

The Spartan Fano quarters of Lt. Ed Kelly of the Skeeters. (Kelly)

Lt. Edwin Plank of the Flying Skulls. He had fifty-eight missions to his credit when the war ended. (Plank)

Loaded down with 500-pound bombs and belly tanks, two Skeeter Thunderbolts wait for another P-47 to land before taxiing out to the active runway at Fano. (Church)

keted by low clouds, fog, and ground haze. Russian and partisan forces were also continuously on the move throughout much of Austria and Yugoslavia, and great care had to be taken lest they accidentally attacked these friendly forces; the political repercussions from such an error would have echoed all the way back to Washington.

Because of these factors, pilots studied maps of the territory for hours; a critique and review of check points was held in the 79th's war room (a Nissen hut outfitted with maps, photos, and a projector for displaying essential information) after each mission, and Colonel Pinkston initiated an intensive foul-weather training program for all pilots. This training and preparation paid off handsomely February 1 when Lieutenant Alfred Hearne led a flight of Comanches on instruments through a solid overcast for over an hour . . . found a small hole in the cloud cover . . . went underneath to collect a large bag of locomotives, railway cars and motor transport . . . then brought his people back out of the soup and safely home. All other DAF and Twelfth Air Force missions to that same area were beaten by the weather that day, and Hearne was awarded the British DFC on the personal recommendation of Air Vice-Marshal Foster, the DAF Air Officer Commanding. Foster had succeeded Air Vice-Marshal Sir William Dickson as the Desert Air Force AOC in December.

After being socked in February 2 and 3, the Group got in a full day of operations on February 4 that netted four locomotives, a rail bridge, and large amounts of rolling stock. On the 6th only one sortie got off the ground – an armed recce to Venice primarily to test the new K-25 camera then being installed on the Group's aircraft – while the next day the skies remained clear long enough for four fighter-bomber missions over northern Italy.

Ten missions on the 8th, and three on the 9th further disrupted the enemy's rail movements, but the 79th lost a man each day. Weather was a definite factor in the death of one, and may also have accounted for the loss of the other. Lieutenant George E. Keppler of Pasadena, California disappeared in the haze while the Skulls were cutting rail lines near Casarsa, Italy, and could have fallen prey to either weather or flak. The next day the Comanches lost Lieutenant Richard Ascenzi. Without radioing the nature of his emergency Ascenzi bailed out over the Adriatic near the mouth of the Po River. Lieutenant Irvin Grandjean immediately made an instrument descent through a solid overcast that extended from the deck in many places to 10,000 feet, relying fully on his altimeter which is usually less than a hundred percent accurate at low altitude. He broke into the clear just above the tops of the waves and spotted Ascenzi struggling with his dinghy in the heavy seas. The Dallas, Texas pilot then made an instrument pattern climb back out of the overcast so ground controllers could get a radio fix. They sent a Wellington to the scene with a dropable lifeboat. The rescue plane spotted the downed flier on its first pass, then lost him as it swung around to drop the boat. Further searches that day and the next failed to find any trace of the Comanche pilot.

A critique and a review of check points was held in the 79th's war room after each mission. (Church)

The weather finally broke on February 19 and held for the remainder of the month. At last they could effectively cover the crowded Austrian rail network, and hardly a day passed that a flight returned from that area without a collection of scalps.

The 79th probed into Germany proper – the Group's first time ever from an Italian base – on February 20 when Major John L. Beck took the Skeeters over the Alps to create havoc with the enemy's rail system near Hitler's private retreat at Berchtesgaden. This foray into *der Fuehrer's* backyard was highly successful – "Our rockets hit an electric train in the station loaded with troops, and they headed for the woods after the first shot was fired"[6] – and gave everyone a boost in morale, but later that day the Comanches were bombing a rail bridge near Casarsa when Lieutenant Irvin Hoerr was knocked down by flak. The Peoria, Illinois pilot was still unaccounted for when the war ended.

Operations were curtailed the next day when a 239 Wing Mustang attempted to land at Fano with two 1,000-pound bombs dangling precariously beneath its wings. As the P-51 touched down, both bombs fell off. One exploded midway down the runway, tearing it up so badly it took the remainder of the afternoon to repair. Miraculously, the pilot escaped with only minor injuries. The pilot involved in another accident the following day also somehow escaped serious injury when his P-38 got out of whack on landing and slid halfway down the runway on its nose. On February 23 the Falcons went back to get the Casarsa bridge.

The bridge – more correctly, a rail diversion – had been a particularly frustrating target since late November. Constructed over a nearly dry river bed it was easily repaired, and time and again the Falcons or some other group would knock it down only to return a few days later to find it back in full operation. It was also well defended by numerous anti-aircraft batteries that exacted a heavy toll from the attacking aircraft; in three consecutive missions the DAF lost five aircraft. After Irvin Hoerr was lost to Casarsa's defenses, the Group returned on February 23 – this time a surprise had been prepared for the German ground gunners.

Three flights armed with rockets and 20-pound fragmentation clusters (frags had been designed solely for bomb bay use, but 79th armament personnel devised a way for them to be mounted on external wing racks) went in ahead of the main strike force to suppress Casarsa's guns. The flak-suppression mission worked so well, that the twelve bomb-toting Thunderbolts coming in behind them enjoyed a flak-free environment and were able to plant ten 500-pound bombs directly on the bridge. The same method was later used with success against targets near Stenghella and Latisana.

Two fighter-bomber shows on the 24th again proved expensive for the Comanches (out of a total of five Falcon pilots killed or missing during February, four were from the 86th Squadron) when Lieutenant Arthur Burnap, Jr. mushed into the ground at the bottom of his bomb run over a bridge north of Rovigo, Italy, and Lieutenant Thomas O'Brien failed to rejoin his formation after rocketing barges near the mouth of the Piave River.

During the period February 19 through March 16 the enemy made a concentrated, large-scale effort to move troops from Yugoslavia and northern Italy to his front in Austria where

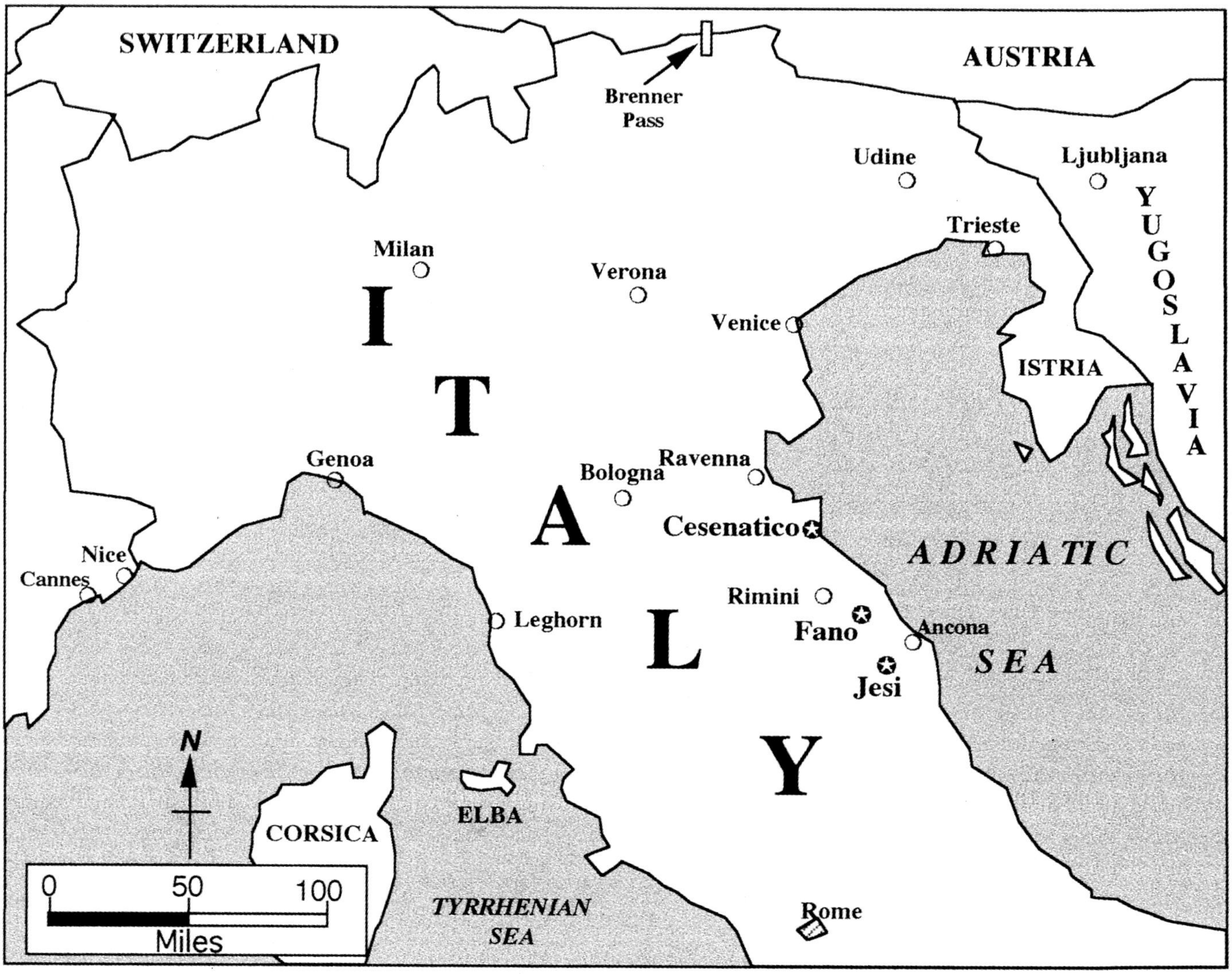

Wingside briefing with Captain Al Hearne (bottom, middle) and Captain Allen Gilbert (top, right). Others are unidentified. (Church)

Despite a heroic effort by Lt. Irvin Grandjean, Lt. Richard Ascenzi (above) was swallowed up by the cruel waters of the Adriatic Sea. (Church)

they were desperately needed to stave off the Russian advance. Despite extremely adverse weather conditions – flying through treacherous mountain terrain heavily obscured by clouds, and facing intense anti-aircraft fire from batteries trained on them from mountain positions above them – the 79th and other Desert Air Force units went all-out to disrupt the enemy's troop movement; each day these targets were not hit a considerable amount of men and material was removed beyond range of the fighter-bombers.

Averaging ten missions a day for the last four days of February, the Group covered the rail lines in the Ljubljana-Klagenfurt-Villach-Dobbiaco area with exceptionally good results, high-lighted by a show on the second to last day of the month when scores of trains and flat cars were worked over with an estimated seventy-five percent either destroyed or damaged. Except for one pilot slightly wounded by debris from a bomb blast, Group casualties were nil during those last four days of February although Lieutenant Robert Moody had a close call. Moody was shooting up a troop train over Yugoslavia when his engine quit. Because anti-aircraft fire was intense, he assumed he had taken a hit, so he rolled back his canopy and prepared to belly it in. Only at the last moment did he remember that he had neglected to switch fuel tanks at the start of his strafing run, and when he did so now his fuel-starved engine sputtered to life again and Moody skimmed over the tops of the trees and headed for home.[7]

After a slow start during the first two days of March when weather grounded the Group's aircraft on the 1st, and prevented them from reaching their targets on the 2nd, they resumed their war against the enemy's transportation system on March 3. For the next four days they flew missions from dawn to dusk as the tempo of the air campaign against communications targets quickened rapidly, reaching a climax March 6 when the 79th won its second Distinguished Unit Citation; the first was for its support of Eighth Army in Tunisia. They would lose a plane a day – resulting in one pilot missing, two taken prisoner, and one seriously injured – but they effectively thwarted the enemy's plan for bringing pressure against the advancing Russians.

Lieutenant Zoltan J. Angyal became the first Falcon casualty March 3 when he and three other Comanches went down low to bomb and rocket a train on the Bassano-Ora-Feltre line in northern Italy. The boxcars were filled with ammunition and in the resulting blast pieces of debris set Angyal's Thunderbolt on fire. Suffering from severe burns he bailed out at 1,000 feet and landed in a tree. Angyal, Merle Blair, Richard Ascenzi and Calvin Arnold had all been tent mates on Corsica. Blair was killed in a jeep accident on that island; Arnold was shot down on the Group's first mission from Jesi in October and taken prisoner; Ascenzi was lost at sea when bad weather foiled attempts to pluck him from the icy Adriatic in February, and now Angyal was seriously injured. It was indeed a dangerous business that they were in.

One hundred and nine sorties on the 4th resulted in heavy claims against rail traffic, motor transport, bridges and gun positions. It was against one of the latter, a flak battery near Rovigo, that the Skeeters lost Lieutenant Donald Montgomery. Hit by a burst of 20-mm flak, he bailed out and was picked up by the Germans. The next day Lieutenant Albert Mathias from Chicago was shot down by ground fire while rocketing a train near Jesenice, Yugoslavia and was still listed as missing at the end of hostilities.

Two South African Spitfires on an early morning reconnaissance north of Venice on March 6 reported almost eight hundred rail transport on the line near Conegliano. Desert Air

Force quickly put up thirty-nine Marauders from 3 SAAF Wing against this target, plus 244 Wing and 7 SAAF Wing Spitfires, as well as Mustangs and Kittyhawks from 239 Wing, and Falcon Thunderbolts. Destruction was widespread as they hit this chokepoint; fighter-bombers alone claimed over two hundred railway cars destroyed or damaged.

Also during the day the 79th's pilots dropped out of overcast skies to knock two spans out of a bridge at Montereale, and drop the northeastern span of a bridge at Cittadella into the water. They also flew anti-flak missions with rockets and frags, attacked oil barges on northern Italy's waterways, and with 239 Wing Mustangs kept up the pressure against enemy rail traffic in the Villach-Klagenfurt area of Austria. It was against one of these Austrian targets that Lieutenant Arthur Pneuman, a Skeeter pilot from Syracuse, New York, was knocked down and captured.

Another highlight of the Group's activities during March was a two-day attack against Campoformido airdrome near Udine, one of the largest airfields in northern Italy. Enemy air opposition no longer posed a serious threat – although there were some 120 enemy fighters based in Italy as of March 1, most flown by RSI pilots, their operations were severely limited by a lack of fuel[8] – but sightings of small enemy formations over northern Italy were again being reported (the Comanches encountered twenty Me 109s while escorting B-26s to Casarsa March 11; no contact was made) and the presence of the enemy base at Udine only a few minutes flying time from the Eighth Army front dictated the need for an attack.

On March 18 the Group sent fifty Thunderbolts sweeping low over the drome in four separate rocketing and strafing missions that did but minimal damage to the enemy (only two Ju 88s were found on the field) while they in turn were badly cut up by the airdrome defenses. Four Skeeter P-47s were shot full of holes by ground fire; Jack Tessier hit a tree while strafing a gun position that had been set up beneath it and limped back to Fano minus several feet of wing – he took out the gun position, but his plane was so badly damaged it needed a new wing, engine, canopy and guns.[9] – and Lieutenant Clarence E. Paff, a fifty-five mission veteran from East Lansing, Michigan was slapped out of the sky and has never been heard from.

Two days later, on March 20, reconnaissance planes reported a large number of enemy aircraft on the field and the 79th returned to Campoformido with a vengeance. This time they hit the known gun positions first with frags, phosphorus and rockets, then returned again and again with the same ordnance to work over the airfield itself. They set a new sortie record – 260 – in twenty-four missions, as they thundered across the drome in an almost unceasing stream. Most of the pilots flew three missions that day as they set buildings on fire, cratered runways, blasted revetments, and destroyed or damaged twenty-one aircraft on the ground. Twelve hours later, after the last Falcon Thunderbolt touched down at Fano, most of the pilots felt they knew Campoformido better than their own landing ground.

Major Fred Zilly (left) and Comanche pilots Lts. Victor Gartzke, Robert White, Jack Boyd, Irvin Grandjean, Richard Powell and Eugene Franco. (Horn)

Lts. Thomas Riley, Tom O'Brien, Al Hearne, Loren Hintz and Harold Hall head for a post-mission debriefing. O'Brien and Hintz were later knocked down over hostile territory and were still listed as missing at the end of the war. (Church)

Despite the record number of sorties no pilots were lost to enemy action (after the initial flak-suppression flights German gunners were reluctant to stick their heads up, and the only opposition in the air was a lone Me 262 jet that quickly darted away when challenged by the Flying Skulls) although

Comanche pilots Lieutenant William Nicholas and Paul Church each had a narrow brush with disaster from mechanical failures.

Nicholas was returning to Fano when he lost a prop and bailed out off the coast. As he paddled around in his dinghy he drew fire from enemy shore batteries and was wounded slightly in the leg before the air/sea rescue people got to him.

Paul Church was taxiing out for his third mission of the day when one of the steel shipping bands that held his frag cluster together broke, spilling several of the lethal bombs on the taxiway. He returned to the revetment to have a new cluster mounted. With the problem "fixed," he taxied back out to take off and was moving down the runway picking up speed when the band broke again. This time, two of the bombs exploded. The P-47's wing took the brunt of the blast, but the plane swerved off the runway and skidded to a blazing halt in front of the control tower. Church made a hurried exit and escaped with minor facial burns. The crash crew quickly extinguished the blaze and Church went back to survey the wreck, hoping to salvage the Thunderbolt's eight-day clock – a valued souvenir. It was already gone! The firefighters had worked fast indeed.[10]

Falcon pilots pound German rail traffic in Yugoslavia. (Horn)

An advance party left Fano on March 21 to prepare a new landing ground forty miles up the coast at Cesenatico. That same day the 79th participated in a unique Desert Air Force effort called Operation BOWLER.

German lines of communication in northern Italy and the Balkans were by now so badly crippled that the enemy had resorted to surface shipping to transport much of his equipment and supplies. Especially heavy was the water traffic at the head of the Adriatic, between Trieste and Venice, where the distance between the two ports was such that crossings could be made entirely under the cover of darkness. Photo reconnaissance Spitfires (known as "Blue Spits" because of their camouflage) of 285 Wing had been watching this activity since late February, and it was soon evident the volume of traffic was increasing steadily. It was also apparent that the harbor at Venice was the focal point. Air-Vice Marshal Foster studied the problem for a few days, then decided to mount a full scale air attack against the Venetian port at the appropriate time.

Lt. Zoltan Angyal was seriously injured March 3 when a railway boxcar he was rocketing blew up in his face. He bailed out and landed in a tree. (Church)

Armed with rockets and frags, this Thunderbolt stands ready for another train hunting expedition to Jugland. (Church)

That time came on March 21 when aerial reconnaissance revealed the 3,200-ton *Otto Leonhardt* (a 340-foot cargo vessel) had moved to an active shipping berth in the harbor at

A frag cluster. Designed for bomb bay use, 79th Armament people devised a way for them to be mounted on external racks. (Horn)

Lt. William Nicholas lost a prop and bailed out off the coast. (Church)

Venice taking on supplies. Also in the harbor were two coastal tankers of 1,000 tons each, a pair of 649-ton torpedo boats, and numerous barges.

Foster's plan called for two squadrons of Thunderbolts and a squadron of Mustangs to take out the harbor's anti-aircraft defenses while Wing Commander G. H. Westlake led in the main strike force of forty-eight 239 Wing Mustangs and Kittybombers. The hitch to the operation, and the reason for naming it BOWLER, was that Venice had been declared an Open City by the Allies and was not to be bombed or shelled under any circumstances. Too many of Italy's historic, age-old monuments had already been demolished or badly battered, and to ruin more at this stage of the war would be inexcusable. The Desert Air Force Commander made it painfully clear that all senior officers involved would be "bowler-hatted" (fired) if bombs missed their mark and fell into the city – the target area was to be strictly confined to the 650x950-yard shipping basin and surrounding docks. To find out just who was doing what, a Spitfire would be overhead at 20,000 feet taking pictures.

Captain Benjamin B. Cassiday, Jr., the Skeeter pilot who had shot down a Me 109 on his first combat mission the previous June and who would become the Skeeters' last wartime commander, was leading the 79th's show and had twenty Falcon Thunderbolts over the harbor at Venice by mid-afternoon on the 21st. They, and a squadron of 239 Wing Mustangs went in first against heavy anti-aircraft fire to sear forty-three gun positions with rockets, frags and machine-gun fire. Then, as the flak-suppression flights wheeled for home, the first wave of fighter-bombers roared in over the breakwater. While hundreds of Venetian civilians watched from rooftops, little realizing they were being treated to a display of infinite pilot skill – or how easy it would have been for someone to overshoot the target and send a bomb hurtling into the crowded city – Westlake's airborne warriors set the *Otto Leonhardt* on fire with two direct hits. Great gouts of flame and smoke gushed high in the air as the ship settled slowly into the muddy basin. Three more waves thundered in as the pilots continued to rain bombs down upon the harbor. Two barges disintegrated, and another was set ablaze. Docks were splintered; warehouses blown apart (one, housing ammunition, erupted with such violence the "Blue Spitty" pilot, dutifully snapping photos 20,000 feet over the holocaust, was flipped over on his back); the tanker flamed and gutted, and a torpedo boat sunk. A near miss on a destroyer at the north end of the west quay sent more debris hurtling into the air.

Then it was over. Only one aircraft (a Kittybomber) had been lost, and the pilot was quickly fished out of the sea by a

Lt. Paul Church had a narrow brush with disaster when a frag cluster broke and exploded as he was taking off for his third mission of the day against Campoformido airdrome at Udine. (Horn)

waiting Walrus, and all of the bombs had been in the target area except one that destroyed a small, private building. As Venice's famous pigeons fluttered back to roosts overlooking the canals, flames and smoke billowed up from the docks testifying to the efficiency and accuracy of Desert Air Force pilots.[11] The next day Air Vice-Marshal Foster sent the following message to the 79th Fighter Group:

> "Full photo coverage has now been received of the attack against Venice harbor installations. The results were excellent, and the maximum amount of military damage has been done by a comparatively small force. Bombing was accurate and no apparent damage has been done to any of the cultural monuments which were in close proximity to the target. The anti-flak attacks were well-timed and accurately delivered. Thanks to this and the efficiency of Air/Sea Rescue, we did not lose a single pilot. My best congratulations to all who took part in this neatly executed operation."[12]

All officers and men from DAF Headquarters down through the squadrons breathed a collective sigh of relief – the bowler hats could be kept on the shelf.

With sunny skies heralding the approach of spring, everyone on both sides of the line realized it was only a matter of weeks – possibly days – before the Allies launched their final ground offensive in Italy. Until that time, however, Desert Air Force continued to fly interdiction missions as it had since the first of the year.

On March 22 the 79th went after rolling stock in Austria and railway bridges in Italy until a mid-morning takeoff accident canceled operations for the remainder of the day. Lieutenant Morrison D. Loftiss, a Skeeter pilot from Indianapolis was killed when a frag cluster broke and exploded as he was accelerating down the runway.

The next day, the last they would operate from Fano, the Group put up nine missions against rail movements, gun positions, bridges and a small airdrome – all in northern Italy. A bridge strike near Udine attracted twenty Me 109s that made a fast pass at the Skulls. One P-47 was slightly nicked by the cannon-firing Messerschmitts flown by Italian pilots of *2° Gruppo*,[13] and Lieutenant Jack Faires had to hit the silk after his Thunderbolt was shot up. Faires' troubles had begun when his Jug ran out of fuel and the engine didn't instantly respond when he switched tanks. This put him about 150 yards behind the rest of the pack, making him easy meat for two 109s who immediately pounced on him from out of the sun while he still had his bombs on. The P-47 was fatally damaged on the 109s' first pass, and Faires was hit by shrapnel and flying glass. In one motion he toggled his bombs . . . did a split-s . . . rolled over on his back . . . and dropped free of the burning Thunderbolt, experiencing a brief moment of panic when he thought he was going to be strafed in his chute, before landing safely in a cornfield near the village of Tarcento. Italian farmers hid him inside a corn shock as a German patrol searched for him, and later sneaked him into town covered up with corn stalks in the back of an oxen-drawn wagon. There he was put to bed, and that evening a local doctor removed the shrapnel and glass from his right leg and thigh, wrist and arm. Faires later returned to Allied control and eventually to the States, where Army doctors took more glass and metal out of his leg, back and thigh, and also found a large piece of shrapnel at the base of his skull that could not be removed.[14] No fewer than three Italian pilots claimed credit for shooting down Faires, but it was probably *Capitano* Ugo Drago, whom 79th pilots had met before on July 26 over Brescia.[15]

The Group also had three other aircraft damaged that day, two by ground fire and one when it flew through exploding

Boilermaker Pete, Paul Church's P-47 after a frag explosion on takeoff. A few weeks later Church lost another aircraft when he got into a flat spin while testing Boilermaker Pete II and had to bail out. He decided not to name his third Thunderbolt, and hasn't named anything Boilermaker Pete since. (Horn)

All missions were canceled for the remainder of the day on March 22 when Lt. Morrison Loftiss was killed in a frag takeoff explosion (above) similar to the one that destroyed Paul Church's Thunderbolt two days earlier. (Church)

Three different views of Lt. Ed Kelly's Thunderbolt. X-71 had Kooley's Comet painted on the starboard side and was Kelly's choice for naming it. Dove Andare Babe? was the choice of Kelly's crew chief, Sgt. Vince Nero, and was painted on the port side. Roughly translated, it means "where are you going baby?" Nero is shown kneeling on the Jug's wing in the center photo. Kelly flew with the Skeeters and had seventy missions by the end of the war. (Kelly)

debris, but they destroyed or damaged eleven enemy aircraft on the ground, flamed a host of motor transport, knocked out several flak batteries, and caved in a railway tunnel.

They had the tunnel closing operation down to a science: an element leader and his wingman would drop down to fifty feet or less, going flat out, and then release their bombs while pulling up and to the left as fast as possible. The bombs would arch up into the tunnel entrance as the planes headed up and off to the side out of harm's way. The second element, trailing far enough behind to allow the smoke and debris to clear, would then repeat the process. The technique was first proposed by Lieutenant Wayne Sherer of the Comanches as an alternative to dive-bombing tunnels, and he and Lieutenants Romie Royce, Ray Hagler and George Huntzberger tried it for the first time on a tunnel north of Rome in April 1944. All four pilots were awarded DFCs for their pioneering work.* Later, the technique would be refined: while one pilot bounced a pair of 1,000-pound bombs into the mouth, another would simultaneously plant a similar load between the two entrances. With a ton of explosives blowing up and another ton blowing down at the same time, the tunnel took a terrific beating.

Later on March 23, the Group's pilots flew forty miles up the coast to join A-Party at Cesenatico, a fashionable pre-war summer resort colony. Located on one of the finest white-sand beaches on the Italian side of the Adriatic, Cesenatico's living conditions were exceptionally good. Billeted in tents at first, the men soon moved into villas along the coast; all officers were housed and fed as a group in a large downtown hotel; tennis courts were available; movies and USO shows were held in an open-air theater on the beach, and well-stocked clubs and bars were opened. Life was far above the mere existence it had been back in North Africa and Sicily.

* Sherer had also submitted to Headquarters AAF an idea for using para-bombs to attack enemy bomber formations. The idea was rejected as impractical, but German fighters later employed para-bombs against American bomber formations over Germany with some success.[16]

Lt. Wayne Sherer (center) of the Comanches proposed a new way to take out railroad tunnels. He and Lts. Romie Royce, Ray Hagler and George Huntzberger tried out the new technique for the first time in April 1944, and by the spring of 1945 the 79th's pilots had it down to a science. (Sherer)

The landing strip was not appreciated as much as the living quarters. The runway, constructed of PSP matting over sand, was short and obstructed at both ends. Takeoffs with 1,000-pound bombs were extremely difficult and dangerous, and were only undertaken when 500-pounders wouldn't suffice. Nevertheless, these last few weeks of the European war spent at Cesenatico proved to be the busiest in the Group's long combat career.

For the remainder of March and during the first eight days of April, Falcon pilots roamed over northern Italy and the Balkans hitting bridges, trains and motor transport. During this period takeoff accidents claimed the life of one pilot and seriously injured another, while one pilot was downed from mechanical failure, and another was missing as a result of enemy action.

Lieutenant Robert S. Robinette, a Skull pilot from Butler, Indiana, was killed March 24 when he struck a building on takeoff (he was carrying two 1,000-pounders); Captain Herbert Hanson lost a prop March 25 while returning from a fighter-bomber show near Nervesa, Italy and bailed out (he later turned up safe), and Lieutenant Warren Bostick was shot down by small arms fire April 2 while the Skeeters were over Austria strafing a train. Bostick, from Manton, Michigan, was on his third combat mission. Another pilot on the mission, William Probst of the Comanches, had his oil line shot away, drenching his cockpit canopy with the lubricant. With his forward visibility obstructed, Probst guided on his flight leader's wing and both made it back to base, the leader tucked in close alongside Probst as he came in over the fence for an otherwise uneventful landing; a happy ending to his first combat sortie.[17]

On April 4, Don Lawless was with seven other Flying Skull pilots bombing a railway bridge near Gorizia, Italy when he almost fell victim to a Messerschmitt Me-262 *Schwalbe* (Swal-

Living conditions at Cesenatico bordered on the deluxe as well as the Adriatic, but the landing strip had obstructions at both ends of the runway, and blowing sand made engine maintenance difficult. (Church)

Ground personnel at Cesenatico work on the tail wheel of a P-47. (Kelly)

Cesenatico was a fashionable, pre-war resort located on one of the finest white sand beaches on the Italian side of the Adriatic. But because of the blowing sand, pilots had to fly with carburetor air filters closed, resulting in loss of engine power which made takeoffs with a heavy bomb load extremely hazardous. (Church)

Jane's Playboy ready to go with rockets and frags. (Church)

low), the first jet fighter to see combat in the war. He had just pulled out of his bomb run and was in a gentle, climbing turn away from the target when his wingman warned there was a "bandit" on his tail. At the same time Lawless saw "golf balls" slowly arcing over his canopy and knew he was being shot at. Without a backward glance and all in one motion he flipped his '47 onto its back . . . pulled the stick back into his stomach . . . jammed the throttle to the firewall . . . and hit the war emergency boost button. His heavy Jug plummeted like a rock. Close behind were two dark green Me-262s, their swastikas outlined clearly on their tails. Jinking once or twice to throw off his pursuer's aim, Lawless planned to hit the deck running and lose the German jets in the trees. But they broke off at about 3,000 feet and streaked north toward Austria at high speed, possibly because they were low on gas, out of ammo, or worried about two British Spitfires that had been hovering overhead like a couple of hawks, ready to swoop down from their high-cover perch. Unknown to Lawless at the time, two other Spits had already scared off a third jet that had made up the trio of enemy fighters snooping around the edge of the Skulls' formation.[18]

It was also in early April that *Lucifer's Ghost* was "retired" from service. The *Ghost* was a Comanche P-47 that had proven to be virtually indestructible. It had gone through five pilots and two crew chiefs, and had survived more than 500 operational hours and 208 combat missions, including 147 in a row, with only two engine changes. It had taken a beating in the air – coming back at times with its wings in tatters and gaping holes in its fuselage – as well as on the ground, operating from rough, bumpy, half-completed runways. But it always came back. "That's it! That's 500 hundred hours!" the crew chief, Sergeant Grady B. Richardson, said when Lieutenant William E. Bishop set the *Ghost* down for the last time "That's one tough Thunderbolt," Bishop added. "It has never let me down!"[19] In addition to Bishop, Ed Lemmon, Walter Manning, Zoltan Angyal and Alfred Hearne all flew the *Ghost* at one time or another, and Sergeant Bates Shuping was its first crew chief.

By April 1945 Adolf Hitler's Third Reich – a vainglorious regime that was to have lasted a thousand years – was near total collapse. The end of Nazi Germany was inevitable. Her cities lay in charred, skeletal ruin, her industry was smashed and shattered, her people starving and homeless. The armies of the Western Allies had crossed the Rhine in March and were now driving deep into the heart of the Fatherland, while in the east Marshal Georgi Zhukov's Red Army hordes, back from the brink of disaster on the cruel, cold steppes of the Ukraine, were within forty miles of Berlin, poised for the final assault. Between them, the Wehrmacht struggled for life in an ever-shrinking salient.

In northern Italy, however, it seemed nothing had changed since the beginning of the winter stalemate four months earlier. Indeed, on the surface at least, the enemy there appeared stronger than ever. They had dug deeply into the north banks of the Senio River, and stoically and methodically strengthened their mountain positions south of Bologna. They had flooded the lowlands near the east coast, their morale was high, and they outnumbered the Allies on the ground by six divisions. Kesselring no longer masterminded the German defense of the northern Apennines (he had been summoned home in March to help shore up the sagging Western Front), but in his place stepped the very capable von Vietinghoff. And Vietinghoff's command, that included several elite panzer and parachute units, was probably the most effective fighting force remaining in the German service.

But the comparison of strength between the two opposing armies was deceiving. Four of von Vietinghoff's divisions were Italian Fascists raised by the exiled Mussolini, and were little more than weak combat groups; over 60,000 partisans were loose behind German lines, forcing the enemy to divert front-line troops to curb their activities; the Allies held a large edge in artillery and armor, and they had absolute command of the air.

Clark's plan to break the long stalemate was ably conceived and designed: his objective was to destroy all German forces in Italy, if possible, south of the Po. Eighth Army would strike first, crossing the Senio and pushing up the Adriatic toward Ferrara to threaten the enemy's flank and draw off his reserves. When von Vietinghoff was committed in the east, Fifth Army would drive on Bologna (by staggering the two ground assaults both Allied armies could be given maximum air support), then continue to advance to Bondeno and link up with Eighth Army. Both forces would then strike to seize Verona, blocking the last escape routes into Germany. The critical phase of the offensive would be Eighth Army's initial assault, when it would have to fight through a narrow gap (the so-called Argenta Gap) between Lake Comacchio and flooded swamp land a few miles to the west. The Gap was expected to be fiercely contested, but a quick breakthrough at that point would unhinge von Vietinghoff's entire line and put the Allies in position to cut off a major German retreat.

Shortly after noon on April 9 over eight hundred heavy bombers droned northward from their bases on the Foggia plain, apparently bound for targets in Austria or Germany. Then, over Cesenatico, they wheeled sharply to the west and unloaded tons of fragmentation bombs (frags were chosen to avoid churning up ground over which Eighth Army would have to travel) on German positions north of the Senio River. Behind them, as Allied artillery laid down five, forty-two minute barrages, came the mediums to pound pre-selected targets. Then the fighter-bombers swarmed over the battlefield – bombing, rocketing, strafing and napalming (the 79th pioneered the use of air-to-ground rockets in the MTO, but never used napalm) – as they assailed enemy gun positions, command posts and strongpoints in blistering, low-level attacks.

Supported by flame-throwing tanks the infantry jumped off at dusk, each man knowing if he survived this battle he had

Engine maintenance at Cesenatico. (Church)

It ran a little rough coming home. Lt. William Waller's P-47 and result of oil leak caused by flak. Waller flew with the Skeeters, and notched the Group's last confirmed victory in the air when he bagged a 109 over Mulhouse on September 24. (Church)

probably survived the war, and they moved swiftly ahead, reducing one strongpoint after another. The enemy fought back as best he could from behind prepared positions, but he was stunned by the furious storm of bombs and shells, and slowly gave up ground. British, Polish and New Zealand troops (Canadian troops, who had fought with Eighth Army since the invasion of Sicily had left the theater shortly before the offensive began and were thus deprived of a share in the final triumph in Italy) were soon across the Senio River and on their way to the next, the Santerno.

That night Bostons, Baltimores and Mosquito bombers flew out of Forli and Cesenatico from dusk to dawn, hitting enemy positions closer to friendly troops than had ever before been attempted in the dark. With first light the heavies returned to saturate the area in front of the advance with a carpet of bombs while the fighter-bombers, directed by ground controllers using a card index of photos to pinpoint specific targets only a few hundred feet from the first line of infantry, provided the mud-sloggers with flying artillery of devastating intensity.

By nightfall on April 11, three Eighth Army divisions had reached the Santerno, and by the 13th Allied ground troops were pouring through Argenta Gap toward Ferrara. The next morning, behind the heaviest air support ever given in Italy, Fifth Army hit the center of the line and drove for Bologna, reaching that city seven days later where it joined advance units of Eighth Army.

By April 19 von Vietinghoff was in serious trouble. His mountain defenses were ruptured; his left wing was reeling under Eighth Army's savage blows; he could no longer stabi-

The enemy's transportation system north of Rome was thoroughly worked over by Falcon Thunderbolts and other DAF units. A Po River bridge under attack. (Church)

Lt. Lou Challet and Dagwood soak up some rare Italian sunshine. (Church)

A Comanche T-bolt taxies back to its hardstand after a successful mission over Yugoslavia. (Church)

A Falcon Thunderbolt undergoes a prop change. (Church)

British crash crew foams down a Flying Skull "auger job." (Church)

lize the front; he was desperately short of fuel, and the last of his reserves had been committed. Only an orderly retreat to the north banks of the Po could hope to stave off complete disaster, but an earlier request to make such a move had been rejected by Berlin. On April 20, when he took it upon himself to disengage and retire to the north, it was already too late.

Allied armor had broken into the flat, open country above Bologna and was racing to cut off his retreat. As the Allies closed up to the Po River, Desert Air Force and XXII TAC struck vigorously against the congested temporary river crossings. All permanent Po River bridges had long been destroyed, and by April 23 so were the pontoon bridges. Many Germans escaped the net by swimming the broad river – where without guns, tanks or transport they were powerless to set up a defense line – but many more were rounded up and taken prisoner. Those units that remained south of the Po were ripe for destruction.

Fifth Army's 10th Mountain Division crossed over the Po on April 23, seized Verona three days later, and fought up the shores of Lake Garda to close the Brenner Pass. Other Allied formations followed, quickly fanning out across the upper Po Valley to block remaining escape routes into Austria. As a major partisan uprising on April 25 further compromised the German position, Allied ground units continued to take town after town. When the British entered Venice April 29, only seventeen days after the start of the offensive, von Vietinghoff agreed to unconditional surrender.

The documents of this surrender were signed in a palace at Caserta, and promptly at midday on May 2, 1945 nearly a million men in Italy and Austria laid down their arms. It marked the first German capitulation of the war.

The long Mediterranean strife was over.

When Alexander launched his spring offensive April 9, the 79th Fighter Group began a period of close-support operations that was without equal in its long combat career. That morning Colonel Pinkston addressed not only the pilots but the ground crews as well. "As he talked every man present felt a tinge of excitement – a rejuvenation of spirit – for the end of their long journey was now plainly in sight. All knew it was here, in the valley of the Po, where they would finally finish an enemy they had been pursuing steadily for two and a half years. Colonel Pinkston asked for a superhuman effort, and he got it."[20]

For seventeen straight days they put more than a hundred planes in the air each day, and from April 16 through the 20th their daily sortie figure rose to over 160. They swarmed over the battlefield from sunrise to sunset day after day, blasting a path for friendly infantry and hounding a fleeing enemy. Results were excellent and congratulatory messages from forward

The end of the war is only a few days away as a Comanche armament crew wheels a 500-pounder into place beneath the wing of a razorback P-47. (Horn)

Captain Ed Payne of the Flying Skulls at Cesenatico, with his X-22 in the background. (Payne)

The long Mediterranean strife is over. Falcon Thunderbolts at rest after a job well done. (Church)

troops poured in regularly. But it was not without loss, made all the more tragic with the end of the war so near.

Lieutenant James McHenry was killed on the first day of the offensive when he and four other Skull pilots were rocketing a fortified house a few miles west of Ravenna; another Skull pilot was seriously injured in a takeoff accident on April 11; Lieutenant Richard Evans, a Comanche pilot, had his electrical system shot out over Rovili April 15 and was seriously injured attempting a belly-landing; Lieutenant Loren E. Hintz, a Comanche pilot from Glendale, California, died April 21 when his P-47 crunched into the ground at the end of his bombing run near Budrio; another pilot from the 85th was missing after a fighter-bomber show on April 22, and Captain Arthur Halfpapp, a Skeeter pilot on what was supposed to have been a milk run, was killed by anti-aircraft fire over the Adige River on April 24. It was Halfpapp 103rd trip into the enemy's backyard. That same day a B-25 crashed and exploded on Cesenatico's runway, canceling all further operations that day while the runway was repaired, and two days later a British Spitfire accidentally dropped a bomb near the 79th's gas and ammo dump, but luckily no one was hurt.

John Kittrell, who was one of the eight Skeeter pilots who had been on the February 20 Berchtesgaden show, and whose good luck airplane (*Zozo*) helped him survive a close call in January when his engine quit on takeoff, had another close call on April 17.

Kittrell, now a captain, was on his 100th mission when hit by ground fire near Bologna. He bellied-in without flaps two hundred yards on the wrong side of the line, and it wasn't long before the Germans spotted his smoking plane and tracked him down. Captured, he managed to escape a few days later and was back with his squadron exactly ten days after being shot down.[21]

From April 25 until the first of May the Group's Thunderbolts roamed over northern Italy attacking enemy troop concentrations, by then virtually the only targets remaining. On the afternoon of May 1 twelve Comanche Thunderbolts (one slightly holed by flak) returned from a fighter-bomber strike against shipping off Trieste. As the pilots set their heavy P-47s down on Cesenatico's short, steel-matted runway all further operations were scrubbed.

They had just flown the 79th's last combat mission of the war.

sixteen

Taking the Scenic Route Home

"Only when freedom has been lost does one appreciate its true value."

*– Yvonne de Ridder Files**

By VE-Day, approximately one of every three pilots who had passed through the 79th Fighter Group at one time or another on the long haul from Cairo to Cesenatico had been killed, was missing, or was a prisoner of war. Countless others had been wounded or injured, some seriously enough to create lifelong health problems. Many of those missing were presumed dead – and would be officially so declared with the passage of time – while others were found to be very much alive when prisoner of war camps were liberated. In all, about one fourth of the Group's total casualties, excluding those injured or wounded, spent part of their war behind barbed wire; "in the bag" in POW parlance.

When captured the first words many of them heard were, *"Fer you da var ist ofer."* In most cases it was, but they now faced a much tougher war – a war to maintain their mental and physical health. Their treatment varied depending on how the war was going for the enemy at that particular moment, and whether their captors were civilians, regular army troops or Luftwaffe personnel. Generally, those who fell into the hands of the Luftwaffe fared best, undoubtedly because of the fraternal bond between fliers of all nations. Wehrmacht, or regular army troops were fairly correct in their treatment of captured American pilots, but civilians were entirely unpredictable. It was not unusual for a captured airman to be insulted, spat upon, beaten, kicked – or murdered – by angry, vengeful civilians, especially as the air war against Germany intensified. In most cases, those captured by the Italians were eventually turned over to German military authorities.

If not seriously injured, a prisoner's first stop was usually a Luftwaffe Intelligence and Evaluation Center. There, the pilot-officer prisoner was invariably surprised to learn that his English-speaking interrogator apparently knew almost as much about him and his unit as he did himself, which of course is what the interrogator *wanted* the airman to believe.

In most instances, the method of interrogation did not include torture or physical violence, as would be the case with American airmen shot down over North Vietnam twenty-five years later. But by engaging in a friendly "we-know-everything-anyway" conversation with the prisoner – the background and breeding of most officers made it difficult for them to be rude, and they felt ill at ease refusing to answer obviously innocent questions[1] – coupled with solitary confinement, withholding of privileges, psychological blackmail, threats, living conditions designed to lower moral and produce mental depression, and taking advantage of the prisoner's shock at finding himself in a situation beyond his control, a skillful interrogator could nevertheless usually obtain information from the prisoner beyond just name, rank and serial number regardless of how determined he was to resist. The object was not to learn any great secrets, as most pilots at the squadron level were not privy to such information. Rather, the interrogator sought out details about tactics and operations, and attempted to gather small talk that would assist in breaking down the resistance of future POWs. For every word spoken beyond name, rank and serial number the interrogator undoubtedly learned or confirmed *something*, but most prisoners were convinced that their words, small talk or otherwise, were of no great value to the enemy's war effort.[2]

* As a member of the Belgian Resistance, Yvonne de Ridder Files helped save downed American and British fliers, She was betrayed, tortured, and when she refused to talk was sentenced to be hanged, but was saved when Antwerp was liberated in September 1944. In 1970 she married Lt.-Colonel Roger Files, a former pilot and squadron commander with the 79th. She is the author of *The Quest for Freedom*, a story about the Belgian Resistance during World War II.

Following his interrogation, which could take anywhere from one to four weeks, the prisoner was usually transported to a transit camp called a Dulag Luft (*Durchgangslager*, or "through-going camp"), which was sort of a distribution center. Eventually, traveling by train, truck, or on foot, the prisoner ended up in a permanent camp called a Stalag Luft where he settled down to the suffocating monotony of life as a *Kriegie* (short for *Kriegsgefangen*, the German word for prisoner of war) and fought to keep his sanity; fought to keep from "going 'round the bend."

Americans in German POW camps generally received better treatment than their counterparts in Japanese prison camps – although their treatment was poor compared to German prisoners in American POW camps – and officers were generally treated better than enlisted men.* But regardless of rank, or whether the prisoner was an airman or a ground-pounder, life as a Kriegie was no picnic. Those who have been "in the bag" all share grim memories of being crammed into filthy, suffocating boxcars, marched for days at a time on frozen, blistered feet, and being bombed and strafed by their own troops. They were perpetually hungry and many had their digestive systems permanently ruined by a steady diet of ersatz coffee, sawdust bread, wormy vegetables, and watery soup flavored with rotten potatoes or rutabaga. If lucky, their diet was occasionally supplemented by Red Cross food parcels.

Medical treatment varied from camp to camp, but most Kriegies were in poor health, and many suffered from dysentery, while others had jaundice or pneumonia. All were continually plagued by lice and fleas. They were also subject to unannounced searches by the Gestapo, and any POW found outside his barracks at night could be shot without warning. And they were dismayed and irritated to learn that their life behind wire was being depicted to those on the home front as one of comfort and leisure, although that impression was undoubtedly designed to calm the fears of their friends and relatives back in the States.[4]

General living conditions were abominable, and life was harsh, but boredom was the prisoner's biggest enemy. To keep from "going 'round the bend" they engaged in an endless series of miscellaneous diversions. According to the Geneva Convention, officers could not be forced to work, which gave them the opportunity to arrange numerous leisure time activities, from planning and producing theatrical productions, to planning and executing escape plans. One of their most popular pastimes was taunting their guards, or "goon-baiting."

What sustained them the most, however, was the knowledge that the war couldn't last forever – that it *must* end some time – and the hope that the Allies would be victorious. In the meantime, they tried as best they could to maintain their mental and physical health and adapt to their unfamiliar environment. And they dreamed of the day when they would finally be "out of the bag." Three Falcon pilots who dreamed that dream were Robert Bell, Donald Claycomb and Albert Bratt.

Robert Bell spent six months "in the bag." A factory worker in Detroit before the war, Bell graduated with pilot class 43-C at La Junta, California and flew PBYs for Air/Sea Rescue out of Ajaccio, Corsica, before moving across the island to join the 79th's Flying Skull squadron at Serragia in August 1944. On October 29, 1944, on his thirteenth mission, he was hit by antiaircraft fire while bombing and strafing an ancient Po River bridge south of Bologna and ditched at sea a few miles off the Italian coast. After three failed rescue attempts – which left him wondering if "unlucky" Mission 13 had something to do with it – Bell eventually made it to shore the next day where he was immediately confronted by three Italian civilians and a German soldier who stuck a rifle in his face. Taken to a nearby house, he was greeted by an older Italian who spoke good English, and the German soon left, leaving him in the custody of the Italians. Bell was allowed to wash the sea salt off his body with a wet cloth, given clean clothes, a slice of bread and a bowl of hot stew. It was his first food in over twenty hours. After sleeping all that night and most of the next day, his underwear and flight suit were returned to him – washed and pressed – and he was taken to a German army hospital:

> "At the hospital I was given a pair of pajamas and a bed in a room to myself, and after a few hours sleep they brought me a slice of dark bread and some ersatz coffee," Bell said. "Later that morning I visited with two wounded American soldiers. They said they had had no food for two days before being captured, but that they were being treated well. I told them the Germans were being pushed back and that they would be home for Christmas. Back in my room I was given a bowl of watery soup and another slice of bread for lunch.
>
> "That afternoon a doctor who spoke fluent English examined me, and asked if I played chess. I did, so we played a game each day for the two days I was in the hospital. We parted with a handshake.
>
> "On the second day a young Italian man was let into my room by someone I didn't see. He was dressed in a gray tee-shirt and pants that looked like he had slept in

* When it was learned that the Germans were also treating sergeant POWs better than privates, the AAF made every enlisted man who flew over Germany a sergeant.[3]

them. Because he wasn't wearing pajamas or hospital apparel I asked what he was doing here. In Italian and broken English he told me he was a partisan and indicated we should escape. If I understood him right he said we would fight the Germans and that there would be plenty of girls available for sex. Thinking he had been sent by the Germans to test me, I shook my head several times and said 'No.' He became annoyed and left in a hurry, leaving me with a weird feeling about what was going on.

"The third morning I was taken to a building occupied by the Germans and a young soldier was assigned as my guard. He was armed with a submachine-gun and spoke some English. He told me we were going to Trento, and we were soon bicycling north along the side of a major road. I spotted an airfield about two miles away where planes were taking off and landing, and fantasized for a moment about stealing a plane before reality set it.

"That night we stayed in a small hotel full of soldiers, and I ate in their mess hall where I was completely ignored. After the meal they burst into song; I knew several of the tunes and almost joined in when they sang *Lili Marlene*.

"Later, in our room with two beds, my guard said he was going to go visit some friends, and he left. As I was lying on my bed I noticed his submachine-gun on the other bed (without an ammunition clip), and being curious I started to field strip it. There I sat with pieces of it on the bed, and finding it was a little more difficult putting the gun back together than it had been to take it apart, when in walked my guard. He looked, laughed, and proceeded to show me how the pieces fit. I slept like a log that night.

"The next morning we went by truck to Padua, and that night we stopped at an army barracks at Venenza. I wondered what kind of quarters we would have that night, as it seemed strange I had not been turned over to the Germans, but supposed arrangements had been made with my guard. This time things were different. I was introduced to a German officer who spoke very good English and he apologized for the lack of decent facilities for officers. The guard was told to bring me back to see him after we had eaten. In the mess hall there were more Italians than Germans, and the Italian songs were more melodious.

"After the meal I was taken to the German officer, who offered me a cigarette, and we sat and talked. He told me he had been on the Russian front, and spoke of Hitler as being a great leader. It was his opinion that the Allies would lose the war. That night I slept on a cot in a locked room.

"In the morning a truck took us to a town above Bolzano, where I was taken to an army administration center. I said 'goodbye' to my guard, and sat around in a locked room the rest of the day. That evening two new soldiers were assigned as guards – both in their forties or older, and armed with rifles – and we soon left the building, walked a few blocks, and got on a street car. During the ride I noticed several citizens wearing black arm bands (which I recognized the significance of) and was sure there were no friendly feelings towards me by some of my fellow passengers, especially since my flight suit identified me as a flier. One man wearing a black arm band pointed at me, and muttered something to those around him, and became very angry and agitated; he advanced toward me cursing, and one of my guards had to step in front of me to end the episode.

"From the street car we took a train, and knowing my geography I knew we were about to leave Italy through the Brenner Pass. During the first hour or so of travel I was the object of attention by five German soldiers, and I was a little apprehensive, but it was not long before we were trading war stories. They were veterans of North Africa, one had parachuted into Crete, and another had been stationed in Italy for the last two years. When I told him that an old stone bridge had been my last target, he became excited, telling me he had been an anti-aircraft gunner at a town with a stone bridge and that maybe he had shot me down.

"We went through several tunnels, and I saw flak guns mounted on railway cars between the tunnels, and after changing trains at Innsbruck we arrived at Frankfort where I was taken to an interrogation center. It was November 10. My interrogator spoke very good English. He offered me an apple, invited me to sit down, and proceeded to tell me all about my group and squadron. German intelligence must have been very good because he showed me photos of the tents we lived in, and even the inside of our mess hall. I denied any knowledge of the place he was talking about, or the names he read from a list as being from my group and squadron. I don't think he believed me. He also told me President Roosevelt had died (he hadn't), and that the war would soon be over. I told him it didn't matter who was president, that the war wouldn't be over until Germany was defeated. I guess that remark didn't go over well as I spent the next ten days in solitary with coffee, bread and soup for meals.

"After being released from solitary I was greeted by an American colonel, the former CO of my group [Colonel Stark] who had been shot down before I joined it. He knew I was in camp, so it seemed the prisoners also had good intelligence.

"After five days of decent food from Red Cross parcels, and the companionship of many Allied fliers, I was on the move again. This time to a permanent camp near the Polish border where I became a resident of Stalag Luft III."

Bell was liberated on April 30, 1945 – "In retrospect, my thirteenth mission and near rescues were not that unlucky, as the bottom line was survival" – and was at Reims, France the day the war in Europe ended. While waiting with a small group of former POWs near the airstrip, word spread that a group of high-ranking officers would be visiting them. Bell was the officer in charge of his small group, and when the officers appeared he called them to attention and saluted a man he had only seen in photographs. "Returning my salute, General Eisenhower gave me an 'at ease' and shook my hand," Bell said. "It was a day to remember."[5]

Following the war, Bell stayed in the service, retiring in 1968 as a chief master sergeant. He died March 8, 2000.

Donald Claycomb's "var vas ofer" – his flying war, at least – on September 4, 1944. That was the day he was shot down while strafing a motor convoy near Dole, France. A student at the University of Colorado at the time the Japanese bombed Pearl Harbor, Claycomb joined the Air Corps in the late spring of 1942 and graduated with pilot class 43-B at Luke Field, Arizona in February 1943. He served as an instructor at Pinellas Army Air Field in Florida before joining the 79th Fighter Group in July 1944. Originally assigned to the 85th Squadron, he was soon transferred to the 86th as a flight leader. On September 4 he was leading the squadron on a search and destroy mission up the Rhone River Valley when they spotted a motor convoy and went down to strafe. On his fifth pass his engine was hit by ground fire, stopping it cold. Without power, he put his '47 down wheels-up in a plowed field, but because he also had no aileron control it was more of a controlled crash than a belly landing, and the impact knocked him unconscious:

"When I regained consciousness I was still in the cockpit, and could smell hot oil but I don't believe the aircraft was on fire," he said. "At any rate, I passed out again when I tried to get out of the plane, and when I came to I was on the ground pulling myself away from the plane with my hands. Shortly thereafter I was picked up by a small group of Germans – soldiers and Red Cross people – who took me to a nearby hospital in a horse-drawn hay wagon. There, there sewed up my forehead and put my leg in a splint, the other injuries not being obvious.

"The next morning I was interrogated by a German officer, but all he got was my name, rank and serial number. Then I was loaded into an ambulance with some wounded German soldiers and we headed for Germany.

"We went north for several days to Strasburg, making stops at hospitals along the way, then east into southern Germany and Austria. My flight suit and dog tags had disappeared at the first hospital I was in, so for the next four months, until the end of what I call my 'hospital tour,' I had no identification, and no clothes except my underwear. I had a cast on my right leg up to my crotch, and a body cast from hip to neck. In January those were removed, and I was shipped off to an interrogation center at Frankfurt. Surprisingly, for all those months no one questioned that I was who I said I was. And fortunately, by the time I reached the interrogation center I had been down so long it was obvious that no worthwhile intelligence could be extracted from me so I was only in solitary on bread and water for one night.

"From the interrogation center I was sent to Kassel, where I finally got some clothes, then it was off to Stalag Luft I on the Baltic coast about 150 miles north of Berlin.

"About a week before the war ended the Germans abandoned the camp, and we were soon liberated by the Russians. From there it was France, and then home."[6]

Al Bratt was born and raised near Boston, Massachusetts. He attended the University of New Hampshire in the fall of 1941, and enlisted in the AAF's College Deferment Program the following June. In September 1942, while attending college, the campus was given a "real buzz job" by a P-40 that Bratt believes had to have been from the 79th as it was the only P-40 outfit then training in New England. Called to active duty in February 1943, he graduated with pilot class 44-C at Spence Field, Georgia, and joined the 79th and the Skeeters in July 1944. He was shot down over northern Yugoslavia on the last day of 1944 while on a two-ship weather recce that turned into a train-busting show:

"Until waking up on the snow-covered ground with the feet of at least a dozen people standing around me, the last thing I remembered was struggling to get out of my airplane," Bratt said. "How I managed to get free of the aircraft and pull the ripcord remains a mystery. From the welts, scrapes and bruises I surmise I must have landed in a tree and that these people, who were apparently local inhabitants, had rescued me from whatever predicament I had been in. My helmet and goggles were gone, and there was no sign of my parachute.

"They took me to a nearby farm house where they gave me something hot to drink. I was still pretty shaky, but tried to convey to them that I wanted to be put in touch with local partisans. From their response I gathered they were already in the process of doing that, but twenty minutes later in walked two German soldiers with machine-pistols.

"I spent the first few days in a very old stone prison in the town of Celje. The cells were about eight by eight with a wooden pallet in one corner, a bucket in the other, and a little barred window high up on the outside wall. About three days later I was awakened in the middle of the night by two guards and taken to a railway station where we boarded a regularly scheduled passenger train and headed north.

"About mid-morning the next day the train was strafed by four British P-51s and everyone, civilian and military, jumped off the still-moving train into the snow and ran for a nearby woods. As some people were killed and others wounded in the attack, I was not very popular and was thankful to have the two guards handy for my protection. Later in the day another train came along and took us to Gratz, Austria where I was held on a military airfield for about ten days. It was a collection point for Allied airmen shot down in the Balkans and by the time we left there were about two dozen of us.

"From there we were transported all the way across Germany in old, unheated coaches, nearly freezing to death in the process. We pulled into the Frankfurt marshaling yards after dark a couple of days later and remained there during a British air raid on the city, with bombs falling all around us. The next day it was on to the Luftwaffe interrogation camp on the outskirts of Frankfurt am Main.

"At the camp it was solitary confinement for ten days, with interrogation sessions toward the end. My interrogator showed me a dossier which was a real eye-opener; they knew almost as much about me as I did myself. From there it was a short train trip to the Red Cross camp at Wetzlar where we were issued some personal items such as a toothbrush and overcoat, and then on to our permanent camp on the outskirts of Nuremberg – Stalag XIII D.

"We arrived early in February, and our stay there lasted only a couple of months, which was fortunate given the near starvation diet and lousy living conditions in this former Russian camp. Perhaps to keep our minds off such things, we were treated to front row seats for a thousand bomber AAF raid on Nuremberg, several British night raids, plus a lone Mosquito bomber that dropped a 2,000-pound bomb almost every night to keep everyone awake.

"By early April, Allied forces were getting near and the camp was evacuated. The entire prisoner population, escorted by guards, marched out and headed south in a column that must have been more than a mile long. Our destination was reportedly the Bavarian Alps, but we never made it. On the day that President Roosevelt died (April 12) we were on the outskirts of Moosburg after approximately a week on the road. Just north of town was a temporary camp of tents surrounded by barbed wire and wooden guard towers. We were there for about ten days, when early one morning the distant shelling, which had been getting progressively closer, was right overhead and a firefight erupted between advance elements of Patton's 3rd Army and an SS unit defending the town. We spent several hours with our noses in the dirt as bullet sang through the air, rendering our tents no longer waterproof.

"Later that day Patton himself entered the main gate and we were officially liberated, but confined to the camp for our own safety. A few days later we were flown out in C-47s to Camp Lucky Strike in France where medical attention and a special bland diet for us Kriegies was the order of the day. Not long thereafter we boarded a ship and stopped at Southampton, England to pick up a contingent of nurses. While we were there every whistle on every ship in the harbor started blowing. It was VE-Day! A week or so later we arrived in Boston and were taken to Camp Miles Standish for processing. We were home for good."[7]

Following the war Bratt got a degree in Air Transportation and went to work at Logan International Airport in Boston as an operations supervisor, eventually working his way up to assistant director of aviation. He retired after 39 years, and today (1999) lives in an airpark community in Florida where he is building an amphibious airplane.

Escape was on the minds of virtually every airman who was taken prisoner, and many spent their entire Kriegie experience scheming and planning how to get out from behind the wire. They dug tunnels, foraged and forged, and joined "escape committees" where they shared their various talents and skills to help themselves and others in the quest for freedom. Few succeeded, and many who did were quickly recaptured and murdered by the Gestapo, as happened following a mass escape from Stalag Luft III in March 1944 that has since been recounted in several books and popularized by a 1963 movie, *The Great Escape*, starring Steve McQueen and James Garner.

By the summer of 1944, as the Allies advanced closer to the German border, and the possibility of escaping successfully became more attractive, the prisoners were put on notice that so-called "death zones" had been created throughout Germany in which all persons found in a "death zone" suspected of being an enemy agent or escapee would be shot on sight. "Escaping from prison camps is no longer a sport," the notice read. "Stay in the camp where you will be safe. Breaking out of it now is a damned dangerous act!"[8]

Attempting to escape was a "damned dangerous act" no matter when one tried it, but at least three pilots in the Group – Thomas McCarty, William Glasgow and John Kittrell – tried it and succeeded. Their secret of success appears to be that they managed to escape before being taken to a permanent POW camp.

McCarty was part of a Comanche flight attacking enemy shipping in the Gulf of Tunis on April 30, 1943, when their formation was bounced by fifteen Me 109s. In the ensuing fight, McCarty and another pilot collided, and the wreckage of their crippled P-40s fell on a third a hundred feet below. The other two pilots were still unaccounted for at the end of the war, but McCarty was fished out of the sea by the crew of an Italian hospital ship and taken prisoner. In the fall of 1943 he escaped from a prison camp at Sulmona, Italy, and successfully made his way back through the lines. When he got to Bari he recounted his story to Captain Thomas J. Semmes, an Intelligence officer with the 79th Fighter Group:

> "I was flying on Captain Turner's wing, and had joined him in firing on a 109 that split-essed off into a vertical dive pouring smoke," McCarty said. "At the bottom of my dive I collided with another P-40 that appeared suddenly from below, and its prop sheared off my left wing near the fuselage. The two aircraft broke clear of each other, and I went into a spin at 9,000 feet. I thought at the time the other pilot was Turner, and I'm almost sure my P-40 didn't fall on a third aircraft as reported.
>
> "I attempted to bail out but was unable to pull my body out of the cockpit because of the terrific centrifugal force until the aircraft somersaulted and threw me clear; my chute opened only about five seconds before I hit the water. At this time I saw another chute go into the water about a mile away. I tried to swim toward it, and fired my pistol twice to attract attention, before losing it in the water.
>
> "The water was very cold, and I found that even with my Mae West on I would be rolled over on my back, and my head would go under every time I stopped swimming. As I swam I saw the Italian destroyer we had attacked being abandoned by her crew. They and I were rescued five hours later by an Italian hospital ship that I soon learned was a former British destroyer that had been captured in Greece. This ship was the same one the 86th had attacked, but not damaged, on April 29, and while on board I observed a large number of armed German troops being evacuated from Tunis to Italy.
>
> "The ship took me to Taranto, where I was kept in solitary confinement for one month. From there I was moved to POW Camp No. 21 at Chieti, where there were 1,200 British and 217 American prisoners. The British were mostly from Tobruk, the Americans were air crews. Previous to my arrival at Chieti, approximately 2,500 Britishers had escaped over a short period of time.
>
> "Following the Italian armistice, the Italians left me unguarded for nine days. Our camp commanders – a British colonel and an American lieutenant colonel – ordered us not to try to escape under threat of court martial. They claimed their orders came from higher Allied command. One officer did escape during this period, and court-martial papers were drawn up against him. Nine days later, when German guards appeared on the walls, we were told we were then free to try to escape. I might add that the British colonel was drunk most of the time.
>
> "On September 23 the Germans moved us to Sulmona where we learned we were to be taken to Germany the following morning. That night I escaped with two other American officers – Lieutenants Beck and Johnson from the 33rd Fighter Group.
>
> "During the five months I was a prisoner food was poor and scarce. We were given only small quantities of rice, macaroni and stale bread, not sufficient to maintain our normal weight. Once a month this was supplemented by a small Red Cross parcel containing a meager amount of cheese and chocolate. There was only one small water faucet in the camp, and I often stood in line over three hours to get a drink. We slept on wooden floors, forty to a room, and were treated rather badly, especially by the Italians, but never subjected to physical torture, and we were not required to work.
>
> "After I escaped it took me one month to reach the Allied lines. Italian farmers hid me, and fed me, and fur-

nished me with civilian clothes. Often I was very close to the enemy, and had several narrow escapes. Before reaching our lines I parted company with my friends from the 33rd. I noticed during my travels that German morale seemed good. A number of German soldiers were wearing mixed Italian-German uniforms, and they were living off the land, taking whatever food they wanted. I did observe, however, that they have a great fear of ground strafing.

"Lieutenant [Harlan] Highfield of the Skeeters was also a prisoner at the same camp I was in, but I don't think he escaped. He had bellied in behind the lines on March 29, and was wounded in the arm by a strafing Me 109. Lieutenants Margolian, Rideout, Adams, Lewellian and one other pilot, all from the 57th Group, were with me in the POW camp at Chieti. I understand some of them escaped."[9]

William Glasgow flew with the Flying Skulls. He bailed out over Italy on December 8, 1943 while on a fighter-bomber show near Orsogna. Captured almost as soon as his feet hit the ground, Glasgow escaped a day or two later to begin a harrowing journey through the enemy lines to freedom. He was back with his squadron by the end of the month:

"I left my heavy wool jacket with my crew chief, and flew the mission in just a khaki shirt, confident I would be back in an hour or so," Glasgow said. "Everything went swell until I started to pull out of the bomb run, and the first burst of ack ack hit my ship. It felt like somebody set a firecracker off under my seat, and I was dazed for a moment. When I recovered, the ship was burning and headed down in a dive. The canopy had been blown off, and I saw that my trousers were torn and bloody. I thought to myself, 'this is it, I've had it, so what th' hell . . .'

"I undid the seat belt and stood up in the cockpit, fully expecting to hit the tail section when I jumped. Somehow I missed it, and the next thing I knew I was sailing peacefully through space. When I started tumbling head over heels I realized it would be smart to pull the ripcord and open the chute. I gave it a good jerk, and the chute jerked back, the chest buckle hit me in the mouth and knocked out three teeth. It seemed to take forever to get down, and I could see flashes from artillery fire and Jerry soldiers running around all over the place.

"I landed in open country and got out of my chute in a hurry. I threw away my flying equipment and beat it for the protection of a small hill. As I ran around the side of the hill I ran right into a group of German soldiers. They yelled at me to halt. They were carrying submachine-guns, so I halted. I was then taken to a car with a British warrant officer seated in it – he had also just bailed out – and the two of us were driven to a small town and given first aid treatment.

"At the town I met the German officer in charge of the ack ack battery that had knocked me down. He kept proudly telling me how the first burst from one of his guns nailed me: *'Vas goot?'* he asked. So I said, *'Ya, vas very goot,'* and that seemed to make him happy.

"The German doc insisted that I be given a tetanus shot, but the Britisher was sick from his, and I didn't want to be in the same boat. I complained loudly, insisting I had been given a shot in the past month, and I finally talked him out of it.

"We were taken to a building that was being used as a clearing station for casualties, and it was filled with victims. The orderlies told everyone I was a bomber pilot, and I half expected one of those bomb happy boys to slit my throat. Some of them had been shocked into insensibility by our raids, and had to be led in like blind men, unable to see, hear or talk.

"No one paid much attention to the Britisher or myself, so after two or three loads of Germans had been taken out by ambulance I decided to try to walk out of the place. There didn't seem to be any guards around, and Italian civilians were walking in and out, so I told the British chap my idea and he gave me his escape kit containing maps, money, and a compass. When I was all set, the ambulance pulled up in front and we were loaded in. After we started moving I tried the rear door, but found it locked. I started to batter it with my feet, but the noise attracted the attention of the German soldiers in the front seat, and they made me quit it.

"We were taken to a hospital at Chieti, and then driven to a large base hospital at Penne. I was treated very good there. The evening meal consisted of mashed potatoes, greens, a piece of meat as big as a baseball, and tea spiked with rum. I feigned more serious injury than I had, groaning and grunting every time I was moved.

"That first night, after a minor injury to my wrist had been treated, I discovered my watch was missing. I complained to the chief surgeon, and a few minutes later the officer brought back three watches and I picked mine out.

"On trips between the ward and the operating room I observed as much as I could of my surroundings, and tried to figure out possible ways to escape. I noticed that the first night a light was left burning in the ward, but the second night it was turned off. So, at three o'clock in the morning, after the orderly had made his last inspection, I got dressed and walked to the washroom. There was a window high off the floor, so I climbed on top of the latrine partition and started to pry it loose. I had been hard at work a few minutes when in walked the orderly. He had his head down, and came into the stall next to the one I was perched on, so close I could have reached out and patted him on the head. I held my breath and tried to keep my knees from shaking. Just as I was about ready to collapse, he left. I was shaking with fright, hurriedly finished breaking open the window, and fell to the ground fifteen feet below. I laid there a few minutes listening to the guard coughing and hacking; he trotted right by me, but never looked in my direction, and finally I got up enough nerve to make a break down the hill and away from the hospital.

"I had seen the snow-capped peaks of the Grand Sasso [sic] mountains to the southwest, so with the aid of the compass and bright moonlight I struck out across country toward the hills. I walked until dawn, plowing through muddy fields, and keeping clear of towns and roads. I spent the entire next day hiding out in the woods – cold, hungry, and wet. At dusk I approached a farm house and received food from the Italians, but no lodging as the farmer feared reprisals.

"For the next two days I traveled only at night, sleeping in barns and hen houses during daylight. On the third day I found three isolated farm houses owned by three brothers who took me in for the next three days and nights. These Italians treated me swell. They fed me plenty of macaroni, brown bread and wine, and farmers came from all around to see me and try out their rusty English. There were also three single girls living in one of the houses, which made a good situation even better.

"One afternoon I was down at the girls' house having lunch when a couple of kids came down to tell me German soldiers were at one of the houses trying to get chickens. I went outside and hid in the bushes, but after they left I decided to leave, as too many people knew my whereabouts.

"I left later that night. About midnight I stumbled across a young Italian who had been visiting his girl friend, and he offered to take me home for dinner. But upon arriving at his house we found four German soldiers there. I waited outside while the kid brought me a plate of cold macaroni and a bottle of wine. The following day, after a good night's sleep in the home of an Italian who had once lived in the States, I was led to the hideout of eight Allied escapees. Some of these Britishers had been captured during Wavell's first push in Libya, and had escaped from the Italians after the armistice.

"The British soldiers had been farmed out to different homes for one or two hot meals a day, and in between they lived on dried figs and bread obtained from nearby farms. They knew little of the battle situation, and were kept in a state of indecision by many rumors. Their clothes were in shreds, and they were in no condition to make the final break across difficult terrain. Their most haunting fear was that some civilian's tongue might wag and they would be found out.

"We had the hell scared out of us one night when we heard German voices at the entrance to our hideout. There was a mad scramble to douse the fire, and then three Italian boys walked in, laughing. We felt like choking them, but had to laugh with them.

"I remained in the hideout for two days, then with a rough and ready British paratrooper, and a red-headed sergeant, both of whom 'knew the ropes,' I decided to make a break for freedom. We left that night, hoping to dodge areas of German military activity while we headed for the snowline on the mountains. It was rough going over almost impassable terrain, and we ran across numerous steep ravines that took hours to navigate. My shoes were soon in tatters, and on one occasion we had to fall to the ground when a lone German soldier passed by a few feet away.

"The first night was spent in a straw hut where civilians had built a fire and fed us roasted rib of lamb. The next morning dawned with a heavy fog, much to our pleasure, and we started out on the last leg of our journey. We went down one side of a very steep ravine, and were then unable to get up the other side. We decided to follow a small path at the bottom of the ravine but it led into a small town a woman said was filled with Germans. We had hurried consultation. We hated to go through the town, but the prospect of back-tracking across the ravine and finding a new way out was even worse. We decided to chance going through the town. We made it! We sneaked through the town and hid in an abandoned house until after dark. We learned from civilians that Eighth Army held a small town only four miles away – but they were to be the longest four miles of our entire trip.

"We started out in darkness to cross the road, which was one of those winding affairs that meant we would have to cross it three or four times before making open country. German soldiers kept walking down the road to chow, and we were shaking in our boots. The paratrooper dashed across first. A few minutes later the sergeant sneaked across. I was waiting my turn when I heard a German voice yell, 'Halt!'

"I felt like digging a hole in the ground and hiding in it. I could hear the mumble of German voices off to my right, so I held my breath, prayed, and dashed across the road away from the sound. I made my way through an orchard filled with slit trenches, and with every tree branch looking like a gun pointed at me. I went to our prearranged rendezvous point, but my friends never showed up. I don't think I could have made it as far as I did without their help, and I sure hated to go on without them – and only a few miles from freedom.

"I slept in a barn after walking about three miles, and was awakened in the morning by the sound of rifle and machine-gun fire. I went to a farm house but an Italian woman excitedly warned me away, telling me the Germans were using the house for an observation post. She directed me to stay in the ravine and make for a small town a few hundred yards away that was held by the British.

"After a short walk I came upon a group of civilians, and I could tell by the way they greeted me that I was out of enemy territory. They escorted me into town, and the Italian clothes I had picked up enroute made such a good disguise the British soldier guarding the road didn't even give me a second look. I was so glad to see him, however, I could have hugged him.

"I never heard what happened to my two friends, but I know now that four miles can be a long way from freedom."[10]

With eighty missions to his credit, Glasgow returned to the States where he was assigned to the Fighter Test Branch at Wright Field in Ohio. He was killed in a flying accident several months later.

John Kittrell was shot down and captured over northern Italy on April 17, 1945, just two weeks before the end of the war. A native of Rochester, New York and a graduate of pilot class 44-A at Mariana, Florida, he joined Skeeter Squadron on Corsica in the summer of 1944. On the April 17 mission – his one hundredth – Kittrell's flight was bombing a fortified house near the front lines when anti-aircraft fire fatally crippled his P-47 (the heretofore lucky *Zozo*), and he bellied it in hot two hundred feet on the wrong side of the lines. Captured almost immediately, he escaped a few nights later:

"After my plane was hit I was so preoccupied with finding a clear spot to put it down in that I forgot to lower my flaps; I greased it in like a bullet," Kittrell said. "I got out and crawled through the grass, but the Germans noticed the smoke from my plane and soon found me. As they were walking me back to their command post we stopped near a pile of stones and wood that had been someone's barn. An Italian farmer was tugging at a long piece of rope, and suddenly a bull appeared from beneath the rubble. The Germans then pointed a finger at me to admonish me for causing this inhumane act. I exclaimed with horror and disbelief that I could never do such a thing.

"During the next two days, while walking north to a POW camp, the Germans picked up seven more prisoners. One day, while we were resting on makeshift cots, I noticed that one of the guards had put his pistol under his pillow. He then left the room. I decided not to take it because I was suspicious that it might be a trap. Sure enough, when he returned he immediately looked under the pillow for his gun. That hunch probably saved my life as they were undoubtedly waiting for me on the other side of the door.

"About four o'clock in the morning of the seventh night we stopped at a house and the guards told us to knock on the door until someone came to let us in. The guards then turned and went out the front gate, leaving us standing there alone. We looked at each other and wondered whether we should go out the front gate ourselves, but decided that was what they wanted us to do so they could shoot us trying to escape.

"Instead, two New Zealanders and myself went over a wall in the rear of the yard and ran away, separating from each other so if one were caught the other two might make it. Earlier that night we had passed through a town where the villagers seemed pro-American, so I backtracked my way there. Up ahead I saw a lone German sentry standing in the road in front of a house. He had already seen me, so I kept on walking, passing by in front of him. After about five yards he called out for me to halt, but I kept on going. He called 'Halt!' again, but I didn't stop until he called out 'Halt!' a third time in a voice I knew he meant business.

"I stopped and turned around. He asked me in Italian where I was going. I pointed to a town in the distance. He started speaking rapid Italian, so I told him I didn't understand Italian because I was French. He looked at me sort of puzzled, then told me to go. I walked away, expecting a bullet in the back at any moment.

"Presently I came upon a group of teenagers, and after telling them who I was they told me to go with them. We went to an old warehouse, where I helped them carry away sacks of sugar. Then they took me to a house where one of their friends gave me a bicycle and the two of us rode together to a farm house in the country where I was hidden in a barn loft until British forces arrived. They gave me a spot of tea, put me in an ambulance, and took me back to my field."[11]

Not every pilot shot down in neutral territory or behind enemy lines ended up being a prisoner of war. Many, with the help of friendly civilians, managed to evade capture entirely, although it was a nerve-wracking experience for the downed pilot, and very risky for the civilians involved. If caught by the Germans aiding or harboring a downed Allied airman, a civilian and his immediate family could expect to be summarily executed.

No two behind-the-lines experiences were exactly alike, but those of two Flying Skull pilots – William P. Feimer and Eugene T. Van Houten – are typical. Feimer, who was seriously injured bailing out of his flak-stricken P-40 over Italy in October 1943, dodged the bullet for eleven days before picked up by the advancing Canadians and returned to Allied control. Van Houten was shot down over Italy almost a year later and successfully evaded capture for the remainder of the war.

Feimer joined the 79th and the Flying Skulls in September 1943. On October 4, shortly after his squadron arrived at Penny Post Landing Ground, he found his name on the list for an eleven o'clock mission. Wolfing down a Spam sandwich, Feimer took off with his flight and headed west. Major Frank Wagner was leading the show and because of Feimer's relative inexperience (his eighth mission) he was flying on Wagner's wing:

"We had been outbound about fifteen minutes when we crossed the bomb line (roughly the Fortore River) and Major Wagner signaled us to echelon right and arm our bombs," Feimer said. "The flak was getting quite heavy, and I may have been hit about this time because I had trouble pulling the arming lever. As two bursts of flak rocked my P-40 I pulled in close to the major and we both flicked over to start our run. When I saw his 500-pounder fall clear I dropped mine, although I never did see what we were trying to hit. As I tried to regain altitude I noticed I couldn't keep up; I pushed the throttle all the way forward, but still the rest of the flight pulled away from me. My coolant temperature gauge was now way over in the red, and when I noticed exhaust fumes stretching the whole length of my aircraft I decided to get out.

"I rolled back the canopy, undid my seat belt and shoulder harness, and tried to exit, but the slipstream kept me pinned. I then trimmed the P-40 so it was in a moderate climb, climbed up on the seat, and when my airspeed got below 100 mph I leaped to my right and up. The wind hit me again and my right foot flew forward under the instrument panel, where it wedged in tightly. The next few seconds were probably the most frightening of the whole affair; I was sure I was going to go down with the plane. Finally, with one last tug, I broke free and cleared the aircraft – well, almost; somehow the antenna wire wound around my right leg and tore a large piece of cloth off my pants.

"I didn't count to three as we were taught, as I found there was an uncontrollable desire to get that chute open. When I reached for the ripcord I got another shock – the handle of the D-ring wasn't in the pocket where it was supposed to be. After a frantic search I found it dangling near my knees, gave it a good yank, and was relieved to see the chute blossom overhead. The first thing I noticed was how quiet it had become.

"Soon I could hear rifle fire and the unmistakable 'burrrp, burrrp' of a German machine-pistol, and thinking I might be getting shot at I pulled on the shroud lines to get me on the ground as soon as possible. I could make out some high tension power lines on the ground, and knowing the ones in the States were about four stories high, I decided to use them to help gauge my distance and cushion my fall. But these towers were only ten feet high, and thinking I still had thirty or forty feet to go, I slammed into a small plowed field with unexpected violence. My head flew down and my chin hit my chest.

"I sat there momentarily stunned for a few moments, and began unbuckling my chute harness, when several Italians ran excitedly up the hill, waving their arms and shouting, 'Go! Go! Germans!' So I ran for a hundred yards or so, then ducked into a shelter fashioned from a pile of rocks that peasant farmers used as protection against sudden rainstorms. The Italians, however, gestured for me to keep moving, so I raced full tilt down the hill and dove into an erosion ditch, completely exhausted and gasping for breath.

"I stayed in the ditch for more than two hours, trying to make myself as inconspicuous as possible while a German patrol beat the nearby woods looking for me. As I got my wind back I checked my Colt .45, and examined the contents of a small escape kit I had tucked inside my shirt.

The kit contained a small compass, an unlabeled tube of toothpaste-like substance I later found out was milk, some water purification tablets, atrabine pills, and four small pieces of chocolate. There was also supposed to be some local currency and a silk escape map, but these were missing. The money was of little consequence as I had been paid earlier that morning and carried a large amount of lire in my shirt pocket. The map was another matter, and I silently cursed whoever it was who stole it, probably to send home as a souvenir. I had another escape kit containing fishing gear, gloves, and more chocolate, but it was attached to my chute pack and left behind.

"As I tried to ease my position I noticed for the first time there was something seriously wrong with my neck. I could only change position with great difficulty, and the pain kept getting worse. By mid-afternoon the Italians came back to look for me, covered my give-away uniform with a long coat, and helped me to a small farm house. As I tried to walk the pain became almost unbearable.

"At the farm house was the wife of one of the men who had found me, his teenage son, and a girl of about ten. The son was very nervous about my presence there, so to show them I meant no harm I offered him my .45. That seemed to satisfy every one; the youth returned my pistol, and I was given something to eat: two raw eggs in a cup. About an hour later a man of about sixty walked in. His name was Calavito Giambatista, and he had lived in the States for thirty years and could speak perfect English. After a short conference it was decided Calavito's place, about ten minutes down the road, would be safer. His summer home was more in the nature of a barn; a two-story brick and stone building with no rooms as such, but a bed in one corner, and an area in another corner where they did their cooking. The loft was filled with hay, while the downstairs was shared with a mule and a flock of scrawny chickens. Behind the building was an enclosure where a few hogs were kept. During the summer Calavito and his wife lived in the building while they worked their land, returning in the winter to the nearby village of St. Elia Piansis. I was given a bowl of chicken soup and put to bed. Even though there were mice scurrying all over the place I had a restful night.

"Early the next morning Calavito woke me up with a start. He was very excited, and told me German troops were searching all the nearby buildings. I dressed quickly and was led outside where I laid down in a weed patch. Calavito covered me with straw, and although it had begun to rain and I was getting soaked, and insects crawled all over my face, I didn't move a muscle. Finally, about two hours later, Calavito took me back to the house. He said a jeep full of Germans had searched all the buildings, and when they left they stole all the chickens and eggs they could carry.

"Shortly after a lunch of spaghetti and ersatz coffee I joined Calavito and three refugees from Yugoslavia, and was taken to a cave dug into the side of a hill. It was about a fifteen minute walk, and we had to hide once when a German patrol came by, but we reached the cave safely and were given some more food. The three Slavic refugees and myself spent the next three nights there.

"The first night we witnessed a terrific artillery barrage – the shells were exploding only a hundred yards from the entrance to the cave, and I thought for a moment the artillery was probing for us. The next day we could see the Germans blowing up bridges as they retreated north. By October 8 Calavito decided it was safe to move back to the house, as he thought the battle line had now moved north and were in friendly (or at least neutral) territory.

"The next six nights were spent at the farm house, and my neck kept getting increasingly worse. One day Calavito brought his son there – a former officer in Mussolini's army – and he shaved me with a straight razor. It was a very weird feeling having that razor going up and down my throat by a man who had been my enemy only a few weeks before.

"On October 11 one of the Italians went down the mountain and came back with seven Canadian soldiers. The Canadians were relieved to find I was American, as they thought they were being led into a trap. They carried me on a stretcher to a small village where we were housed in a school house, and the whole village turned out for a celebration. Someone cooked a large omelet – it was about three inches thick and eighteen inches across – and someone else started to play an accordion.

"The next morning the Canadians started carrying me again, but I noticed their hands were blistered from the day before. Finally, I was put on some sort of runner with no wheels, and padded with straw, that was pulled by a cow. It was a rough trip, but better than walking. As we went down the road Italians came up and offered us grapes, peaches, apples and other fruit.

"After an all-day trip we reached a dry river bed where a jeep was waiting. I was loaded on it and taken to a hospital in Bari."[12]

William Feimer returned to Italy in 1954 and found the cave he had hidden in after being shot down eleven years earlier. (Feimer)

Feimer's wife, Louise, with the men who helped him hide from the Germans in October 1943. (Feimer)

Feimer's injury was diagnosed as a fracture-dislocation of the second cervical vertebrate. He was transferred to hospitals in Sicily and North Africa before going home on the hospital ship *Arcadia*, arriving at Charleston, South Carolina in January. In 1954, Feimer and his wife, Louise, returned to Italy on vacation where he was reunited with the Italian family that had befriended him during the war.

Van Houten was born and raised on a small farm near Hamlin, New York. With only two years of high school, he took and passed the entrance exam for cadet training, and graduated with pilot class 44-B. He joined the 79th and the Flying Skulls in July 1944, and flew his first mission on August 3, one year and a day from his first ever flight in an airplane. Hit and forced down while bombing a railway station near Imola, Italy on November 8, 1944, Van Houten hooked up with friendly civilians almost immediately. He watched from his hiding place as the Germans siphoned off the gas from his downed P-47. Later, after the Germans had gone, the Italians blew it up:

> "I spent my first nine days in a farm house near Imola," Van Houten said. "The house and barn were all part of the same building and at night, or whenever the Germans came snooping around, we lived in a small ten by seven foot room the Italians had dug out beneath one of the cow stables. The room was only about four feet high, and en-

The stone farmhouse where Bill Feimer spent the fifth, sixth and seventh nights after his bailout. (Feimer)

Lt. Eugene T. Van Houten was shot down over Italy in November 1944 and spent the rest of the war hiding from the Germans. Most of the time he was holed up in a church, where he never missed a meal. (Van Houten)

trance was through a small hole in the floor covered with a concrete block that could be lifted out. Every night six or seven of us slept in that room with the concrete cover in place covered with a little hay to disguise the opening.

"After nine days I decided to move. I wore a brown suit and a derby hat, and bicycled down the road about a hundred yards behind an Italian girl on another bicycle. After only about three or four miles I got to wave at my first Nazi, and he waved back.

"I moved in over a cow barn where I lived for the next twelve days. At night, I would lift boards out of the ceiling above the manger and pull myself up into a small opening only a few feet square and replace the boards. After twelve days I moved again, on a bicycle again, and got to wave at another Nazi.

"This time I holed up in a church, sleeping in a small room above the janitor's room. There were two Polish boys there named Vincent and Alfrezdo who had deserted from the German Army. This is where I stayed until April, never missing a meal. The water wasn't potable so I drank one-year-old wine during the day, and three-year-old wine in the evening. Every day we saw German soldiers in the area, and on Sundays they would dress up and go to church.

"In April, a Scottish regiment came through when the front opened up and I last saw my two Polish friends with a bunch of Nazi prisoners. I waved good bye to them."[13]

After the war, Van Houten flew DC-6s for United Airlines out of Chicago for three years, then went into business for himself as a power shovel operator. In 1980 he took up flying again as a hobby, doing aerial photography for a New York firm. Today, he and his wife live in Hamlin, New York about two "country blocks" from where he was born.

seventeen

The Last Tally-ho

"Not in vain may be the pride of those who survived, and the epitaph of those who fell."

– Winston Churchill

The capitulation of von Vietinghof's forces in Italy and Austria on May 2 was only the first of three official acts of surrender before all the guns in Europe ceased firing. Two days after the surrender in Italy German divisions in Northwest Europe gave up to Montgomery, and on May 7 a surrender document covering all German forces was signed at Eisenhower's headquarters at Reims, France.

During those few days between the surrender at Caserta and the signing at Reims, the 79th continued to fly reconnaissance patrols over northern Italy and the Balkans to ensure that surrender terms were being complied with. It was also during this period that the 79th severed its long relationship with the Desert Air Force.

To mark the occasion, Air Marshal Sir Guy Garrod, RAF Commander-in-Chief, Mediterranean; and the DAF Air Officer Commanding, Air Vice-Marshal Foster, visited the Group on May 4 to thank the men for a job well done. Colonel Pinkston had the men assembled on the beach in front of the open air theater to hear the Britishers' farewell address and, as part of the ceremony, Captain Philip Bagian was to lead three Thunderbolts low across the beach in a symbolic fly-over.

Bagian was a 120-mission vet with the Skeeters and generally considered the Group's "hottest" pilot at the time; arguably, he was also its most unforgettable character. Seldom seen on the ground without a toothbrush in his mouth, he was a wild man in the air. More than once he had flown inverted down the length of the runway, and at Fano he once landed out of a loop, throwing his gear and flaps down at the last moment before setting his heavy Jug down smoothly on the runway.[1] He had a chest full of medals that included the coveted Silver Star and British DFC, but was usually in hot water with his superiors for his wild flying antics. Today would be no exception.

After thoroughly buzzing the beach and doing slow rolls off the deck, he came in low across the water and cut a volleyball net that was stretched just a few feet from the stage where Air Marshal Garrod was giving his victory speech. Bagian's "buzz job" promptly ended the ceremony, and Colonel Pinkston was more than just a little upset over the incident. The rest of the troops thought it was a "helluva good show"[2] and a fitting way to end their long association with the British. Because of their extended periods of isolation from American military jurisdiction, the 79th had developed a rather refreshing personality that was unique from other American units. A visiting colonel once told Colonel Pinkston: "You have no ordinary men in your command – just a collection of characters."[3]

Shortly after VE-Day Colonel Pinkston was ordered to return to the States for special assignment, and Lt.-Colonel Johnny Martin assumed command of this "collection of characters." For Martin, the promotion capped a long, outstanding career with the 79th. One of the original members of the Group, he served as commanding officer of the Skulls for several months during the winter of 1943-44 and had been deputy group commander since July 1944. By the end of the war he had logged 200 combat missions – a Group high – and was credited with the destruction of one and one-half enemy aircraft in the air. After his return to the States in 1946 he was given command of the Virginia Air National Guard. In 1947, while on a routine P-51 flight from Miami, Florida to Richmond, Virginia, this country lost an outstanding air leader and fighter pilot when the popular Johnny Martin was lost at sea off the North Carolina coast. Probable cause was that gasoline siphoned off at altitude because of an improperly secured gas cap, and the plane ran out of fuel.[4]

Martin wasn't the only former squadron commander to die in "the saddle," so to speak, during peacetime or in a training accident after surviving many hours of combat. Fred Borsodi and George Lee, who had been popular fighter leaders of the Comanches and Skeeters, respectively, met similar fates.

Borsodi, the second commanding officer of the Comanches, was assigned as a test pilot in the Fighter Flight Test Section of the Air Technical Service Command at Wright Field after he completed his combat tour with the 79th, and while running high-speed compressibility dives in a P-51 he became the first man to photograph a shock wave. He was killed in England in January 1945 while demonstrating a Lockheed P-80 Shooting Star, America's first operational jet fighter.* At the time, only four P-80s were overseas – two in Italy and two in England – and Borsodi, who had test flown the jet numerous times was in England to demonstrate the plane to Eighth and Ninth Air Force fighter pilots who would use it in simulated combat with piston-engined aircraft to develop techniques to use against the German Me-262. Borsodi took the plane up on January 29, and was circling the field at about 700 feet when there was a puff of smoke from the tail exhaust and the entire tail assembly fell away. The rest of the airplane tumbled a few times and hit the ground, in flames but right side up. Borsodi never had a chance. He made no attempt to get out of the airplane, and was either unconscious or already dead when the plane crashed. He was buried in the US Military Cemetery at Cambridge, England. It was later determined that an automatic shut-off switch which was supposed to stop the transfer of fuel from the wing tip tank into the main tank continued to operate after the main tank was full, causing it to rupture or break, and the fuel drained into the aft section of the fuselage where it ignited.[5] As a result of Borsodi's fatal crash, fire warning sensors were installed in future models of the Shooting Star and other jet fighters, which ultimately saved the lives of numerous pilots.[6]

Like Borsodi, Lee had also been with the Group from the beginning and was one of the original "Desert Rats." When "Duke" Uhrich went home in the fall of 1943, Lee took over as CO of the Skeeters. By September 1944 he had accumulated 191 combat missions – more than double the number usually considered a "tour" – but instead of going home he transferred to the 86th Fighter Group at the request of Colonel Bates. Bates had taken over that group in August and arranged for the transfer of several veteran pilots from the 79th (including Lee) to boost the experience level of his new outfit. Lee served as a

* The P-80 arrived on the scene too late for World War II combat but would be used extensively during the Korean War.

In one of those rare moments when he wasn't in hot water for his wild flying antics, Captain Philip Bagian receives the Silver Star from General Myers. (Church)

Colonel Pinkston had the men assembled on the beach (above) to hear the Britisher's farewell address when Bagian's buzz-job promptly ended the ceremony. (Horn)

One of the original "Desert Rats," Lt.-Colonel Johnny Martin took command of the 79th on May 17. He was killed in a flying accident off the North Carolina coast two years later. (Church)

Four Falcon Thunderbolts representing Headquarters flight and each of the Group's three squadrons take part in the large aerial victory parade over Udine. (Church)

squadron commander under Bates until February 1945, then took over the group when Bates went home; his pilots became known as "Lee's Lieutenants." By the end of the war he had logged a total of more than 250 missions. Lee was killed in 1955 when the Republic F-84 Thunderjet he was flying crashed during a routine flight over Missouri.

After a large aerial victory parade over Udine on May 28, and the return to the States of most of the older members of the Group in late June, the 79th moved to Horsching Air Base near Linz, Austria on July 26. There it became part of the United States Air Forces in Europe, assigned to the Ninth Air Force. The Group's mission was "to maintain a display of airpower to back up surrender terms, and to be ready to suppress any revolts or disturbances that might occur in the area."[7] Despite the formidable sounding mission, day-to-day activities evolved into a normal peacetime training program; newly assigned pilots were checked out in the P-47 and got in their flying time, while ground crews kept at their tasks of maintaining and servicing aircraft. The 79th also furnished a small detachment to maintain an airfield at Salzburg.

Aerial view of Horsching Air Base near Linz, Austria, where the 79th Fighter Group became a part of the United States Air Forces in Europe. (Horn)

Ladies Night at the Officers' Club at Horsching Air Base where those not yet eligible to go home try to forget they are part of the United States Air Forces in Europe. (Horn)

They barely had a chance to settle in at Horsching when they ran into a hornet's nest of international intrigue. Pierre Laval, the French politician who became the symbol of collaboration with the Nazis as head of the Vichy regime, flew in from Barcelona, Spain in a Ju-188 flown by two former Luftwaffe pilots to give himself up. The base swarmed with "brass," VIPs and reporters, and for weeks the men were swamped with newspaper clippings from friends and relatives in the States showing the 79th's "capture" of Monsieur Laval. He was extradited to France and tried for treason. Following a quick trial Laval was convicted. After a failed suicide attempt, he was executed by a French firing squad on October 15, 1945 at Fresnes Prison in Paris.

French traitor Pierre Laval with (left to right) Captain Ragnar C. Lind; Group Adjutant Major Henry Wood, and Deputy Group Commander Lt.-Colonel Roger Files. Laval was later put on trial in France, convicted of treason and executed. (Church)

The base at Linz was in rundown condition, and littered with wrecked German aircraft. Since the end of the war, it had served as a convalescent hospital for thousands of starved concentration camp victims, refugees and other displaced persons, and about five hundred still remained on the base when the 79th moved in. American appetites diminished over the next several weeks as these victims of Nazi tyranny shuffled their weary skeletons to the Group's mess hall doors each mealtime, and queued-up patiently in long lines to wait for leftovers. "They rarely spoke, even to each other, and when they did it was with unnatural sounds, the tongue fearful and unaccustomed. They reached out their improvised mess gear – tin cans, glass jars, old pails, whatever they could find – with palsied hands, stared with fanatical absorption at the food as it was ladled out; then, without once taking their eyes from the food in their possession, would hobble a few feet away, gulping the food as they went. Here was not propaganda; here was the reason we had left home."[8]

The plight of the refugees notwithstanding, Horsching Air Base was quickly put back into shape. Quarters were fixed up, and featured steam heat and hot and cold running water. The use of Austrian waitresses – nervous at first, but put at ease after learning they wouldn't be punished if they made a mistake – and food on plates instead of in mess kits went a long way toward improving both the officers and enlisted mens' mess. PW labor took care of the heavy housekeeping chores on the base, two Red Cross girls operated a doughnut shop and library, horseback riding was available, and hunting and skiing lodges were set up for both officers and enlisted men. Eisenhower's ban on fraternization was soon discarded as a bad idea, and local entertainment included a show nearly every night in the base theater (*Diamond Horseshoe* with Betty

Laval's wife accompanied him when he flew in from Spain to give himself up. (Church)

Grable was playing the night that Japan surrendered) and softball, baseball and football were incorporated into a physical training program.

By the end of November the football team had completed a winning season – capturing the Southern League championship, but losing to the 86th Fighter Group for the European Theater Fighter Group title – and the ski lodge had been taken over by Headquarters, United States Forces in Austria. Because of a shortage of personnel (enlisted men with 60 points or more were leaving for the States), the squadrons were consolidated into the Group under one headquarters, leaving only a CO and first sergeant at the squadron level. Because of the lack of ground crews pilots pre-flighted their own aircraft and performed first echelon maintenance, and flying was greatly reduced. Morale varied from day to day as rumors about going home waxed and waned, but it undoubtedly was low the day news came down from on high that the willful firing of weapons on base, or bringing cats and dogs into the mess hall would be severely dealt with.

But the big question on everyone's mind was: "How long will the occupation last?"

By August 1946 the Group rounded out its thirteenth month of occupational duty, and its forty-sixth month of continuous service overseas. Colonel Martin had left in May – he was married to Miss Mary McElroy (an American Red Cross girl from Latrobe, Pennsylvania) in the village church at nearby Traun in March, precipitating a boisterous celebration that is still talked about to this day, and his place as both Group and base commander was taken over by Colonel German P. Culver.

The 79th Fighter Group completed its occupational duty in May 1947. By that time, personnel in Group Headquarters and in each of the three squadrons had been reduced to one officer and one enlisted man. In June, the Group and its three squadrons were transferred, less personnel and equipment, from Austria to Langley Field, Virginia and assigned to the Tactical Air Command. Before it could be brought back up to full strength it was inactivated on July 15, 1947.

These two former Luftwaffe pilots flew Laval and his wife in from Barcelona, Spain in a Ju-188. (Church)

Even though the war was over, there were still the hazards of routine flight operations. A P-47 sporting 79th Group "buzz numbers" on its fuselage but with 57th Group rudder markings comes to a sorry end in an Austrian drainage ditch . . . (Church)

. . . while another Thunderbolt, this one with tail markings of the 350th Fighter Group's 345th Squadron, sits burned out on the runway at Horsching after a bad taxiing accident. (Church)

With flying time at a minimum, Lts. Paul Church (left) and Robert Norris of the Comanches wile away the long hours with a game of cribbage in their billet at Horsching. (Horn)

The officer's Mess at Horsching Air Base in Austria was a long way from North Africa in more ways than one. (Horn)

The 79th Fighter Group remained on the inactive list for just over eight years. On June 20, 1955 the Department of the Air Force announced the redesignation of the Group to Headquarters, 79th Fighter Group (Air Defense) and assigned it to the Air Defense Command, and two months later it was reactivated at Youngstown Municipal Airport, Youngstown, Ohio. Its last known commander was Colonel Benjamin H. Emmert, Jr. Later, it was once again placed on the inactive list, but the date of that order has not been established.

Following the war, some former members of the Group opted to stay in the service and make the military a career. Several attained field grade rank before they retired, and at least three – Lee "Goose" Gossick, Tarleton "Jack" Watkins, and Benjamin B. Cassiday, Jr. – became general officers. Others returned to civilian life but remained in the Army or Air Force Reserve and were called to active duty again during the Berlin Crisis, or when the cold war in Korea suddenly turned hot. Most, however, counted up their points and when the time came they traded their khaki for mufti and returned home to pick up their lives again. They went their separate ways – got married, raised families, pursued careers – but stayed in touch with wartime buddies. In February 1974 several former members of the 85th Squadron who had kept in touch over the years – Leonard Beckerman, Willis Johnson, Matthew Purchla, Peter Jasitis, Orion Jones, Edward Lukas and Jack Beeks – and their wives met informally at the home of Ed and Betty Newbould in South Holland, Illinois to plan a reunion. Frank Sanders,

Shortly after the end of the war, this P-47 flown by Flight Officer Wilbert Norton of the Comanches became part of the Wings of Victory Exhibition in Amsterdam in the Netherlands. (Beentjes)

Left: This large granite memorial to the 79th Fighter Group was dedicated at the Air Force Museum Memorial Gardens at Dayton, Ohio on October 1, 1988. Right: Another view of the memorial at the Air Force Museum. A pyramidal design was chosen to symbolize the origin of the Group's combat career in Egypt. Two propellers, one from a P-40 and another from a P-47, flank the monument. (Author's photos)

Ben Cassiday, Elmer Johnson and Roger Files soon joined that group, and their combined efforts resulted in an 85th/79th reunion in Chicago eighteen months later. Nearly 300 people attended the three-day event, and another was held two years later, beginning a tradition that continues to this day.

By 1981, nearly 500 former members of the 79th – about a fourth of all who served with the Group during the war – had been located, and a 79th Fighter Group Association was formed. Seven years later Association members dedicated a large granite memorial to the 79th Fighter Group in the Memorial Gardens at the Air Force Museum in Dayton, Ohio. A pyramidal design was chosen to symbolize the origin of the Group's combat career in Egypt, and inscribed on the base, the words: "Dedicated to those who served and those who waited – October 1, 1988." A re-dedication ceremony was held at the memorial eleven years later.

It has been nearly sixty years since the men of the 79th went to war – ancient history if you're under fifty-five; yesterday if you're not. There would be no easy road to victory, President Roosevelt warned, but like their comrades-in-arms around the globe the men of the 79th were fast learners and quickly became very good at what they did.

The ground personnel worked long, arduous hours in all kinds of weather at seemingly unending tasks that were both physically and mentally challenging. Not exposed to enemy fire, at least on a regular basis, their jobs were nevertheless dirty, demanding, mostly boring, and oft-times hazardous, and most of them spent upwards of thirty-six months overseas away from family and loved ones.

The average pilot was overseas for much less time, and had privileges envied by many. But he faced extraordinary danger every time he climbed into the cockpit of an airplane, and nearly one of every three was either killed, missing or a prisoner of war long before he would have been eligible to rotate back to the States.

Together they helped to win the war. They were not super patriots but they knew where they came from and they believed in their country, their mission, and themselves. They formed a combination that was unbeatable. As part of what has been called "The Greatest Generation" they not only played a key role in the defeat of Fascist Italy and Nazi Germany to remove the yoke of tyranny and win a generation of peace in Europe, they also helped to make the United States the leader of the free world after the war was over.

They are in their seventies and eighties now – those who are left – and how they managed to get through the Great Depression and history's most destructive war without benefit of television, recreational drugs, computers, free love, fast food and political correctness is undoubtedly a total mystery to their children and grandchildren.

But thanks to them and all the other fine young men (and women) of their generation this is still the land of the free – they proved beyond doubt that it is the home of the brave – and one of the few countries in the world where one can still voice displeasure with the workings of the Government without fear of repercussion or reprisal. Obviously, there are many things wrong with our country today, and it has become almost a full-time job just making sure the politicians and special interest groups don't give away with one stroke of the pen everything the World War II generation fought and died for, but thanks to them the United States is still the best place in the world to live, and stands head and shoulders above whatever ranks second.

Appendices

Appendix I

Summary of 79th Fighter Group Combat Operations

The following is based on information obtained from the National Archives and Records Center; the Albert F. Simpson USAF Historical Research Center at Maxwell AFB, Alabama; 79th Fighter Group War Diary, and through correspondence or interviews with former members of the 79th Fighter Group. Every effort has been made to ensure the accuracy of this summary but it is, nevertheless, an unofficial listing.

Data on combat losses were, with few exceptions, taken from information made available shortly after the end of the war. It is therefor possible that some personnel listed here as missing or killed in action later turned up safe when Allied forces liberated German prison camps.

In compiling the list of individual aerial victories, claims made by pilots of the attached 324th Fighter Group and 99th Fighter Squadron are included, as are claims made by 79th pilots while on detached service with the 57th Fighter Group, although the latter were eventually credited to the 57th and do not appear on the 79th's group total. Only aircraft confirmed "destroyed" or "probably destroyed" are included on this list, as sortie and operational records reflecting individual claims for enemy aircraft "damaged" in air-to-air combat are incomplete and show only the Group total. In addition, Group records show one additional enemy plane destroyed in the air, and one probably destroyed, but the date of combat and individual credit for those victories have not been established.

Aircraft Markings and Radio Call Signs

To identify individual aircraft and the units to which they belonged, 30-inch high numbers, prefixed by the letter "X" were painted on both sides of the fuselage. On P-40 aircraft the "X" was about eight inches shorter than the numbers; on P-47s, numbers and letters were usually the same height. Aircraft were numbered as follows:

Headquarters – 1 through 9
85th Squadron – 10 through 39
86th Squadron – 40 through 69
87th Squadron – 70 through 99

In the spring of 1945 the Group painted the vertical tails of its Thunderbolts light blue with three yellow lightning flashes fanning out across the tail.

Radio call signs were changed occasionally to confuse the enemy, but most of the time squadrons were assigned the following:

85th Squadron – Dickey
86th Squadron – Crowfoot
Squadron – Tadpole

Mission Summary

(Operating 589 days out of 787)

Bombing	2,599
Strafing without bombs	518
Patrol and fighter sweeps	349
Bomber escort	299
Convoy and naval escort	128
Reconnaissance	107
Air/Sea rescue assistance	27
Miscellaneous	36
TOTAL	**4,063**
Number of effective sorties	37,006

Damage to Transportation System

	Destroyed	Damaged
Motor transport	2,290	2,541
Horse drawn vehicles	243	165
Horses and mules	712	
Highway bridges	52	106
Roads		562
Locomotives	171	327
Railroad cars	1,452	4,236
Railroad bridges	69	156
Rail cuts	1,292	

Damage to Ground Installations

	Destroyed	Damaged
Tanks	23	30
Mobile guns	56	5
Railroad guns	5	2
Armored vehicles	9	12
Gun positions	239	92
Buildings and fortified positions	439	460
Ammo, supply and fuel dumps	30	28
Bivouac areas		34

Aerial Victories (by squadrons)

Squadron	Destroyed	Probably Destroyed	Damaged
Unknown	1	1	
85th	36	9	22
86th	32	6	17
87th	52	7	24
99th	16	2	4
316th	1		
TOTAL	**138**	**25**	**67**

Damage to shipping

	Destroyed or sunk	Damaged
Destroyers	2-1/2	2
Aircraft carriers	1	
Boats	126	155
Barges	58	107

Aircraft Claimed on the Ground (Group total)

Destroyed	Probably Destroyed	Damaged
59	31	150

Individual Aerial Claims

Date	Name	Sqd.	Dest.	Prob.
15 Dec 42	Capt. Fred Borsodi	86	Me-109	
11 Jan 43	Lt. Jesse Jory	87		Me-109
22 Mar 43	Lt. Asa Adair	87	Me-109	
22 Mar 43	Lt. Robert Ligett	87	1/2-Me-109	
22 Mar 43	Lt. Paul McArthur	87	1/2-Me-109	
22 Mar 43	Lt. Kensley Miller	87		Me-109
23 Mar 43	Lt. George Maxwell	86	Me-109	
2 Apr 43	Lt. Charles Jaslow	87	Me-109	
7 Apr 43	Lt. Lee Gossick	87	Me-109	
20 Apr 43	Lt. William Abbott	85	Me-109	
20 Apr 43	Capt. Fred Borsodi	86	Ju-88	
20 Apr 43	Capt. Fred Borsodi	86	Me-109	
20 Apr 43	Lt. Pete Bedford	86	Ju-88	
20 Apr 43	Lt. Pete Bedford	86	Me-109	
21 Apr 43	Lt. Leo Berinati	87	Me-109	
21 Apr 43	Lt. Charles Bolack	85		Me-109
21 Apr 43	Lt. Ed Fitzgerald	87	Me-109	
21 Apr 43	Lt. John Kelly	86	Me-109	
29 Apr 43	Lt. William Hanson	86	MC-202	
29 Apr 43	Major Tarleton Watkins	86	Me-109	

20 Apr 43	Capt. Barney Turner	86	MC-202	
29 Apr 43	Lt. Jack Kauffman	86	Me-109	
29 Apr 43	Lt. Conly	86	Mc-202	MC-202
29 Apr 43	Lt. Brewer	86		Me-109
30 Apr 43	Capt. Barney Turner	86	Me-109	
30 Apr 43	Lt. Wayne Rhynard	86	Me-109	
30 Apr 43	Lt. Robert Allard	86		Me-109
30 Apr 43	Lt. Sammy Say	85	Me-109	
30 Apr 43	Lt. Malcolm McNall	85	MC-202	
5 May 43	Lt. William Ryburn	85	Me-109	
8 May 43	Capt. Robert Dempsey	316	Me-109	
8 May 43	Lt. Sammy Say	85	Me-109	
8 May 43	Lt. John Hoagland	85	Me-109	
8 May 43	Lt. Fred Hale	85	Fi-156 Storch	
8 May 43	Lt. Fred Hale	85	Me-109	
10 May 43	Lt. George Lee	87	FW-190	
7 Jun 43	Lt. Milton Clark	85	2 MC-202s	
7 Jun 43	Lt. Richard Bunker	85	2 MC-202s	
8 Jun 43	Lt. Milton Clark	85	Me-109	
8 Jun 43	Lt. William Ryburn	85	Me-109	
8 Jun 43	Capt. John Cimaglia	85	Me-109	
8 Jun 43	Capt. John Cimaglia	85	MC-202	
8 Jun 43	Lt. Charles Bolack	85	MC-202	
8 Jun 43	Lt. John Martin	85	MC-202	
8 Jun 43	Lt. John Hoagland	85		Me-109
9 Jun 43	Lt. Richard Morrissey	86	1/3 FW-190	
9 Jun 43	Lt. Pete Bedford	86	1/3 FW-190	
9 Jun 43	Capt. Fred Borsodi	86	1/3 FW-190	
9 Jun 43	Major Tarleton Watkins	86	Me-109	
10 Jun 43	Lt. Joseph Connelly	85	1/2 MC-202	
10 Jun 43	Lt. John Martin	85	1/2 MC-202	
10 Jun 43	Lt. John Kirsch	87	Me-109	
10 Jun 43	Lt.-Col. Charles Grogan	87	Me-109	
10 Jun 43	Lt. Paul McArthur	87	2 MC-202s	
10 Jun 43	Lt. Paul McArthur	87	2 Me-109s	
10 Jun 43	Lt. Morris Watkins	87	Me-109	
10 Jun 43	Lt. Kensley Miller	87	Me-109	
10 Jun 43	Lt. Asa Adair	87	Me-109	
10 Jun 43	Lt. Leo Berinati	87	Me-109	
10 Jun 43	Lt. Wyman Anderson	87	Me-109	
10 Jun 43	Lt. Wyman Anderson	87	2 MC-202s	
10 Jun 43	Lt. Lee Gossick	87	Me-109	
10 Jun 43	Lt. Frank Huff	87	Me-109	
3 Aug 43	Lt. John Hoagland	85		Me-109
12 Aug 43	Lt. Willis Johnson	85		Me-109
12 Aug 43	Lt. Charles Bolack	85		Me-109
12 Aug 43	Lt. Fred Hale	85	FW-190	
12 Aug 43	Lt. Harold Burns	85		Me-109

12 Aug 43	Lt. Robert Kelley	85		Me-109
13 Aug 43	Lt. Paul McArthur	87	Me-109	
13 Aug 43	Lt. Leo Berinati	87	FW-190	
13 Aug 43	Capt. William Rogers	87	Me-109	Me-109
13 Aug 43	Lt. Morris Watkins	87	Me-109	
30 Nov 43	Capt. George Lee	87	FW-190	
30 Nov 43	Lt. Jack Wainwright	87	FW-190	
22 Jan 44	Lt. Clinton Owen	87	2 FW-190s	
22 Jan 44	Lt. David Vandivort	87	FW-190	
22 Jan 44	Lt. William Dean	87		FW-190
22 Jan 44	Lt. Walter Peterman	87	FW-190	
22 Jan 44	Lt. Frank Nicolai	87	2 FW-190s	
23 Jan 44	Lt. Robert Skotnicky	86	1/2 ME-109	
23 Jan 44	Lt. Erwin Silsbee	86	1/2 Me-109	
24 Jan 44	F/O Ed Bozzi	87	FW-190	
24 Jan 44	Lt. William Colgan	87		Me-109
25 Jan 44	Lt. John Beck	87	FW-190	
25 Jan 44	Lt. Gaston Callum	85	FW-190	
25 Jan 44	Lt. Robert Duffield	85	FW-190	
27 Jan 44	Lt. Willie Ashley, Jr.	99	FW-190	
27 Jan 44	Lt. Leon Roberts	99	FW-190	
27 Jan 44	Lt. Robert Dietz	99	FW-190	
27 Jan 44	Lt. Ed Toppins	99	FW-190	
27 Jan 44	Lt. Harold Baugh	99	1/2 FW-190	
27 Jan 44	Lt. Clarence Allen	99	1/2 FW-190	
27 Jan 44	Capt. Lemuel Custis	99	FW-190	
27 Jan 44	Lt. Charles Bailey	99	FW-190	
27 Jan 44	Lt. Wilson Eagleson	99	FW-190	
27 Jan 44	Lt. John Rogers	99		1/2 FW-190
27 Jan 44	Lt. Elwood Driver	99		1/2 FW-190
27 Jan 44	Lt. Robert Lawrence	99		FW-190
27 Jan 44	Lt. Albert Benz	85	FW-190	
27 Jan 44	Lt. Gaston Callum	85		FW-190
27 Jan 44	Lt. Carl Stewart	85		FW-190
28 Jan 44	Capt. Charles Hall	99	2 FW-190s	
28 Jan 44	Lt. Robert Dietz	99	FW-190	
28 Jan 44	Lt. Lewis Smith	99	FW-190	
28 Jan 44	Lt. William Colgan	87	FW-190	
28 Jan 44	Lt. Gordon AcMoody	87		FW-190
28 Jan 44	Lt. Clinton Owen	87	FW-190	
28 Jan 44	Lt. William Dean	87	FW-190	
28 Jan 44	Lt. Risden Wall	86	FW-190	
28 Jan 44	Lt. Leonard Penar	86	1/2 FW-190	
28 Jan 44	Lt. Herman Leuther	86	1/2 FW-190	
5 Feb 44	Lt. Elwood Driver	99	FW-190	
7 Feb 44	Lt. George Bolte	85	Me-109	
7 Feb 44	Lt. Wilson Eagleson	99	FW-190	
7 Feb 44	Lt. Leonard Jackson	99	FW-190	

7 Feb 44	Lt. Clinton Mills	99	FW-190	
7 Feb 44	Lt. Raymond Higgins	85	Me-109	
7 Feb 44	Lt. Robert Duffield	85	FW-190	
7 Feb 44	Lt. Robert Bartlett	85	FW-190	
7 Feb 44	Lt. William McLane	85	FW-190	
7 Feb 44	Lt. Donald Gravenstine	85	FW-190	
7 Feb 44	Lt. Carl Stewart	85	FW-190	
7 Feb 44	Lt. Martin Granberg	85	FW-190	
7 Feb 44	Lt. Jack Wainwright	87	FW-190	
10 Feb 44	Lt. Jack Wainwright	87	FW-190	
19 Feb 44	Lt. Carl Stewart	85	FW-190	
17 Mar 44	Capt. Carl Stewart	85	Me-109	
17 Mar 44	Lt. Charles DeFoor	85	Me-109	
30 Mar 44	Capt. Carl Stewart	85	FW-190	
30 Mar 44	Capt. Ed Byron	86	2 Me-109s	
18 Apr 44	Capt. Risden Wall	86	FW-190	
18 Apr 44	Lt. William West	86	1/2 FW-190	
18 Apr 44	Lt. Raymond Hagler	86	1/2 FW-190	
13 May 44	Lt. Robert Crawford	86	FW-190	
13 May 44	Lt. Malcolm Hayles	86	Me-109	
13 May 44	Capt. Roger Files	85	Me-109	
15 May 44	Lt. Damon Adkins	87	Me-109	Me-109
15 May 44	Lt. Walt Peterman	87	FW-190	
15 May 44	Lt. Wilton Thompson	87	Me-109	
25 May 44	Lt. William Fuestel	87	Me-109	
25 May 44	Lt. James Blassingham	87	Me-109	
25 May 44	Lt. Walt Peterman	87		Me-109
25 May 44	Lt. Robert Noell	87	Me-109	
25 May 44	Lt. Ferdinand Tichenor	87	Me-109	
26 Jun 44	Unknown	86		Me-109
30 Jun 44	Lt. Ben Cassiday	87	Me-109	
30 Jun 44	Lt. David Shuttleworth	87	Me-109	
13 Jul 44	Major George Ewing	86	Me-109	
26 Jul 44	Lt. Eugene Gilmore	86		Me-109
26 Jul 44	Major George Ewing	86	FW-190	
26 Jul 44	Lt. Warren Tallent	86		Me-109
26 Jul 44	Lt. Charles Hancock	86	2 Me-109s	
26 Jul 44	Lt. Billy Head	86	2 Me-109s	
26 Jul 44	Lt. Richard Hilgard	86	Me-109	
26 Jul 44	Lt. Robert Steiner	86	Me-109	
24 Sep 44	Lt. Ronald Faison	87	Me-109	
24 Sep 44	Lt. William Waller	87	Me-109	

Losses

6 Nov 42	Lt.-Colonel Peter McGoldrick, Group CO., KIA strafing motor convoy near Charing Cross, Egypt.
10 Dec 42	Lt. Robert Guillebeau, 86th Sqd., KIA after encounter with enemy aircraft near El Agheila, Libya.
16 Jan 43	Capt. Raymond Palermo, 87th Sqd., killed in mid-air collision near Hamuriet, Tunisia.
21 Mar 43	Lt. Melvin K. Davis, 85th Sqd., MIA after encounter with enemy aircraft near Mareth, Tunisia.
25 Mar 43	Lt. Franklin T. Johnson, 85th Sqd., POW strafing near Gabes, Tunisia.
26 Mar 43	Lt. Robert Spurgin, 86th Sqd., POW strafing near El Hamma, Tunisia.
26 Mar 43	Lt. Robert Ligett, 87th Sqd., POW strafing near El Hamma, Tunisia.
26 Mar 43	Lt. Arthur Weldon, 86th Sqd., POW strafing near El Hamma, Tunisia.
26 Mar 43	Lt. Dave Brown, 86th Sqd., POW strafing near El Hamma, Tunisia.
29 Mar 43	Capt. Kenneth Boggs, Asst. Group Ops Officer, KIA after encounter with enemy aircraft near Mahares, Tunisia.
29 Mar 43	Lt. Harlan Highfield, 87th Sqd., POW strafing near Mahares, Tunisia.
2 Apr 43	Lt. Ed McDonnel, 87th Sqd., MIA after encounter with enemy aircraft near Wadi Akarit, Tunisia.
6 Apr 43	Lt. George Harris, 86th Sqd., MIA strafing near Achichina, Tunisia.
6 Apr 43	Lt. Donald McKay, 86th Sqd., MIA strafing near Achichina, Tunisia.
6 Apr 43	Lt. Ober Leatherman, 86th Sqd., KIA strafing near Achichina, Tunisia.
6 Apr 43	Lt. George W. Gilpin, 316th Sqd., KIA strafing near Achichina, Tunisia.
8 Apr 43	Lt. Ralph Lind, 85th Sqd., KIA strafing near Messouna, Tunisia.
21 Apr 43	Lt. John Anderson, 85th Sqd., MIA after encounter with enemy aircraft off Cape Bon, Tunisia.
22 Apr 43	F/O Chester Janicke, 87th Sqd., killed in flying accident during gunnery practice near Hani, Tunisia.
30 Apr 43	Lt. Perry Bailey, 86th Sqd., MIA after mid-air collision over Gulf of Tunis.
30 Apr 43	Lt. William Hanson, 86th Sqd., MIA after mid-air collision over Gulf of Tunis.
30 Apr 43	Lt. Thomas McCarty, 86th Sqd., POW after mid-air collision over Gulf of Tunis. Later escaped.
6 May 43	Lt. Cahill, 316th Sqd., POW, strafing near Tunis, Tunisia.
16 Jul 43	Lt. Charles Lowndes, 86th Sqd., killed in flying accident near Causeway LG, Tunisia.
31 Jul 43	Lt. Frank E. Newton, 86th Sqd., MIA dive-bombing shipping in Messina Strait.
3 Aug 43	Lt. James Pittard, 87th Sqd., POW dive-bombing shipping in Messina Strait.
3 Aug 43	Lt. Daniel H. Mayer, 86th Sqd., KIA strafing near Randazzo, Sicily.
3 Aug 43	Capt. Frank M. Huff, 87th Sqd., POW strafing near Randazzo, Sicily.
3 Aug 43	Lt. Farrel E. Yocum, 85th Sqd., KIA strafing near Mt. Etna, Sicily.
11 Sep 43	Lt. Carl L. Simpson, 85th Sqd., killed in landing accident at Palagonia LG, Sicily.
26 Sep 43	Lt. Whitman R. Smith, 86th Sqd., MIA on armed recce near Avellino, Italy.
6 Oct 43	Lt. Henry P. Steele, 86th Sqd., KIA strafing near Termoli, Italy.
2 Dec 43	Lt. Ernest H. Kellerman, 85th Sqd., KIA strafing near Ancona, Italy.
8 Dec 43	Lt. Charles Kehr, 86th Sqd., KIA bombing near Orsogna, Italy.
8 Dec 43	Lt. William Glasgow, 85th Sqd., POW bombing near Orsogna, Italy. Later escaped.
12 Dec 43	Lt. Burke Allen, 87th Sqd., MIA bombing and strafing near Chieti, Italy.
12 Dec 43	Lt. Howard A. Smith, 85th Sqd., POW bombing and strafing near Chieti, Italy.
18 Dec 43	Lt. Ralph C. Specht, 87th Sqd., KIA bombing near Orsogna, Italy.
18 Dec 43	Lt. Wendell Simmons, 87th Sqd., KIA bombing near Orsogna, Italy.
18 Dec 43	Lt. William B. Marshall, 85th Sqd., MIA bombing near Orsogna, Italy.
30 Dec 43	Lt. William A. Martin, 85th Sqd., KIA strafing near mouth of Sangro River, Italy.
2 Jan 44	Lt. George R. Greer, 86th Sqd., MIA bombing and strafing near St. Benedento, Italy.
3 Jan 44	Lt. John H. Morgan, 99th Sqd., killed in landing accident at Madna LG, Italy.
9 Jan 44	Lt. Lawrence Varner, 85th Sqd., KIA strafing near Pescocostanzo, Italy.
10 Jan 44	Lt. Richard Wiener, 87th Sqd., MIA strafing near Pescocostanzo, Italy.
15 Jan 44	Lt. William Griffin, 99th Sqd., POW bombing and strafing near Eighth Army bomb line, Italy.
22 Jan 44	Lt. Jack Maye, 87th Sqd., POW after encounter with enemy aircraft over Anzio beachhead, Italy.

28 Jan 44 Lt. Samuel Bruce, 99th Sqd., MIA after encounter with enemy aircraft over Anzio beachhead, Italy.
17 Feb 44 Lt. Paul Hartman, 87th Sqd., KIA strafing near Anzio beachhead, Italy.
18 Feb 44 Lt. Albert R. Mace, 86th Sqd., KIA bombing and strafing near Anzio beachhead.
21 Feb 44 Lt. Alwayne Dunlap, 99th Sqd., killed in landing accident at Nettuno, Italy.
23 Feb 44 Lt. Harry J. Daniels, 99th Sqd., MIA while on patrol off west coast of Italy near Anzio.
29 Feb 44 Lt. George McCrumby, 99th Sqd., MIA during routine patrol off Gaeta Point, Italy
11 Mar 44 Lt. Ray Higgins, 85th Sqd., killed on P-47 transition flight near Naples, Italy.
11 Mar 44 F/O Vincent Wall, killed in landing accident at Venosa, Italy.
18 Mar 44 Lt. Clemenceau Givings, 99th Sqd., KIA on patrol over Italy.
24 Mar 44 Lt. Ward T. Pringle, 85th Sqd., MIA after encounter with enemy aircraft near Orvieto, Italy.
27 Mar 44 Lt. Herbert Anderson, 87th Sqd., KIA on patrol over Anzio beachhead, Italy.
28 Mar 44 Lt. Edgar Jones, 99th Sqd., killed in takeoff accident at Capodichino airfield, Italy.
28 Mar 44 Lt. William H. Rueschoff, 87th Sqd., killed in landing accident at Capodichino airfield, Italy.
31 Mar 44 Lt. Norvell Stoudmire, 99th Sqd., killed in takeoff accident at Capodichino airfield, Italy.
6 Apr 44 Lt. Charles W. DeFoor, Jr., 85th Sqd., KIA near Anzio beachhead, Italy.
6 Apr 44 Lt. Robert Paul, 87th Sqd., MIA during routine patrol near Anzio beachhead.
18 Apr 44 Lt. Donald W. Mulkey, 86th Sqd., KIA dive-bombing near Lake Bolsena, Italy.
21 Apr 44 Lt. Berning T. Edds, 87th Sqd., killed on P-47 transition flight near Naples, Italy.
21 Apr 44 Lt. James Scofield, 85th Sqd., killed landing with hung bomb at Capodichino airfield, Italy.
7 May 44 Colonel Charles W. Stark, Group CO, POW dive-bombing near Fabro, Italy.
7 May 44 Lt. Merle E. Stafford, 86th Sqd., POW dive-bombing near Fabro, Italy.
9 May 44 Lt. Maurice Wilson, 86th Sqd., killed attempting emergency landing, Italy.
9 May 44 Lt. Lawrence Borsheim, 85th Sqd., POW after encounter with enemy fighters near Rome, Italy.
10 May 44 Lt. Frank T. Seres, 86th Sqd., KIA bombing and strafing near Rome.
13 May 44 Lt. Donald Richer, 86th Sqd., KIA bombing near Cassino, Italy.
13 May 44 Lt. Michael J. Slater, 86th Sqd., KIA after encounter with enemy aircraft near Cassino, Italy.
16 May 44 Lt. Louis Rouleau, 86th Sqd., killed while slow-timing P-47 near Marigliano, Italy.
17 May 44 Capt. Clarence Stevens, 87th Sqd., POW bombing near Rome, Italy.
17 May 44 Lt. Raymond Ermis, 87th Sqd., KIA bombing near Rome, Italy
22 May 44 Lt. Edward Letzkus, 86th Sqd., KIA bombing near Rome, Italy.
23 May 44 Lt. Robert Biting, 87th Sqd., KIA in mid-air collision over Italy.
24 May 44 Lt. Charles P. Logel, 87th Sqd., KIA bombing north of Rome, Italy.
25 May 44 Lt. Robert Swenson, 87th Sqd., MIA bombing near Viterbo, Italy.
25 May 44 Lt. Garth Thornton, 87th Sqd., MIA bombing near Viterbo, Italy.
6 Jun 44 Lt. Charles Landers, 87th Sqd., POW bombing and strafing near Tarquinia, Italy.
9 Jun 44 Lt. Stuart Bartlett, 86th Sqd., KIA strafing near Foligno, Italy.
10 Jun 44 Lt. John Winslow, 87th Sqd., KIA bombing near Orvieto, Italy.
10 Jun 44 Lt. Damon Adkins, 87th Sqd., KIA strafing north of Rome, Italy.
13 Jun 44 Lt. William Pritchard, 87th Sqd., killed in takeoff accident, Serragia Airdrome, Corsica.
13 Jun 44 Lt. David Moss, 87th Sqd., killed landing with hung bomb at Alto Airdrome, Corsica.
26 Jun 44 Lt. John H. Bothe, 86th Sqd., KIA after encounter with enemy aircraft near Imola, Italy.
11 Jul 44 Lt. Sam Rospo, 86th Sqd., killed in flying accident, Corsica.
13 Jul 44 Lt. Robert Patin, 86th Sqd., killed in flying accident, Corsica.
26 Jul 44 Lt. George Vaccaro, 87th Sqd., KIA strafing Valence Airdrome, southern France.
1 Aug 44 Lt. Noel Sonnichsen, 87th Sqd., MIA bombing and strafing Villafranca Airdrome at Verona, Italy.
2 Aug 44 Lt. Vincent Millican, 85th Sqd., KIA strafing Bergamo-Seriate Airdrome, Italy.
3 Aug 44 Lt. James Green, 85th Sqd., KIA bombing and strafing near Verona, Italy.
5 Aug 44 Lt. George W. Beers, 85th Sqd., killed in takeoff accident at Serragia Airdrome, Corsica.
13 Aug 44 F/O Herbert H. Woerpel, 87th Sqd., KIA strafing La Jasse Airdrome, southern France.

13 Aug 44 Lt. Robert H. Williams, 85th Sqd., KIA strafing La Jasse Airdrome, southern France.
15 Aug 44 Lt. James P. Williams, 87th Sqd., KIA bombing and strafing near Cannes, France.
16 Aug 44 Lt. William Ramsdell, 85th Sqd., killed in takeoff accident at Serragia Airdrome, Corsica.
25 Aug 44 Lt. Harry Mitchell, 85th Sqd., killed in landing accident at Serragia Airdrome, Corsica.
28 Aug 44 F/O Russell Jennings, 87th Sqd., KIA strafing near Montelimar, France.
28 Aug 44 Lt. Percy Brown, 86th Sqd., MIA strafing, southern France.
29 Aug 44 Lt. Leonard Charpentier, 86th Sqd., POW/WIA strafing near Montelimar, France. Later returned to Allied control.
4 Sep 44 Lt. Donald Claycomb, 86th Sqd., POW bombing and strafing, southern France.
11 Sep 44 Lt. Jack Fortune, 86th Sqd., killed in landing accident at Valence, France.
11 Sep 44 Lt. John Winschell, 86th Sqd., killed in landing accident at Valence, France.
28 Sep 44 Lt. Marion Zipperer, 86th Sqd., KIA on weather recce near Belfort, France.
7 Oct 44 Lt. Calvin J. Arnold, 86th Sqd., POW bombing near Cesena, Italy.
9 Oct 44 Lt. James Menifee, 86th Sqd., KIA bombing near Rimini, Italy.
9 Oct 44 Lt. Robert Stahl, 86th Sqd., KIA bombing near Rimini, Italy.
11 Oct 44 Lt. Victor Phelps, 87th Sqd., POW bombing and strafing near Imola, Italy.
12 Oct 44 Capt. Gordon Bell, 87th Sqd., killed in landing accident at Jesi, Italy.
29 Oct 44 Lt. Robert Bell, 85th Sqd., POW bombing bridge near Argenta, Italy.
31 Oct 44 Capt. Keith Croskery, 87th Sqd., KIA strafing and rocketing near Venice, Italy.
6 Nov 44 Lt. Robert Norman, 87th Sqd., POW bombing bridge near Ravenna, Italy.
6 Nov 44 Lt. William Peters, 86th Sqd., killed in takeoff accident at Jesi, Italy.
9 Nov 44 Lt. James Anderson, 86th Sqd., KIA strafing and rocketing near Forli, Italy.
4 Dec 44 Lt. Ronald Faison, 87th Sqd., POW strafing and rocketing near Cotignale, Italy.
17 Dec 44 S/Sgt. Gerald V. Ervin, 86th Sqd., killed when P-51 crashed in squadron dispersal area at Fano, Italy.
31 Dec 44 Lt. Albert Bratt, 87th Sqd., POW strafing train near Ljubljana, Yugoslavia.
31 Dec. 44 Lt. Richard Gorsuch, 87th Sqd., MIA over Italy.
4 Jan 45 Lt. William Harding, 85th Sqd., KIA rocketing rail traffic near Sarajevo, Yugoslavia.
4 Jan 45 Lt. Harry Bartley, 87th Sqd., KIA bombing bridge near Stenghella, Italy.
11 Jan 45 Lt. Archibald McIlwaine, 85th Sqd., killed in takeoff accident at Fano, Italy.
21 Jan 45 Lt. Robert Hewitt, 86th Sqd., KIA reason unknown, near Bodres, Italy.
23 Jan 45 F/O Wesley Stage, 85th Sqd., POW bombing and strafing near Padova, Italy.
27 Jan 45 Lt. James F. Hannon, 86th Sqd., KIA bombing railroad tracks near Giorgio, Italy.
8 Feb 45 Lt. George E. Keppler, 85th Sqd., KIA near Casarsa, Italy.
9 Feb 45 Lt. Richard Ascenzi, 86th Sqd., MIA over Adriatic Sea.
20 Feb 45 Lt. Irvin Hoerr, 86th Sqd., MIA bombing bridge near Casarsa, Italy.
24 Feb 45 Lt. Arthur Burnap, 86th Sqd., KIA bombing bridge near Rovigo, Italy.
24 Feb 45 Lt. Thomas O'Brien, 86th Sqd., KIA rocketing barges on Piave River, Italy.
4 Mar 45 Lt. Donald Montgomery, 87th Sqd., POW rocketing flak battery near Rovigo, Italy.
5 Mar 45 Lt. Albert Mathias, 87th Sqd., MIA rocketing train near Jesenice, Yugoslavia.
6 Mar 44 Lt. Arthur Pneuman, 87th Sqd., POW rocketing rail traffic near Klagenfurt, Austria.
18 Mar 45 Lt. Clarence E. Paff, 85th Sqd., MIA strafing Campoformido Airdrome at Udine, Italy.
22 Mar 45 Lt. Morrison Loftiss, 87th Sqd., killed when frag cluster exploded during takeoff at Fano, Italy.
24 Mar 45 Lt. Robert S. Robinette, 85th Sqd., killed in takeoff accident at Cesenatico, Italy.
2 Apr 45 Lt. Warren Bostick, 87th Sqd., MIA strafing train in Austria.
9 Apr 45 Lt. James McHenry, 85th Sqd., KIA rocketing fortified house near Ravenna, Italy.
21 Apr 45 Lt. Loren E. Hintz, 86th Sqd., KIA bombing near Budrio, Italy.
22 Apr 45 Unknown, 85th Sqd., MIA bombing and strafing, northern Italy.
24 Apr 45 Capt. Arthur Halfpaff, 87th Sqd., KIA bombing and strafing over Adigo River, Italy.
12 May 45 Lt. James W. Fanning, 87th Sqd., KIA.
25 Oct 45 Lt. Marlin E. Klassie, 85th Sqd., killed in flying accident near Salzburg, Austria.

Appendix II

Assignments

Third Air Force: 9 February 1942

First Air Force: I Fighter Command: 22 June 1942. During this period the Group was part of the Eastern Defense Command and Boston Air Defense Wing.

Ninth Air Force; IX Fighter Command: November 1942. From November 1942 through the conclusion of the Tunisian campaign the Group was under the administrative control of the Desert Air Task Force, an advanced administrative headquarters established for the purpose of administering Ninth Air Force units operating under the RAF's Desert Air Force. For operational purposes AAF and RAF units in the Mediterranean were integrated into operational commands. During the period from March 1942 to 22 August 1943 the 79th fitted into the integrated AAF-RAF operational command structure as follows:

Northwest Tactical Air Forces (NAAF); Northwest African Tactical Air Force (NATAF); Desert Air Force: 14 March 1943.
NAAF: NATAF; XII Air Support Command: 4 June 1943.
NAAF; NATAF; Desert Air Force: 14 June – 22 August 1943.
Twelfth Air Force: 22 August 1943. Throughout the period the 79th remained assigned directly to Headquarters, Twelfth Air Force, but was attached for operational control as follows:
NATAF; Desert Air Force: 22 August 1943. Mediterranean Allied Tactical Air Force (MATAF; NATAF redesignated): Desert Air Force: 1 January 1944.
MATAF; XII Air Support Command (XII ASC); 64th Fighter Wing: 18 January 1944.
MATAF; XII ASC: 11 February 1944.
MATAF; XII ASC; 64th Fighter Wing: 27 February 1944.
MATAF; XII Tactical Air Command (TAC – XII ASC redesignated); 64th Fighter Wing: 15 April 1944.
MATAF; XII TAC: 20 April 1944.
MATAF; XII TAC: 87th Fighter Wing: 11 June 1944.
MATAF; XII TAC; 64th Fighter Wing: 9 September 1944.
MATAF; XII Fighter Command: 20 September 1944. In the September 1944 division of Twelfth Air Force units between France and Italy, the 79th was allotted on paper to XII Fighter Command, but actually remained in France under the operational control of XII TAC until it returned to Italy in October.
MATAF; Desert Air Force: 1 October 1944.
MATAF; XXII TAC: 9 May 1945. United States Strategic Air Forces in Europe; Ninth Air Force; XII TAC; 70th Fighter Wing: 31 July 1945.
United States Air Forces in Europe; Ninth Air Force; XII TAC; 70th Fighter Wing: 16 August 1945.
United States Air Forces in Europe; XII TAC; 70th Fighter Wing: 15 November 1945.
Tactical Air Command: 25 June-15 July, 1947.
Air Defense Command; Eastern Air Defense Force; 4708th Air Defense Wing: 18 August 1955.

Appendix III

Commanding Officers

Group Commanders

2nd Lieutenant Thomas G. Mitchell	11 Feb 42
Lt.-Colonel J. Stanley Holtner	17 Feb 42
Lt.-Colonel Peter McGoldrick	July 42
Colonel Earl E. Bates	6 Nov 42
Colonel Charles W. Stark	21 Apr 44
Lt.-Colonel Melvin J. Nielsen	12 May 44
Colonel Gladwyne E. Pinkston	28 Nov 44
Lt.-Colonel John F. Martin	17 May 45
Colonel German P. Culver	Aug 45
Lt.-Colonel Bascom A. Brooks	5 Feb 47
Lt.-Colonel John M. Thacker	Apr 47
Colonel Benjamin H. Emmert, Jr.	1955

85th Squadron

Captain J. L. Cole	9 May 42
Major Jacob F. Schoellkopf IV	July 42
Major Frank B. Wagner	23 Sep 43
Major John F. Martin	24 Dec 43
Captain Carl W. Stewart (acting)	Apr 44
Major Eugene Kleiderer, Jr.	21 Jul 44
Major Earl P. Maxwell	16 Oct 44
Lt.-Colonel Roger Files	Feb 45
Major Edwin Payne	Unknown

86th Squadron

Captain W. R. Compton	9 May 42
Captain L. C. Lydon	30 Jun 42
Captain Jack C. West	Aug 42
Captain Tarleton Watkins	Sep 42
Major Fredric A. Borsodi	20 Jun 43
Lt.-Colonel Melvin J. Nielsen	16 Oct 43
Major George W. Ewing, Jr.	8 May 44
Major E. J. Byron	14 Aug 44
Major Frederick J. Zilly	16 Oct 44
Major Alfred Fetters	30 Apr 45

87th Squadron

Lt.-Colonel Charles E. Grogan	Jul 42
Major Benjamin F. Uhrich	26 Jan 43
Major George T. Lee	Nov 43
Major John L. Beck	Sep 44
Major Benjamin B. Cassiday, Jr.	Jan 45

Appendix IV

Station List

Dale Mabry Field Florida	9 Feb 42	28 Apr 42
Morris Field North Carolina	28 Apr 42	15 Jun 42
Hillsgrove, Rhode Island (Hqs Sqdn & 8th)	15 Jun 42	2 Jul to 28 Sep 42
East Boston, Massachusetts (86th Sqdn)	15 Jun 42	2 Jul 42
East Hartford, Connecticut (87th Sqdn)	15 Jun 42	28 Sep 42
Bedford, Massachusetts (Hqs Sqdn & 85th)	2 Jul 42	28 Sep 42
Enroute overseas	28 Sep 42	12 Nov 42
Landing Ground 174, Egypt	18 Nov 42 to 28 Jan 43	20 Jan
LG 150, Gazala, Egypt (A-Party)	23 Jan 43	7 Feb 43
Darraugh North LG, Libya	7 Feb 43 to 15 Feb 43	23 Feb to 25 Feb 43
Castel Benito LG, Libya	25 Feb 43 to 26 Feb 43	11 Mar to 14 Mar 43
Causeway LG, Tunisia	11 Mar 43 to 14 Mar 43	8 Apr 43 to 14 Apr 43
Hani LG, Tunisia	17 Apr 43 to 18 Apr 43	2 Jun to 6 Jun 43
El Houaria LG, Tunisia (B-Party)	2 Jun 43	14 Jun 43
Bou Grara, Tunisia (A-Party)	6 Jun 43	14 Jun 43
Causeway LG, Tunisia	14 Jun 43 to 13 Aug 43	25 Jun
Syracuse, Sicily (A-Party)	16 Jun 43	26 Jul 43
Cassibile LG, Sicily	26 Jul to 28 Jul 43	31 Jul 43
Palagonia LG, Sicily	32 Jul 43 to 15 Sep 43	13 Sep
On 18 August a small detachment which had remained at Causeway joined the Group at Palagonia		
Isole LG, Crotone, Italy	13 Sep to 15 Sep 43	22 Sep to 24 Sep 43
Firmo LG, Italy (A-Party)	24 Sep 43	24 Sep 43
Pisticci LG, Italy	24 Sep 43 to 29 Sep 43	26 Sep
Penny Post LG, Italy	26 Sep to 29 Sep 43	4 Oct to 9 Oct 43
Foggia No. 3, Salsola, Italy	4 Oct to 9 Oct 43	19 Nov to 23 Nov 43
Madna LG, Italy	19 Nov to 23 Nov 43	15 Jan to 10 Feb 44
Capodichino Airdrome, Italy	17 Jan to 10 Feb 44	1 May 44
Pomigliano Airdrome, Italy	1 May 44 to 20 Jun 44	11 Jun
Serragia Airdrome, Corsica	11 Jun to 20 Jun 44	22 Aug to 30 Aug 44
St. Raphael, France	22 Aug to 30 Aug 44	1 Sep to 5 Sep 44
Valence Airdrome, France	1 Sep to 5 Sep 44	15 Sep to 22 Sep 44
Bron AD, France (A-Party; flt ech)	15 Sep 44	1 Oct 44
Le Vollon AD, France (B-Party)	22 Sep 44	29 Sep 44
Enroute from France to Italy	29 Sep 44	11 Oct 44
Jesi Landing Ground, Italy	3 Oct to 11 Oct 44	5 Dec to 7 Dec 44
Fano Landing Ground, Italy	5 Dec to 7 Dec 44	20 Mar to 24 Mar 45
Cesenatico LG, Italy	20 Mar to 24 Mar 45	22 Jul to 28 Jul 45
Horsching Air Base, Austria	22 Jul to 28 Jul 45	25 Jun 47
Langley Field, Virginia	24 Jun 47	15 Jul 47
Youngstown Municipal Airport, Ohio	18 Aug 55	

Appendix V

Insignia

79th Fighter Group insignia (Falcons)

The historians of ancient Egypt recorded on their obelisks the story of Horus the hawk. Some three thousand years ago, these scribes told of a son born to Osirus, one of the gods of the sun. This was Horus, who was orphaned in his youth when Osirus was killed by the sun god Set. With manhood, Horus assembled an army, killed Set, and regained the throne that was rightfully his. The hieroglyphics on the obelisks tell how Horus, the hawk, became known to these ancients as the avenger of his father.

It is peculiarly significant that the 79th Fighter Group carried on the ancient tradition of Horus. The design recalls Egypt, in whose burning skies they first met the enemy. It suggests that this land of history and sand was the beginning of the British Eighth Army's advance up the Western Desert road to Tunis, and to victory. It points up the role played by the 79th in this victory as it supported Montgomery and his men. Finally, it is a tribute to Colonel Peter McGoldrick, the Group commander, and the first member of the 79th Fighter Group to die in combat.

Horus the hawk symbolized the determination of the 79th to avenge, like Horus, the death of its brilliant leader. With the speed of the hawk, they dove out of the sun and struck with the swift deadliness of the cobra, and their deeds, like those of Horus, will be recorded with the immortals.

The significance of the component parts of the design is as follows: The blue strip at the top of the insignia is the Egyptian representation of the sky, symbolic of the medium in which their planes operated. Below this, in the upper left corner are the Egyptian numerals for "79," the numerical designation of the Group. The inverted U-shaped characters each represent ten; the straight lines, one; hence 79. In the upper right corner is a device always seen in connection with any depiction of a sun god. First the red sun, suggesting the origin of these gods, and also symbolic of the fact that fighters frequently dive on an enemy from out of the sun. Hanging over the sun is an uraeus, or cobra, shown to represent the fact that the gods were protected, and thus symbolic of one function of fighter aircraft, namely protection. Also symbolized are the qualities of deadliness, swiftness, and death to the enemy, which are characteristics of the cobra. Suspended from the neck of the serpent is the Egyptian Key of Life, which was always shown with a god to symbolize immortality. The Key of Life also may symbolize good fortune, a charm to bring good luck. The hawk or falcon is the chief figure in the design, and is the symbolic representation of the sun god Horus. Its form is typically Egyptian, standing dominant, erect and fearless, the symbol of swift flight, unerring aim, strength, endurance, winged skill, and destruction of its prey. These qualities are all symbolic of the same qualities of the fighter planes of the Group, of those who flew them, and of those who kept them flying.

With the aid of Mr. Alan Rowe, conservator of the Graeco-Roman museum in Alexandria, Egypt, and Mr. Badie Effendi, the museum artist, the Falcon insignia was designed while the Group was at Landing Ground 174 in the fall of 1942.

85th Squadron (Flying Skulls)

The 85th Squadron insignia, the Flying Skull, was designed by Corporal Joseph Pumphrey in July 1942. The insignia, with its white death's head and yellow wings on a field of blue, is symbolic of winged death and destruction to be inflicted on all enemies of the United States.

When the design was first submitted to Washington for approval, squeamish War Department officials rejected it as being "too gruesome." They were quickly convinced by Major Schoellkopf, the squadron commander, that his pilots were preparing to fight a war that was little less gruesome itself, and the insignia was officially approved.

86th Squadron (Comanches)

Fred Borsodi first proposed the Comanche name for the squadron when it was based at LG-174 in Egypt. The Comanche Indian tribe was constantly at war during early American pioneer days, recognized no superior, and were victorious in every battle.

The cartoon character has his left arm outstretched over the clouds, and with his beckoning finger, challenges all comers. The satisfied smirk on his face signifies the pleasure he had disposing of his last victim, as blood can be seen dripping from his tomahawk. The battle headdress of red, white and blue feathers is waving defiantly in the breeze.

The insignia was designed by Sergeants Charles A. Farquhar and Everly J. McGrath.

87th Squadron (Skeeters)

The Skeeter insignia, showing an armed airborne mosquito prowling the skies in search of the enemy, was inspired by a poem written by Lieutenant Frank W. Hamilton while the squadron was stationed at Rentschler Field, Connecticut. The poem told of the hordes of mosquitoes that plagued them during the summer of 1942, that would "come screaming down in a dive . . . wouldn't quit; would try again for another hit . . . and we needed that spirit if we were going to beat the Axis."

Appendix VI

Citations

Extract from General Orders No. 23, War Department, Washington, DC, 24 March 1944:

". . . citation of the following unit . . . is confirmed . . . in the name of the President of the United States as public evidence of deserved honor and distinction. The citation reads as follows:

"For outstanding performance of duty in action against the enemy in direct support of the British Eighth Army in the Middle East theater in the North African campaign from March 1943 to the capitulation of the enemy forces in Tunisia and Sicily.

"Entering the campaign as the ground forces were advancing across the North African desert and were in great need of effective air support, this unit, though lacking in experience at that time, immediately and continuously rendered tactical air support of our allied army, directly contributing to the success of the advance.

"Through the bravery, skill and efficiency of its pilots, and the initiative, ingenuity, untiring efforts, and devotion to duty of its ground personnel, despite personal hardships and difficult desert conditions, the 79th Fighter Group advanced with the front lines of the British Eighth Army, operating continuously under all types of weather conditions to carry out fighter patrols, to dive bomb and strafe enemy troops, positions, and supplies; to engage and destroy enemy aircraft, and to provide fighter escort for our own and allied bombardment airplanes and ship convoys.

"By the skillful, courageous, efficient, and carefully coordinated efforts and performance of duty in action against the enemy, this organization, throughout its participation in the North African campaign, rendered an invaluable contribution vital to the success of our forces and in keeping with the finest tradition of our armed forces."

Extract from General Orders No. 97, War Department, Washington, DC, 1946:

"The 79th Fighter Group is cited for outstanding performance of duty in action during the period 16 to 20 April 1945. The 79th Fighter Group, flying as the only American fighter-bomber unit coordinating its efforts with the British Eighth Army's drive to pierce the heavily defended Santerno River line to reach Bologna and Ferrara, signally distinguished itself by the resolute manner in which it overcame hazardous conditions to contribute materially to the defeat of the German armies in Italy.

"Flying their P-47 type aircraft in daring minimum altitude attacks, only a few hundred yards in front of our forward positions, despite continuous enemy anti-aircraft fire of such intensity that two aircraft and pilots were lost and nineteen aircraft were damaged, the gallant pilots of the 79th Fighter Group made their attacks with consummate skill and accuracy, in the face of the rapidly changing ground situation, which allowed less than an hour between the instant the target was received and the pilots were briefed and airborne. On no occasion was any target declined and on each mission the objective was struck at the time specified, although in two instances, pilots continued on to the attack after their aircraft had been turned completely over by bursting shells, while flying at a speed of 400 miles an hour at an altitude of 100 feet.

"Taking off from a short runway with obstructions at either end, forced to fly with carburetor air filters closed because of blowing sand at the airdrome, and as a result of which there was loss of engine power, briefed at a central point rather than in the usual manner by squadrons on the complicated nature of the close-in targets to be attacked, pilots bombed, strafed and rocketed such pin-point targets as fortified houses, camouflaged pillboxes, and motor transport with devastating effect.

"In these five days of intensive effort, during which each pilot of the Group flew approximately eight sorties, the unprecedented total of 845 sorties were flown, resulting in the destruction or damage of 173 fortified houses, six guns, four tanks, eight armored cars, eighty-four motor transport, eight bridges, eighteen barges, and numerous casualties to fleeing enemy troops.

"The extraordinary performance of the 79th Fighter Group's air and ground personnel in overcoming the greatest of aerial hazards and maintenance difficulties was typical of their esprit de corps and bravery and reflected the highest credit on themselves and the military service of the United States."

Extract from Twelfth Air Force General Orders No. 165, 23 July 1945:

". . . the 79th Fighter Group is cited for outstanding performance of duty in action against the enemy in the Mediterranean Theater of Operations on 6 March 1945.

"During the months of February and March 1945, the German Army made desperate attempts to withdraw troops and equipment from Yugoslavia in order to utilize them against the Russian drive through Austria. Taking full advantage of characteristically poor weather, darkness, and a terrain which made effective fighter-bomber attacks extremely hazardous, he would have succeeded were it not for the unceasing, resolute attacks made by the 79th Fighter Group, which, as the sole American fighter-bomber group operating in this area, displayed so outstanding a unit courage and determination that the enemy's attempts to withdraw were frustrated. This battle reached its climax on 6 March 1945.

"Despite extremely adverse weather and with full knowledge of exceptionally strong anti-aircraft defenses which had destroyed eight of their aircraft and damaged twenty-two others in the preceding fifteen days, the pilots of the 79th Fighter Group, in complete defiance of the hazards involved, returned again and again in attacks against vital communications routes and targets, taking off from runways 1,500 feet short of the safety margin for bomb-laden P-47s and flying through treacherous mountain terrain heavily obscured by overcast.

"Undeterred by swiftly changing weather and intense anti-aircraft fire from batteries accurately trained on them from mountain positions higher than their attacking altitude, the gallant pilots of the 79th Fighter Group bombed, strafed and rocketed rail and motor vehicles with devastating effect, disabling twenty-eight locomotives, destroying or damaging more than 300 railroad cars, fifty motor transport and five barges, and knocking out two bridges.

"The extraordinary heroism, determination and consummate skill of both ground and air crews of the 79th Fighter Group on this day, during which they flew 114 sorties despite the loss of one and heavy damage to two other aircraft, disrupted the enemy's plan for bringing pressure to bear against the advancing Russian forces and climaxed an outstanding period of attack and interdiction of the Yugoslav battle area."

NOTE: No evidence has been found in the records available in the USAF Historical Division that this citation was ever confirmed by the War Department.

Appendix VII

Equivalent ranks and units

Ranks

USAAF and SAAF	RAF	German	Italian
Flight Officer/2nd Lt.	Pilot Officer	Leutnant	S. Tenente
1st Lieutenant	Flying Officer	Oberleutnant	Tenente
Captain	Flight Lieutenant	Hauptmann	Capitano
Major	Squadron Leader	Major	Maggiore
Lt.-Colonel	Wing Commander	Oberstleutnant	Tenente Colonello
Colonel	Group Captain	Oberst	Colonello
Brig-General	Air Commodore	Generalmajor	
Major-General	Air Vice-Marshal	Generalleutnant	
Lt.-General	Air Marshal	Generaloberst	
General	Marshal of the RAF	Generalfeldmarschall	

Units

American

Basic unit – squadron
Three squadrons – one group
Various number of groups – one wing

British and Commonwealth

Basic unit – squadron
Three or four squadrons – one wing
Various number of wings – one group

German

Basic unit – staffel
Three staffeln – one gruppe
Three gruppen – one geschwader
jagdgeschwader – fighters
kampfgeschwader – bombers
stukageschwader – dive bombers

Italian

Basic unit – squadriglia
Three squadriglia —one gruppo
Three gruppa – one stormo

79th Fighter Group Aircraft in Profile

2Lt. Charlie Bolack, 85 FS, D.A.F., P-40F X-15 s.n. unk., Hani West air base, Kairouan, Tunisia, April-June 1943. One kill confirmed on 8 June in this Warhawk.

Capt. Carl Stewart, CO 85 FS 12 AF - possible P-47D-26RE, X39 *WEST BY GAWD VIRGINIA s.n.* unk., Serragia air base, Corsica, late summer of 1944. Two kills in Warhawks and two in earlier P-47, including the first Thunderbolt kill for the Group.

Capt. Fred Borsodi, Flt Ldr 86 FS, D.A.F., P-40F-10 CU X-42 s.n. unk., Hani West airdrome, Kairouan and El Houaria (Cape Bon) air base, Tunisia, April-June 1943 with three confirmed kills.

Purported P-47D of Lt. Billy Head, 86 FS, 12 AF, s.n. unknown, Serragia air base, Corsica, in *Operation Dragoon*, southern France, August 1944. Two confirmed kills possibly in this A/C on 26 July over Brescia, Italy.

Lt. Paul McArthur, 87 FS, D.A.F., P-40L X-83 *SPRING*, possibly 41-19936, Hani West air base to El Houaria air base, Apr-Jun 1943. Four confirmed kills in *SPRING* on 10 June before the future ace had to bail out.

Lt. Ben Cassiday, Jr., 87 FS, 12 AF P-47D-23RA X-75 *LADY BE GOOD* s.n. 42-27956, Serragiaair base, Corsica, summer 1944. Single confirmed victory likely in A/C on 30 June over Bozanno, Italy.

Lt. Ed Toppins, 99 FS D.A.F., P-40L-1CU A-19 *TOPPER II* s.n. 42-10461, Madna air base, Italy. His first kill was confirmed in this well used A/C over Anzio on 27 January 1944.

Capt. Charlie "Buster" Hall, 99 FS, D.A.F., purportedly the P-40L-5CU A-30 s.n. 42-210582, Madna air base, Italy, used to attain his second and third confirmed kills on 28 January 1944.

Col. Earl Bates, CO 79 FG, D.A.F., P-40L X-01 *LI'L JOE III* s.n. unk., last *LI'L JOE* based at Palagonia, Sicily, mid-summer of 1943. Distinguished Unit Citation for his Group's action, March thru August 1943.

Col. Gladwyn Pinkston, CO 79 FG, P-47D X01 s.n. unk., based at Casenatico, Italy. His group won their second D.U.C. for support of the Santero River crossings in the Po River campaign of April 1945.

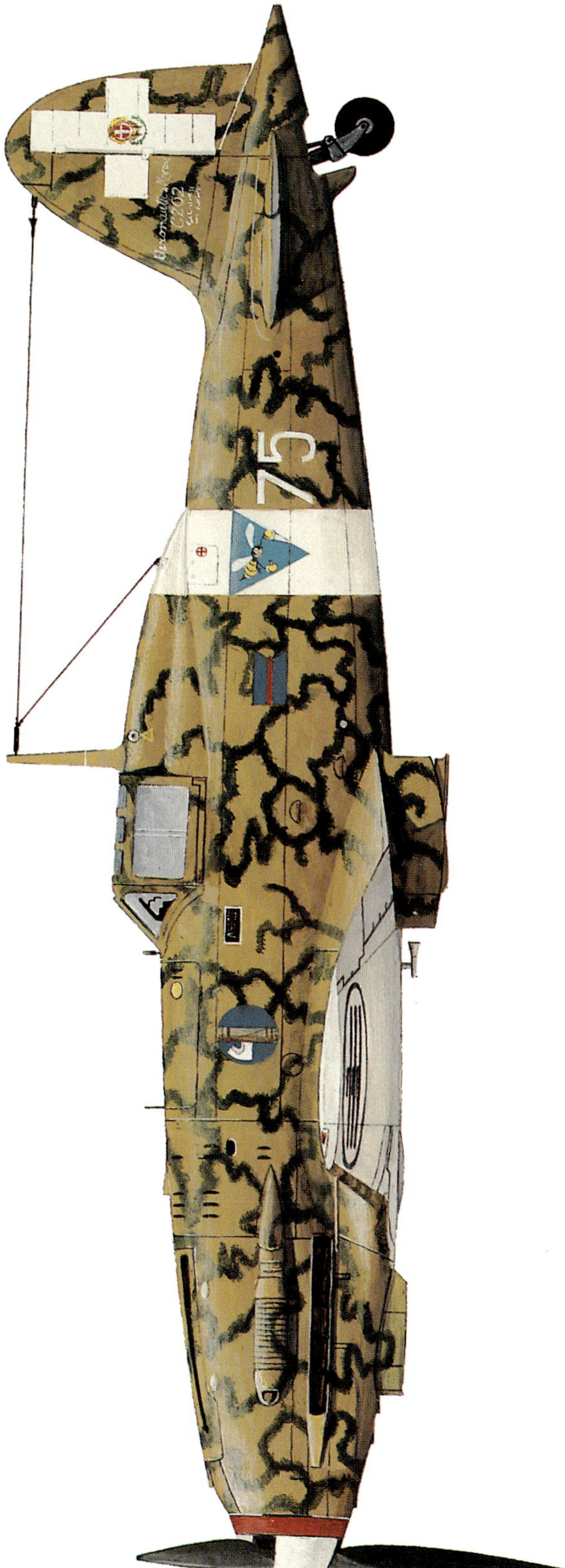

Maggiore Luigi Filippi, CO 23 Gruppo, 3 Stormo, Macchi C-202 series VII, s.n. uncertain, operations from Gabes and Medenine air dromes in Tunisia, January thru March and April thru July, 1943, at Ciampino air field in defense of Rome.

Major Franz Gotz, Gruppe Kom. III./JG 53 Bf 109G w.n. unk., based at Orvieto air field in January 1944 against the Anzio beachhead and later in northern Italy at Maniago air field until their recall to Germany in July.

End Notes

Chapter 1: El Hamma

1. Letter, Morrissey to author, 1976.

Chapter 2: The Balloon Goes Up

1. Richard Collier, editor, *The War in the Desert* (Time-Life Books, 1997).
2. Anthony Heckstel-Smith, *Tobruk, the Story of a Siege* (W. W. Norton & Co., Inc. 1959), p. 14.
3. Winston S. Churchill, *The Second World War,* Vol. II (Houghton Mifflin Co., 1949).
4. W. F. Craven and J. L. Cate, *The Army Air Forces in World War II,* Vol. II (Univ. of Chicago Press, 1949), p. 14.
5. No author, *The Eighth Army.* Booklet prepared for the British War Office by the Ministry of Information (HMSO, London, 1944), p. 52.
6. Ibid.
7. Ibid.

Chapter 3: To Find a War

1. Letter, Jaslow to author, May 1999. Cochran, who had a reputation as a tactical fighter genius, served as a trouble shooter for General Doolittle in North Africa, and later in Burma his air commando group supported British Brigadier Orde Wingate's Special Force, and employed the first helicopters ever used in combat. A brigadier general by war's end, Cochran became a close personal friend of Britain's Lord Louis Mountbatten who became Supreme Allied Commander in Southeast Asia. Ironically, Cochran was killed when he fell off a horse in upstate New York in August 1979, just one week after Mountbatten was killed by IRA terrorists in Ireland.
2. 79th Fighter Group War Diary.
3. Ibid.
4. Ibid.
5. Ivan Dmitri, *Flight to Everywhere* (McGraw Hill, New York), p. 26.
6. C. H.Laughlin, *Journal* of the American Aviation Historical Society, Spring 1978.
7. Jaslow letter, May 1999.
8. No author, *The Eighth Army*, p. 9.
9. Collier, *The War in the Desert.*
10. Letter, Watkins to author via Jack Kelly, July 1999.
11. Kelly letter, July 1999.
12. War Diary.
13. Letter, Fred Wright to author, August 1974.
14. Ibid.

Chapter 4: All Out For Monty

1. Walter J. Boyne, *Clash of Wings* (Simon & Schuster, New York, 1994), p. 171.
2. Robert H. Adleman and Col. George Walton, *Rome Fell Today* (Little Brown & Co., Boston, 1968), p. 177.
3. Major-General W. G. Stevens, *Bardia to Enfidaville, Official History of New Zealand in the Second World War* (R. E. Owen, Government Printer, Wellington, 1962), p. 213.
4. Chaz Bowyer, *Men of the Desert Air Force* (William Kimber & Co., Ltd., London, 1984), p. 231.
5. Stevens, *Bardia to Enfidaville*, p. 202.
6. War Diary.
7. Christopher F. Shores, Hans Ring, and William N. Hess, *Fighters Over Tunisia* (Neville Spearman Ltd., London, 1975), p.274.
8. Letter, Richards H. Hoffman, MD, to author, 1976.
9. Shores, Ring and Hess, *Fighters Over Tunisia*, p. 283.
10. Ibid.

11. Letter, Thomas Anderson to author, July 1999.
12. Hoffman letter.

Chapter 5: Cape Bon

1. Paul J. Vercammen, editor, *Air Combat* magazine, Vol.2, No. 5, 1969.
2. Rhynard, interview with author, October 1999.
3. Craven and Cate, *The Army Air Forces in World War II*, Vol. 11, p. 193.
4. Marc' Antonio Bragadin, *The Italian Navy in World War II* (US Naval Institute Press, Anapolis, Maryland, 1957), pgs. 249-50.
5. Johannes Steinhoff, *The Straits of Messina* (Andre´ Deutsch, Ltd., London, 1971), p. 24, and Shores, Ring and Hess, *Fighters Over Tunisia*, pgs. 375-76.
6. Shores, Ring and Hess, *Fighters Over Tunisia*, pgs. 375-76.
7. Ibid, p. 365.
8. Ibid, pgs. 376-77.
9. Jaslow letter.
10. 79th Fighter Group newsletter, 1943.
11. Shores, Ring and Hess, *Fighters Over Tunisia*, p. 379. According to the authors this was the only FW-190 lost over Tunisia that day.
12. David Fraser, *Knight's Cross* (HarperCollins Publishers, New York), p. 415.
13. John North, editor, *The Alexander Memoirs,1940-45.* (Casell, London,1969),p. 39.

Chapter 6: Turkey Shoot

1. Craven and Cate, *The Army Air Forces in World War II*, Vol.II, p.425.
2. Bragadin, *The Italian Navy in World War II*, p.257.
3. Ibid, p. 258.
4. Roderic Owen, *The Desert Air Force* (Hutchinson & Co., Ltd., London, 1948), p. 93.

Chapter 7: The Straits of Messina

1. Hanson W. Baldwin, *Battles Lost and Won* (Harper & Row, New York, 1966), p. 192.
2. Adleman and Walton, *Rome Fell Today*, p. 73.
3. Baldwin, *Battles Lost and Won*, p. 217.
4. Steinhoff, *The Straits of Messina*, p.187.
5. Ibid, pgs. 187-88.
6. Baldwin, *Battles Lost and Won*, p. 218.
7. War Diary, report of senior medical officer.
8. Baldwin, *Battles Lost and Won*, p. 220.
9. Mark M.Boatner III, *The Biographical Dictionary of World War II* (Presido Press, Novato, California, 1996), pgs. 242-43.
10. Kelly letter.
11. Martin Blumenson, *Sicily, Whose Victory* (Ballentine Books, Inc., New York), p. 144.

Chapter 8: Not So Sunny Italy

1. David Mason, *Salerno, Foothold in Europe* (Ballentine's Illustrated History of the Violent Century, New York, 1972), p. 144.
2. Letter, Norman L. R. Franks to author via 79th Fighter Group Association, April 1994. Franks is author of *Another Kind of Courage*, a history of RAF air/sea rescue Walrus operations.
3. Letter, Grogan to author via Richards H. Hoffman, MD, 1975.
4. Lt.-Colonel G. W. L. Nicholson, *The Canadians in Italy, 1943-45* (Minister of National Defense, Ottawa, 1966), p. 205.
5. Owen, *The Desert Air Force*, p. 187.
6. Nicholson, *The Canadians in Italy*, p. 215.
7. Owen, *The Desert Air Force*, p. 186.
8. Barrie Pitt, editor, *History of the Second World War,* Part 52 (Marshall Cavendish USA Ltd., 1973), p. 1,453.
9. Owen, *The Desert Air Force*, p. 197.
10. Letter, Tom McIntosh to author, September 1982. McIntosh was an armorer with the 87th Fighter Squadron.
11. Lt.-Colonel J. P. "Pete" Bedford, USAF (Ret.), Winter 1987 *Friends Bulletin* of the Air Force Museum Foundation.
12. Owen, *The Desert Air Force*, P. 200.
13. Pinkham, interview with author; Jaslow letter.

Chapter 9: Stalemate

1. Eric Linklater, *The Campaign in Italy* (HMSO, London, 1951), p.106.
2. Hoffman letter.

Chapter 10: The Stranded Whale

1. Martin Blumenson, *Anzio, The Gamble That Failed* (J. B. Lippincott Co., Philadelphia & New York, 1963), p. 48.
2. Ibid.
3. Letter, Merlin Eltzroth to author, April 1999. Eltzroth was a pilot with the 85th Fighter Squadron.
4. Christopher Shores, *Pictorial History of the Mediterranean Air War,* Vol. 3 (Ian Allen Ltd., London, 1974), p. 117.
5. Owen, *The Desert Air Force*, p. 209.
6. Charles B. MacDonald, *The Mighty Endeavor* (Oxford Univ. Press, New York, 1969), p. 200.

7. Charles E. Francis, *The Tuskegee Airmen* (Bruce Humphries, Inc., Boston, 1955), p. 45.

8. Stanley Sandler, *Segregated Skies* (Smithsonian Institution Press, Washington, DC, 1992), p. 57.

9. Letter, Silsbee to author, June 1999. Of the eighty-four missions Silsbee flew during the war, this was his longest at two hours and fifty-five minutes.

10. War Diary.

11. Blumenson, *Anzio, The Gamble That Failed*, p. 103.

12. Craven and Cate, *The Army Air Forces in World War II*, Vol. III, p. 352.

13. Blumenson, *Anzio, The Gamble That Failed*, p. 112.

14. Jerry Scutts, *Bf 109 Aces of North Africa and the Mediterranean* (Osprey, London, 1994), p. 63.

15. Blumenson, *Anzio, The Gamble That Failed*, p. 112.

16. Ibid, p.113.

17. Sherer, letter to author, June 1999.

18. Blumenson, *Anzio, The Gamble That Failed*, p. 124.

19. Pitt, *History of the Second World War*, p. 1,622.

20. Ibid.

21. War Diary.

Chapter 11: Cassino, Strangle and Rome

1. Adleman and Walton, *Rome Fell Today*, p. 151.

2. Geoffrey Perret, *Winged Victory* (Random House, New York, 1993), p. 233.

3. Letter, Duffield to author, July 1999.

4. Ernest R. McDowell, *The P-40 Kittyhawk* (ARCO Publishing Co. Inc., New York, 1958), p. 20.

5. Eltzroth letter.

6. Letter, Dave Rouleau to author, May 2000.

7. War Diary.

8. Ibid.

9. Letter, Scheumack to author, August 1999.

10. Sandler, *Segregated Skies,* p. 53.

11. Ibid.

12. Craven and Cate, *AAF in World War II*, Vol. III, p. 378.

13. Eltzroth letter.

14. Ibid.

15. Raymond Toliver, *Nazi Interrogator* (Zebra Books in arrangment with Aero Publishers, 1978), pgs. 187-89. Despite the unfortunate title, this excellent book has a wealth of information on Colonel Stark.

16. Adleman and Walton, *Rome Fell Today*, p. 211.

17. Letter, Royse to author, June 1999.

18. War Diary.

19. Ibid.

Chapter 12: Corsican Summer

1. General Chuck Yeager with Leo Janos, *Yeager* (Bantam Books, New York, 1985), p. 61.

2. Letter, Taddei Dominique to author, 1999. Dominique is one of a group of Corsicans working to document the presence of Allied airmen on Corsica during the war, and honor them with a memorial.

3. Eltzroth letter.

4. Ibid.

5. Samuel Eliot Morrison, *The Two-Ocean War* (Little, Brown & Co., Boston, 1963), p.364.

6. Bragadin, *The Italian Navy in World War II*, p. 99.

7. Ibid, p. 346.

8. Letter, Woerpel to author via Raymond Woerpel, 1944.

9. MacDonald, *The Mighty Endeavor*, p.321.

10. Eltzroth letter.

11. Bill Colgan, *World War II Fighter-Bomber Pilot* (Sunflower University Press, Manhattan, Kansas, 1985), p. 96.

12. Letter, Ferdinando D'Amico to author, March 1988; Nick Beale, D'Amico and Gabriele Valentini, *Airwar Italy: 1944-45* (Airlife Publishing Ltd., London, 1996), pgs. 72-73.

13. D'Amico letter.

14. Letter, Cochran to author, June 1999.

15. Letter, Brittian to author, April 1999.

16. Letter, Bratt to author, June 1999.

17. Letter, Remble to author via Andre´ Besson, August 1999.

18. Letter, Edward McLaughlin to author, June 1999. McLaughlin was a pilot with the 86th Fighter Squadron.

Chapter 13 : Rhone Valley Massacre

1. Harry Powell (85th pilot), interview with author, October 1999.

2. Letter, Robert Bell (85th pilot) to author, July 1999.

3. Letter, Lawless to author, September 1999.

4. Colgan, *Fighter-Bomber Pilot*, p. 107.

5. Ibid, p. 108.

6. Letter, Bagian to author, March 1999.

7. Colgan, *Fighter-Bomber Pilot*, p. 111-12.

8. Lawless letter.

9. Letter, Charpentier to author, March 2000.

10. William B. Breuer, *Operation Dragoon* (Presido Press, Novato, California, 1987), p. 246.

11. Letter, Claycomb to author, July 1999.

12. Hall, interview with author, October 1999.

13. Lawless letter.

Chapter 14: Back in the Gumbo Again

1. Owen, *The Desert Air Force*, p. 229.
2. Ibid, p. 235.
3. Letter, Arnold to author, October 1973.
4. Letter, Sweeney to author, August 1999.
5. Owen, *The Desert Air Force*, p. 235.
6. Franks letter.
7. Letter, Bell to author, July 1999.
8. War Diary.
9. Letter, Norman to author, June 1999.
10. Letter, Van Houten to author, July 1999.
11. War Diary.
12. Ibid.

Chapter 15: Italian Finalé

1. Letter, Dick Hilgard (86th pilot) to author, July 1999.
2. Bratt letter.
3. Letter, Kittrell to author, September 1999.
4. Sally Van Wagenen Keil, *Those Wonderful Women in Their Flying Machines* (American Book-Stratford Press, Saddle Brook, New Jersey, 1979), p. 243.
5. Lawless letter.
6. Kittrell letter, and *New York Tribune*, 1945.
7. Letter, Moody to author, June 1999.
8. Beale, D'Amico and Valentini, *Airwar Italy:1944-45*, pgs. 170-71.
9. Letter, Tessier to author, June 1999.
10. Letter, Church to author, November 1976.
11. Owen, *The Desert Air Force*, p. 246.
12. War Diary.
13. Beale, D'Amico and Valentini, *Airwar Italy: 1944-45*, p. 178.
14. Letter, Faires to author, August 1999.
15. D'Amico letter.
16. Letter, Sherer to author, March 2000.
17. Letter, Probst to author, June 1999.
18. Lawless letter.
19. *The Stars and Stripes* (Mediterranean edition), April 12, 1945.
20. War Diary.
21. Kittrell letter.

Chapter 16: Taking the Scenic Route Home

1. Toliver, *Nazi Interrogator*, p. 387.
2. Ibid, p. 15.
3. Stephen E. Ambrose, *Citizen Soldiers* (Simon & Schuster, New York, 1997), p. 293.
4. David A. Foy, *For You The War Is Over: American Prisoners of War in Nazi Germany* (Stein & Day, New York, 1984), p. 135.
5. Bell letter.
6. Claycomb letter.
7. Bratt letter.
8. Alan Burgess, *The Longest Tunnel* (Grove Weidenfeld, New York, 1990).
9. War Diary.
10. Ibid.
11. Kittrell letter.
12. Letter, Feimer to author, 1975.
13. Van Houten letter.

Chapter 17: The Last Tally-Ho

1. Sweeney letter.
2. Ibid, and Church letter.
3. War Diary.
4. Letter, John F. Martin Jr. to author, August 1999.
5. Richard A. Morley, *Profile of a Test Pilot, Engineer, Pilot Patriot* (USAF Museum *Friends Journal*, Fall 1996 and Winter 1997).
6. Donald S. Lopez, *Fighter Pilot's Heaven* (Smithsonian Institution Press, Washington, DC, 1995), p. 54.
7. War Diairy.
8. Ibid.

Glossary

AAF: Army Air Forces
AOC: Air Officer Commanding (RAF)
ASC: Air Support Command
Bandit: Enemy aircraft
Bogie: Unidentified aircraft
CCS: Combined Chiefs of Staff
CO: Commanding Officer
DAF: Desert Air Force
DFC: Distinguished Flying Cross
Djebel: Mountain, Tunisia
DSC: Distinguished Service Cross
F/O: Flight Officer
Frags: Fragmentation bombs
FW: Focke-Wulf (German single-engined fighter)
Jug: Nickname for Republic P-47 Thunderbolt
KIA: Killed in Action
LCT: Landing Craft, Tank
LCVP: Landing Craft, Vehicle, Personnel
LG: Landing Ground
LST: Landing Ship, Tank
MAAF: Mediterranean Allied Air Forces
MIA: Missing in Action
Mission: More than one aircraft completing an assigned combat task
MP: Military Police
Ops: Operations
Panzer: German tank, or armored unit
POW: Prisoner of War
PSP: Pierced Steel Planking (perforated steel sheets used for rapid construction of runways)
RAF: Royal Air Force
SAAF: South African Air Force
Snapper: Enemy aircraft
Sortie: One aircraft completing a combat operational flight
Spit or Spitty: Nickname for Supermarine Spitfire (British fighter)
TAC: Tactical Air Command
VIP: Very Important Person
Wadi: River, or dry river bed, Tunisia
WDAF: Western Desert Air Force

Bibliography

Adleman, Robert H., and Walton, Colonel George *Rome Fell Today*. Boston: Little, Brown & Co., 1968.

Baldwin, Hanson, *Battles Lost and Won*. New York: Harper & Row, 1966.

Barnett, Correll, *The Desert Generals*. The Viking Press, 1960.

Beal, Nick, D'Amico, Ferdinando, and Valentini, Gabriele *Air War Italy: 1944-45*. Shrewsbury, England: Airlife Publishing Ltd., 1996.

Blumenson, Martin, Anzio, *The Gamble That Failed.* Philadelphia & New York: J. P.Lippincott Co., 1963.

— *Bloody River.* Boston: Houghton Mifflin Co., Boston, 1970.

— Sicily, *Whose Victory?* New York: Ballantine Books, 1968.

Boatner, Mark M. III. The *Biographical Dictionary of World War II.* Novato, California: Presido Press, 1996

Bowyer, Chaz. *Men of the Desert Air Force.* London: William Kimber & Co., 1984

Bragadin, Marc' Antonio. *The Italian Navy in World War II.* Maryland: US Naval Institute, 1957.

Breuer, William B. *Operation Dragoon.* Novato, California: Presido Press, 1987.

Carell, Paul. *The Foxes of the Desert.* New York: E. P. Dutton & Co., 1961.

Cate, J. L. & Craven, W. F., editors. *The Army Air Forces in World War II, Vols. II and III.* Chicago: University of Chicago Press, 1949.

Cavigli, Henry J. *Escapades in the Blue.* New York: Vantage Press, Inc., 1996.

Colgan, Bill. *World War II Fighter-Bomber Pilot.* Manhattan, Kansas: Sunflower University Press, 1985.

Collier, Richard, editor. *The War in the Desert.* New York: Time-Life Books, 1977.

Constable, Trevor J., & Toliver, Colonel Raymond F. *Horrido, Fighter Aces of the Luftwaffe.* New York: Ballantine Books, 1968.

Deighton, Len. *Blood, Tears and Folly.* New York: Harper-Collins Publishers, 1999.

Dodds, Wayne S. *The Fabulous Fifty-Seventh Fighter Group of World War II.* Missouri: Walsworth Publishing Co., 1985.

Dmitri, Ivan. *Flight to Everywhere.* New York: McGraw-Hill.

Durand, Arthur A. *Stalag Luft III (The Secret Story):* Baton Rouge, Louisiana: Louisiana State University, 1988.

Foy, David A. *For You The War is Over (American Prisoners of War in Nazi Germany).* New York: Stein & Day, 1984.

Francis, Charles E. *The Tuskegee Airmen.* Boston: Bruce Humphries, Inc., 1955

Graham, Dominch. *Cassino.* New York: Ballantine Books, 1970

Hess, William N. *Allied Aces of World War II.* New York: ARCO Publishing Co., 1966.

Jackson, Maj.-Gen. W. G. F. *The Battle for Rome.* London: Batsford, 1969.

Lewin, Ronald. *Montgomery as Military Commander.* New York: Stein & Day, 1971.

Lind, Ragner C., editor. *The Falcon.* Munich: F. Bruckmann, 1946.

Linklater, Eric. *The Campaign in Italy.* London: His Majesty's Stationery Office, 1951.

MacDonald, Charles B. *The Mighty Endeavor.* New York: Oxford University Press, 1969.

Mason, David. *Salerno, Foothold in Europe.* New York: Ballantine Books, 1972.

Maurer, Maurer. *Air Force Combat Units of World War II.* Washington, DC: Government Printing Office, 1961.

McDowell, Ernest R., and Hess, William N. *Checkertail Clan: 325th Fighter Group in North Africa and Italy.* Fallbrook, California: Aero Publishers, Inc.,1969.

McDowell, Ernest R. *The P-40 Kittyhawk.* New York: ARCO Publishing Co.,1969.

Mizrahi, Joseph U. *Knights of the Black Cross.* Granada Hills, California: Sentry Books, 1972.

Morison, Samuel Eliot. *The Two-Ocean War.* Boston: Little, Brown & Co.,1963.

Nicholson, Lt.-Col. G. W. L. *The Canadians in Italy, 1943-45.* Ottawa: Ministry of National Defense, 1966.

North, John, editor. *The Alexander Memoirs, 1940-45.* London: Cassell,1962.

Orgill, Douglas. *The Gothic Line.* London: Pan Books, 1969.

Owen, Roderic. *The Desert Air Force.* London: Hutchinson & Co., 1948

Parrish, Thomas, editor. *The Simon & Schuster Encylopedia of World War II.* New York: Simon & Schuster, 1978.

Perret Geoffrey. *Winged Victory.* New York: Random House, 1993.

Phillips, N. C. *New Zealand in the Second World War: Vol. I, Italy: The Sangro to Cassino.* Wellington: New Zealand War History Branch, 1957.

Richards, Denis, and Saunders, Hilary St. George. *Royal Air Force* (3 vols). London: His Majesty's Stationery Office, HMSO, 1953-54.

Rust, Kenn C. *The Ninth Air Force in World War II.* Fallbrook, California: Aero Publishers, 1967.

— *Twelfth Air Force.* California: Historical Aviation Album Publications, 1975.

Sandler, Stanley. *Segregated Skies.* Washington, DC: Smithsonian Institution Press, 1992.

Shamburger, Page, and Christy, Joe. *The Curtiss Hawks.* Kalamazoo, Michigan: Wolverine Press, 1972.

Shores, Christopher F., and Ring, Hans. *Fighters Over The Desert.* New York: ARCO Publishing Co., 1969.

Shores, Christopher F., Ring, Hans, and Hess, William N. *Fighters Over Tunisia,* London: Neville Spearman, 1975.

Steinhoff, Johannes. *The Straits of Messina.* London: Andre Deutsch Ltd., 1971.

Stevens, Maj.-Gen. W. G. *New Zealand in the Second World War: Bardia to Enfidaville.* Wellington: New Zealand War History Branch, 1962.

Strawson, John. *The Battle for North Africa.* New York: Charles Scribner's Sons, 1969.

Thruelsen, Major Richard, and Arnold, Lieutenant Elliott. *Mediterranean Sweep.* New York: Duell, Sloan and Pearce, 1944.

Toliver, Raymond. *Nazi Interrogator.* New York: Zebra Books, 1978.

No Author. *The Eighth Army.* London: His Majesty's Stationery Office, 1944.

No Author. *History of the 82nd Fighter Control Squadron.* Printed in Germany, 1946.

Index

79th Fighter Group Personnel

(Includes 99th and 316th squadrons)

Surname, first name and middle initial (where known). See text for rank.

Abbott, William G., 8, 38, 58, 225
AcMoody, Gordon R., 118, 121, **124**, 149, 150, 227
Adair, Asa A., 14, 15, 48, **52**, **66**, 74, 75, **84**, 86, 90, 225, 226
Adkins, Damon, 141, 146, 228, 230
Aldrich, Donald, **151**
Allard, Robert H., 62, 226
Allen, Burke F., 105, 108, 229
Allen, Clarence, 119, 227
Anderson, Herbert A., 119, 136, 230
Anderson, James E., Jr., 179, 231
Anderson, John R., 59, 229
Anderson, Wyman D., 8, 14, 55, **66**, 74, **75**, **84**, 226
Anderson,Thomas S., 8, 55
Angyal, Zoltan J., 189, **191**, 197
Arnold, Calvin J., 8, 174, 175, 181, 189, 231
Ascenzi, Richard, 187, **189**, 231
Ashley, Willie 119, 227
Austin, Alan Y., 118, 124

Bachetti, Leonard, 39
Bagian, Philip, 8, 163, 164, 216
Bailey, Charles, 120, 227
Bailey, Perry E., **55**, 62, 229
Baker, Thomas M., 152
Balega, John L., 134, **151**
Bartlett, Robert, 123, 124, **167**, 228
Bartlett, Stuart L., 141, 146, 230
Bartley, Harry E., 183, 184, 231
Bates, Earl E., 26, **28**, 30, 51, **76**, **87**, **89**, **106**, 128, 133, 137, 138, 139, 217,218, 233
Baugh, Howard, 119, 227
Beck, John L., 109, 119, 187, 227, 233
Beckerman, Leonard, **142**, **167**, 221
Bedford, John P. "Pete," 9, 58, **59**, 72, 99, **100**, 225, 226
Beeks, Jack C., 8, **142**, 152, 221
Beers, George W., 156, 230
Bell, Gordon A., 121, 145, 174, 231
Bell, Robert B., 8, 176, 204, 206, 231
Benz, Albert, 120, 128, 227
Berinati, Leo G., 59, 74, 75, 86, 89, 225, 226, 227
Bishop, Wiliam E., 8, 197
Biting, Robert M., 143, 230
Blair, Basil H., 8, **104**, 105, 125
Blair, James 111n
Blair, Merle, 189
Blare, George O., 14, 59, 66
Blassingham, James, 8, 144, **145**, 228
Boggs, Kenneth, 52, 229
Bolack, Charles "Kim," **59**, 62, 71, 72, 88, 89, 225, 226
Bolte, George, 123, 128, 134, 227
Boone, John, 163, 164
Borsheim, Lawrence, 139, 230
Borsodi, Frederic A., 9, 10, 11, 12, 13, 37, 51, 58, 59, **60**, 67n, 72, 86, 98, 99, **100**, 139, 217, 225, 233, 235
Bostick, Warren R., 196, 231
Bothe, John H., 151, 230
Boyd, Jack G., **190**
Bozzi, Edward M., **88**, 118, 227
Bratt, Albert V., Jr., 8, 157, 158, 182, 183, 184, 204, 206, 207, 231
Brewer, Al, 61, 226
Brittian, William "Doug," 8, 156, 157
Brooks, Bascom, 233
Brown, David H., 13, 51, 229
Brown, Percy E., Jr., 164, 231
Brown, Robert S., **162**
Bruce, Samuel, 120, 123, 230
Bunker, Richard, 13, 71, 226
Burch, Frank, 138
Burnap, Arthur E., Jr., 188, 231
Burns, Harold R., Jr., 89, 226
Bush, Cecil T., 152
Byron, Edward J., 136, 174, 228, 233

Cahill, John C., 65
Callum, Gaston, 95, 98, 119, 120, 227
Campbell, Chet, 8
Campbell, Ed, **150**
Cassiday, Benjamin B., Jr., 8, **150**, **151**, 152, 192, 221, 222, 228, 233
Challet, Louis L., **199**
Charpentier, Leonard A., 8, **160**, 165, 231
Church, Paul B., 8, **191**, **192**, **193**, 221
Churchill, Clyde, 8
Cimaglia, John O., 14, 47, 66, 71, 226
Cirrito, Anthony J., **88**
Clark, Milton L., 14, 71, 92, 93, 94, 226
Claycomb, Donald E., 8, **165**, 167, 204, 206, 231
Claycomb, William, 8
Cochran, John C., Jr., 8, **151**, 156n
Cole, J. L., 233
Colgan, William B., 8, 118, 121, 163, 164, 227
Colmer, Ralph, 8
Compton, W. R., 233
Conly, 60, 61, 226
Connelly, Joseph W., 14, **72**, 73, 226
Cox, Jack, 8
Cox, Thomas E., **73**
Craig, Henry, 8
Crawford, Robert, 141, 228
Cronk, Carl E., **160**
Croskery, Keith S., **151**, 176, 177, 231
Cross, Richard, **151**
Crossley, Harold, **66**
Culver, German P., 220, 233
Cumberland, Horace W., 72
Cummings, Charles, 97
Custis, Lemuel, 120, 227

Daniels, Harry J., 230
Davis, "Pop," 39
Davis, Melvin K., 47, 229
Davis, Robert, 97
Dean, William R., 116,121, 227
DeFoor, Charles W., Jr., 105, 134, 137, 228, 230
DeHay, Dale F., 114
Delaney, Fred, 13, 48
Dempsey, Robert, 66, 67n
Dietrick, Emery, **52**
Dietz, Robert, 119, 121, 227
Doughtie, Jack, 111n
Dozeman, Milton, 8
Driver, Elwood, 119, 123, 227
Drum, Robert, 8
Duffield, Robert J., 8, 119, 123, 124, 132,134, 227, 228
Dunlap, Alwayne, 128, 230
Dzamba, John P., 74, 97

Eagleson, Wilson, 120, 123, 227
Edds, Berning T.,138, 230
Einstanding, Harry, 8
Eltzroth, Merlin S., 8, 136, 139, **142**
Emmert, Benjamin H., Jr., 221, 233
Erick, Allen, 8
Ermis, Raymond A., 55, 143, 230
Ervin, Gerald V., **184**, 231
Estes, Delmar L., **142**, 176
Evans, Edward G., 8, **142**
Evans, Richard D., 202
Ewing, George W., Jr., 139, 152, 154, 228, 233

Faires, Jack, 8, 193
Faison, Ronald M., 169, 181, 228, 231
Fanning, James, 231
Farquhar, Charles A., 236
Feimer, William P., 8, 98, 212, 214, 214n
Fernebok, Irving J., **31**, 36
Fetter, Alfred L., 8, **176**, 177, 233

Files, Roger B., 8, 141, 164, 203n, **219**, 222, 228, 233
Finklestein, Herman,8
Fitzgerald, Edward P., 14, **49**, 55, 59, **66**, 74, **75**, 225
Foreman, Milo, 8
Fortune, Jack C., 168, 231
Franco, Eugene A., **190**
Fuestal, William, 144, 228

Gagliardo, Anthony J., 8, 93
Gartzke, Victor, 190
Geers, Jospeh, 8
Gibson, Charles, 85
Gilbert, Allen, 174, **189**
Gilmore, Eugene O., 154
Gilmore, Jackson, 8
Gilpin, George W., 54
Givings, Clemenceau, 230
Glasgow, William C., 59, **61**, 105, 107, 108, 109, 208, 209, 211, 229
Gorsuch, Richard P., 182, 231
Gossick, Lee V., 8, 14, **34**, 38, 49, 55, 66, 74, 75, **83**, 221, 225, 226
Gower, William, 8
Granberg, Martin J., 8, 124, 152, 228
Grandjean, Irvin L., 187, **189**, **190**
Gravenstine, Donald J., 123, 124, **153**, 154, **160**, 228
Green, James L., 155, 156, 230
Greer, George, 109, 229
Grier, Robert K.,125
Griffin, William, 229
Grogan, Charles E., 26, 52, 73, 74, 94, 226, 233
Gruver, Jay R., **142**, 157
Guilfoyle, Donald W., 8
Guillebeau, Robert, 38, 229
Gumbleton, John, "Jack," **55**, 61

Hagler, Raymond, 138, 195, 228
Hale, Charles F., "Fred," 14, 66, 89, 92, 66n, 226
Halfpapp, Arthur E., 202, 231
Hall, Charles, 119, 121, 227
Hall, Harold, B., 8, **165**, 167, **190**
Hamilton, 134
Hamilton, Frank W., 236
Hancock, Charles, 155, 228
Hannon, James F.,185, 231
Hanson, Herbert L., 8, 196
Hanson, William D., **55**, 60, 62, 225, 229
Harding, William, 184, 231
Harlocker, Frank, **160**
Harris, George L., 52, **53**, 54, **55**, 229
Hartman, Paul L., 127, 230
Hawk, Thomas, 150
Hayles, Malcolm,8, 141, 228
Hazzard, Herbert M., 8
Head, Billy, 155, 228
Hearne, Alfred, 148n, 187, **189**, **190**, 197
Hennin, Francis W., 59, **66**, 74, 89, 90
Hewitt, Robert F., 185, 231
Higgins, Raymond L., 123, 133, 228, 230
Highfield, Harlan E., 52, 209, 229
Hilgard, Richard W., 8, 155, 228
Hintz, Loren, **190**, 202, 231
Hoagland, John G., 13, 51, **59**, 66, 72, 86, 226
Hodge, William E., 161
Hoerr, Irvin, 187, 231
Hoffman, Richards H., 7, 8, 52, 55, **58**, **78**, 105, 110, 111
Holland, Wilbert, 39
Holtner, Stanley, 233
Horn, William, 8
Huff, Frank, 14, 48, 54, **66**, 74, **75**, 86, **87**, 90, 226, 229
Hundley, James, **66**, **75**, **83**
Huntzberger, George E., 144, 195
Hutt, John C., 62, **73**

Jackson, Charles F., **58**
Jackson, Leonard, 123, 227
Jamison, Clarence, 123
Janicki, Chester, 59, 229
Jasitis, Peter, 221
Jaslow, Charles, 8, 26, 31, 54, 55, 66, 74, **75**, **83**, 100, 101, 225
Jennings, Russell K., 163, 164, 231
Joh, Edwin, "Leo," 104, 121
Johnson, Elmer, 222
Johnson, Franklin T., 48, 229
Johnson, Willis R., 88, 221, 226
Jonas, Lloyd P., **84**
Jones, Charles, **75**, **83**
Jones, Edgar, 136, 230
Jones, Frank, 8
Jones, Orion, **150**, 221
Jones, Reidy, 87, 90
Jory, Jesse "Fred," 38, 43, **49**, 52, **66**, **74**, 75, **84**, 225

Kauffman, Jack, 8, 60, **61**, **63**, **65**, **69**, **84**, **94**, 336
Keene, John E., 123, 125
Kehr, Charles H., 105, 107, 229
Kellerman, Ernest H., 105, 229
Kelley, Robert P., 8, 88, 227
Kelly, Edward J., 8, **186**, **194**
Kelly, John C., "Jack," 8, **33**, 38, 39, 59, 61, **82**, 84, 85, 90, **94**, 225
Kelly, Russell R., 8
Keppler, George E., 187, 231
Kettenbrink, Albert R., 105
Killeward, Matthew, **64**
Kinkle, Lou, 8
Kirsch, John L., **49**, **66**, 74, **75**, 97, 226
Kittrell, John C., 8, **151**, 202, 208, 211
Klassie, Marlin, 231
Klear, Milo, 136
Kleiderer, Eugene, Jr., 152, 159, 160, 233
Knighten, James, 123

Laird, Robert F., 132
Land, Harold D., 8, 136, 175n
Landers, Charles, 145, 230
Lane, Allen, 120
Lankford, Charles, 154
Lansing, Joseph, **160**
Lappin, Vincent, 8
Lawless, Don, 8, 162, 164, **168**, **172**, **178**, 186, 196, 197
Lawrence, Robert, 120, 227
Leatherman, Ober N., 54, 229
Lee, George T., 66, 74, 90, **75**, 104, 110, 116, 133, 217, 218, 226, 227, 233
Lemmon, Edmund T., 141,148n, 197
Letzkus, Edward, 143, 230
Leuther, Herman, 104, 121, 137, 227
Ligett, Robert, 13, 15, 48, 51, 225, 229
Lincicome, Albert, E., 118, 121
Lind, Ragnar G., 8, **219**
Lind, Ralph, 14, 55, 229
Loftiss, Morrison D., 193, 231
Logel, Charles, 143, 230
Long, Richard, **142**, 152
Lownders, Charles, 90, 229
Lukas, Edward, 221
Lyans, Glenn M., 8, 132, 133
Lydon, L. C., 233

Mace, Albert R., 128, 230
Magness, Stephen, **75**, **78**, **83**, 94, 111n
Malone, Richard, **64**
Manning, Walter, 197
Marshall, William B., 105, 108, 229
Martin, John F., 8, 66, **67**, 71, 72n, 73, 93, 94, 108, 134, **160**, 185, 216, 217, 220, 226, 233
Martin, William, 105, 229
Martino, Saverio P., 125, 138
Mathesius, William, 105, 119
Mathews, Hugh, 92
Mathias, Albert, 189, 231
Mauritz, Michael, 123
Maxwell, Earl, 161, 168n, **172**, 233
Maxwell, George, 48, 225
Maye, Jack, 97, 116, 123, 229
Mayer, Daniel, **55**, 86, 90, 229
McArthur, Paul G., 8, 15, 48, 66, 73, **74**, 75, 89, 225, 226, 227
McCarty, Thomas H., 62, 208, 229
McCrumby, George, 119, 123, 128, 230
McDonnel, Ed, 54, 229
McEwen, John, **117**
McGoldrick, Peter, 25, **28**, 30, 32,37, 38, 139, 229, 233, 235
McGrath, Everly J., 236
McGuire, James, 8
McHenry, James, 202, 231
McIlwaine, Archibald G., 157, 184, 231
McIntosh, Thomas, 8
McKay, Donald W., 52, 54, 229
McLane, William, 123, 124, 228
McLaughlin, Edward M., 8
McNall, Malcolm, "Joe," 8, 14, 62, 226
Melonakis, Peter, 134
Menger, Richard, 184
Menifee, James, 174, 231
Merrill, Hollis, **176**, 177
Miller, Kensley, 48, **66**, 74, 225, 226
Miller, Phillip G., 48, 55
Millican, Vincent, 155, 156, 230
Mills, Clinton, 123, 227, 228
Milstead, Frank H., 8, **151**
Minett, Robert T., 8, 38, 87
Mitchell, Harry, 162, 231
Mitchell, Thomas G., 233
Montgomery, Donald, 189, 231
Moody, Robert P., 8, 189
Morgan, John, 110, 229
Morgan, Warren, 8
Morrison, Bruce L., 15, **75**
Morrissey, Richard P., 8, 13, **14**, 15, 38, 72, 226
Moschberger, Fredrick J., 181
Moss, David, 148,230
Mulkey, Donald N., 138, 230
Mullin, Bernard, **11**, **78**, **142**
Murto, George, 8

Nashold, George H., Jr., 123
Nero, Vincent, **194**
Newbould, Edwin P., 8, 221
Newton, Frank E., 85, 90, 229
Nicholas, William, 8, 191, **192**
Nicolai, Frank T., 124, 135
Nielsen, Melvin J., 98, 109, 125, 139, **140**, 177, 182, 233
Noell, Robert E., 144, 228
Norman, Robert P., 8, **177**, 178, 231
Norris, Robert, **221**
Norton, Wilbert, **221**
Nystrum, Raymond E., **144**

O'Brien, Thomas A., **162**, 188, 231
Odle, Conrad H., "Harry," 8, **142**, **150**
Ogden, William W., 157, 164
Owen, Clinton, V., 14, 59, **75**, 86, 97, 110, 116, 121, 227

Paff, Clarence E., 190, 231
Palermo, Raymond, 38, 229

Palmer, Arthur J., 167
Patin, Robert L., 141, 152, 230
Paul, Robert, 138, 230
Payne, Edwin, 8, 176, **201**, 233
Peickert, 138
Penar, Leonard J., 121, **127**, 227
Pepper, Robert, 125, 141
Perry, Henry, 119
Peterman, Walter G., 116, 121, 141, 227, 228
Peters, Robert M., **179**
Peters, William E., 178, 231
Phelan, James, **178**
Phelps, Victor L., 174, 231
Phillips, Richard, 8
Pinkham, John, 8, 100
Pinkston, Gladwyn E., 182, **183**, 187, 200, 216, 233
Pittard, James G., 8, 55, 86, 90, 229
Plank, Edwin L., 8, **186**
Pneuman, Arthur H., 190, 231
Porter, Ralph, **49**, **88**
Powell, Harry K., 8
Powell, Richard, **190**
Pringle, Ward T., 135, 230
Pritchard, William F., 148, 230
Probst, William J., Jr., 8, 196
Proctor, Robert W., 119, 124
Pumphrey, Joseph E., **32**, 37, **73**, 235
Purchla, Mathew F., 136, 145, 221

Ramsdell, William M., **160**, 161, 231
Reutershan, James H., 38, **65**, **84**
Rhodes, John R., 176
Rhynard, Wayne E., 8, 54, **55**, 62, **64**, 85, 226
Richardson, Grady B., 197
Richer, Donald, 141, 230
Richmond, Robert, 146
Riley, Thomas, **190**
Roarke, Sherrill, 8
Roberts, George S., 100, 119
Roberts, Leon, 119, 227
Robinette, Robert S., 196, 231
Roehrdanz, Elroy C., 152
Rogers, John, 119, 227
Rogers, Leslie, 39
Rogers, William, 15, 48, 55, 71, 227
Rospo, Sam, 141, 148n, 152, 230
Rouleau, Louis T., 134, 137, **139**, 143, 230
Rowe, Walter, **31**, 36
Royse, Romie R., 8, 144, 145, 195
Rueschoff, William H., 136, 230
Ryan, Robert M., 152
Ryburn, William L., 65, 71, 226

Sachleben, Clifford E., 95
Sanders, Frank E., 8, 221
Sanderson, Richard G., 8, **153**
Say, Samuel L., 14, 37, **38**, 43, 62, 66, 266
Scheumack, Powell A., 8, 109, 120, 128, 136
Schoellkopf, Jacob F., 13, 26, 48, 77, **78**, 93, 233
Schuchman, Kenneth W., 8
Scofield, James B., 136, 138, 230
Sears, Frank J.,139, 230
Semmes, Thomas J., 208
Shapira, Elliott K., 8
Sherer, Wayne, 8, **104**, 125, 195
Shuping, Bates, **64**, 197
Shuttleworth, David H., 134, 141, 144, 152, 228
Silsbee, E. R., "Randy," 8, 110, 118, 121, 227
Simmons, Wendell, 105,108, 229
Simpson, Carl L.,43, 58, 95, 229
Sirman, Donald S., 121,128
Skotnicky, Robert, 118, 227
Slater, Michael J., 141, 230
Slatton, Jack, **160**, 176
Smith, Howard A., 105, 108, 229
Smith, Lewis, 121, 227
Smith, William R., 98, 229
Sonnichsen, Noel, 149, 155, 230
Spanhut, Fred, 8
Sprecht, Ralph C., 105,108, 229
Spurgin, Robert, 8,13, 51, 229
Stafford, Merle E., 139, 230
Stage, Wesley, 185, 231
Stahl, Robert S., Jr., 174, 231
Stalter, William J., 152, **153**
Stark, Charles W., 139, **140**, 206, 230, 233
Steele, Henry P., 98, 99, 229
Steiner, Robert B., 155, **166**, 228
Stern, William, **78**
Stevens, Clarence E., 143, 230
Stewart, Carl W., 120, 124, 128, 134, **135**,136, 227, 228, 233
Stewart, Guy A., 55
Stoudmire, Norville, 230
Sweeney, Robert M., 8, 175, 181
Sweeting, James F., 8
Swenson, Robert, 143, 144, 230

Tallent, Warren H., 155, 228
Taylor, Robert, 8, 14
Taylor, William R., 13, 15, 60, **62**
Temple, Alva, **108**
Tessier, Jack, 8, 190
Thacker, John M., 233
Thompson, Wilton A., 141, 143, 228
Thornton, Garth, 143, 144, 230
Tichenor, Ferdinand, 144, 183, 228
Tobin, John J., "Jack," 8, **181**
Toppins, Ed., 119, 227
Trafton, Earl, 8
Trittipo, George, **88**
Trumbo, Charles E., Jr., 118
Turner, Barney E., **11**, 60, 62, **63**, 208, 226
Tyson, Vernon, 55

Uhrich, Benjamin B., 14, 52, **75**, **83**, 94, 104, 110, 217, 233

Vaccaro, George W., 154, 230
Van Houten, Eugene T., 8, **168**, 179, 212, 214, 215
Vandivort, David H., 8, **88**, **100**, 101, 110, 116, 227
Varner, Lawrence, 109, 110, 229

Wadja, Raymond F., 128
Wagner, Frank, 109, 233
Wainwright, Jack, 104, 116, 118, 125, 227, 228
Wall, Risden, 121, **132**, 134, 138, 227, 228
Wall, Vincent, 133, 230
Wallace, Clifford, 93,
Waller, William C., 169, 198n, 228
Walsh, Edward M., 145, 154
Ward, Frank, 8
Waring, Donald, 93
Watkins, Morris H., 15, 54, 66, 74, **75**, 89, 90, 226, 227
Watkins, Tarleton H., "Jack," 12, 13, **33**, 37, 38, 47, **53**, 60, 72, 86, 221, 225, 226, 233
Weaver, Daniel, 8
Weinheimer, Claire, 8
Weldon, Arthur J., 13, 51, 229
West, Jack C., 26, 233
West, William, **110**, 125, 138, 146, 228
White, Robert, **190**
Wiener, Richard, 110, 229
Williams, James P., 161, 231
Williams, Robert H., 157, 158, 231
Wilson, Maurice W., 139, 230
Winsauer, Henry J., 8, 78
Winschell, John E., 168, 231
Winslow, John R., 141, 146, 230
Woerpel, Herbert H., 7, 151, 157, 158, 230
Wood, Henry, **219**
Wooten, William O., Jr., 93
Wright, Fred A., Jr., 8, **25**, **27**, 32, 40, 43, 48, 52
Wyson, Max, 8

Yocum, Farrel E., 86, 90, 229

Zilly, Fred, 148n, **162**, 174, **175**, **190**, 233
Zipperer, Marion M., 169, 231

Other American Personnel

Arnold, Henry H., 108, 130
Benny, Jack, 97, **98**
Brereton, Lewis H., 23, 41
Caniff, Milton, 26, 48, 76n
Cannon, John K., **106**, 108, 109, 121, 132
Clark, Mark Wayne, 91, 92, 96, 103, 116, 121, 122, 127n, 129n, 142, 148, 172, 173, 184n, 198
Cochran, Jacqueline, 185
Cochran, Philip G., 26
Darcey, Thomas C., 148
Davis, Adele, 151
Davis, Benjamin O., 100
Dever, Jacob L., 166, 173
Doolittle, James H., 24, 99
Drummond, Tom, **185**
Eaker, Ira, 129, 130, 132
Eisenhower, Dwight D., 49, 69, 79, 81, 91, 95, 109, 153, 159, 166, 206
Ellor, Helen, 151
Fairland, "Fuzzy," 38
Feimer, Louise, **214**
Files, Yvonne de Ridder, 203n
Garner, James, 208
Grable, Betty, 219, 220
House, Edwin J., 114, 125
Ingram, Virgil, Jr., 48
James, Teresa, 185
Kartveli, Alexander,133
Lucas, John P., 113, 116, 122, 123, 127
McElroy, Mary, 220
McQueen, Steve, 208
Mears, Frank, 25
Myers, 217
Newbould, Betty, 221
Nielsen, Ariel, 139
Patch, Alexander M., 160, 165
Patton, George S., 47n, 81, 83, 86, 87, 160, 166, 207
Pyle, Ernie, 102
Radke, Katherine, 26
Remington, Peter H., 180
Rickenbacker, Edward V., 76n
Roosevelt, Franklin D., 23, 79, 107, 109, 113, 152, 153, 207
Rouleau, David, 134
Salisbury, Arthur, 76n
Saville, Gordon P., 130, 131
Seller, Lillian, 182
Silver, Gershon, 108
Smith, Walter Bedell, 95
Spaatz, Carl A., 47, 76n, 108, 109
Strickland, Auby C., 41
Truscott, Lucian K., Jr., 127n, 140, 142, 160
Urquhart, Donald, 152
Wade, Lance, **107**, 111
White, Walter, 137
Zipser, Albert, 38

British Commonwealth and other Allied Personnel

Alexander, Harold R. L. G., 33, 47n, 63, 67, 81, 90, 103, 107, 122, 141, 173, 184n, 200
Auchinleck, Claude, 21, 22
Broadhurst, Harry, **40**, 41, 50
Burton, H. F., "Billy," 11
Churchill, Winston S., 19, 21, 23, 33, 67, 79, 91,

101, 107, 112, 113, 114, 152, 153, 159, 160
Clutterbuck, W. E., 76
Collishaw, Raymond, 18
Conningham, Arthur, 107
Cunningham, Alan, 21, 22
Cunningham, Andrew, 18
Darwen, Jackie, 50, 51
DeLuy, Claude, **158**
Dickson, William, 187
Drake, Billy, **29**
Effendi, Badie, 37, 235
Foster, R. M., 187, 193
Freyberg, Bernard, 50, 129
Garrod, Guy, 216
Giambatista, Calavito, 213
Giraud, 147,149
Gouachon, Pierre, 136
Guingand, W. F. de, 50, 51
Hayes, R. J., 85
Heysham, David, 100
Horbaczewski, Eugeniusz, 52
Horrocks, Brian, 50, 51
Juin, Alphonse, 142
Kirkman, Sidney, 141
Klopper, H. B., 16
Leese, Oliver, 172, 184n
McCreery, Richard, 184n
Montgomery, Bernard Law, 10, 15, 33, 34, 39, 47n, 48, 49, 50, 51, 55, 63, 80, 81, 86, 87, 91, 96, 97, 98, 103, 104, 107, 109, 173
O'Connor, Richard N., 18, 21
Remble, Vincent, 157, **158**
Ritchie, Neil, 22
Rowe, Alan, 37, 235
Skalski, Stanislaw, 52, 59
Stalin, Joseph, 20, 23, 107
Tassigny, Jean de Lattre de, 161
Taylor, Cyril, 85
Tedder, Arthur, 47, 69, 81, 90, 91, 96, 107
Wavell, Archibald, 17, 20, 21
Westerna, J. F., 65
Westlake, G. H., 192
Wilson, Henry, 130, 153, 159
Zhukov, Georgi, 197

Enemy Military and Civilian Personnel
Arnim, Jurgen von, 49, 50, 51, 55, 67, 71
Baade, Ernst Gunther, 80
Badoglio, Pietro, 84, 95n, 102
Bär, Heniz, 44,46
Berres, Heinz-Edgar, 46, **48**
Bonomi, Ivan, 142
Bucholz, Ulrich, 57, 58
Canaris, Wilhelm, 117
Drago, Ugo, 193
Emmanuel, King Victor III, 84
Etterlin, Fridolin von Senger und, 80, 129
Freytag, Siegfried, 46
Gariboldi, Gen. 20
Giusepe Castellano, 95
Goering, Hermann, 82
Grasser, Hartmann, 47
Graziani, Rudolfo, 18
Guzzoni, Alfredo
Hackl, Anton, 46, 55
Hitler, Adolf, 17, 20, 22, 22n, 55, 84, 98, 126, 128, 149, 159, 171, 187, 197
Hosman, Karl, 66
Hube, Hans Valentine, 80, 84, 87, 90
Kaiser, Herbert, 46
Kesselring, Albrecht von, 49, 80, 90, 96, 102, 112, 116, 117, 118, 122, 125, 128, 140, 142, 143, 147, 148, 153, 171, 172, 173, 179, 198
Koechy, Karl, 64
Kohler, Arnim, 46
Laval, Madame, **220**
Laval, Pierre, 219, **220**
Mackensen, Eberhard von, 102, 112, 125, 126, 127, 128, 142
Meese, Giovanni, 49, 50, 54, 55
Münchberg, Joachim
Mussolini, Benito, 17, 18, 19, 20, 32, 41, 67, 68, 84
Nagumo, Chuichi, 132
Neumann, Eduard, 180
Omert, Emil, 46
Pavesi, Gino, 69, 75, 76
Psczolla, Alfredo, 66
Reinhart, Ernst Wilhelm, 46, **47**, 52
Rommel, Erwin, 16, 17, 20, 21, 22, 23, 25, 32, 33, 34, 47n, 49, 50, 51
Rudorffer, Erich, 47
Scharff, Hanns, 139
Steinhoff, Johannes, 44, **46**, 64
Tone, Wolfgang, 47
Ubben, Karl, 46
Vietinghoff, Heinrich von, 95, 96, 102, 112, 116, 117, 118, 140, 142, 198, 199, 200, 216
Zangren, Gustav Adolph von, 140

American Air Units
2nd Air Combat Control Squadron (Amphibious), 159
16th Service Supply Squadron, 148n
64th Fighter Squadron, 86
66th Fighter Squadron, 38
82nd Fighter Control Squadron, 116
315th Fighter Squadron, 56
316th Fighter Squadron, 10n, 13, 41, 48, 54, 56, 60, 62, 65, 66, 67n
328th Fighter Control Squadron, 116
345th Fighter Squadron, **220**
358th Service Squadron, 103

1st Fighter Group, 57, 109
4th Fighter Group, 77
12th Bomb Group, 48, 71, 95, 108
16th Fighter Group, 136
27th Fighter Group, 152
31st Fighter Group, 115,122
33rd Fighter Group, 23, 24, 115, 119, 122, 208, 209
56th Fighter Group, 77
57th Fighter Group, 10, 23, 24, 25, 26, 30, 31, 32, **33**, 37, 38, 43, 57, 58, 63, 67n, **76**, 82, 86, 92, 108, 111, 133, 147, 148, 159, 179, 209, **220**, 224
81st Pursuit Group, 25
82nd Fighter Group, 57
86th Fighter Group, 138, 148, 217
310th Bomb Group, 180
320th Bomb Group, 156
321st Bomb Group, 108
324th Fighter Group, 10, 41, 56, 77, 78, 92, 115, 119, 122, 137, 224
325th Fighter Group, 26, 108, 133
332nd Fighter Group, 137
340th Bomb Group, 95, 156
350th Fighter Group, 139, 147, **220**
449th Bomb Group, 116

64th Fighter Wing, 115
87th Fighter Wing, 148, 182

Air Technical Service Command, 217
IX Fighter Command, 41, 47n
XII Air Support Command,47, 92, 111n, 114,130
XII Bomber Command, 47
XII Tactical Air Command, 137, 147, 148, 154, 155,156, 159, 162, 173
XXII Tactical Air Command, 173,179, 180

Eighth Air Force, 77
Fifteenth Air Force, 91, 125, 137, 153, 175, **176**, 178 181
Mediterranean Air Command, 47
Mediterranean Allied Air Forces, 127, 132, 156, 158
Mediterranean Allied Strategic Air Force, 179
Ninth Air Force, 51, 92
Northwest African Air Forces, 47, 73
Northwest African Coastal Air Force, 47
Northwest African Tactical Air Force, 47n
Twelfth Air Force, 51, 99, 121, 147, 168, 173
United States Army Middle East Air Force, 23

Other Allied Air Units
1 South African Squadron, 59
3 South African Wing, 174, 190
7 South African Wing, 10, 58, 95, 190
13 Hellenic Greek Squadron, 37
55 Squadron RAF, 52
92 Squdron RAF, 57, 60
112 Squadron RAF, **26**, **29**
145 Squadron RAF, 52, 95
167 Maintenance Squadron RAF, 174
211 Group RAF, 42, 60, 92
233 Wing RAF, 32
239 Wing RAF, 10, 11, 32, 46, 82, 95, 174, 180, 187, 190, 192
241 Group RAF, 47n
244 Wing RAF, 10, 52, 95, 114, 115, 116, 190
283 Squadron RAF, 75
284 Squadron RAF, 85, 92
285 Wing RAF, 191
322 Wing RAF, 10, 85
324 Wing RAF, 114
417 Squadron RAF, 59
601 Squadron RAF, 65
Desert Air Force, 10, 39, 41, 43, 44, 46, 47, 50, 51, 54, 57, 76, 77, 92, 95, 98, 100, 103, 114, 147, 172, 173, 179, 184, 187, 188, 191, 193, 200, 216
French Lafayette Squadron, 135
RAF Middle East, 23
Western Desert Air Force, 18, 23, 31, 32, 33, 39

Enemy Air Units
Aeronautica Nazionale Repubblicanna, 155n
Fliegerkorps Tunis, 49, 58
Fliegerkorps X
JG 4, 126
JG 51, 47, 126
JG 53, 46, 47, 126
JG 77, 43, 44, 46, 52, 84
KG 26, 154
KG 100, 154
Luftflotte II, 80, 82, 154, 155, 180
Luftflotte IV, 180
Luftgau, 64
Regia Aeronautica, 43, 47, 71, 82
Republica Sociale Italiana, 180, 190
SKG 10, 123n
20 Gruppo Caccia, 155n, 193
20 Gruppo, JG1 (Italien), 180
60 Gruppo, 47
160 Gruppo, 47
180 Gruppo, 47
I/JG 77, 44, 46, **48**, 66
II/JG 2, 47
II/JG 77, 46, 52
III/JG 77, 46
II/SG 2, 66

Allied Ground Units
Sixth Army Group, 166, 173
Fifteenth Army Group, 81,152, 184
Eighteenth Army Group,47
Armee d´Afrique, 147
First Army (Br.), 47n, 63
Third Army (US), 166
Fifth Army (US), 91, 95, 96, 98, 103, 113, 115, 117, 127n, 128, 129, 131, 137, 140, 147, 152, 172, 173,184, 198, 199, 200
Seventh Army (US), 80,81, 83, 86, 160, 161, 166, 173

Eighth Army (Br.), 10, 21, 22, 23, 32, 33, 34, 39, 41, 47n, 49, 50, 51, 54, 60, 63, 80, 81, 83, 86, 92, 94, 95, 96, 97, 98, 99, 100, 103, 107, 110, 140,147, 152, 172, 173, **177**, 179, 180, 184n, 189, 190, 198, 199, 235, 237
British V Corps, 147
British X Corps, 50, 51, 117, 129
British XIII Corps, 22, 141
British XXX Corps, 22, 50, 54
French II Corps, 161, 166
French Expeditionary Corps, 47n, 129, 142
New Zealand Corps, 50, 129
Polish Corps, 141, 142
US II Corps, 47n, 49, 50, 54, 63, 117, 129, 142
US VI Corps, 113, 116, 117, 122, 123, 125, 126, 127, 140, 142, 153, 160, 161, 184
Americal Division, 160
1st Airborne Division (Br.), 92
1st Airborne Task Force, 160
1st Armored Division (Br.), 50
1st Armored Division (US), 122
1st Infantry Division (Br.), 122
1st Infantry Division (Canadian), 81
2nd South African Division, 16
2nd New Zealand Division, 129, 130
3rd Infantry Division (US), 86, 122, 126, 127n, 128, 142
4th Indian Division, 18, 63, 129, 130, 131
4th Infantry Division (Br.), 179
5th Infantry Division (Br.), 81
7th Armored Division (Br.), 18, 63
10th Mountain Division (US), 200
36th Infantry Division (US), 129, 142
45th Infantry Division (US), 126, 127
50th Infantry Division (Br.), 81
51st Infantry Division (Br.), 81
78th Infantry Division (Br.), 81, 101, 129
82nd Airborne Division (US), 81, 83
3rd Canandian Brigade, 95
5th New Zealand Brigade, 12
2nd Royal Tank Regiment (Br.), 18
7th Royal Tank Regiment (Br.), 18
Coldstream Guard, 52
French Forces of the Interior, 168
Long Range Desert Group, 25
Middle East Command (Br.), 17, 33
Nova Scotia Battalion (Canada), 97
21st Mobile Field Hospital, 105, 110
70th Station Hospital, 136
95th Evacuation Hospital, 124
Task Force 88 (Navy), 156
US Rangers, 122
Western Desert Force, 18, 21, 23
XII TAC Advance, 159

Enemy Ground Units
Army Group Afrika, 49-50
Comando Supremo, 20, 63, 95
Deutsches Afrika Korps, 13, 17, 20, 21, 22, 32, 34, 49, 67
Kommandant Messina Strait, 80
Panzerarmee Afrika, 34
First Army (Italian), 49, 54, 55
Fifth Panzer Army (German), 49
Sixth Army (Italian), 80, 91
Tenth Army (German), 95, 96, 102, 112, 117, 118, 122, 140, 142, 172
Tenth Army (Italian), 18, 21
Fourteenth Army (German), 102, 112, 117, 125, 130, 172
Nineteenth Army (German), 159, 161, 166
XIV Panzer Corps (German), 80, 129
1st Parachute Division (German), 81, 97
15th Panzer Division (German), 16, 54, 81
21st Panzer Division (German), 13
26th Panzer Division (German), 97
29th Panzer Division (German), 81
90th Light Division (German), 16, 54
164th Light Division (German), 54
Hermann Goering Division (German), 81, 83, 126
5th Panzer Regiment (German), 16
Infantry Lehr Regiment (German), 126

Place Names (United States)
Akron, Ohio, 141
Anderson, South Carolina, 176
Augusta, Georgia, 168
Bedford, Massachusetts, 25, 95
Bonners Ferry, Idaho, 109
Boston, Massachusetts, 206, 207
Brazil, Indiana, 119
Brooklyn New York, 54, 55, 138, 143
Buffalo, New York,161
Butler, Indiana, 196
Cedartown, Georgia,148n
Charleston, South Carolina, 214
Charlotte, North Carolina, 25
Chicago, Illinois, 189, 152, 222
Cleveland Heights, Ohio, 132
Cleveland, Ohio, 155
Cohoes, New York, 141
Copperton, Utah, 37
Cranford, New Jersey, 134
Dallas, Texas,187
Dayton, Ohio 99, 222
Detroit, Michigan, 85,182
Dillsboro, Indiana, 155
Dixon, Missouri, 136
East Lansing, Michigan, 190
Enid, Oklahoma, 86
Erwin, Tennessee, 65
Etna, Pennsylvania,168
Falconer, New York, 105
Farmingdale, New York, 133
Fort Wayne, Indiana, 156
Fort Wayne, Texas, 128
Fort Worth, Texas, 143
Garfield, Kansas,167
Gladwyne, Pennsylvania, 133
Glendale, California, 202
Groton, Connecticut, 25
Gulfport, Mississippi, 25
Hamlin, New York, 214, 215
Hanson, Mississippi, 164
Hartford, Connecticut, 26
Hillsdale, New York, 143
Hillsgrove, Rhode Island, 10, 26
Holcomb Rock, Virginia, 161
Idaho Falls, Idaho, 139
Indianapolis, Indiana, 86, 193
Indiantown Gap, Pennsylvania, 27
Jamestown, New York, 59
Johnstown, Pennsylvania, 109
Kansas City, Missouri, 146
Lakeport, New Hampshire, 95
Los Angeles, California, 48, 99
Madison, Wisconsin, 132
Manchester, New Hampshire, 30, 141
Manton, Michigan, 196
Marion, Wisconsin, 178
Marshall, Wisconsin, 151
Medford, Wisconsin, 152
Meyers Hill, South Carolina, 184
Miami, Florida, 30, 99,216
Milwaukee, Wisconsin, 116
Mineral Springs, Arkansas,161
Montgomery, Alabama, 159
New York City, New York, 136
Norfolk, Virginia, 27, 178
Oak Hill, West Virginia,146
Olyphant, Pennsylvania, 157
Omaha, Nebraska, 184
Orlando, Florida, 182
Oshkosh, Wisconsin, 47
Pasadena, California, 187
Peoria, Illinois, 187
Philadelphia, Pennsylvania, 163
Quincy, Florida, 143
Richmond, Virginia, 216
Rochester, New York, 211
Roxbury, Massachusetts, 154
Royal Oak, Michigan,89
San Antonio, Texas, 152
Sarver, Pennsylvania, 184
Savannah, Georgia, 170
Scarsdale, New York, 177
Seattle, Washington, 120
Selina, Alabama, 105
Shaker Heights, Ohio, 143
South Holland, Illinois, 221
South Orange, New Jersey, 151
Southwick, Massachusetts, 174
St. Charles, Illinois, 164
Susanville, California, 138
Tacoma, Washington, 175
Tallahassee, Florida, 25
Van Buren, Arkansas, 148
Washington, DC, 151
Waterloo, Wisconsin, 26
Weehawken, New Jersey, 105
Welsh, Louisiana, 174
West Haven, Connecticut, 133
Westville, New Jersey, 105
Wichita, Kansas, 162
Willimantic, Connecticut, 155
Wilmington, Delaware, 52
Wilmington, North Carolinaa,148
Ziegler, Illinois, 59

79th Fighter Group Bases
Bedford, Massachusetts, 25
Bou Grara, Tunisia, 81
Bron, France, 168
Capodichino, Italy, **109**, 110, 111, 114, **117**, **118**, **120**, 127, 132, 136, 138
Cassibile, Sicily, 84, 95
Castel Benito, Libya, 41, 48
Causeway, Tunisia, 10, 11, 13, 41, 43, 48, 52, 55, 81, 82
Cesenatico, Italy, 195, 196, 198, 199, 202, 203
Dale Mabry Field, Florida, 25, 157
Darraugh North, Tunisia, 40
El Houaria, Tunisia, 71, 77, 81
Fano, Italy, 181, 182, **183**, 185, 186, 191, 216
Firmo, Italy, 97, 98
Foggia #3 (Sal Sola), Italy, 99, 103
Hani West, Tunisia, 56, 59, 71, 81
Horsching, Austria, 218, 219, **221**
Isole, Italy, 97
Jesi, Italy, 170, 174, **175**, 176, 178, 181, 182
La Fauconnerie, Tunisia, 55, 56
Langley Field, Virginia, 220
LG 150, Libya, 40
LG 174, Egypt, 30, **33**, 35, 36,37, 38, 40, 235
Madna, Italy, 114
Morris Field, North Carolina,25
Palagonia, Sicily, **83**, **84**, 85, **86**, 87, **88**, 89, 92, 93, 97
Penny Post, Italy, 98, 212
Pisticci, Italy, 97, 98
Pomigliano, Italy, 136, 138, 143, 146
Rentschler Field, Connecticut, 26, 236
San Raphael, France, 162, 165, 166, 167
Septemes, France, 170
Serragia, Corsica, 147, 148n, 150, 152, 158, 159, **161**, 162, 204
Syracuse, Sicily, 83, 84
Theodore Green Field, Rhode Island, 26
Valence, France, **164**, 167, 168, 170
Youngstown Municipal Airport, Ohio, 221